Anonymous

Knight and Co.'s Elwood, Alexandria, Ind.

and Madison County Biennial Directory

Anonymous

Knight and Co.'s Elwood, Alexandria, Ind.
and Madison County Biennial Directory

ISBN/EAN: 9783337290658

Printed in Europe, USA, Canada, Australia, Japan

Cover: Foto ©Suzi / pixelio.de

More available books at **www.hansebooks.com**

KNIGHT & ELWOOD, ALEXANDRIA, —AND— MADISON COUNTY

GENEALOGY
977.201
M26K
1893-1894

Biennial Directory
1893-4.

J. H. MATTHEWS, Compiler.

EMBRACING A COMPLETE ALPHABETICAL LIST OF BUSINESS FIRMS AND PRIVATE CITIZENS; A CLASSIFIED LIST OF ALL TRADES, PROFESSIONS AND PURSUITS; A MISCELLANEOUS DIRECTORY OF CITY AND COUNTY OFFICERS; LISTS OF SOCIETIES; PUBLIC AND PRIVATE SCHOOLS, CHURCHES, BANKS, INCORPORATED COMPANIES, &C., &C.

—ALSO—

A DIRECTORY OF MADISON COUNTY, INCLUDING TOWNS AND VILLAGES.

PRICE, $3.00.

KNIGHT & CO.,
PUBLISHERS,
CINCINNATI, O., 1892.

KNIGHT & CO.'S
Biennial Directory
ELWOOD, INDIANA,
AND MADISON COUNTY,
1893-4.
MISCELLANEOUS INFORMATION.

CITY GOVERNMENT.

Mayor,
HON. WM. A. DEHORITY.
Office: Main.

City Officers.
lerk.........Orla A. Armfield
reasurer....Thomas L. DeHority
:arshal........Frank M. Hunter
COMMISSIONERS.
dward H. Peters........1st Dist
enry Bronnenberg.....2d Dist
ndrew J. Cunningham...3d Dist
ttorney, George M Ballard

City Council.
t Ward.... { George W. Brier
Ward.... { F. M. Harbit
{ James Boyer
Ward.... { W. L. Austill
{ Theodore Hasnock
{ Sam'l H. Cochran
1 Ward... { C C Kestner
{ W B Willitts

Board of Education.
iniel Sigler, President
:nry Callaway, Secretary
E Leeson, Treasurer
of Thomas Fitzgibbons, Superintendent Schools

Churches.
ristian Church, w Main
thodist Episcopal Church, n e cor n B and Anderson
thodist Protestant Church, s D
esbyterian Church, s e cor 18th nd A
tholic Church, n e cor s A & 14th

Post Office.
J M Overshiner, Postmaster
Arthur V Overshiner, Dpty Postmaster
A F Bourden, Delivery Clerk
Beecner Willitts, Delivery Clerk
U G Kingman, Mailing Clerk
Post Office hours, 7 a m to 7 p m

Incorporated Companies.
American Tin Plate Co The, incorporated 1891, capital $300,000, A L Conger pres, John F Hazen, v pres, C S Tarlton sec'y, W B Leeds treas, s w cor s K and 27th
Citizens' Gas & Mining Co, incorporated 1887, capital $50,000, E C Heck pres, W A DeHority sec'y and treas, n e cor n B & 16th
Diamond Plate Glass Co The, A L Conger pres, E G Keith v pres, F M Atterholt sec'y, W D Preston treas
Elwood Electric Light & Power Co, incorporated 1891, capital $25,000, C M Greenlee pres, J E Jeffries sec'y and treas, 207 n 16th
Elwood Machine Works, incorporated 1891, capital $5,000, L D Shively pres, J E Jeffries sec'y & treas, 209 n 16th
Elwood Natural Gas & Oil Co, incorporated 1887, capital $5,000, J M Overshiner pres, D Sigler treas, Wayne Leeson sec'y, R L Leeson supt, 201 s Anderson

GENERAL INDEX.

ria (Alphabetical Arrangement of Names).......... 89
:d Business Directory (Elwood)...................... 83
 (Alphabetical Arrangement of Names)............... 5
aneous Directory................................... 3
a County Gazetteer................................. 161
and Villages....................................... 130

Index to Advertisements.

ALEXANDRIA.

dria Investment Co, left
e lines
dria Investment Co..... 90
dria Marble and Granite
)rks............................. 91
, W H............................ 92
ick Bar.......................... 94
m Lumber Co The.................. 95
1, M E........................... 96
 & Hughes........................ 97
J P & Son, right side lines
Villkie, right bottom lines
& Mathews........................ 108
1, John A........................ 105
r I.............................. 107
nsperger, Frank.................. 106
1, L M........................... 109
Sheffield, left side lines.
) H.............................. 110
G. orge S........................ 111
d, Harvey J...................... 118
oog, John L, left bottom
 :es
e & Binkley...................... 115
& Meyer.......................... 117
 Scott........................... 119
.... 120
& Schatz......................... 122
)n, John S...................... 123
y & Davis........................ 124
o Hotel.......................... 124
ll & Armstrong................... 125
ison, N E........................ 126

ELWOOD.

& Finan........................... 8
l & Binford...................... 10
, D C............................ 12
& Pauley......................... 15
Daugherty........................ 21
ity Real Estate Co, back
/er
l Land Co....back cover
on, L & Co....................... 28
1 & Nearon....................... 40

(ELWOOD—Continued.)

Knotts, David C.................. 47
Miller, B F...................... 55
Rummel Bros...................... 64
Roop & Haynes, left bottom
 lines
Schnasse, G Jr & Co.............. 67
Spruce, Will J................... 70

FLORIDA.

Thomas Bros...................... 133

FRANKTON.

Grandview Hotel.................. 134
Jones, Perry..................... 135
Ring, J J........................ 136

GILMAN.

Parker & Kirkman................. 137

LAPEL.

Hecker, James W.................. 138
Ingalls, P N..................... 139
McKinster House.................. 140
Tinker, Dan A.................... 141
Woodward Bros.................... 142

ORESTES.

Plackard, E S.................... 143

PERKINSVILLE.

Dean & Willits................... 145

PENDLETON.

Alexander, L Ed.................. 146
Craven, A B...................... 148
Goodrich & Burdette.............. 149
Jordan, M L...................... 150
Lewis Bros....................... 151
Sturm, G W....................... 153
Welch, Thomas G.................. 154

SUMMITVILLE.

Bear, L F........................ 155
Fear, W C & Co................... 156
Hundley, J M..................... 157
Kinley, C C...................... 158
Summitville Bank................. 159
Gas Center Land Co............... 160

Elwood Iron Works, incorporated 1892, capital $10,000, John Halloran pres and mgr, J W Littler v pres, Francis Kramer secy, Gustave Kramer treas, J B Baird supt, n e cor s J and 22d

Jay Grain Co The, incorporated 1888, capital $50,000, Oliver Jay pres, J K Heap v pres, D W Jay sec'y and treas, E B Harvey mgr, 401 s Anderson

McCloy W R Glass Co, incorporated 1892, capital $50,000, W A McCloy pres, W R McCloy sec'y and treas, West End, n J

Secret Societies.

MASONIC.

Quincy Lodge, 230 F and A M, instituted 1858, meets before the full moon of each month in Masonic Hall

Elwood Chapter No 71, O E S, meets second and fourth Wednesday in each month in Masonic Hall

I. O. O. F.

Quincy Lodge No 200, I O O F, instituted 1858, meets every Friday evening in I O O F Hall

Elwood Encampment No 168, instituted 1887, meets every first and third Tuesday of each month in I O O F Hall

Elwood Canton No 33, instituted 1890, meets first Monday night in each month

Elwood Rebecca Degree Lodge No 253, meets first and third Tuesday of each month in I O O F Hall

K. OF P.

Elwood Lodge No 160, K of P, instituted 1887, meets every Wednesday evening in Castle Hall, n w cor Anderson and s A

Court Elwood No 1097, instituted July, 1892, meets second & fourth Monday nights in each month in G A R Hall

I. O. R. M.

Seneca Tribe No 113, I O R M, instituted 1890, meets every Thursday in Wigwam on s A

G. A. R.

Elwood Post No 61, G A R, instituted 1868, meets first and third Tuesday nights of each month in their G A R Hall

C. B. L.

Cardinal Manning Council No 376, Catholic Benevolent Legion, organized 1892, meets first & third Tuesday nights of each month at St Joseph's School Building

Elwood Club, incorporated 1891, capital $1,000, Charles S Tarlton pres, G V Newcomer secy, Thos L DeHority treas, rooms 6 and 8, 120 s Anderson

Banks.

Citizens' Exchange Bank, organized 1891, B F Callaway pres, H C Callaway cashr, E C Heck asst cashr, s e cor Main and Anderson

First National Bank The, organized 1892, John R Page pres, James H DeHority v pres, James M Barton cashr, J A DeHority asst cashr, n w cor Main and Anderson

Township Officers.

George C Noland, Trustee
Joseph E Sigler, Assessor
Justices of the Peace—Ward L Roach, George B Hartley, Chas L Armington

WM. J. DOVE, Real Estate, Loans and Insurance,
NEELEY BLOCK.   8½ N. Meridian, ANDERSON, IND.

LARMORE BROS., ICE CREAM, WHOLESALE MANUFACTURERS AND DEALERS, also OYSTERS IN SEASON. 513 Nichol Ave., ANDERSON, IND.

ELWOOD City Directory.

ABBREVIATIONS.

gt............agent	e s............east side	propr.......proprietor
sst......assistant	h..............home	Rev........reverend
ve.........avenue	lab...........laborer	S or s..........south
ds..........boards	mach......machinist	s e..........southeast
et..........between	mkr............maker	s s.........south side
ookpr....bookkeeper	mnfg...manufacturing	s w.........south west
ldg........building	mnfr....manufacturer	sec........secretary
lk............block	nr..............near	supt....superintendent
arp........carpenter	N or n..........north	trav sales
lk............clerk	n e..........northeast	traveling salesman
ol'd........colored	n s..........northside	treas.......treasurer
or..........corner	n w.........northwest	w s.........west side
or e...........east	opp.........opposite	wid...........widow
e.........east end	pres......president	W or w..........west

ALPHABETICAL LIST OF NAMES.

A

.bbot Daniel L, lab, h. 1512 n B
bbott Charles, painter, h. 2012 s A
bbott George W, feed mill, dealer in all kinds of feed, 1504 n B, h. 2012 s A
.bner Susie, wid, h. 1901 n E
.chenbach Zeffeni N, teamster, h. 612 s 16th
.ckles Frank, lab, h. 1930 n B
.dair Bertha, laundress, h. 1820 s B
.dair Mrs Elizabeth R, dressmkr, 1820 s B, h. same
.dair Minnie, h. 1820 s B
.dams Elmer, bookpr, S B & H J Adams, h. s C, near 22d
.dams Express Co, F M Hunter agt, 104 s Anderson
.dams H J (S B & H J Adams), h. New Castle, Ind
.dams James W, with S B & H J Adams, h. 1220 Main
.dams Matilda, wid, h. 1821 e Boulevard
.dams Ora, clk, h. 1220 Main

nderson Foundry and Machine Works, Manufacturers of BRICK AND TILE MA-CHINES, SAW MILLS, ETC.
5 N. Jackson Street,   'Phone 53.   ANDERSON, IND.

Jackson & Burr Do the Largest INSURANCE Business. Insure in the good old Companies they represent.

69½ N. Meridian, - - ANDERSON, IND.

Adams Stephen B (S B & H J Adams), h. New Castle, Ind.
Adams S B & H J, wholesale poultry; rear gas office, n Anderson
Adamson L Dow, clk, 1525 Main, bds 1111 Main
Addison Mary, clk, 201 s Anderson, b. 224 s 19th
Addison Solomon, lab, h. 223 s 19th
Aholt Frank, wks Rodefer's Brick Works
Albert Dolph, glass wkr, bds 803 Main
Albert Theophalis, glass wkr, bds 803 Main
Albert Wm, glass wkr, bds e s 10th bet n A and C
Albright Edward, plumber and gas fitter, h. 1615 e Boulevard
Albright Emily, wid, h. 1335 s D
Albright Frank A, lab, h. n s s C bet 23d and 24th
Aldridge James F, lab, h. 1018 n 17th
Alexander Australia, lab, h. e s 22d bet s B and L E & W Ry
Alexander Thomas, painter, h. 2006 n C
Alford Franklin, h. 2302 Main
Alis Elmer, gatherer, bds 431 n 9th
Allen Albert, carpenter, h. 1811 n C
Allen Esta, h. n w cor s A and 19th
Allen Lydia, dressmkr, bds 1814 s A
Allen Mary E, wid, h. n w cor s A and 19th
Alley Cryus P, glass wkr, h. 1913 n A
Allison Everett, yardmaster, P C C & St L, h. 913 n A
Allison Joseph, glass wkr, bds 417 n 7th
Alt Philip, bartender, 1524 Main, h. s D
Alterholt F M, secy Diamond Plate Glass Co
Alturdoff Frederick, lab, bds 1604 n C
Alvay Druie, domestic, 1344 s C
Ambler Alfred, glass wkr, bds 2500 Main
American Tin Plate Co The, A L Conger pres, John F Hazen v-pres, W B Leeds treas, C S Tarlton secy, s w cor 27th and s K
Amerman John, glass wkr, bds 418 n 12th
Amidon Wm L, eng, h. w s 9th bet A and C
Amons Oliver, glass wkr, h. 1108 Main
Anderson Allison, glass wkr, bds 1004 n F
Anderson Anna L, h. n s s J bet 11th and 12th
Anderson Henry, farmer, h. n s s J bet 11th and 12th
Anderson Hiram F, wks Electric L & P Co, h. 222 n 13th
Anderson John W, teamster, h. 2126 Main
Anderson Ulysses, carp, h. 2129 n A
Andres Bros (Edward M Andres), variety store, 1530 Main
Andres Edward M (Andres Bros) h. 1530 Main
Antle George W, h. 1816 s H
Antle Henry, tin plate mkr, h. 1816 s H

George B. Epperson, Contractor and Builder of Felt and Gravel ROOFING.

89 E. 9th St., - - ANDERSON, IND.

Anwyll Joseph, glass wkr, rms 1521 n B
Apple Frederick, glass blower, h. n w cor 9th and n A
Arbuckle Edward, lab, h. 1430 n 7th
Arbuckle King, glass wkr, h. 1430 n 7th
Arbuckle Levi, teamster, h. 1430 n 7th
Arbuckle Wm, student, h. 1430 n 7th
Arehart Frank, stone mason, h. s s s J, bet 13th and 14th
Armfield Gertie, laundress, bds s B
Armfield John D, physician, 1224 Main, h. same
Armfield Orla A, atty at law, also city clk, 1526½ Main, h. 1224 Main
Armfield Stella, h. 622 n 16th
Armfield T O, physician and surgeon, also secy Board of Health, 1515½ Main, h. 1802 s A
Armstrong Samuel, brick mason, h. 508 n 16th
Armstrong Wm H, glass wkr, h. 1209 Main
Asher Harry, harness mkr, wks 119 s Anderson, h. s A
Ashley John H, mgr The R H Horne Produce Co, h. 2328 Main
Ashman John, watchman, h. 1329 s C
Ashton Peter J, glass wkr, h. 1116 n F
Ault George S, teamster, bds n s 8th bet n K and L
Ault Martin L, glass wkr, h. n s 8th bet n K and L
Austill Henry C, student, h. 104½ n 16th
Austill Oscar S, h. 104½ n 16th
Austill Wm H, furniture & undertaking, 1534 Main, h. 104½ n 16th
Austill Wm L, undertaker, 1534 Main, h. 2012 n B
Austin Barney, teamster, h. 2119 s A
Austin Charles M (C M Austin & Bro), h. 2119 s A
Austin C M & Bro (Charles M and Owen L Austin), saddlery and harness, 1524 s A
Austin Myrtle, clk, 201 s Anderson, h. 2119 s A
Austin Olive, h. 2119 s A
Austin Owen L (C M Austin & Bro), h. 1005 n 17th
Austin Warren B, h. 2119 s A

B

Bachfield Charles W, jewelry, 104 s Anderson, h. Main
Bailey Frank M, candy mkr, wks 1704 s D, h. 312 s 17th
Bailey George T, blksmith, h. cor 4th and n A
Bailey Monroe, plasterer, h. w s Anderson, near n A
Bailey Rebecca, wid, h. 1925 s A
Bailey Samuel, lab, h. n s L E & W Ry bet 24th and 25th
Bailey Wm R, teamster, h. e s 26th bet s A and B
Bailey Wm T, glass wkr, h. 1518 n A

HUGH FISHER, Manufacturer Screen Doors and Windows all sizes. Furniture repairing a specialty.
198 and 200 N. Milton St., ANDERSON, IND.

BAUER & FINAN,
———DEALERS IN———
Lumber, Lath, Shingles,
And all kinds of BUILDING MATERIAL. Manufacturers of

FURNITURE *and all kinds of SPECIALTIES in the Furniture Line.*

Office & Mill, Nos. 2123 to 2131, Cor. J and 22nd Sts.,
ELWOOD,   ~   ~   ~   INDIANA.

Baird James B, supt Elwood Iron Works, h. 1818 s J
Baker Andrew J, meat market, 123 s Anderson, h. 2007 s B
Baker Charles L, carp, bds 1643 s A
Baker Clinton, lab, h. n s s C bet 23d and 24th
Baker Frank, gas well driller, bds 1527 n C
Baker James A, lab, h. 1930 n D
Baker James F, lab, h. n s s C bet 23d and 24th
Baker Seth, h. n s s C bet 23d and 24th
Baldauf Edward A, boxmkr, bds 736 n Boulevard
Baldauf George P, glass blower, h. 730 n Boulevard
Baldauf Jacob H, glass blower, h. 736 n Boulevard
Baldin Calvin, wagon mkr, 1522 s A, h. s A
Balentine Wm, glass wkr, bds 1329 s C
Ball George W, painter, bds 1529 s B
Ball Theodore M, painter, h. 1529 s B
Ballard Benj F, carp, h. 2012 n F
Ballard Richard, glass wkr, bds 1048 n 14th
Ballenger John, carp, bds 1515 n B
Balser Bernard C, lab, h. s e cor L E & W Ry and 22d
Balser George T, lab, h. 1929 s W
Balser Philander A, lab, h. s e cor L E & W Ry and 22d
Bambrough Wm H, glass blower, h. 1314 n 9th
Bambrough Jonas, glass blower, h. 240 n 6th
Bannon Jerry, glass wkr, h. 426 n 7th
Barber Herman, glass wkr, bds 408 s Anderson
Barber James, propr Erie Hotel, h. same
Barber John S, tailor, h. 408 s Anderson
Barber Joseph, lab, h. 1626 n F
Bark Frank, glass wkr, h. rear 824 Main
Barkdull John A, glass wkr, h. 1439 n 7th
Barktell Philip, hod carrier, rms 2122 Main
Barlow Elmer, glass wkr, bds 803 Main

---

ohn O. Miller, Practical Watchmaker & Jeweler. Eleven Years' Experience in the Manufacturing of Watches.
I. Meridian,   -   -   -   ANDERSON, IND.

J. A. Munchhof & Bros. Undertakers and Funeral Directors and Practical Embalmers. Office and Warerooms,
Telephones 189, 24 and 51. No. 98 N. Main St., ANDERSON, IND.
☞ OFFICE OPEN DAY AND NIGHT. ☜

Barnes Bros (E E, Walter, Wood and Charles Barnes), barber shop, 216 s Anderson
Barnes Charles (Barnes Bros), h. 1523 s F
Barnes Elmer E (Barnes Bros), h. s F bet 14th and 15th
Barnes Walter (Barnes Bros), h. s F bet 14th and Anderson
Barnes Wood (Barnes Bros), h. s G bet 14th and Anderson
Barnhardt Charles, carp, h. w s 10th bet n H and I
Barnhart John M, carp, h. 1633 n F
Barr John, gatherer, bds 812 n 11th
Barr Madison, lab, h. 2300 n F
Barr Wm T, carp, h. 2329 s A
Barrett John, glass wkr, bds 807 Main
Barrett Patrick, glass wkr, bds 807 Main
Barton James M, cashier The First Natl Bank, h. 1933 s A
Barton Samuel, glass wkr, bds 825 n 9th
Bartow Joseph, gatherer, bds 526 n Boulevard
Bassler Laura, dressmkr, 1517 Main, rms same
Batch Charles, glass blower, bds 1604 n C
Batchfield Charles, jeweler, h. 1215 Main
Baumgartner Levi L, clk, 100 s Anderson, h. 412 n 13th
Bauer Benj, h. 1722 s F
Bauer Bernhard (Bauer & Finan), h. 526 n Boulevard
Bauer & Finan (Bernhard Bauer and John Finan Jr), lumber, lath, shingles and all kinds of building material, 2123 to 2131 s J (see adv)
Bauer Jacob, gatherer, bds 526 n Boulevard
Baugher Joseph T, h. 1709 e Boulevard
Bauser Wm H, carp, 1716 s H
Bawtee Lewis T, clk, h. 1912 Main
Baxter Edward M, tinner, wks 213 s Anderson, bds 211 n 13th
Beach Walker, clk, 212 s Anderson, h. s F bet 14th and Anderson
Beale Abbie J, h. 1620 n A
Beale Kate F, h. 1620 n A
Beale Pearl E, domestic, 1634 n B
Beale Samuel, eng, h. 1620 n A
Bearnard Coyl, box mkr, bds 803 Main
Beasley Walter C, polisher, h. 1934 n C
Beaty Mary A, wid, h. w s 10th bet n F and G
Beaty Nettie, wks tin plate mill, bds 1913 n A
Beaver Wm, carp, h. 1600 n D
Bebee Wm H, plasterer, h. 1800 s H
Bechter Joseph, porter, 526 n Boulevard, bds same
Beck Jennie, wid, h. 320 s Anderson
Beck W Melvin, baggage mstr, L E & W Ry, h. 320 s Anderson
Becker Albert W, glass blower, bds 414 n 14th

WOOLLEY FOUNDRY AND MACHINE WORKS,
Engineers, Founders and Machinists.
N. W. Cor. 14th and C. W. and M. R. R.

WHEN — THE — Anderson Clothiers & Hatters.
ONE PRICE TO ALL.

B. J. Binford
We may live without friends, we may live without books,
But civilized man can not live without cooks;
We can live without love—what is passion but pining?
But where is the man who can live without dining?
R. B. Binford.

ELWOOD · RESTAURANT,
BINFORD & BINFORD, Proprietors.
WARM ✢ MEALS,

Oysters in Season. Hot and Cold Lunch. Cigars & Tobacco. Short Orders a Specialty.

OPEN NIGHT & DAY.

11 S. Anderson, - - - ELWOOD, IND.

ecker Henry C, glass blower, bds 414 n 14th
eckett John, teamster, h. n s s J bet 12th and 13th
eckey John, roofer, 108 s Anderson, bds 213 s Anderson
eeler Carolina, wid, h. 685 s Anderson
eher D E (Beher & Maddock), h. 1505½ Main
eher Edward, barber, rms 1505½ Main
eher Jefferson, carp, h. 1627 n C
eher & Maddock (D E Beher and J E Maddock), barbers, n w cor Anderson and s A
eher Marcus, carp, rms 1505½ Main
eher Samuel, clk, 1584 Main, bds 104½ n 16th
ehr Frank A, glass wkr, h. 416 n 7th
ehymer Andrew J (Behymer Bros also Behymer, James & Co), h. 1601 n D
ehymer Bros (A J and Perry Behymer), attys, 118½ s Anderson
ehymer, James & Co (A J & Perry Behymer and Frank James), real estate and ins, 118½ s Anderson
ehymer Perry (Behymer Bros also Behymer, James & Co.), h. 846 n Anderson
ll Emma, clk, 201 s Anderson, h. 1525 n E
ll George T, clk, 1526 Main, h. 1525 n E
ll John, eng, h. rear 1204 Main
ll Joseph, glass wkr, bds 807 Main
nedict Benj P, drayman, h. 1823 n B
nedict Daniel (Elwood Crystal Ice Co), h. 612 n Anderson
nedict David H, driver, h. 1823 n B
nedict George W, lab, h. 1823 n B
nedict Josina S, h. 612 n Anderson
nedict Marshall, teamster, bds 1815 Main
edict Wm G, h. 1608 s A
edict Wm H, lab, h. 1904 s J
efield Isham, h. 1922 s A

oop & Haynes, Real Estate,
LOANS AND INSURANCE.
210½ S. Anderson, - - - ELWOOD, IND.

Benefield Lynn R, mach, bds 2304 n A
Benge George, carp, h. 2307 n F
Bennett George, hod carrier, h. 622 s 16th
Bennett George, glass wkr, bds 1053 n 14th
Bennett Samuel, glass wkr, h. 413 n 10th
Bennett Wm, glass wkr, bds 1000 n F
Benton John, mach, bds 1925 n D
Beroker Lee, painter, rms 202½ s Anderson
Bereman Charles, lab, h. 2323 n B
Berry Clara E, h. 2302 Main
Berry C J (Smith & Berry), h. 2302 e Main
Berry Una D, h. 2302 Main
Besch Jacob, carp and contractor, w s n Anderson, h. same
Besch Tehresa, wid, h. 1709 s F
Bhinylol Andrew, lab, bds s s L E & W Ry bet 23d and 24th
Bick Vallorous, meat market, 2507 n D, rms same
Bicknell Merideth E, clk, 123 s Anderson, h. 2100 s A
Biegel Rev Balthasar, pastor St Joseph's Catholic Ch, h. 1320 s A
Biegel Mary, housekeeper, 1320 s A
Biglow John, lab, bds 2525 s B
Binegar J W, frame mkr, cor n B and 13th, h. 217 n Anderson
Binford & Binford (E J and R B Binford), proprs Elwood Restaurant, 111 s Anderson (see adv)
Binford Elmer J (Binford & Binford), rms 123½ s Anderson
Binford Elma, stenographer, 1527½ Main, bds 2317 s A
Binford R Bailey (Binford & Binford), rms 123½ s Anderson
Bingaman Mrs Belle, boarding house, 2118 s A, h. same
Bingaman Wm H, photographer, 400 s Anderson, h. 1011 s A
Birkett Cuthbert, glass wkr, h. 417 n 7th
Birkett Mary E, h. 417 n 7th
Birt John S, tinner, 108 s Anderson, h. e s 11th near s A
Birt Robert W, roofer, 108 s Anderson, h. e s 11th near s A
Birt Wm, tinner, h. e s 11th bet s A and B
Bishop Berner F, glass blower, h. 900 n 13th
Bishop Olerick, water wks, bds 412 n 12th
Bishop Wm, lab, h. 2409 n A
Bitner Albert L, lab, h. 1018 s B
Blackburn Rose, domestic, s s s H bet 13th and 14th
Blot Harry, glass wkr, rms 1612 s D
Bodemer Sallie, teacher 1st grade, Linwood Bldg
Boggs Martin, glass blower, bds 851 n 11th
Boglmann Ernest, glass wkr, h. 2413 n C
Boldon Calvin, carp, h. 1635 South
Boling Walter W, bartender, 106 s Anderson, h. 1428 Main
Bolinger Burton, lab, bds 2334 n C

Deal & Willkie, We will write your Insurance in none but Standard Companies; All parties are treated alike, no cut-rates and no wildcat Insurance.
REAL ESTATE AND NOTARY PUBLICS.

WHEN — YOUR MEASURE TAKEN, AND *SUITS OR OVERCOATS* MADE TO ORDER.

ELWOOD CITY DIRECTORY.

he Pittsburgh Saloon & Restaurant,

D. C. BOWSER, Proprietor.

Choice Wine, Beer, Liquors and Cigars.

EALS AND LUNCHES. **OYSTERS** AND GAME IN SEASON.

113 S. Anderson, - - - ELWOOD, IND.

oll John, glass wkr, h. 831 n 12th
oll Wm G, glass wkr, h. 831 n 12th
olle Eugene, glass wkr, bds s w cor 11th and n C
olse George W, glass wkr, h. n w cor 8th and n L
olt Lincoln, teamster, h. 623 n 17th
ond George H, cigar mnfr, 115½ s Anderson, bds Boston House
ond Waldo, cigar mkr, wks 115½ s Anderson, rms same
oner John N, glass wkr, h. 224 n 13th
oher David M, glass wkr, h. 1302 n D
one Harrison, lab, h. 207 n 13th
oring Frank M, agricultural implements, buggies, &c, 1514½ Main, h. 1800 n C
oring James W, merchant, h. 1610 n E
oring John, lab, bds 1345 s A

ston House The, Myers & Dickerson proprs, rates $2.00 per day, 1531 and 1533 s A
ottorff John R, agt, h. n s s J bet 13th and 14th
oulden Mary J, wid, h. 1802 s B
ourden A F, genl delivery clk, p o, h. s s s F bet 14th and Anderson
ourden G W (Stokes, Glaspy & Co), h. 1413 s F
ousman Adison A, carp, h. e s 23d bet s M and N
owker Wm C, contractor, res 1526 n A
owser De-Witt C, The Pittsburg Saloon and Restaurant, fine wines, beer, liquors, cigars, meals and lunches, 113 s Anderson, h. s w cor 12th and Main (see adv)
owser Perry B, correspondent, h. 1626 n A

John L. Lindskoog, Fashionable MERCHANT TAILOR. First-Class Work and Fit GUARANTEED.
H. H. Block, N. E. Cor. Church and Harrison, ALEXANDRIA, IND.

WM. J. DOVE, Insures against loss by Fire, Cyclone, Accident and Death.
NEELEY BLOCK.   61½ N. Meridian, ANDERSON, IND.

Bowyer Lorenzo D, lab, h. 1614 n F
Bowyer Wm L, carp, h. 1614 n F
Boyden Cora L, h. 1532 n B
Boyden Isaac T, clk, h. 1515 n A
Boyden Wm, student, h. 1515 n A
Boyden Wm W, h. 1532 n B
Boyer Abraham H (Morrison & Boyer), h. 1521 s D
Boyer Joseph R, lab, h. 1634 n C
Boyland Thomas W, carp, h. 2325 n C
Bozell Effie N, h. 1010 n 17th
Bozell John, lab, h. 1010 n 17th
Bozell Wm H, lab, h. 1010 n 17th
Bracher W R, butcher, 116 s Anderson, h. 2033 s A
Brackneg Philip, glass wkr, bds 1512 s A
Bradfield Lee T, glass wkr, h. 941 n 13th
Bradley James M, teamster, h. 2500 n E
Bradley Wm, lab, bds 1901 s A
Brady James, h. 1610 n B
Brady Terrence I, glass wkr, h. 857 n 11th
Brady Wm E, plumber, J M Livingston, bds 1610 n B
Branch James, glass wkr, h. 400 n 7th
Branch Wm, glass wkr, h. 1819 n C
Brann James, gatherer, bds 404 n Boulevard
Brannen Frank, glass finisher, h. n w cor 10th and n C
Brannen James, bartender, n w cor 10th and n C, h. same
Brannon John, glass blower, bds s s n C, 1st w Anderson
Brannum Joseph G (P Kuntz Lumber Co), h. Alexandria, Ind
Brannum Wm S (P Kuntz Lumber Co), h. Hartford City, Ind
Brasher Wm R, butcher, h. 2033 s A
Brasson Wm, glass wkr, bds 404 n 12th
Bratton Ella, domestic, 118 n 16th
Breedlove Wesley, glass wkr, bds 1000 n F
Breen James, glass blower, bds 1226 n D
Brenner Caddy P, h. 1522 s A
Brenner Ernest E, glass wkr, bds 1522 s A
Brenner Samuel, boarding, 1522 s A, h. same
Bridgeman G, driver, n e cor 10th and n C
Bridgman Wm G, clk, h. 2325 s A
Brier George W, bookeeper, Citizens' Exchange Bank, h. cor 16th and s F
Brier G Morton, clk, P C C & St L, h. s F and 16th
Briggs Alfred O (Briggs & Pauley), h. 409 n 10th

Anderson Foundry and Machine Works, Manufacturers of Portable and Stationary **Steam Engines.**
265 N. JACKSON STREET, ANDERSON, IND. 'Phone 53.

Is Your Property Insured? If not, CALL AT ONCE on **JACKSON & BURR,** 69½ N. Meridian, - - ANDERSON, IND.

ELWOOD CITY DIRECTORY.

Briggs & Pauley (A O Briggs and J W W Pauley), furniture and upholsterers, 1401 Main (see adv)
Bright Margaret, wid, h. 1345 s D
Britton Joseph, finisher, bds 929 n 12th
Brittenham Daniel, driver, Elwood B Wks, h. 1824 n F
Brizendine Leroy, teamster, h. 2525 Main
Broadbent Richard F (Griffin & Broadbent), h. 1832 n B
Brobst Arlletta M, h. 426 n 11th
Brobst Caleb, grocer, 424 n 11th, h. 426 n 11th
Broderick John, watchman, L E & W Ry, bds s C
Brooks Edward, lab, h. 1620 n F
Broughman Frank, glass wkr, h. 232 n 12th
Brower Fleming, drayman, h. 1350 s B
Brower Luther, lab, h. 1350 s B
Brown Benj F, carp, h. 211 n 11th
Brown Charles V, lineman, h. w s 21st bet s N and O
Brown Duncan A, carp, h. 1806 s A
Brown Edward, carp, h. 422 n 14th
Brown Francis D, dressmkr, h. 1515 n B
Brown Frank, brickmason, h. 422 n 14th
Brown Frank, lab, h. 2317 s A
Brown George, cook, 1514 Main, rms same
Brown H M, dentist, rm 1, 120½ s Anderson, h. rear 2425 Main
Brown John, carp, h. s w cor 23d and Main
Brown John R, grocery and restaurant, 2401 s M, h. same
Brown Joseph, plasterer, h. 422 n 14th
Brown Lesta, h. 1334 s C
Brown Martin, gatherer, bds 911 n 14th
Brown Mary E, wid, h. s w cor 23d and Main
Brown May, wks lamp factory, bds 412 n 12th
Brown Milow, blksmith, bds 1534 n C
Brown Murdock, barkeeper, 113 s Anderson, bds 1350 s A
Brown Rudolph, atty, notary and real estate, 104½ s Anderson, h. 422 14th
Brown Theodore, hod carrier, h. 810 s 16th
Brown Thomas S, teamster, h. 1515 n B
Brown Vard, h. 820 s Anderson
Brown Wm, carp, h. 1575 n B
Brown Wm, plasterer, bds 2020 s A
Browning Katherine, wks 1704 s D, bds s 14th
Bruce Caselman L, glass wkr, bds 1620 s E
Bruce Hallack A, glass wkr, bds 1620 s E
Bruce Samuel S, glass wkr, bds 1620 s E
Brum Adam A, driver, h. 2301 n A
Brum George W, carp, h. 2301 n A

George B. Epperson, Paints, Oils, Varnishes and Painters' Supplies.
80 E. 9th St., - - ANDERSON, IND.

John Donnelly will sell your property, and insure quick returns. Place your business in his hands.
10 East 10th Street, - ANDERSON, IND.

ELWOOD CITY DIRECTORY. 15

A. O. BRIGGS. J. W. N. PAULEY.

BRIGGS & PAULEY,
※ Furniture Dealers ※
UPHOLSTERERS.

Manufacturers of ALL SIZES STEP LADDERS.

Upholstering and Furniture Repairing a Specialty.

1401 Main, - - - - - ELWOOD, IND.

Brum John, glass blower, bds n e cor 14th and n C
Brunnon Benj, wks box factory, h. 2408 s A
Bryen Ja??, glass wkr, h. n w cor 8th and n B
Buchanan John, shoemkr, 1533 Main, h. 1808 s B
Buchanan Sophia, milliner, 1529 Main, h. 1808 s B
Buckley Harry J, glass wkr, h. n e cor 4th and n E
Bui Charles S, lab, h. 817 n 16th
Bull Charles R (Mason & Bull), bds 2302 n A
Bumgardner Levi L, clk, h. 412 n 12th
Bunce Hetty, wid, h. n s s I bet 13th and 14th
Bunch Sarah, wid, h. 2400 s A
Burdie Wm, rms 1528 Main
Burger James, painter, h. 2310 n D
Burk Frank, glass wkr, h. 912 n 12th
Burk George W, supt Elwood Planing Mill Co, h. 503 s Anderson
Burk John, glass wkr, h. 912 n 12th
Burke Anna, domestic, 1421 s G
Burke Daniel M, saloon, 106 s Anderson, h. 1108 Main
Burke James S, glass blower, h. 1108 Main
Burke Winifrede, wid, h. 1108 Main
Burkhart Samuel, glass wkr, h. 1529 n A
Burnett Allen F, h. 927 n 13th
Burnett Burnie E, glass wkr, h. 927 n 13th
Burnett Wm J, glass wkr, h. 927 n 13th
Burnett Wilson S, glass wkr, h. 927 n 13th
Burns Charles, glass wkr, bds 419 n 9th
Burress Solomon A, carp, h. 2414 Main
Burress Wm L, tel opr, L E & W pass station, h. 2414 Main
Burroker Elmus, painter, bds 2019 n A
Burroker Leander, painter, bds 1629 n F
Burrows Louis, baker, h. 2100 n B
Burrows Thomas, glass wkr, h. 1103 s H

PICTURE FRAMES of all sizes and prices at Hugh Fisher's Novelty Works,
198 and 200 N. Milton St., - - - ANDERSON, IND.

J. T. Knowland & Son, Brass & Iron, Steam, Gas and Water Goods.
111 N. Main St., ANDERSON, IND. 'Phone 30.

Burrows Wm, glass wkr, h. 417 n 8th
Burry Andrew, clk, 100 s Anderson, h. 412 n 13th
Bush Daniel W, carp, h. 2414 n E
Bush Jacob, milk depot, 2120 n E
Bushey Taylor, carp, h. 2322 Main
Butler Benj D, clk, 111 s Anderson, rms 123½ s Anderson
Butler Jesse, teamster, bds 1925 n A
Butler Wm, glass wkr, bds 1925 n A
Butler Wills H, h. 1931 s K
Byer Peter, glass wkr, bds 515 Main
Byrne P P, agt U S Express Co, h. 1633 n B

C

Cain Agnes, h. 431 n 9th
Cain Lizzie, h. 431 n 9th
Call Herbert I, h. 2425 Main
Call John W, street contractor, h. 2425 Main
Callahan John, glass blower, h. 1108 n F
Callahan Timothy, glass wkr, bds 233 n 12th
Callaway Beniah Z, physician, pres Citizens' Exchange Bank, h. 1204 Main
Callaway Frank W, clothier, h. 1210 Main
Callaway Henry C, cashier Citizens' Exchange Bank, h. 1204 Main
Campbell Daisy, wks 1704 s D, h. 314 s 13th
Campbell Dora, h. 2133 n A
Campbell Edward, lab, h. 318 s 13th
Campbell Elmer, wks Tin Plate Co, h. 1625 s K
Campbell George, driver, h. 1625 s K
Campbell George W, brickmkr, h. 2133 n A
Campbell G W, clk, 100 s Anderson, h. 721 s Anderson
Campbell James, glass wkr, h. 940 n Anderson
Campbell John, tin plate wkr, h. w s 23d bet s M and N
Campbell Joseph, cook. 113 s Anderson, rms 1528 Main
Campbell Letta A, h. 800 s 18th
Campbell Milo, drayman, h. 1625 s K
Campbell Mollie, dining room, The Stevenson House, bds same
Campbell Richard S, janitor, Linwood School Bldg, h. 1625 s K
Campbell Robert, lab, h. 318 s 13th
Campbell Roy, tin plate wkr, h. 1625 s K
Campbell Wm, eng, h. 318 s 13th
Campbell Wm H, farmer, h 800 s 18th
Canady Wm, wks Rodefer's Brick Works.
Cannon Alice, domestic, 1345 s A
Carey Frank, glass wkr, bds 927 n 13th

John O. Miller, Dealer in WATCHES, CLOCKS & JEWELRY, SILVERWARE and OPTICAL GOODS.
3 N. Meridian, - - - ANDERSON, IND.

ey Thomas, glass wkr, bds 927 n 13th
lisle Joshua, cooper, h. n. s s I bet 14th and Anderson
lton Mrs Harriet, h. 1618 s D
lton May A, tailoress, wks 113½ s Anderson, h. 500 n 14th
lton W J (W J Carlton & Co), h. 500 14th
lton W J & Co (W J Carlton and John Garner), saloon, s w cor Anderson and s A
os John, glass wkr, bds 412 n 10th
penter Alonzo, barber, 216 s Anderson, h. s G and 13th
penter Elana, clk, h. 220 n 12th
penter George, wks saw mill, h. 220 n 12th
penter George O, clk, 201 s Anderson, h. 1827 n B
penter Herbert P, bookpr and stenog, Citizens' Gas & Mining Co, h. 220 n 12th
penter James F, lab, h. 2132 n B
penter Lena, clk, 201 s Anderson
penter Simpson, drayman, h. 1827 n B
penter Wm, lab, bds n s L E & W Ry bet 23d and 24th
penter Wm E, drayman, h. 1827 n B
r Isaac (Gillespie & Carr), rms 1609 s D
: Joseph, plasterer, bds 1009 n 10th
: James E, glass blower, h. 719 n 14th
:oll James, glass wkr, h. 735 n 14th
:oll Elizabeth, wid, h. 1623 s D
son Charles, blksmith, rms 2025 Main
son Kit, oysters, &c, 1528 s A, rms n e cor A and Anderson
:er Andrew, lab, h. 1102 s A
ter Anna, h. 1102 s A
ter Cassius, barber, h. 1320 s B
ter Elmer, clk, 201 s Anderson, h. Frankton, Ind
:er Laura, domestic, 1303 s D
ter Louis, tin plate wkr, bds 1401 s I
ter Stella, h. 1629 n F
:er Wm H, del clk, 212 s Anderson, h. 1401 s I
ey James, lab, bds n e cor s N and 23d
ner John, blacksmith, h. 2402 Main
s Stella, domestic, 415 s Anderson
to Allen B, teamster, h. 1509 n F
to George T, lab, h. 1509 n F
dl Edwin R, wks Elwood Water Wks, bds 817 s B
anaugh Thomas, glass blower, h. 431 n 9th
lor Walter S (Shore and Caylor), h. 2011 s B
mbers Minerva, wid, h. s s s I bet 14th and Anderson
mness Anthony, h. 1613 Main
mness Clara, comp, h. 1613 Main

WOOLLEY Foundry and Machine Works,
Designers and Manufacturers of **Heavy Machinery, Engines, Boilers and Rolling Mill Work.**
N. W Cor. 14th and C. W. and M. R. R.

STUART, THE FLORIST, Cut Flowers and Floral Work a specialty. 99 to 111 W. 3d. Telephone 73. ANDERSON, IND.

WHEN — The Most Reliable CLOTHING House
✷ IN ANDERSON. ✷
PRICES ALWAYS THE LOWEST.

Chamness Clinton, brick mason, h. 2021 n C
Chance Matthew S, clk, 201 s Anderson, h. 1822 n F
Chaney Ernest, iron wkr, bds 1818 s K
Chapin Almeson T, real estate dealer, h. 1818 Main
Chapin Maud A, h. 1818 Main
Chapman Finel, glass wkr, bds w s 7th bet n E and F
Chappell Edward, glass wkr, bds 810 n 11th
Charles Alfred R, milk depot, 2122 Main, h. same
Charles Thomas, tin plate wkr, bds 1800 s H
Chelds Wm, tin plate wkr, bds w s 22d bet s M and N
Cheney Alonzo, teamster, h. 2013 s A
Chew John, lab, h. 1902 n A
Christie H, lab, rms 1528 Main
Christy John, glass wkr, bds 426 n 10th
Ciegler Lewis, stonemason, h. 1621 n F
Cipion Jacob, glass wkr, h. 420 n 7th
Cisseront John B, glass wkr, bds s w cor 11th and n C
Citizens' Exchange Bank, B T Callaway pres, H C Callaway cashier, E C Heck asst cashier, s e cor Main & Anderson
Citizens' Gas & Mining Co, capital $50,000.00, incorporated 1887, E C Heck pres, W A DeHority secy and treas, n e cor n B and 16th
City Prison, rear 1511 Main
City Treasurer's Office, T L DeHority treas, 112 s Anderson
Clancy Frank A, bartender, 432 n 9th, h. same
Clancy Stephen, saloon, 432 n 9th, h. same
Clark Alexander, carp, h. n s s D, bet 13th and Anderson
Clark Benj B, drayman, h. 1603 s D
Clark Edgar M, glass wkr, h. 1603 s D
Clark George, lab, bds 2119 s A
Clark H H, photographer, s s Main w of Anderson, h. 2024 n B
Clark J Alexander, lab, wks 1511 Main, h. 1534 n 16th
Clark Sarah G, h. n s s D
Clark Thomas, lab, bds 1604 n C
Clary Henry L, teamster, h. 114 n 13th
Clary John, farmer, h. 114 n 13th
Clary Lucinda C, h. 114 n 13th
Class John F, school teacher, h. n s s I bet 14th and Anderson
Clatterbaugh Mary J, wid, h. 2100 s A
Clause W L, asst secy Diamond Plate Glass Co, h. Kokomo, Ind
Clayball Howard, carp and builder, 2540 n B, h. same
Clayball James, carp, h. 1813 n C
Clements Mrs Barbara, dressmkr, 2301 n A, h. same
Clengenpeel Isaac, carp, h. 1527 s J
Clifford Charles E, bartender, h. n s s J bet 13th and 14th

Insure with ROOP & HAYNES,
IN THE STANDARD COMPANIES THEY REPRESENT.
210½ S. Anderson, • • • • • • ELWOOD, IND.

Robinson & Glasseo, Real Estate, Loans and Insurance. Building and Loan money procured in 15 days.
Room 9 "When" Building, - ANDERSON, IND.

ELWOOD CITY DIRECTORY.

Clifford Mrs Emma J, dressmkr, w s 11th, 1st s n F, h. same
Clifforn Lena, h. w s 11th, 1st s n F
Cline James, lab, bds 2787 s A
Cline John F, lab, h. 2787 s A
Closnit Paul (Mayor & Closnit), bds 410 n 9th
Cloud Wm C, lab, h. 1512 s A
Clous John, glass wkr, bds 232 n 7th
Clover Wm, glass wkr, bds 1053 n 14th
Cluggish Jennie, dining room, The Stevenson House, bds same
Clutsbaugh John, brickmason, h. 228 n 7th
Clymer Jefferson C, clk, h. 1615 n C
Clymer Myrtle L, h. 1512 s B
Clymer Royal H (R H Clymer & Son), h. 1512 s B
Clymer R H & Son (R H and Wm Clymer), livery, 1600 s A
Clymer Wm E (R H Clymer & Son), h. 1527 s A
Cochran Francis M, iron wkr, h. s w cor s O and Pan Handle Ry
Cochran Henry, teamster, h. 405 Main
Cochran James M, wks sash factory, h. s e cor 12th and n A
Cochran Jane, wid, h. 1924 s A
Cochran Lizzie, h. w s 9th bet A and C
Cochran Mary, wid, h. w s 9th bet A and C
Cochran Sadie L, h. s w cor s O and Pan Handle Ry
Cochran Samuel H, propr saw mill, h. s e cor 12th and n A
Cochran Samuel, lather, h. n s s C bet 23d and 24th
Cochran Wm F, sawyer, h. 208 n 13th
Cody Edward, lab, h. 2512 s B
Cody John, lab, bds 2512 s B
Coffman Emma, domestic, 1722 s H
Cohen Isaac, jeweler and druggist, 1510 Main, h. 1802 s A
Coibin Michael, glass wkr, h. 1222 n D
Cole A M, photographer, 108½ s Anderson, h. 1234 n D
Cole Charles A, glass wkr, h. 405 n 7th
Cole George, carp, h. 847 n 12th
Cole John, tin plate wkr, bds w s 22d bet s M and N
Cole John R, glass wkr, h. 405 n 7th
Cole Martha J, h. 847 n 12th
Coleman John I, miller, h. 1818 n D
Coleman Maud, h. 1818 n D
Coleman Moses M, lab, h. 1818 n D
Coleman Samuel, miller, 1513 Main, h. 1818 n D
Collard Henry, glass wkr, h. 420 n Boulevard
Collier Charles, glass wkr, h. 1218 n D
Collins Absolom, section foreman, h. 1323 s C
Collins Con, molder, bds 1802 s B
Collins Edwin (Trader & Collins), bds 1522 s A

Deal & Willkie, have placed 85 loans in six months, Farm loans at 6%. All parties desiring to secure loans
WILL SAVE MONEY BY CALLING ON US.

J. P. CONDO & SON, FURNITURE DEALERS, ...ABLISHED 1856. ALEXANDRIA, IND.
We have the largest stock, latest styles, latest designs, sold on EASY WEEKLY PAYMENTS.

WHEN—The Only Retail Clothiers
In the State of Indiana
That Manufacture their OWN CLOTHING.

Collins Melvin, glass wkr, bds 1429 n 7th
Collins Norah L, teacher, 4th grade, 2d Ward Bldg, bds 1900 Main
Collins Wm, blksmith, wks 1522 s A, bds same
Colly David, glass wkr, bds 419 n 9th
Colter C M, scroll wkr, bds 1005 Main
Comer David W, fruit stand, 1518 Main, h. 1985 n C
Cones Edward, lab, h. 1614 n D
Confer Charles M, bartender, 1522 Main, h. 1936 n A
Congor A L, pres Diamond Plate Glass Co and American Tin Plate Co, res Akron, O
Conley Jacob, teamster, h. 1908 s A
Conner Dell, glass wkr, bds 2133 n A
Conner Thomas (Hupp & Conner), bds Stevenson House
Conover Edwin W, reporter, The Elwood Leader, rms Boulevard
Conrad Leonidas P, glass wkr, h. 1111 n F
Conton Michael, glass wkr, bds 1226 n D
Conway Michael W, glass wkr, h. 2008 n B
Cook Alonzo, mgr plate glass wks, h. s s s H bet 13th and 14th
Cook Alvin P, blksmith, wks 1522 s A, h. 1004 n 17th
Cook Wm, glass wkr, bds 1103 s H
Cooley Albert, clk, 118 s Anderson, h. 1519 E Boulevard
Cooley Harry, wks Tin Plate Mills, bds 1315 s A
Cooley Wellington, carp, h. 1315 s A
Coombes John A, lab, h. 1821 n F
Coombes Wm L, lab, h. 420 n 16th
Cooper Effie, teacher 3d grade, 2d Ward School, bds 1900 Main
Cooper John, glass wkr, bds 417 n 7th
Cooper Lewis B, lab, h. 2027 s B
Cooper O Howard, wks Tin Plate Mills, bds 1622 Main
Cooper Samuel B, glass wkr, h. 407 n 8th
Cope George, hoop mkr, h. w s 22d bet s M and N
Copeland Claud, clk, 201 s Anderson
Copeland Thomas, painter, h. 1622 s H
Coppock Lincoln, plasterer, 1622 s D, h. same
Cotton James S, lab, h. 1025 n 17th
Cotton Wilbur, stonemason, h. s s s J bet 13th and 14th
Cox Alfred T (McCord & Cox), h. 1810 Main
Cox A Elmer, clk, 103 s Anderson, h. 1932 n A
Cox Charles, grocer, 1512 Main, rms same
Cox & Daugherty (W A Cox, C H Daugherty), agents Singer Mnfg Co, 1356 s A (see adv)
Cox Edmond M, drayman, h. 2320 s B
Cox Elmer, clk, h. 1932 n A
Cox George O, janitor, 2d Ward School Bldg, h. 2020 s A
Cox Isaac M, lab, h. 1816 s M

John L. Lindskoog, The Leading Tailor of Alexandria.
All the Latest Novelties in Suitings and Trouserings.
H. H. H. Block, N. E. Cor. Church and Harrison, ALEXANDRIA, IND.

WM. J. DOVE Can give you choice in 20 of the oldest and best Insurance Companies represented. Note this fact when placing your insurance.
NEELEY BLOCK.   61½ N. Meridian, ANDERSON, IND.

Singer Mfg. Company
COX & DAUGHERTY, Agents.
1356 South A,   · · ·   ELWOOD, IND.

Cox Jesse W, carp. h. 802 n 11th
Cox John W, lab, h. 1316 s M
Cox Lizzie N, h. 802 n 11th
Cox Martha J, h. 1310 Main
Cox Mary E, h. 1310 Main
Cox Thomas, farmer, h. 1310 Main
Cox Thomas A, physician, n s s G bet 13th and 14th, h. same
Cox Thomas, carp, bds 1925 s J
Cox Wm, carp, bds 1111 Main
Cox Wm A (Cox & Daugherty), h. 1313 n A
Cox Wm H, lab, h. 1316 s M
Coxen Emanuel, carp and builder, 1510 n E
Coxen Kittie, h. 1005 w Main
Coxen Omer W, carp, h. 1510 n E
Coy Hiram, lab, h. 2027 n D
Coyle George W, glass wkr, h. 847 n 11th
Craig Wm, glass blower, h. e s 10th bet n A and C
Cramer Claud, W U messenger, h. 1210 Main
Cramer Edward, carp, bds 1709 s F
Cramer Harry, iron wkr, bds s I
Cramer John, meat market. 1521 Main, h. 415 n 14th
Cramer Joseph, carp, bds 1709 s F
Crandall Charles O, carp, rms 1613 s A
Creagmile Alexander, teamster, h. 625 s 17th
Creagmile Alonzo, glass wkr, h. 625 s 17th
Creagmile Edward, glass wkr, h. 625 s 17th
Creagmile James, teamster, h. 907 s B
Creesperment Constant, glass wkr, h. 917 n 13th
Criste Cora, clk, bds 900 n Anderson
Criss Cyntha, wid, h. 1612 n B
Criss Wm, h. 1612 n B
Criswell Edward, mach, bds 1923 s J
Crittenaur Maurice, glass wkr, h. rear 801 n 9th
Crittin Cleve, glass wkr, h. rear 801 n 9th
Crook Charles D, paper hanger, h. 1613 n E
Crook John W, carp, h. 1613 n E
Croy Commodore P, h. s G

Anderson Foundry and Machine Works, Manufacturers of **BOILERS,** Steam Heaters, Castings, and General Machinery.
265 N. JACKSON STREET,   'Phone 53.
ANDERSON, IND.

LARMORE BROS. 513 Nichol Avenue, ANDERSON, IND. Telephone 220. Will deliver you your ICE CREAM, OYSTERS AND MILK any place in the city, and guarantee first-class goods.

Croy Hugh S, h. s G
Crouch Lincoln, h. s w cor Main and 12th
Crume Jacob N, glass wkr, h. s w cor 10th and n C
Culbertson Celia, h. 1400 s G
Cummings Daniel, glass wkr, h. n w cor 12th and n F
Cummings John H, glass blower, h. n w cor 12th and n F
Cummings Louis, clk, 1532 Main, h same
Cummins Edward, glass wkr, h. 1726 s A
Cummins Walter H, h. 1609 s D
Cunningham George W, glass wkr, h. 1608 s E
Cunningham Michael, glass blower, bds n w cor 10th and n C
Curl Richard, lab, h. 1513 n D
Curnett Wm, wks lumber yard, bds 404 n 6th
Curran Dennis, h. cor 4th and n A
Curtis W G, supt The Elwood Water Works, h. 1320 s D
Cutinger Herman, glass wkr, h. 1105 n F
Cuzick Cynthian, wid, h. 1853 s B

D

Daffron Grant, eng, h. s s s I bet 12th and 13th
Daffron Merrit M, eng, h. 1400 s I
Dailey James, glass wkr, h. 929 n 12th
Dailey John, glass wkr, h. 929 n 12th
Daily Wm, lab, bds s w cor 8th and n C
Dair Arthur, glass wkr, h. 1343 s C
Dair James M, section hand, h. 1343 s C
Dale John W, lab, h. 1822 n F
Danner Frank O, barber, wks 1516 s A, h. 1912 n D
Daugherty Charles H (Cox & Daugherty), h. 117 n Anderson
Daugherty Lizzie, h. n Anderson
Daunenbauer Anna F, domestic, 851 n 11th
Dauenhoml John, gatherer, h. 938 n 12th
Dauenhorn Maxwell, glass wkr, h. 938 n 12th
Davidson Joseph, lab, h. 1623 n F
Davidson Marion, lab, h. 1623 n F
Davidson Mary, h. 1623 n F
Davin Michael, glass wkr, bds 428 n 9th
Davis Andrew, lab, h. 2015 n A
Davis Andrew, stonemason, h. 1520 n C
Davis Elizabeth, wid, h. 1900 Main
Davis Grant, glass wkr, bds 2100 n A
Davis James D, stonemason, h. 115 n 13th
Davis John, carp, bds 1624 n D
Davis John W, lab, h. 1333 s A

eal Estate Exchange does a general Real Estate business. The finest lots in the world for sale or trade at our office.
0 East 10th Street, - ANDERSON, IND.

ELWOOD CITY DIRECTORY. 23

avis Lane, stonemason, h. 1609 n F
avis Minta F, clk, 1418 Main, h. 1900 Main
avis Neonta, h. 1609 n F
avis Oliver M, eng, h. w s 9th bet A and C
avis Rosser, tin plate wkr, bds n e cor s N and 23d
avis Wm, tin plate wkr, bds w s 24th
avison James, glass wkr, bds 833 n 11th
awson James W, roofer, 108 s Anderson, h. 2132 n F
'awson Lydia, wid, h. 2132 n F
'awson Thos J, foremn, 108 s Anderson, h. n s s G bet 13th and 14th
eal John T (Deal & Willkie), bds Boston House
eal & Willkie (John T Deal and Herman F Willkie), attorneys, loans and ins, 120½ s Anderson (see left bottom lines)
)ean Gertie L, dining room, 1528 Main, bds same
)ean James H, carp, h 1439 n 7th
)ean Zuchariah T, real est and auctioneer, 1516½ s A, h. 1526 n G
)eBrussell Benj, glass wkr, h. n w cor 10th and n G
)ecker Clara I, cashier, 201 s Anderson, h. 1911 Main
)ecker Jane, wid, h. 1911 Main
)ecker Jasper N, carp, h. s w cor 19th and A
)ecker Sherman, lab, h. 910 s B
)eely Lawrence, glass wkr, h. 1226 n D
)eely Maggie, h. 1226 n D
)eHority Charles C (DeHority Real Estate Co), h. 1514 n A
)eHority David C, real estate, 1535 n C, h. same
)eHority Edward C, student, h. 1629 Main
)eHority Frank, student, h. 117 n Anderson
)eHority James H, vice-pres The First National Bank, DeHority Real Estate Co, h. 1629 Main
DeHority Mrs Jane W, h. 117 n Anderson
DeHority Joseph A, asst cashier The 1st Natl Bank, h. 1629 Main
DeHority Real Estate Co, James H, Wm A, Charles C DeHority and E C Heck, real estate (see lower card outside cover)
DeHority Susanna, wid, h. 117 n Anderson
DeHority T L, pharmacist, also city treasurer, 112 s Anderson, h. 1817 s G
DeHority Hon Wm A (DeHority Real Estate Co), mayor, also pres and secy The Citizens' Gas & Mining Co, h. n w cor 18th and n B
Delvans Emile, glass wkr, bds 419 n 8th
DeMoss Wm S, carp, bds s w cor 11th and n H
Denney Abel, lab, h. 2315 Main
Denney Austin A, lab, h. 1624 n D
Denney Jasper, h. 1624 n D

Hugh Fisher's Novelty Works! Jig and Scroll Saw Work in all the latest designs and patterns. Call and examine my work.
98 and 200 N. Milton St.,
✶ ANDERSON IND. ✶

J. T. Knowl[...] & Son, MAKERS AND DESIGNERS OF NATURAL GAS Fixtures and Fittings.
111 N. Main St., ANDERSON, IND. 'Phone 80.

24   ELWOOD CITY DIRECTORY.

✦ T. F. DOAN, ✦
House, Sign and Fresco Painter,
Artistic Paper Hanging and Frescoing a Specialty.

Work executed in all parts of the State. Estimates furnished on application.

A SHARE OF YOUR PATRONAGE SOLICITED.

1602 South A, · · · ELWOOD, IND.

Denney Lorbine, h. 1624 n D
Denney Lillie E, clk, 204 s Anderson, h. 1634 n D
Denson Thomas, glass gatherer, bds n w cor 10th and n C.
Desfayes Ernest, boarding house, 825 n 9th, h. same
Desfayes Lizzie, h. 825 n 9th
Deshon James, glass wkr, bds 244 n 7th
Destaggs David, lab, h. 1610 e Boulevard
Destaggs Della, clk, h. 1610 e Boulevard
Detrich Peter, glass wkr, h. 230 n Boulevard
Detrich Matthew, glass wkr, h. 230 n Boulevard
Detrich Matthew Jr, glass wkr, h. 230 n Boulevard
Deutenberg Francis C, glass wkr, bds 807 Main
Dewese Charles, glass wkr, rms 1221 n D
Dewitt Newton J, glass wkr, bds n s 10th bet n F and G
Dexheimer Frederick, teamster, h. 2212 s B
Diamond Plate Glass Co, A L Congor pres, E G Keith v-pres,
 F M Atterholt secy, W D Preston treas, cor 9th & n E
Dickerson Wm H (Myers & Dickerson), h. Boston House
Dickover Fary G, h. 1332 s A
Dickover Lewis L, tin plate, h. 1332 s A
Dickover Mrs L J, boarding, 1332 s A
Dickson John W, carp, h. 193 n 13th
Dickson Wm, glass wkr, bds 213 n Anderson
Dill Mrs Catharine (F B Hand & Co), rms 1529 Main
Dill Ishmael, lab, bds s s J bet 13th and 14th
Dill Wm W, mgr F B Hand & Co, rms same
Dillenleger August, glass wkr, h. 803 n 11th
Diller Charles, tin plate wkr, bds 1800 s H
Diller John U G, clk, 1532 Main, bds 1800 s H
Dillon George W, city transfer, h. 1319 s B
Dilts Ollie, glass wkr, bds 1514 s D
Dipboye Charles, wks tin plate, bds 2020 s A

JOHN O. MILLER'S For FINE WATCH REPAIRING and DIAMOND SETTING.
3 N. Meridian, - - - ANDERSON, IND.

Dipboye Rev Jonathan, h. 1812 s B
Dipboye Rev Joseph W, h. 1812 s B
Ditz Frank, glass wkr, bds 515 Main
Dixon Wm S, glass wkr, h. 800 n 11th
Doan Theron F, house, sign and fresco painter and paper hanger, 1602 s A, rms 1528 Main (see adv)
Dockter John, glass wkr, bds 1009 n 10th
Dockter Theodore, glass wkr, bds 1009 n 10th
Dodge John, gatherer, bds 710 n Anderson
Donaldson D S, storekeeper, Diamond Plate Glass Co, h. 2030 n A
Doran Charles, glass wkr, h. 2517 n A
Dorlac Sipiho, glass wkr, bds 800 n 11th
Douge Luther (L Ferguson & Co), bds 1603 s D
Douglass Philander, glass wkr, h. 1314 s E
Douglass Tessie L, domestic, 1625 n B
Downs Arthur, glass wkr, bds 417 n 7th
Downs Solomon F, teamster, h. 1010 s A
Doyle John, section hand, h. 1714 e Boulevard
Doyle Joseph H, eng, h. 1801 n B
Doyle Louis L, h. 1801 n B
Dozois Peter (P O Dozois & Co), h. Tilberry, Canada
Dozois P Omer (P O Dozois & Co), h. 1421 s G
Dozois P O & Co (P O and P Dozois); dry goods, notions, &c, 204 s Anderson
Dragoo James P, plumber, 1425 Main
Drake Charles, teamster, h. w s s J bet 12th and 13th
Drepperd Anna, domestic, 1604 n C
Drouard Joseph, glass wkr, h. 412 n 10th
Duc Jacob, glass wkr, h. rear 801 n 9th
Dudgeon Andrew J, lab, h. 612½ s Anderson
Dugan Mrs Anna A, milliner, 1517 Main, rms same
Dugan Veach, glass wkr, rms 1017 s A
DuHadaway John, carp, h. 2000 Main
DuHadley Thomas, mach, h. 2003 n A
Duncan Charles E, carp, h. 223 n 16th
Duncan Ebernea, street contractor, bds 211 n 11th
Duncan Joseph, carp, 223 n 16th, h. same
Duncan Joseph W, grocer, n s L E & W Ry bet 23d and 24th, h. n s L E & W Ry bet 24th and 25th
Duncan Monroe, carp, h. 223 n 16th
Dunlap A J, livery, feed and sale stable, 1624 s A, h. 1620 s A
Dunlap Wm S, hostler, wks 1624 s A, bds 1620 s A
Dunlap John R, clk, 201 s Anderson, h. 1326 s E
Dunn Frank, glass wkr, bds 405 n 12th
Durham Louise, domestic, 2414 Main

WOOLLEY Foundry and Machine Works,
General Machinery, Heavy and Light Castings, and Sheet Iron Work.
N. W. COR. 14th AND C W. AND M. R. R.

WHEN—The Largest Stock of CLOTHING, HATS, CAPS and Gents' FURNISHING GOODS in ANDERSON.

Dwiggins Amos, carp, h. 1622 e Boulevard
Dwiggins James M, plasterer cont, h. 2531 Main
Dwiggens Leroy F, painter, h. 2025 Main
Dwiggens Martha, wid, h. 1635 s A
Dyer John, glass blower, bds n w cor 10th and n C
Dyer Thomas, foreman Plate Glass Co, h. s w cor 12th and n H

E

Eads Frank C, lab, h. 2107 n B
Eagle Flouring Mills, N H House propr, 817 s Anderson
Eash Charles, carp, h. 1521 n E
Eastburn Thomas C, carp, h. 1902 n A
Eavens Wm, brickmason, bds 1610 n E.
Eberhart Louis T, cigar mkr, wks 115½ s Anderson, rms 1528 Main
Ebert Wm H, glass wkr, h. 909 s B
Edwards Locy D, domestic, 1624 s A
Edwins & Heath (S W Edwins, W N Heath), physicians and surgeons, 202½ s Anderson, Opera Block
Edwins S W (Edwins & Heath), h. 1020 Main
Edwins Theodore K, shipping clk, h. 1020 Main
Efflander Andrew, glass wkr, h. 515 Main
Efflander Frederick, glass wkr, h. 515 Main
Egan Walter, eng, P C C & St L Ry, bds 1359 s B
Eggerton Wm, glass wkr, h. 222 n 11th
Egginton Robert H, glass wkr, h. 828 n 12th
Egolf Adam J, lab, h 2507 n D
Eider Peter, glass wkr, h. 920 n 12th
Eikenberry Elias, drayman, h. 2021 s A
Elbert Frank A, glass wkr, h. 413 n 8th
Elbert John J, glass wkr, h. 413 n 8th
Elbert Joseph L, glass wkr, h. 906 n F
Elickson John, glass cutter, bds 1332 n 9th
Elliott Effie I, h. n s s G bet 13th and 14th
Elliott Emma B, cook, 1528 Main, bds same
Elliott Harry B, variety store, dealer in notions, toys, glass and queensware, stationery, &c, 125 s Anderson, h. 1810 s A
Elliott J H, livery and feed, 1819 s A, h. Boulevard
Elliott M P, supt Diamond Plate Glass Co, res Kokomo, Ind
Elliott Thomas, glass wkr, bds 807 Main
Ellis Marion, bartender, 1524 Main, h. s s L E & W Ry bet 23d and 24th
Ellison, yard master, rms 1528 Main
Elwood Bottling Wks, Phillip Hamm propr, rear 319 s Anderson
Elwood City Cemetery, w s 13th bet s C and E

Roop & Haynes Are Agents for FIVE of the BEST BUILDING & LOAN COMPANIES in Indiana.
210½ S. Anderson, - - - - ELWOOD, IND.

To Buy or Sell Real Estate, To procure money to build with promptly, for Insurance or Loans, Call on **Robinson & Glassco,** Room 9 "When" Building, ANDERSON, IND.

Elwood City Postoffice, J M Overshiner P M, 214 s Anderson
Elwood City Roller Mills The, Kidwell & Goode proprs, 1513 Main
Elwood City Water Works, W G Curtis supt, 721 and 723 s B
Elwood Club, Charles S Tarlton pres, G V Newcomer secy, Thos L DeHority treas, rms 6, 7 and 8, 120½ s Anderson
Elwood Crystal Ice Co (P Hamm, G Kramer and D Benedict), s w cor Anderson and n F
Elwood Daily Call, Will J Spruce editor and propr, 118½ s Anderson
Elwood Daily Press The, Mellette & Staley proprs, 207½ s Anderson
Elwood Electric Light & Power Co, C M Greenlee pres, J E Jeffries secy and treas, 207 n 16th
Elwood Elevator, Harting & Co proprs, 1509 and 1511 Main
Elwood Fire Department, Patrick O'Brien chief, 1411 s Main
Elwood Heading Co The (S C Reid and J H S Keller), slack barrel heading, s w cor 19th and s B
Elwood Iron Works, John Holloran pres and mgr, J W Littler v-pres, Gustave Kramer treas, Francis Kramer secy, James B Baird supt, n e cor 22d and s J
Elwood Land Co, H D Seymour secy and treas, 1611 s A (see adv outside front cover)
Elwood Leader The, Elmer E Fornshell publisher and propr, 115½ s Anderson
Elwood Machine Works, L D Shively pres, J E Jeffries secy and treas, 209 n 16th
Elwood Natural Gas & Oil Co, J M Overshiner pres, Wayne Leeson secy, D Segler treas, R L Leeson supt, 201 s Anderson
Elwood Opera House, P T O'Brien propr and mgr, s Anderson
Elwood Planing Mill Co, B T Callaway pres, F M Headley secy, H C Callaway treas, G W Burk supt, cor C and Pan Handle Ry
Elwood Real Estate Co (T J Gardner, D E McDonald and D L Green), 1534 s A
Elwood Restaurant, Binford & Binford proprs, 111 s Anderson
Elwood Steam Laundry, Schaeffer & Martin proprs, 1422 Main
Elwood Water Co The, W G Curtis supt, rm 3, 120½ s Anderson
Elwood Weekly Free Press The, Mellette & Staley proprs, 207½ s Anderson
Emerson Frank, tin plate wkr, bds 1800 s H
Emmons James, glass wkr, h. 1225 n A
Enders Arthur J, glass blower, h. 831 n 11th
Enders Frank, gatherer, bds 831 n 11th
Engelhart John, glass wkr, bds 407 n 10th
Enlot Christopher, gatherer, bds 1045 n 14th
Erana Amos, glass wkr, h. 901 s A

Herman F. Willkie, J.P.
COLLECTIONS PROMPTLY MADE.

WHEN—Children's Department
A SPECIAL FEATURE.
Always well Stocked with the **LATEST NOVELTIES.**

L. FERGUSON.   L. DOUGE.

L. FERGUSON & CO.,
Wholesale Confectioneries.

Dealers in EXTRACTS, NUTS AND CIGARS.

1704 South D Street,   •   •   •   ELWOOD, IND.

Erhart Joseph, glass wkr, bds s w cor 11th and n C
Erie Hotel, James Barber propr, 408 s Anderson
Erwin George F, glass wkr, h. 1221 n D
Erwin Otto, glass wkr, bds 413 n 12th
Estle Barton, lab, h. 2012 n F
Etchison Clinton E, lab, h. 2003 Main
Etchison Francis, teamster, h. 1330 s B
Etchison Henry, h. 602 s Anderson
Etchison I G, saloon, rear 112 s Anderson, h. 2003 Main
Etchison Jacob, glass wkr, h. 1340 s B
Etchison James, glass wkr, h. s B
Etchison James, lab, h. 1513 s F
Etchison Malinda, domestic, 305 s Anderson
Etchison Minerva, wid. h. 1613 s F
Etchison Samuel, glass wkr, h. 1340 s B
Etchison Walter, lab, h. 1513 s F
Etchison Wm D, school teacher, h. s w cor s Anderson and J
Etherington Omer, glass wkr, bds w s 10th bet n F and G
Evans Candace M, trimmer, 1517 Main, h. s Anderson
Evans Morgia, tin plate wkr, bds 1812 s H
Evans Rhoda, wid, h. 1643 s B
Evans Wm, tin plate wkr, bds 1527 n C
Evelink Wm, glass wkr, h. w s 8th bet n K and L
Everhart Arthur L, restaurant, 1514 Main, rms 1515½ Main
Everling Frank R, glass wkr, h. n w cor 10th and n L
Everman Wm, lather, bds n s s C bet 23d and 24th
Ewing Albert M, lab, h. 2306 n E
Ewing George W, carp, h. 2306 n F

F

Fagan Joseph P, glass wkr, bds 411 n 8th
Faith Isaac, gatherer, bds 526 n Boulevard
Fall Martin, gas fitter, wks 213 s Anderson, bds Erie House
Falls Albert D, glass wkr, h. w s 8th bet n C and D

John L. Lindskoog, Fine Tailoring in Suits and Pants. An examination solicited. A FIT GUARANTEED.
H. H. H. Block, N. E. Cor. Church and Harrison, ALEXANDRIA, IND.

WM. J. DOVE Is Agent for National Home Building and Loan Ass'n of Bloomington, Ill You can get all the money you want on short notice.
NEELEY BLOCK.   61¼ N. Meridian, ANDERSON, IND.

TELEPHONE LARMORE BROS. for your ICE CREAM, MILK AND OYSTERS, and be sure of prompt delivery and first-class goods. 513 Nichol Ave., ANDERSON, IND. TELEPHONE 220.

Falls Wm D, glass wkr, h. w s 8th bet n C and D
Farr Elihu, foreman, Starkey Brick Works, h. 1339 s A
Farr Jesse, glass wkr, h. 1921 n A
Farr Lemuel, glass wkr, bds 1339 s A
Farr Myrtle, h. 1339 s A
Farrell Michael, packer, bds 710 n Anderson
Farret Virgil, glass wkr, h. 409 n 12th
Faussett Jasper, trav sales, 1704 s D, h. s 17th
Feil Edmond, glass wkr, bds Boston House
Fenstemaker James, glass wkr, h. 1609 n C
Fenstemaker Wm, glass wkr, bds 1609 n C
Ferguson Henry, eng, Elwood Water Works, h. 213 s 19th
Ferguson Lafayette (L Ferguson & Co), h. 1700 s D
Ferguson L & Co (L Ferguson and L Douge), wholesale confections, extracts, nuts and cigars, 1704 s D (see adv)
Ferguson Milton, carp, h. s s 23d bet L E & W Ry and s C
Ferguson Sidney M (Webb & Ferguson), h. cor 16th and n C.
Ferguson Sydney, farmer, h. 1601 n C
Ferree Wm M, wks planing mill, h. 1611 Main
Fettig E, dry goods, 206 s Anderson, h. 322 n Anderson
Fidelity Building & Savings Union, Roop & Haynes agts, 210½ s Anderson
Fiedler Albert, gatherer, bds 839 n 12th
Fiedler Wm, glass blower, h. 839 n 12th
Fieser Edward, gatherer, bds e s 4th bet n E and F
Finan James P, tel opr, P C C & St L Ry, h. 233 n 12th
Finan John, glass wkr, h. 233 n 12th
Finan John, architect, 2131 s J, h. 213 n 12th
Finan John Jr (Bauer & Finan), h. 213 n 12th
Finan Kate, domestic, 1520 s B
Finch Mary, wid, h. 1809 Main
Finch Weldon, druggist, h. 121 n 18th
Finch W A (W A Finch & Co), h. cor 18th and n A
Finch W A & Co (W A Finch, J E Kirkpatrick), druggists, 200 s Anderson
Finey James, glass wkr, bds n e cor 14th and n C
Firn Elmer E, lab, h. 1911 s A
First M E Church, Rev Thomas M Guild pastor, n e cor Anderson and n A
First National Bank The, John R Page pres, James H DeHority v pres, James M Barton cashr, n w cor Main & Anderson
Fisher Andrew, glass blower, h. 240 n Boulevard
Fisher John W, lab, h. 2313 n B
Fitzgerald Edward, glass wkr, h. n e cor 11th and n F

Anderson Foundry and Machine Works, REPAIRS and Job Work of all Kinds A SPECIALTY.
PHONE 58.
263 N. Jackson Street, - - - ANDERSON, IND.

INSURE WITH JACKSON & BURR. Latch string always out and light in the window, until the last man's **INSURED.**
69½ N. Meridian, - - ANDERSON, IND.

Fitzgibbon Mrs Francis, teacher 1st Grade, Linwood Building, h. 1914 s G
Fitzgibbon Thomas F, supt public schools, Linwood School Bldg, h. 1914 s G
Flaherty John, saloon, 109 s Anderson, bds Boston House
Flanigan Thomas, section foreman, h. 911 s Anderson
Flinn John, glass wkr, h. n s of s G, bet 13th and 14th
Flood Rev S H, pastor Methodist Church, h. 5210 s E
Flowers Harry, glass gthr, b. 224 n 13th
Flowers Lorenzo D, glass blower, h. 224 n 13th
Foland Ansil, wks Starkey's Brick Wks, h. 2112 Main
Foland Charles, lab, h. 2022 n A
Foland Claud O, wks Starkey's Brick Wks, h. 2112 Main
Foland Mrs Elizabeth, wid, h. 1810 Main
Foland Geo W, tmstr, h. 2112 Main
Foland John D, lab, h. 1642 s A
Foland L C, sew mach agt, 125 s Anderson, rms 123½ s Anderson
Foland Oliver M, painter, h. 2112 Main
Foland Silas, gas fitter, wks 213 s Anderson, h. 2112 Main
Foland Walter, wks heading factory, bds 1643 s A
Foland Wm, glass wkr, h. 512 n 14th
Foley James, glass blower, bds 1009 n. 10th
Fontaine Louis D, clk, 204 s Anderson, h. Main
Forcum Curtis, wks planing mill, h. cor 12th and n A
Forcum Jane, dressmkr, cor 12th and n A, h. same
Ford Otto, lab, bds 1512 n B
Forney Peter F, saloon, 824 Main, h. same
Fornshell Elmer E, editor and propr The Elwood Leader, b. s s Boulevard, bet 13th and 14th
Fossett Jasper, driver, h. 621 s 17th
Foster Sherman H, drug clk, 105 s Anderson, bds 708 s Anderson
Foster Wm, glass wkr, bds 419 n 9th
Fox Charles, glass packer, h. 2105 s A
Fox John W, boss packer, Geo A Macbeth Co, h. 2105 s B
Foust Cyrus J, painter, h. 2107 n A
Fowles James M, carp, h. 1812 n B
Francis Albert, glass wkr, h. 1351 s A
Francis Alice, h. 1814 n D
Francis Nancy, wid, 1814 n D
Francis Vina, h. 1814 n D
Frank John H, carp, h. 1935 s B
Franks Harold, tin plate wkr, h. 1611 e Boulevard
Franks Joseph B, h. 1611 e Boulevard
Franks Otho, glass wkr, h. 1611 e Boulevard
Frankeberger Simeon O, L E & W Ry agt, h. 1409 s G

George B. Epperson, Carriage Paints and Varnishes A Specialty.

onnelly & Romenger, Livery, Feed and Sale **BARN,**
48 West 9th St. Telephone 76. ANDERSON, IND,
rses and Buggies always on hand, at reasonable prices. Driver furnished when re-
Also office at John Donnelly's Real Estate Office, 10 E. 10th St. Tel. 166.

rnal Building & Loan Assn, of Indianapolis, 120½ s Anderson
l Allen W, vet surgeon, 1600 s Main, bds 1350 s A
e Lewis, clk, bds Boston House
e Wm, hostler, 1317 s A, rms 1319 s A
:r Alexander, shipping clk, bds 2010 n A
:r Everett, clk, b. n s s J bet 14th and Anderson
:r John P, carp, h. n s s J bet 14th and Anderson
:r Lewis, lather, h. n s s J bet 14th and Anderson
:r Oliver, glass wkr, bds 2010 n A
:r Oliver V, farmer, h. 718 s Anderson
ınd Frank, wks Tin Plate Co, h. 2406 n A
ıhd Rus R, lab, h. 2406 n A
ıan Ed, stonemason, rms 1528 Main
ıan H S, civil eng, 104½ s Anderson, h. 1612 s D
h John R, candy mkr, 1704 s D, bds 1700 s D
h Louis, lab, bds 1829 s C
Harry J, electrical eng, h. 610 s Anderson
John, hardware, stoves and house furnishing goods, agricul-
    tural imp, 208 and 210 s Anderson, h. 614 s Anderson
George, carp, h. 2100 n A
:tzko Ludwig, glass wkr, bds 515 Main
Robert, glass wkr, h. 620 s 18th
John, lab, h. 1713 s F
Lillie A, cashier, 212 s Anderson, h. 1713 s E
Sadie E, clk, 201 s Anderson, h. 1713 s F
Wm, bricklayer, h. 1621 Main
Harry M, mach, h. 1613 s F
son Thomas, glass wkr, h. 2113 n B

G

her Terrence, glass blower, bds n w cor 10th and n C
:r Alexander, glass wkr, bds 911 s Anderson
ıay Gilbert N, drayman, h. 2401 s B
John W, h. 1812 n F
šamuel H, carp, h. n w cor 19th and s A
er David, tin plate wkr, h. 1319 s D
er Marion, lab, h. 1625 n D
er Robert, glass wkr, bds 735 n 14th
:r Robert, lab, h. 1934 s B
:r Robert, lab, h. 2309 s B
:r Thomas J (Elwood Real Estate Co), h. 1613 n F
es Edward, clk, h. 1828 n B
r Philip, cigarmkr, h. 410 n Boulevard
John, saloon, 1355 s A, bds Boston House

velty Works, **HUGH FISHER, Propr.,** man-
ıND 200 N. MILTON ST, ufacturer and dealer in Step Ladders,
ınDERSON, IND. Garden Wheelbarrows, Screen Doors
          and Windows, Picture Frames, etc.

J. T. Knowland & Son, WHOLESALE PLUMBERS *and Gas Fitters' Supplies*
111 N. Main St., ANDERSON, IND. 'Phone 80.

Garner Sylvester, glass wkr, bds 819 n 13th
Garner Wm, lab, h. 1333 s C
Garrett Nathan L (Garrett & Snively), h. 408 n 12th
Garrett & Snively (N L Garrett & Samuel Snively), incubators, 111 n Anderson
Gaskill John W, eng, h. 2405 s A
Gates George, glass wkr, bds 416 n 7th
Gatwood John, contractor, w s 14th bet s F and G, h. same
Gauntz James, wks Rodefer Brick Works, h. 2109 n C
Gavin Elizabeth, wid, h. 1621 n C
Gavin Mary E, cook, 111 s Anderson, h. 1617 n B
Geard Charles, lab, bds 2309 s B
Geis Michael, lab, bds 1610 n D
Genell Powell, glass wkr, bds 42 n 12th
George Burt, glass wkr, bds 1303 s D
Gephart Frank, grocer, h. 1915 n E
Gephart Samuel, carp. h. 2524 Main
Gerkin Cornelius, tin plate wkr, bds 1111 Main
Gibbons Samuel, glass wkr, bds 430 n 7th
Gibbs Walter, glass wkr, bds 419 n 9th
Gibson Boston M, glass wkr, h. 1052 n 14th
Gibson Martin S, wks Rodefer Brick Wks
Gifford Albert M, circulating editor The Elwood Daily Call, h. 2118 Main
Gifford James B, clk. 1512 Main, h. 2113 Main
Gifford John S, teacher, h. 2113 Main
Gifford Samuel G, teacher, h, 2113 Main
Gift Wm D, carp, h. 1107 s A
Gilchrist David A, carp, h. s w cor s C and 22d
Gillespie Allen H (Gillespie & Carr), rms 1609 s D
Gillespie & Carr (A H Gillespie & I Carr), fruits, oysters & fish, etc., 121 s Anderson
Gillespie Michael, plumber, h. 118 n 19th
Gilson Samuel R, tmster, h. 5524 s A
Ginzer Frank C, stenographer, The American Tin Plate Co, rms 1705 s F
Gipson Mahlon, lab, h. 2400 s B
Gipson Robert W, lab, h. 2400 s B
Gipson Samuel, lab, h. 2400 s B
Glaspy Michael (Stokes, Glaspy & Co), h. n 19th
Glell Michael J, lab, bds 228 n 6th
Glens Falls Fire Insurance Co of Glens Falls, N Y. net surplus, $1,175,321, Roop & Haynes agts, 210½ s Anderson
Goar Oliver, lab, h. 1820 n F
Gobel John H, carp, h. n s s C w of 24th

JOHN O. MILLER, ELEVEN YEARS' EXPERIENCE in Watchmaking. Finisher six years in Elgin & Springfield Watch Factories.
I GUARANTEE MY WORK. 3 N. Meridian, ANDERSON, IND.

Goddard Charles (Kramer & Goddard), h. Bringhurst, Ind
Goddard John L, student, bds 1811 s B
Goebel Louis, blacksmith, h. 1119 n F
Goin Robert, iron wkr, bds 1917 n A
Golding Oliver, brick mason, h. 1347 s C
Goldnamer David B, clk, 103 s Anderson, h. n Anderson
Goldnamer Esther E, clk, 103 s Anderson, h. n Anderson
Goldnamer E & Co (Mrs Menees Goldnamer); dry gooods, 103 s Anderson and 1507 Main
Goldnamer Mrs Menees (E Goldnamer & Co), h. n Anderson
Goldnamer Millia, h. n Anderson
Goldnamer M Nathan, mgr 103 s Anderson, h. n Anderson
Goldsmith Charles E, watchman, h. 1824 n B
Goldsmith Greenup R, wagon mkr, wks 1522 s A, h. 1824 n B
Goldsmith Maggie, h. 1824 n B
Goldsmith Phoebe E, h. 1824 n B
Goldsmith Wm R, tin plate wkr, h. 1824 n B
Gomer Philip, cigar mkr, Rummel Bros, h. s I
Good George, glass wkr, bds 2531 n A
Good Joseph W, gas fitter, bds 417 n 12th
Goode Martin E (Kidwell & Goode), h. 1920 Main
Goodman George, gatherer, bds 710 n Anderson
Goodman Thomas A, gas well driller, h. 414 n 14th
Goodwin Selmer, plasterer, h. 2322 n A
Gootee C H, barber, 1427 w Main, h. 1526 n H
Gordon Albert E, barber, wks 1516 Main, h. 2035 n A
Gordon Walter, teamster, bds 114 n 13th
Gorins Asa, lab, h. 743 n 14th
Gorman Mrs Jane, dry goods and notions, 1527 Main, h. same
Gorman Mrs Lizzie, h. 1009 n 10th
Gorman Patrick, mgr 1527 Main, h. same
Gorman Wm, plasterer, bds 912 n 13th
Goshorn Nellie, cook, 1514 s A, h. 1932 n B
Goshorn John, city watchman, h. 1932 n B
Govro Donor, glass wkr, h. 411 n 10th
Govro Filesty, h. 411 n 10th
Govro Flora, h. 411 n 10th
Govro Thomas, glass wkr, h. 411 n 10th
Graham Charles, painter, bds 1829 s M
Graham James W, harness mkr, wks 1524 s A, bds s Anderson
Graham Nathan, carp, h. 1829 s M
G A R Hall, 205 s Anderson
Grant John, lab, h. 1933 s A
Grant U S, lab, h. 2517 s B
Grass Charles, clk, 201 s Anderson

WHEN—CLOTHING,

HATS AND MEN'S FURNISHINGS.

Grassestreuer Joseph, tailor, wks 114½ s Anderson, h. 1524 s B
Gray Alonzo F, hod carrier, bds 426 n 11th
Gray James, lab, h. e s 20th bet s B and L E & W Ry
Gray Wm H, drayman, h. 1302 s B
Greathouse Frank, clk, 202 s Anderson, h. 1625 n B
Green Alfred, furniture, 1409 s Main, h. 1403 s Main
Green Daniel L (Elwood Real Estate Co), h. 1526 n B
Green David L, teamster, h. n s s C, e of 26th
Green E E, druggist, n w cor Anderson & s A, h. 608 s Anderson
Green F W, drug clk, n w cor Anderson & s A, h. 608 s Anderson
Green James, glass cutter, h. 414 n 7th
Green Lewis J, brick mason, h. 1602 n E
Green Stella M, h. 608 s Anderson
Green Samuel, tin plate wkr, bds 800 s 18th
Greenlee Cassius M, attorney and notary, pres Elwood E & P Co, 202½ s Anderson, h. 1347 s D
Greenlee Ida B, stenographer, h. 1349 s D
Greenlee John, carp, h. 1349 s D
Greenlee Robert H. carp, h. 2409 s A
Gregg Joseph, carp, h. 1914 s M
Greulich Albert B (Greulich Bros), h. 1901 Main
Greulich Bros (A B & R Greulich), wholesale fresh and salt meats and sausages and bologna, e e Main
Greulich Rheinhold (Greulich Bros), h. e e Main
Griffith Alfred L, bookpr, Diamond Plate Glass Co, h. 1350 s E
Griffin Bertha, h. 417 n 12th
Griffin & Broadbent (E S Griffin, F R Broadbent), attorneys, 105½ s Anderson
Griffin Charles D, lab, bds 207 n 13th
Griffin Elbent S (Griffin & Broadbent), h. 1900 n B
Griffin Michael, glass wkr, h. 1000 n F
Griffin Wm F, lab, h. 417 n 12th
Griffin Wm J, lab, bds 207 n 13th
Grim James F. physician, 322 s Anderson, h. 1327 s D
Grimes Oliver N, wks lumber yard, h. 1312 n D
Griswold James, sect foreman, h. 1334 s C
Groff Edith E, school teacher, h. 806 s Anderson
Groff Lulu E, comp, The Elwood Press, h. 806 s Anderson
Groff Mary E. h. 806 s Anderson
Groff Philip T, miller, 317 s Anderson, h. 806 s Anderson
Groover Wm M, carp, h. 814 s C
Gruey Joseph H, gatherer, h. 404 n Boulevard
Gruey Sophia, wid, h. 404 n Boulevard
Gruey Steven C, gatherer, h. 404 n Boulevard
Guild Rev Thomas M, pastor M E Church, h. 1508 n A

Place Your Real Estate and FARM PROPERTY in the Hands of ROOP & HAYNES,
AND BE SURE OF QUICK RETURNS.
210½ S. Anderson, - - - - ELWOOD, IND.

MONEY TO BUILD WITH PROCURED WITHIN 15 DAYS. Robinson & Glassco, Loan, Real Estate&Insurance agents
Room 9 "When" Building, - - ANDERSON, IND.

Gullion Wm, glass wkr, bds 1713 s F
Gunder John, glass gatherer, bds 812 n 11th
Gunn Louis, h. n s s I bet 13th and 14th
Gunn Nelson, carp, h. n s s I bet 13th and 14th
Gurding Alexander, lab, bds 1803 n D
Guyer Melissa, domestic, 2418 n B
Guynan Michael, molder, bds 1350 s A

H

Haas Anthony, gatherer, h. 917 n 12th
Haas Joseph, glass blower, h. 921 n 12th
Haas Lizzie, h. 917 n 12th
Haas Louis, clk, 120 s Anderson, h. 917 n 12th
Haas Theresa, h. 917 n 12th
Hackelman Carrol, teamster, h. 1801 e Boulevard
Hackelman Judson, lab, h. 1345 s A
Hackleman Pleasant, lumber dealer, h. 1801 e Boulevard
Hackelman Wm, cigarmkr, h. 1345 s A
Hacket Frank S, lab, h. 2106 n C
Hagerty David H, bench boy, bds 1332 s A
Haines Guy, tin plate wkr, bds n e cor s N and 22d
Haines John C, glass wkr, h. 2529 n A
Haines Wm, tin plate wkr, bds 1303 s D
Haislup Oscar L, lab, bds 2013 n F
Halfin Wm E, carp, h. n s s C bet 23d and 24th
Hall John S, driver, h. 715 n 14th
Hall Martin, plumber, bds 408 s Anderson
Hallarman Frank W, bottler, E B Wks, bds Boston House
Hamel Wm, glass blower, bds 408 n Boulevard
Hamilton Andrew H, teamster, h. 2336 n B
Hamilton Charles E, farmer, h. 2741 s A
Hamilton Henry S (Hamilton & Stam), h. 2215 s B
Hamilton James, farmer, h. 1617 n D
Hamilton Matthew, school teacher, h. 1617 n D
Hamilton & Stam (Henry S Hamilton and Alonzo Stam), blacksmiths, 1508 n B
Hamilton T Woodson, carp, h. 1643 s A
Hamlin Findlay H, brickmason, h. 2318 n A
Hamm Phillip (E C Ice Co and E B Wks), h. 1515 s E
Hancher P W, drug clk, 104 s Anderson, h. 1812 e Main
Hand Darby T, lather, h. 706 n Anderson
Hand Ella R, clk, h. 1614 n A
Hand Hiram, bookpr, h. 1614 n A
Hand Martha, wid, h. 1909 n D

Deal & Willkie, **ATTORNEYS AT LAW.** We wi attend to your legal business promptl and charge you no exhorbitant fees.

WHEN—Originators of the One Price System
IN SELLING CLOTHING.
FAIR AND SQUARE DEALINGS WITH ALL.

Hand Thomas J, glass blower, h. 1909 n D
Hann George W (Hann & Moffot), h. Muncie, Ind
Hann & Moffot (G W Hann and Mrs Jessie Moffot), installment goods, 1525 Main
Hanna James C, h. 1910 Main.
Hanna John, carp, h. 1910 Main
Hanshew James R, farmer, h. 1602 e Boulevard
Hanshew Jesse L, wks Electric Light Co, h. 1602 e Boulevard
Hanshew Philander W, druggist, h. 1812 Main
Hanson John A, glass wkr, h. 1508 n D
Harb John, clk, rear 1418 Main
Harbit Nonie, clk, 115 s Anderson, h. 1820 s A
Hardesty Ella, h. 1802 s B
Hardesty Wm, brakeman, bds 2121 n A
Harding Sarah J, wid, h. 1880 n F
Harlon Marlow, glass wkr, bds 802 n 11th
Harley Thomas, tin plate wkr, bds 800 s 18th
Harnack Theodore F, supt, Geo A Macbeth Co, h. 826 n Anderson
Harrell Anna Z, h. 426 n 10th
Harrell Elmer N, watchman, h. 426 n 10th
Harrell John M, glass wkr, h. 426 n 10th
Harrell Mary F, boarding, 426 n 10th, h. same
Harrington Wm, tin plate wkr, bds 800 s 18th
Harris Edward, glass wkr, bds 404 n 12th
Harris Henry, tin plate wkr, bds n w cor s N and 23d
Harris Mrs Martha, boarding house, 835 n 12th, h. same
Harris Paul A, glass wkr, h. 2009 Main
Harris Winifred, school teacher, bds n s s I bet 14th and Anderson
Harrison Henry, gatherer, bds 431 n 9th
Harrold David C, dentist, 202½ s Anderson, h. 1901 n C
Harrold Frank W, dental student, h. 1901 n C
Harry Frank, lab, h. 213 s 19th
Harshman Alonzo, glass wkr, h. e s 11th, 2d s n F
Hartebeck Wm, hostler, wks 1600 s A, bds s A
Harting & Co (H G & S B Harting), elevator and grain, 1509 and 1511 Main
Harting Harmon G (Harting & Co), h. 1520 n A
Harting Sherman B (Harting & Co), h. n end Anderson
Hartman Edward, glass gatherer, bds n w cor 9th and n A
Harvey Edwin B, mgr The Jay Grain Co, h. 818 n 13th
Harvey Ella, house keeper, 1204 Main
Harvey Jessie, h. 1204 Main
Harvey Malinda, wid, h. 1609 n A
Haskett John H (Havens, Haskett & Co), h. 612 n 16th
Hattman Francis A, foreman, Geo A Macbeth Co, h. 851 n 11th

John L. Lindskoog, Leads in the Merchant Tailoring Line English and French Worsteds, imported, always in stock.
Do not buy until you have seen them.
ALEXANDRIA, IND.

Hattman Frederick, foreman, flue works, h. 851 n 11th
Hausecuster Henry, lab, h. 2029 n C
Havens Daniel F (Havens, Haskett & Co), h. 622 n 16th
Havens, Haskett & Co (D F Havens, John Haskett and M M Jackson), gas fitters, 1604 s A
Huvers George, glass blower, bds 835 n 12th
Havey Patrick, gatherer, bds n w cor 10th and n C
Hawkins George W, barber, wks 1520 s A
Haynes Nellie, h. cor 10th and n C
Haynes George E (Roop & Haynes), atty-at-law, h. 2400 s B
Haytin John B, glass wkr, h. 814 n 10th
Hayward Louis, hod carrier, bds 2322 n A
Hayworth Mattie, h. n s L E & W Ry, bet 24th and 25th
Hazen John F, v pres The American Tin P'Co, h. Cincinnati, O
Headley Alonzo, lab, h. 1302 s A
Headley Frances M, secy Elwood Planing Mill Co, h. 1005 Main
Headley Reuben L, lab, bds 1005 Main
Heapley Wm C, h. 1005 Main
Heap James K, v pres The Jay Grain Co, h. Ft Recovery, O
Heath Harry W, clk, 1532 Main, h. 322 n 17th
Heath Thomas C, carp, h. 1831 n B
Heath Wm N (Edwins & Heath), h. 322 n 18th
Heater John, glass gatherer, bds 236 n Boulevard
Heaton Alonzo, carp, h. 2123 n D
Heaton James, painter, h. 2123 n D
Heaton Wm I, bar tender, 1518 s A, rms n Anderson
Heck Alice, milliner, 1418 Main, h. n Anderson
Heck C, glass blower, h. 948 n 12th
Heck D H, clk, 100 s Anderson, h. s s n C
Heck Elmer C, asst cashier, Citizens' Exchange Bank, h. n Anderson
Heck George, gatherer, bds 404 n Boulevard
Hedrick Alonzo, wks Rodefers Brick Works
Heffner David, sawyer, h. 312 s 17th
Heffner Geo W (Geo W and Lewis Heffner), h. 607 s Anderson
Heffner Geo W and Lewis, lumber, 1533 s B
Heffner James D, bookpr, h. 1602 s D
Heffner James Y, mach hand, bds 1602 s D
Heffner John S, carp, h. 615 s Anderson
Heffner Lewis (Geo W and Lewis Heffner), h. 1602 s D
Heffner Thomas, carp, h. s s I bet 14th and Anderson
Heffner Vinnia C, h. 1602 s D
Helms Albert, driver, h. 419 n 9th
Helms Charles W, glass wkr, bds 421 n 9th
Helms Sibbie F, h. 419 n 9th

Jackson & Burr Do the Largest INSURANCE Business. Insure in the good old Companies they represent.

69½ N. Meridian, - - ANDERSON, IND.

ELWOOD CITY DIRECTORY.

Heller Jesse C, real estate, 120½ s Anderson, bds Boston Hotel
Henderson James, glass wkr, h. 2103 n B
Henderson Minnie, h. 2103 n B
Hendricks Ira, plasterer, bds 1009 n 10th
Henegan Patrick, glass wkr, h. 427 n 9th
Hensley Lizzie, wid, h. 1st e 2008 s A
Hepworth Harry, glass wkr, h. 404 n 7th
Herel George M, eng, h. 2501 n A
Herrie Emma E, wid, h. s w cor 20th and s A
Hersch Edward, gatherer, bds 1045 n 14th
Hess Philip, glass wkr, h. 908 n 12th
Hess Wm, glass wkr, h. 826 n 12th
Hesser Herman, bartender, rms s s s J bet 14th and Anderson
Hester Robert, glass blower, bds 911 n 14th
Hester James E, lab, h. 1909 n E
Hester Wm, gatherer, bds 911 n 14th
Hetzel Wm, glass gatherer, h. 228 n 6th
Heverbeck Louis, gatherer, bds 431 n 9th
Hewitt Theodore C, bds 2008 s A
Hiatt Levi W, clk, h. 1010 s B
Hickman Wm C, lab, h. 2328 n C
Hicks James, glass wkr, bds 1533 Main
Hiers James W, plumber and gas fitter, h. n s s N bet 24th and Pan Handle Ry
Hiers Nancy, wid, h. n s s N bet 24th and Pan Handle Ry
Hiers Wm, gas fitter, h. 515 s Anderson
Hiet Delania, painter, h. w s 10th bet n F and G
High Phœbe, domestic, n w cor 10th and n L
Hileman Alonzo, trav sales, h. 1004 s Anderson
Hileman James, glass wkr, h. n s Anderson
Hill George W, glass wkr, h. 1048 n 14th
Hill Ida, domestic, 710 n Anderson
Hill Peter, glass wkr, bds s w cor 8th and n C
Hillard Samuel T, glass wkr, h. w s 11th bet Main and s A
Hillen Anthony, glass wkr, h. 918 n 12th
Himes Euphemia J, h. 1829 n F
Himes Rev Lewis, pastor, Christian Church, h. 1829 n F
Hinds Birdie, h. 1428 Main
Hinds Jessie, h. 1428 Main
Hinds Mrs S A, wid, h. 1428 Main
Hinkle Edward, glass wkr, bds 426 n 10th
Hire Jennie, h. 1800 n F
Hire Mollie A, domestic, h. 1912 s A
Hiser George B, city editor The Elwood Daily Call, h. 1907 n A
Hiser Nellie, h. 1907 n A

George B. Epperson, Contractor and Builder of Felt and Gravel ROOFING.

39 E. 9th St., - - ANDERSON, IND.

John Donnelly, The Real Estate Dealer of Anderson. If you wish to buy, sell or rent, call at 10 E. 10 St., ANDERSON, IND.

Hite Wm H, glass blower, h. 900 n Anderson
Hobaugh Daniel, glass wkr, h. 430 n 7th
Hobbs Lida, wid, h. 1623 n A
Hock Frank, gatherer, h. 837 n 11th
Hock Watsel, gatherer, bds 837 n 11th
Hockett Wm B, plasterer, h. 2311 n C
Hockstrausen Louis, glass flatner, h. 2515 Main
Hodson Frank O, asst city eng, bds 2329 n A
Hodson Jonathan, teamster, h. 2329 n B
Hoffman Charles J, glass blower, h. 2521 Main
Hoffman Jonathan, glass mnfgr, h. 1647 Main
Hoffman May, milliner app, 1529 Main, h. 1647 Main
Hoffman Minnie E, h. 1647 Main
Hoffman Wm C, clk, 117 s Anderson, rms same
Hogan Adeline, wid, h. 1052 n 14th
Hogan Minnie, cook, 111 s Anderson, rms 123½ s Anderson
Hogle George J, saloon, h. 108½ s Anderson
Holden Wm, clk, h. 1609 n E
Holdinghausen Frederick, glass wkr, h. e s 4th bet n E and F
Hollinsworth Wm T, fireman, h. 1828 n B
Hollis Frank, glass wkr, bds 810 n 11th
Holloran John, pres and mgr Elwood Iron Wks, h. 1901 s I
Holmes Frank, glass wkr, h. n e cor 10th and n C
Holmes Isiah F, carp, h. 211 n 24th
Holt Albert, glass wkr, rms 1612 s D
Holt Anna M, h. 1004 n F
Holt Ellen, h. 1004 n F
Holt Joseph, glass cutter, h. 1004 n F
Holt Nellie, domestic, 1005 Main
Holt Roy, h. 1005 Main
Holt Wm L, lab, h. 2534 n E
Home Ins Co, of New York, 1527½ Main
Hommel Arminta, h. 2023 s A
Hommel James A, lab, h. 2023 s A
Hood Charles M, teamster, h. 2028 s N
Hood John, lab, h. 2001 s A
Hood Sherman, lab, h. 1836 n F
Hood Sherman, lab, h. 1523 n F
Hook Stephen, stonemason, h. 2013 n C
Hooton Greene C, clk, h. 1639 Main
Hoover Andrew, tel opr, The American T Plate Co, h. 1609 n D
Hopkins Wm, tin plate wkr, h. w s 22d bet s M and N
Hopper Albert L, gas fitter, h. 1534 n D
Hopper Albert H (Hopper & Hutchison), h. 1534 n D

HUGH FISHER, Manufacturer Screen Doors and Windows all sizes. Furniture repairing a specialty.
198 and 200 N. Milton St., ANDERSON, IND.

BUCK, BRICKLEY & CO., THE LEADING DRUGGISTS, Cor. Ninth and Meridian Streets, ANDERSON, IND.

J. T. Knowland & Son, SANITARY PLUMBERS. *Gas and Steam Fitters.*
111 N. Main St., ANDERSON, IND. 'Phone 30.

40　　　　　ELWOOD CITY DIRECTORY.

JAMES E. HUSTON.　　　O. E. NEARON.　　　JOHN NEARON.

HUSTON & NEARON,
Restaurant and Lunch Counter,
CIGARS AND TOBACCO, CONFECTIONERY AND FRUITS,

OYSTERS IN SEASON, served in Every Style.

SPECIAL RATES TO DAY BOARDERS.

1514 South A,　　·　·　·　·　·　·　·　ELWOOD, IND.

Hopper & Hutchison (A H Hopper & Wm Hutchison), blksmiths, 1612 Main
Hoppenrath Wm, medical student, bds 2019 n A
Horan Wm, iron wkr, h. 1925 s J
Hornaday Charles, brickmkr, bds 812 s B
Horne R H Produce Co The, J H Ashley mgr, 113 n 16th
Horner George E, foreman, h. n s s C e of 26th
Horrell Charles, boarding, 1350 s A, h. same
Horrell Caroline, h. 1350 s A
Hosck Joseph, glass blower, h. 829 n 11th
Hosper Cary, lab, bds 907 s B
Hoting Margaret E, wid, h. 1924 s A
Houck John W, baker, wks 118 s Anderson, h. 616 s 16th
House Newton H, propr Eagle Flouring Mills, h. 1609 s F
House Joel, carp, h. 2123 n F
House Ora Z, clk, 317 s Anderson, h. 1609 s E
Housand Benj, glass wkr, h. 253 n A
Houser Job, eng, 1513 Main, h. 1611 n B
Houstrosser Louis, glass wkr, bds 2418 n B
Howard Charles E, carp, h. s s 23d bet L E & W Ry and s C
Howard James, mach, h. 938 n Anderson
Howard John, glass wkr, h. 570 n 14th
Howe Wesley C, ship clk, h. 1020 Main
Hubert Augustus, finisher, bds 835 n 12th
Hueber John, gatherer, bds 526 n Boulevard
Huffer W L, yard hand, cor n B and 13th, h. 1918 n D
Huffman Wm, glass wkr, bds 2402 n B
Hughes Alford A, lab, h. 215 n 13th
Hughes Charles, carp, h. 1812 n B
Hughes Edward, bds 431 n 9th
Hughes Harry, section hand, h. 1822 s H

John O. Miller, Practical Watchmaker & Jeweler. Eleven Years' Experience in the Manufacturing of Watches.
3 N. Meridian, 　-　-　-　ANDERSON, IND.

Hughes Mary, h. 416 s Anderson
Hughes S A, principal 2d Ward Public School Bldg, h. 2020 s A
Hughes Wm, lab, h. 215 n 13th
Hughes Wm, glass wkr, bds 2121 n A
Hughes Wm, hoop mkr, h. 1822 s H
Hughes Wilson, lab, h. 1825 n C
Hughs James H, lab, h. 2609 s A
Hughs John, blksmith, bds w s 24th bet s N and O
Humbert Julius, glass wkr, h. 419 n 8th
Humerickhouse Clara C, h. 1915 n B
Humerickhouse Emma E, h. 1915 n B
Humerickhouse Jonathan, fish dealer, rear 1418 Main, h. 1915 n B
Humerickhouse Oliver L, glass wkr. h. 1915 n B
Humler Charles, tailor, bds 408 s Anderson
Humner Mrs Annie, wid, h. 424 n 7th
Hungerford Stanley, gas fitter, h. 211 n 13th
Hunt Alexander, eng, bds 335 n 12th
Hunt Dora, h. s w cor 3d and n G
Hunt Mrs Ellen, boarding house, 710 n Anderson, h. same
Hunt Otto, butcher, h. s w cor 3d and n G
Hunter Charles S, lab, h. w s n Anderson
Hunter Edward, carp, bds 417 n 12th
Hunter Francis M, druggist,, agt Adams Exp Co, h. 1608 Main
Hunter Frank M, city marshal, h. 115 n 18th
Hunter Joseph A, clk, 208 s Anderson, h. 1512 s E
Hunter Robert, glass wkr, h. 735 n 14th
Hunter Robert M, carp, h. 912 n 13th
Hunter Stella A, student, h. 1608 Main
Huntsinger Wm, lab, wks 401 s Anderson
Huntsinger Wm I, lab, h. 1901 s B
Huntsinger Wm Jr, lab, wks 401 s Anderson
Hupp & Connor (W A Hupp and Thomas Conner), boots and shoes, 107 s Anderson
Hupp George W, ins agt, 105½ s Anderson, h. 415 s Anderson
Hupp Samuel, roofer, h. 415 s Anderson
Hupp Wm A (Hupp & Conner), h. 1200 s A
Hurlock Joseph, plasterer, h. 1016 s A
Huser Pierre, glass wkr, bds 409 n 12th
Husser Herman, bartender, 109 s Anderson, rms s Anderson
Hussong Bertha, h. 2412 s B
Hussong John W, lab, h. 2412 s B
Huston James E (Huston & Nearon), h. 2016 n A
Huston & Nearon (J E Huston and C E & J Nearon), restaurant and lunch counter, 1514 s A (see adv)

WOOLLEY FOUNDRY AND MACHINE WORKS,
Engineers, Founders and Machinists
N. W. Cor. 14th and C. W. and M. R. R.

WHEN—THE—**Anderson Clothiers & Hatters.**
☞ ONE PRICE TO ALL.

Hutchings Lemuel, lab, h. 1820 n F
Hutchison Wm (Hopper & Hutchison), h. 1522 n D
Hutson Albert, plasterer, bds 1515 n B
Hutt Wm H, glass wkr, h. 820 n 12th

I

Ice Charles, lab, h. 817 s B
Indiana Mutual Building & Loan Association, Roop & Haynes agts, 210½ s Anderson
Indiana Underwriters' Ins Co, of Indianapolis, Ind, 1510 Main
Ingram Mary E, wid, h. 2300 n E
Ingram Robert, lab, h. 1836 n F
Ingram Thomas J, glass wkr, h. 232 n 6th
Inter-State Building & Loan Association, of Bloomington, Ill, 120½ s Anderson
Irons Charles, well driller, h. 1918 n B
Iseley Marion F, glass wkr, h. 2024 s N
Iseley Samuel, wks Starkey's Brick Wks
Iseminger Amos, teamster, h. 1738 s D
Iseminger John, lab, h. 1738 s D
Iseminger Wm, h. 2111 Main
Isenour Mary, wid, h. 2331 Main

J

Jack Benj M, glass wkr, h. 910 s B
Jack John W, teamster, h. 815 s 16th
Jack Mary C, dressmkr, wks 801 s 16th, h. 815 s 16th
Jacken Joseph, glass wkr, bds 419 n 8th
Jackley Everett, glass wkr, bds 2418 n B
Jackley Thomas, glass wkr, bds 2418 n B
Jackson Joseph H, glass wkr, h. 901 s B
Jackson Monroe M (Havens, Haskett & Co), h. ½ mile n w city
Jackson Samuel, glass wkr, bds 901 s B
Jacobs James (Schofield & Jacobs), bds 1850 s A
James Frank (Behymer, James & Co), rms 846 n Anderson
James Mrs Sarah, carpet weaver, rear 1926 n A, h. same
James Wm S, mgr W R McCloy Glass Co, h. cor 11th and n A
Jamison Rev Philip, pastor First Presbyterian Ch, h. 807 s 16th
Jarret Harry, teamster, bds rear 1108 Main
Jay Daniel W, secy and treas The Jay Grain Co, res St Marys, O
Jay Grain Co The, Oliver Jay pres, J K Heep v-pres, D W Jay secy and treas, E B Harvey mgr, 401 s Anderson

Roop & Haynes, Real Estate,
LOANS AND INSURANCE.
210½ S. Anderson, • • • ELWOOD, IND.

Robinson & Glassco, Real Estate, Loan and Insurance Agents, room 9 "When" Building Agents Fidelity Building and Savings Union.
ANDERSON, IND.

Jay Oliver, pres The Jay Grain Co, res St Marys, O
Jeffries Joseph E, secy and treas Electric L & P Co, h. 2015 Main
Jenkins George, tin plate wkr, bds e s 22d bet s M and N
Jenkins Harry C, glass wkr, h. 810 n 11th
Jenkins Lewis, iron wkr, bds s w cor s O and Pan Handle Ry
Jenkins Ollie, catcher, bds 1700 s D
Jenner Almond L, carp, h. 2009 n D
Jenner Charles, dining room, 111 s Anderson, h. 1912 s A
Jenner Daniel T, harness mkr, h. 1908 s A
Jenner Moses G, boarding house, 1912 s A, h. same
Jennings Flora J T, wid, h. 1615 n A
Jessup Mrs Mary F, dressmkr, 801 s 16th, h. same
Job Robert R, lab, h. 1331 s A
John David, tin plate wkr, bds 1319 s D
John Sarah A, wid, h. 800 s 16th
John Wm, tin plate wkr, bds w s 24th bet s N and O
Johnson Grant, glass wkr, bds 1620 s E
Johnson Laura, bds 1351 s A
Johnson Maggie A, h. 403 n 9th
Johnson Nancy, bds 1331 s A
Johnson Victoria, bds 1351 s A
Jones Byron D N, city editor, The Elwood Daily Press, bds 2019 n A
Jones Cora D, domestic, 2010 n A
Jones Corda, dining room, 1528 Main, bds same
Jones Delbert, glass wkr, bds e s 4th bet n E and F
Jones Harry, carp, bds 1624 n D
Jones James, teamster, h. 2327 n F
Jones John, catcher, bds 1700 s D
Jones Major A, clk, h. 500 n 19th
Jones Peter, tin plate wkr, bds 1527 n C
Jones Theophilus, tin plate wkr, bds 1527 n C
Jones Thomas M, h. 2419 n C
Jones Wm, tin plate wkr, bds e s 23d bet s M and N
Jones Wm H, carp, h. 1806 n F
Jones Wm I, clk, h. 500 n 19th
Jones Wm T, lab, h. 2419 n C
Jordan Edward, lab, h. 1434 n 7th
Jordan G Horace, real estate, rms 1933 Main
Jordan Wesley S, real estate, rms 1933 Main
Jordan Richard, lab, h. 1039 n 14th
Jordan Wm E, mach, h. 1484 n 7th
Joshy Eugene, glass wkr, bds s w cor 2nd and n F
Jumper Newton, lab, bds 1802 s B
Jumper Oliver, lab, bds 1802 s B

Deal & Willkie, We will write your Insurance in none but Standard Companies; All parties are treated alike, no cut-rates and no wildcat Insurance.
REAL ESTATE AND NOTARY PUBLICS.

K

Kahler Wm, saloon, n w cor 10th and n G, h. same
Kahn Anna, wid, h. 1520 s B
Kahn Julius, M J Wolf mngr, clothing, etc, 110 s Anderson
Kahawl Fannie, chambermaid, The Stevenson House, bds same
Kahn Thomas, glass gatherer, bds n w cor 9th and n A
Kapp Wm H, carp, h. s B
Kapphan Albert (O'Brien & Kapphan), h. 208 n 11th
Kapphan Albert, glass wkr, h. w s 11th, bet n A and C
Kapps John, glass blower, bds 812 n 11th
Kastler Henry, teamster, h. 1822 s G
Keeber Henry, glass blower, bds 1912 s A
Keel Hugo, glass wkr, bds 413 n 12th
Keith E G, v-pres Diamond Plate Glass Co, res Chicago, Ill
Keith S B, carp, h. 1333 s B
Keller Adda, trimmer, 100 s Anderson, h. 1814 n C
Keller Elizabeth, h. n s L E & W Ry, e 22d
Keller John H S (The Elwood Heading Co), h. 1811 s B
Keller John K, drayman, h. n s L E & W Ry, e.22d
Keller Rillia, h. n s L E & W Ry, e 22d
Keller Wm, lab, h. n s L E & W Ry, e 22d
Kelley Aaron P, lab, h. 1511 n E
Kelley Daniel, lab, h. 1511 n E
Kelley George, glass blower, h. 1608 n F
Kelley James, lab, h. 1511 n E
Kelley Joseph C, glass blower, h. 1608 n F
Kelley Wm, glass blower, h. 1608 n F
Kelley Wm, brkman, bds n w cor s A and 19th
Kelly James, glass wkr, bds 1000 n F
Kelly John, glass wkr, bds 1000 n F
Kemp James W, sawyer, h. 1514 s G
Kemp Sherman, baker, h. 1302 s A
Kemp Peter S, teamster, h. 2004 n E
Kemptner Wm L, carp, h. 2032 Main
Kennedy Michael, molder, bds 1802 s B
Kenneday Wm, lab, bds 2519 s A
Kent John, glass wkr, h. e s 4th bet n E and F
Kent Theodore, glass wkr, bds 2133 n A
Kerr Lulu, trimmer, Alice Heck
Keslet David, tailor, h. 1924 s B
Kesot John T, glass wkr, h. 710 n Anderson
Kessler D, tailor, 206½ s Anderson, h. s B
Key Newton, glass wkr, h. 2031 s N

WM. J. DOVE, Insures against loss by Fire, Cyclone, Accident and Death.
NEELEY BLOCK. 61½ N. Meridian, ANDERSON, IND.

Keyser George W, glass blower, h. 1523 n D
Kidwell Amanda, wid, h. 1901 Main
Kidwell George W, carp, h. 1813 n A
Kidwell & Goode (I A Kidwell & M E Goode), flour, 1513 Main
Kidwell Ira A (Kidwell & Goode), h. 2024 Main
Kidwell Jesse M, clk, P C C & St L, h. 1815 n A
Kidwell John, stock buyer, h. n e cor s J and 14th
Kidwell Maggie, h. 1321 s B
Kidwell Wm, sand dealer, h. 2430 n A
Kilrain Charles, glass wkr, h. 820 s B
Kilrain John, glass blower, h. 820 s B
Kilsoe Noble, brickmason, h. 1516 n E
Kincaid Clyde, lab, bds 1526 n G
Kincaid John, carp, bds 1526 n G
Kinder Ada, domestic, 2400 s B
Kinder Lavina, wid, h. 1534 n C
King Daniel B, druggist, h, 1907 n C
King Murray, glass wkr, bds s w cor 8th and n C
King Russell, barber, 1427 w Main, rms 1428 Main
Kingman Mary E, wid, h. 1809 n E
Kingman U G, mailing clk, P O, h. 1809 n E
Kingman Wm, carp, h. 1929 s A
Kinley Joseph, glass wkr, bds 211 n 11th
Kinley Noah, glass wkr, bds 211 n 11th
Kinzie Elmer I, lab, h. 2334 n C
Kinzie Aaron T, lab, h 2006 s N
Kinzie Wm L, agent, h. 1816 s n
Kirch Peter, glass wkr, bds 515 Main
Kirkham Phora B, cashier, 201 s Anderson, bds 1712 south G
Kirkley Daniel, lab, h. s e cor L E & W R R and 22d
Kirkman Wm H, drayman, h. 1813 e Boulevard
Kirkpatrick James E, frgt and pass agt P C C & St L, h. 1359 s B
Kirtley Daniel V, lab, 2120 n D
Kistler Fannie B, h. rear 910 n F
Kistler C G, glass wkr, h. rear 910 n F
Kitchen Charles, h. 1517 n E
Klapp Albert L, wks foundry, h. 1319 n 7th
Klapp Clinton C, wks Plate Glass Co, h. 1319 n 7th
Klapp Henry C, tin, plate wkr, h. 1319 n 7th
Klapp Madison, teamster, h. 1319 n 7th
Kluth C, tailor, 114½ s Anderson, h. n C, nr 14th
Knepper C A, foreman the Elwood Daily Call, bds 1400 s A
Knight Clarence L, cigar mkr, wks 115½ s Anderson, h. n C
Knight Isaac N, carp, h. 422 n 11th
Knott Andrew E, mgr, 1518 s A, h. 1527 n D

Anderson Foundry and Machine Works, Manufacturers of Portable and Stationary
265 N. JACKSON STREET, 'Phone 53.

Is Your Property Insured? If not, CALL AT ONCE on **JACKSON & BURR,** 69½ N. Meridian, - - ANDERSON, IND.

46 ELWOOD CITY DIRECTORY.

Knotts Charles, lab, bds 1302 s A
Knotts David C, staple and fancy groceries and daily meat market, 2216 s B, h. 2214 s B (see adv)
Knotts Dora E, domestic, 111 s Anderson
Knotts Eveline, wid, h. 1615 n A
Knotts Foster, teamster, h. n s L E & W Ry, bet 20th & 22d
Knotts Frank S, bartender, 1524 s Main, h. 608 n 12th
Knotts James, bartender, 1526 s A, h. 610 n 12th
Knotts Jane, wid, h. 1925 n A
Knotts Joseph F, saloon, h. 1624 s A
Knotts Joseph W, student, h. 1615 n A
Knotts Minerva J, h. 1624 s A
Knotts Noble, student, h. 1615 n A
Knotts Rachel, wid, h. 1333 s A
Knotts Wm H, sr, salesman, 1526 s A, h. 1634 s A
Knotts Wm R, glass wkr, bds 612 n Anderson
Knott John, saloon, 1518 s A, h. 1626 s A
Kolling Mrs Mary, wid, h. 228 n 6th
Koons Samuel J, h. 931 n 12th
Kountz Henry, glass wkr, bds 1013 Main
Kracke Frank, tailor, wks 113½ s Anderson, bds Boston House
Kramer Anna, h. 221 s Anderson
Kramer Francis E, secy Elwood Iron Works, h. 221 s Anderson
Kramer Gustave, (Kramer & Goddard), treas Elwood Iron Works, h. 221 s Anderson
Kramer & Goddard (G Kramer & C Goddard), Excelsior Factory, Junc, L E & W Pan-Handle Tracks
Kramer Joseph A, teamster, h. 221 s Anderson
Kranz Edward D, tailor, h. 1804 n A
Kranz Emmel F, tailor, h. 1804 n A
Kranz Lulu, h. 1804 n A
Kraus Jacob (J Kraus & Co), 120 s Anderson, h. 1519 n B
Kraus J & Co, clothing, 120 s Anderson
Kremer Charles, glass wkr, bds 1812 s G
Krebs Emil, blacksmith, h. 909 n 13th
Kremer Peter, glass wkr, bds 1812 s G
Kummell Frank, lab, bds 1013 Main
Kuntz John, gatherer, bds 411 n 7th
Kuntz Peter (P Kuntz Lumber Co), h. Chicago, Ill
Kuntz P Lumber Co (P Kuntz, F L Mener, A J Winters, J G and W S Brannum, rear 1534 s A
Kuntz Samuel I, carp, bds 2404 s A
Kye George, glass wkr, bds 419 n 9th

George B. Epperson, Paints, Oils, Varnishes and Painters' Supplies.
39 E. 9th St., - - ANDERSON, IND.

John Donnelly will sell your property, and insure quick returns. Place your business in his hands.
10 East 10th Street, - ANDERSON, IND.

◄DAVID C. KNOTTS►
❋ ❋ STAPLE AND FANCY ❋ ❋
GROCERIES.
Daily Meat Market.
2216 South B, · · · · · ELWOOD, IND.

L

Labue Henry, wks Starkey's Brick Works, bds 308 Main
Laboyteaux Hiram, carp, h. 2741 Main
Lake Erie & Western Pass and Frgt Station, S O Frankenberger, agt, n e cor Anderson and L E & W Track
Lamb Charles L, glass wkr, h. 948 n 13th
Lamerton James, lab, bds 228 n 6th
Lamm Wm G, lab, h. 1431 n 7th
Lane Ernest, lab, h. s w cor 20th and n E
Lane John, lab, h. s w cor 20th and n E
Lane Mordecai, shoemkr, h. 1616 s A
Lane Obediah, glass wkr, bds 2124 Main
Lane Robert, lab, bds 2120 n D
Lane Warner W, carp, h. s w cor 20th and n E
Lane Sandy T, carp, h. s w cor 20th and n E
Lane Wm, glass wkr, bds 1000 n F
Langenbacker T, foreman Geo A Macbeth & Co, h. 851 n 11th
Langenbacker Wm, glass blower, bds 851 n 11th
Langley Mrs. Mary, wid, h. 211 n 19th
Langley Wm, lab, h. 211 n 19th
Lanstofer Joseph, gatherer, bds 1039 n 14th
Lare John, glass wkr, h. 939 n 12th
La Rue Cora, dressmkr, 1812 s H, h. same
La Rue Knowles S, barber, wks 1516 Main, h. 1812 s C
La Rue Sheridan, tin plate wkr, h. 1812 s H
Laughlin Adolphus, h. 1821 n D
Laughlin Jeremiah, clk, h. 2106 n D
Laughlin Laura T, h. 1821 n D
Laughlin Patrick O, clk, h. 2106 n D
Lawrence Jesse, lab, h. n s L E & W Ry bet 24th and 25th

PICTURE FRAMES of all sizes and prices at **Hugh Fisher's Novelty Works,**

J. T. Knowland & Son, Brass & Iron, Steam, Gas and Water Goods.
111 N. Main St., ANDERSON, IND. 'Phone 80.

Lawrence John, lab, bds 1013 Main
Lawson Andrew (Lawson & Swanfelt), bds 405 n 10th
Lawson Charles, eng, h. 2011 n A
Lawson Chase F, foreman Brick Wks, h. 2011 n A
Lawson Charles A, eng, h. n s L E & W Ry bet 20th and 21st
Lawson & Swanfelt (Andrew Lawson and Victor Swanfelt), meat market, 403 n 10th
Layman Pearl, domestic, 814 s Anderson
Layne W Riley, huckster, h. 1745 s D
Layton Samuel, lab, h. 2300 s B
Larah Andrew, grocery, 1508 Main, h. Main
Lecoil Florent, glass wkr, h. 801 n 9th
Lee Daniel, glass wkr, bds n e cor 14th and n C
Lee Edward P, painter, h. 2108 n B
Lee Emma A, h. 1013 Main
Lee Ernest V, harness mkr, wks 119 s Anderson, h 814 s 16th
Lee Fielding E, carp, h. 1013 Main
Lee Harry, glass wkr, bds 419 n 9th
Lee James H, glass wkr, h. cor 11th and n D
Lee James W, carp, h. 1013 Main
Lee Mrs Sarah E, boarding, 1013 Main, h. same
Lee Wm, glass wkr, bds n w cor 11th and n L
Lee Wm, harness, etc, 119 s Anderson, bds 814 s 16th
Leeds Warner M, timekpr, The American Tin P Co, h. 2101 s A
Leeds Hannah A, wid, h. 2101 s A
Leeds Wm B, treas The American Tin Plate Co, h. Richmond, Ind
Leer Charles, lab, h. 2316 n C
Leer Edward, glass wkr, h. 2316 n C
Leer Wm, lab, Brick Works, h. 2406 n B
Leeson Edgar D E, clk, h. 1115 Main
Leeson Elbridge R, clk, h. 1630 s A
Leeson Florence, clk, 201 s Anderson, h. 508 s Anderson
Leeson Richard L, dry goods, &c, 201-3-7, h. 518 s Anderson
Leeson Richard L Jr, clk, 201 s Anderson, h. 502 s Anderson
Leeson Silas O, street inspector, h. 1712 s H
Leeson Wayne, clk, 201 s Anderson, h. 508 s Anderson
Lefforge Charles, lab, h. 612½ s Anderson
Legg Benton, carp, h. n w cor s J and 13th
Legg Edward, glass wkr, h. 2301 Main
Legg Frank, carp, h. n e cor s B and 11th
Legg Harry, glass wkr, rms 2113 Main
Legg John E, pat mkr, h 1521 n B
Legg Wm A, teacher, h. 2030 n C
Lemare Victor, glass wkr, bds 412 n 10th
Lembert Leon, glass wkr, h. 805 n 12th

John O. Miller, Dealer in WATCHES, CLOCKS & JEWELRY, SILVERWARE and OPTICAL GOODS.
3 N. Meridian, - - - ANDERSON, IND.

Leonard Thomas, gatherer, bds 851 n 11th
Leslie Charles, clk, bds 2214 s B
Level John, tin plate wkr, h. n e s H, bet 14th and Anderson
Levy David (D Levy & Co), bds 1401 s E
Levy D & Co (D and Y Levy), boots and shoes, 127 s Anderson
Levy Emanuel, clothing, etc., 202 s Anderson, h. 1401 s E
Levy Yette (D Levy & Co), h. Detroit, Mich
Lewis Charles, glass wkr, bds 710 n Anderson
Lewis David, tin plate wkr, bds e s 23d bet s M and N
Lewis David, glass blower, bds 1534 n C
Lewis Evan, tin plate wkr, bds 1527 n C
Lewis Reece, tin plate wkr, h. 616 s 18th
Lewis Samuel, tin plate wkr, h. 1614 s H
Lewis Wm H, lab, bds 1930 n D
Libler Frank, glass wkr, h. 419 n 7th
Libler George, oysters, etc, 401 n 9th, h. same
Lickenbaugh Joseph, gatherer, bds 1324 n 9th
Lidster Henry, eng, 317 s Anderson
Lighty Lewis E, photographer, h. 2516 s B
Lindley James R, glass wkr, h. 221 n 12th
Lindstrom Charles, glass wkr, h. 816 s B
Lineberry Addison, carp, h. 2422 s B
Lineberry Edgar, carp, h. 2422 s B
Lineberry Samuel Jr, carp, h. 1304 s D
Lines Aaron N, carp, h. 1614 n C
Linskey John, polisher, h. 1626 n C
Linville Martin W, groceries, 613 s Anderson, h. 1821 s J
Linwood School, s 19th, bet s J and K
Lister Sadie J, h. 1609 n A
Little B F, physician, 108¼ s Anderson, h. 1927 n E
Little Charlotte C, wid, h. 1512 s A
Little James H, lab, h. 1512 s A
Little Perry D, clk, h. 2523 s A
Littler Joseph W, v-pres Elwood Iron Wks, h. Indianapolis, Ind
Livingston John M, plumber, 1348 s A, h. 1610 n B
Llewellyn Elmer, baker, bds 1345 s A
Loarh Andrew, butcher, h. 1802 Main
Loarh Ella, bookpr, h. 1802 Main
Loarh Flora, milliner, h. 1802 Main
Loarh Grant, hostler, h. 1802 Main
Logan Frank E, carp, h. 213 n Anderson
Long Allie, clk, h. 1321 s D
Long Henry M, brick contractor, h. 120 n 13th
Long Lawrence, glass wkr, bds 1000 n F
Long Lottie, domestic, 1513 s B

WOOLLEY Foundry and Machine Works,
Designers and Manufacturers of Heavy Machinery, Engines, Boilers and Rolling Mill Work.
N. W Cor. 14th and C. W. and M. R. R.

WHEN — The Most Reliable CLOTHING House
✴ IN ANDERSON. ✴
PRICES ALWAYS THE LOWEST.

Long Morris, plasterer, h. 928 s B
Long Nannie, clk, h. 1321 s D
Long Samuel, lab, h. n w cor 16th and n E
Long Walter, lab, bds 2334 n C
Loser Charles, carp, h. n e cor s N and 22d
Lotz Harry, glass blower, h. 921 n 12th
Louzy Alphonse, glass wkr, bds s w cor 11th and n C
Louzy Frank, glass wkr, bds, s w cor 11th and n C
Love Edward T, glass wkr, h. 218 n 7th
Love George, glass wkr, h. 218 n 7th
Love Mrs Margaret, wid, h. 602 s Anderson
Love Wm, lab, h. n s L E & W R R, bet 23d and 24th
Lowery Nettie, dining room, rms 2122 Main
Loyd David, glass blower, bds e s 10th, bet n A and C
Loyd Ida M, cook, 111 s Anderson
Loyd Wm, gatherer, bds 710 n Anderson
Luckey Daniel W, carp, h. 2111 n E
Ludwig John, plasterer, h. 2009 s M
Lumpkins Sherman, clk, h. 90 ½ s A
Lynch Charles A D, restaurant, 1528 Main, h. same
Lynum Oscar, dining room, 111 s Anderson, rms 123½ s Anderson
Lyrus George, gatherer, bds 710 n Anderson
Lyst Charles, bricklayer, h. 2021 Main
Lyst Henry C, brickmason, h. 2001 s B
Lyst John, brick contractor, 2021 Main, h. same
Lyst Samuel C, plasterer, h. 1807 n F
Lytle David A, contractor, s w cor 8th and n C, h. same
Lytle Moses M, glass wkr, h. s w cor 8th and n C

Mc

McBarron Andrew, glass wkr, bds 419 n 9th
McCallister Wm, carp, h. 1525 n A
McCann John, glass wkr, bds 233 n 12th
McCann Wm W, glass wkr, bds 2133 n A
McCarty Albert, lab, bds 2020 s A
McClain Charles P, stonemason, bds n w cor 12th and n E
McCloy W R Glass Co, W A McCloy pres, W R McCloy secy and treas. w e n J
McCloy Washington R, secy and treas, W R McCloy Glass Co, rms 1635 s A
McCloy Wm A, pres W R McCloy Glass Co
McCool Elizabeth, milliner, bds 1828 n B
McCord & Cox (M M McCord & A T Cox), barber shop, 1512 s A

Insure with ROOP & HAYNES,
IN THE STANDARD COMPANIES THEY REPRESENT.
210½ S. Anderson, • • • • • • ELWOOD, IND.

McCord M Marion (McCord & Cox), h. 2133 n C
McCormic Bridget A, wid, h. 1640 s B
McCormic & Co (James McCormic), saloon, 1524 Main
McCormic James (McCormic & Co), h. 1640 s B
McCormick Andrew, glass blower, bds 730 n Boulevard
McDaniel Frank, lab, h. s s s F bet 14th and 13th
McDaniel Joseph, painter, h. s s s F bet 14th and 13th
McDermet Phoebe, wid, h. 1613 s F
McDonald A M, tailor, wks 114½ s Anderson, bds 201 s Anderson
McDonald Darius E (Elwood Real Estate Co), h. 1528 Main
McDonald Fannie, comp, The Elwood Press
McDonald Ola, clk, 201 s Anderson
McDonald Thomas, glass wkr, bds 411 n 10th
McElfresh Albert, clk, 118 s Anderson, h. 1610 n E
McEwen Harry M, eng, bds 1610 n E
McGaugren James, glass finisher, bds n w cor 10th and n C
McGhee Anna, wid, h. 2500 Main
McGinnis Edward, carp, h. 1014 s B
McGinniss John W, lab, h. 2324 s B
McGovern Benjamin A, gatherer, bds 835 n 12th
McGowan Elwood, glass wkr, bds 426 n 10th
McGowan Joseph A, brickmason, h. 1306 s C
McIntosh John, glass wkr, bds 911 s Anderson
McKeoun Arthur, heading mkr, bds 1713 s F
McKinley Leonidas, teamster, h. 1912 n D
McKinley Samuel N, glass wkr, h. 908 n 13th
McKinney James, h. 2102 Main
McKiney Martha J, h. 203 n 13th
McMahan Enoch, eng, h. 914 s B
McMahan Flora, clk, 120½ s Anderson, h. 718 s Anderson
McMahan Joseph L, painter, h. 618 s 17th
McMahan Mrs Sarah, wid, h. 718 s Anderson
McMahan Thomas, grocer, 819 n 11th, h. same
McMahan Wm, carp, bds 1341 s B
McMillen Henry, glass wkr, bds n e cor 14th and n C
McMindes Morris, plasterer, 1604 Main, h. same
McMullen Jas A, brickmason, h. w s 21st, bet s B and L E & W Ry
McMullen Lee T, glass wkr, bds 1721 s A
McNew Chester, hod carrier, h. 1117 s A
McNew James, lab, h. n s s C, bet 23d and 24th
McNew Newt, hod carrier, h. 1345 s B
McNew Otto, lab, bds 1345 s B
McNutt George T, physician and surgeon, 1527½ Main, h. same
McNutt Jule, h. 1344 s B

WHEN — The Only Retail Clothiers
In the State of Indiana
That Manufacture their OWN CLOTHING.

52 ELWOOD CITY DIRECTORY.

McShafrey Frank P, glass blower, h. s s n C, 3d w Anderson
McShafery Harvey J, glass gatherer, b. s s n C, 3d w Anderson
McVicker Asberry, real estate, h. 1925 Main
McVicker John, h. 1356 s B

M

Macbeth Geo A, pres Geo A Macbeth Co, res Pittsburg, Pa
Macbeth Geo A Co, Geo A Macbeth pres, C Rott secy and treas, T F Harnack supt, mnfrs lamp chimneys and globes
Mace Wm O, heading wkr, b. s s s I bet 14th and Anderson
Mack Timothy E, glass wkr, h. s e cor 11th and n D
Mackelflesh James, lab, 2008 s B
Maddock Edgar E, carp. h. 1921 Main
Maddock Herman A, job printer, Elwood Leader, h. 1921 Main
Maddock J E (Beher & Maddock), h. 1921 Main
Maddock Thomas R, carp and contractor, 1921 Main, h. same
Madison Charles, glass wkr, h. 1125 n F
Madison Edward L, glass wkr, h. 1125 n F
Madison George, glass wkr, h. 1125 n F
Madison Reuben, eng, h. 1125 n F
Madlock Smith, glass wkr, bds 927 n 13th
Magel Nicholas, gatherer, bds n w cor 10th and n C
Mager Nicholas, gatherer, bds 812 n 11th
Mahon Charles H C, fine groceries and produce, cigars and tobacco, confectioneries, &c, 212 s Anderson, h. 1331 s B
Maholm Frances, h. 1907 s B
Maholm John R, cooper, h. 1907 s B
Maines Lona, h. 2200 s B
Maley Patrick, glass wkr, bds 233 n 12th
Manly Bert F, mach, h. 420 n 13th
Manley Michael, tin plate wkr, h. e s 22d bet s M and N
Mansfield John, lab, bds 1604 n C
Markley Samuel T, lab, h. 907 s Anderson
Marley Martha, domestic, 825 Main
Marsh Clayton, lab, bds 2525 s B
Marsh Wm, lab, bds 2209 s B
Marshall August, glass wkr, h. 1110 n F
Marshall Charles, glass wkr, bds 810 n 11th
Marshall Hazard, h. 622 s 16th
Marshall Marion, lab, h. 622 s 16th
Martz Joseph, glass blower, bds 851 n 11th
Martz Joseph, gatherer, bds 812 n 11th
Martin John E, packer, bds 710 n Anderson
Martin Joseph V (White & Co), h. 1356 s B

John L. Lindskoog, The Leading Tailor of Alexandria. All the Latest Novelties in Suitings and Trouserings.
H. H. H. Block, N. E. Cor. Church and Harrison, ALEXANDRIA, IND.

M. J. DOVE — Can give you choice in 20 of the oldest and best Insurance Companies represented. Note this fact when placing your insurance.
NEELEY BLOCK.   61½ N. Meridian, ANDERSON, IND.

LARMORE BROS. 813 Nichol Avenue, ANDERSON, IND. Telephone 220. Will deliver you your ICE CREAM, OYSTERS AND MILK any place in the city, and guarantee first-class goods.

ELWOOD CITY DIRECTORY.   53

p Myrtle, h. n s s C, e of 26th
p Wm N, glass wkr, h. 1927 n C
p Wm T, glass wkr, bds 1927 n C
& Bull (Jas D Mason, Chas R Bull), grocers, 2122 Main
James D (Mason & Bull) bds 2334 n C
Thomas T, glass wkr, h. n e cor 11th and n F
he Hall, 112 s Anderson
y Mrs Ada, cook the Stevenson House, bds same
y Herbert, cook the Stevenson House, bds same
y Lillie, clk, 100 s Anderson, h. Boulevard
y Robert B, glass wkr, h. n s s G, bet 13th and 14th
y Mrs Sophia A, wid, h. n s s G, bet 13th and 14th
s Alfred H, carp, h. s s 23d, bet L E and W R R and s C
s Greenberry B, lab, h. s s L E & W R R, bet 23d and 24th
Jacob, h. 1538 s B
s Frederick, gatherer, h. 1045 n 14th
ws James, agent, saloon, 1506 s A, bds Boston House
ws Mrs John, wid, h. 730 n Boulevard
s Manford, bartender, bds 2207 s A
August (Mayor & Closnit), h. 1607 n D
& Closnit (August Mayor & Paul Closnit), saloon, 410 n 9th
s Office, Hon W. A. DeHority mayor, 1526½ Main
eanie, h. 119 n 18th
Mary, bds 2309 s B
harles, glass wkr, bds 2124 Main
Dennis, lab, bds 1603 n F
Charles, glass wkr, bds 1829 s C
.nderson, wks Brick Works, h. 2319 n C
harles S, prin high school
eorge, well digger, bds 1913 s N
hn H, h. 2317 n C
John, glass wkr, h. 910 n F
Jesse (Mellette & Staley), publisher The Elwood Daily and Weekly Press, h. 1934 Main
Loring, teacher, h. 2123 n C
& Staley (Jesse Mellette & E H Staley), proprs The Elwood Daily & Weekly Free Press, 207½ s Anderson
Maggie, wid, h. 1844 s A
Raymond, lab, h. n s L E & W Ry, e 22d
Wm A, bartender, h. n s L E & W Ry, e 22d
all F F, clk, 100 s Anderson, h. 1604 n C
ielding L (P Kuntz Lumber Co), h. Chicago, Ill
larence, carp, bds 1520 n D
ames, wks planing mill, bds 1902 n A
ris, glass blower, h. 406 n Boulevard

n **Foundry and Machine Works,** Manufacturers of BOILERS, Steam Heaters, Castings, and General Machinery.
KSON STREET,   'Phone 53.
ANDERSON, IND.

Jackson & Burr
69½ N. Meridian,

Represent the Largest Lines and the Strongest INSURANCE Companies.
ANDERSON, IND.

54   ELWOOD CITY DIRECTORY.

Metcalf Joseph, glass wkr, bds 1053 n 14th
Methodist Protestant Church, Rev S H Flood pastor, s s s E bet s Anderson and 16th
Metsker Cornelius, groceries and boarding, 803 Main, h. same
Metsker John, clk, h. 803 Main
Metzler Joseph W, clk, 819 n 11th, h. same
Meyer John, jewelry, 211 s Anderson, h. same
Meyer Minnie, h. 857 n 11th
Michael Charles, lab, h. 2028 s B
Michael Robert, glass blower, bds 1610 n E
Michigan Fire and Marine Ins Co, of Detroit, 1527½ Main
Miers Michael, notions, 1000 n 14th, h. same
Miles Calvin, lab, bds 1800 n E
Miller Alfred (Wiley & Miller), h. cor 18th and B
Miller Benj F, carp, h. 937 n 13th
Miller B F, millinery and fancy goods, 312 s Anderson, h. 314 s Anderson (see adv)
Miller Charles, glass wkr, bds 215 n 13th
Miller Charles, lab, bds 1925 n D
Miller Edward (Whitaker & Miller), bds 1621 Main
Miller Edwin, clk, 121 s Anderson, h. 1828 n A
Miller John, lab, h. 1517 n C
Miller Joseph M, glass blower, h. 236 n Boulevard
Miller Mrs Nora, milliner, 312 s Anderson, h. 314 s Anderson
Miller Thomas, hostler, 1634 n B
Miller John E, lab, bds 2126 Main
Millikan Jabez H, physician, 1505½ Main, h. 1802 Main
Millross George, carp, bds 814 s C
Mills Henry M, lamp trimmer, Elwood E & L Co, h. 1901 s B
Mills Hugh, fireman, P C C & St L, h. 508 s 16th
Mills James, carp, h. 2418 n B
Mills Retta, wid, h. 508 s 16th
Minor Bert R, paper carrier, h. 1922 s A
Miner Benona, h. 1922 s A
Minnick Joseph, real estate, h. 1830 Main
Misner John A, clk, 1506 Main, h. 1508 n D
Mitchell Adolphus O, h. 1388 s C
Mitchell Minnie, stenographer, 207 n 16th, h. 1338 s C
Mitchell Oran D, watchman, h. 5527 Main
Mitchell Oran D, flagman Main st crossing, h. 2527 Main
Mittenberger August, glasswkr, h. 949 n 13th
Moffot Mrs Jessie (Hann & Moffot), h. Muncie, Ind
Mohler J Edmund, baker, rms 123½ s Anderson
Montgomery Alexander C, h. 1531 s J
Montgomery Frank, lab, h. w s 21st bet s N and O

George B. Epperson, Contractor & Builder of Concrete Side Walks.
39 E. 9th St.,   ANDERSON, IND.

Estate Exchange does a general Real Estate busi... ER,
The finest lots in the world, IND.
sale or trade at our office. ways
ast 10th Street, - ANDERSON, IN

ELWOOD CITY DIRECTORY. 55

B. F. MILLER, ✻
e Millinery and Fancy Goods.

ALL THE LATEST STYLES

Millinery in Stock. Fine Trimmings and Frames.

HATS MADE TO ORDER A SPECIALTY.

ith Anderson Street, - - - ELWOOD, IND.

omery Isaac W, meat market, 117 s Anderson, h. 2108 Main
omery James W, lab, h. 1505 n E
omery Reece, clk, 117 s Anderson, h. 2108 Main
Flora B, dressmkr, 1631 s A
George L, clk, h. n s s H bet 14th and Anderson
Hugh P, carp, h. 1921 n E
Ira, baker, rms 123½ s Anderson
Jennie, domestic, 1602 s D
Jesse, carp, h. 1921 n E
John H, carp, h. 1910 n A
Josiah M, carp, h. 2415 n B
Joseph D, teamster
Malissa E, h. 2415 n B
Otis F, drug clk, h. n e cor 14th and n C
Thomas R, h. n e cor 14th and n C
Walter, glass wkr, bds 803 Main
Wm E, lab, h. 2415 n B
Amazaih J, teamster, h. 2114 n F
Arthur, tin plate wkr, bds n e cor s N and 22d
David, tin plate wkr, bds w s 24th bet s N and O
Edward, agt, bds 1643 s A
Garfield, lab, Brick Wks, h. 2031 n B
Jacob, glass wkr, bds 405 n 12th
John, tin plate wkr, bds n e cor s N and 22d
John, gas well driller, bds 1627 n C
John H, iron wkr, h. w s 25th bet s N and O

Fisher's Novelty Works! Jig and Scroll Saw Work in all the latest designs and pat-
and 200 N. Milton St.; terns. Call and examine my work.
✻ ANDERSON IND. ✻

J. Ck, Brickley & Co., Anderson, Ind.

THE LEADING DRUGGISTS,
FINE WALL PAPER AND DECORATIONS.

Morgan Joshua J, brickmolder, 2031 n B
Morgan Kate, tailoress, wks 118½ s Anderson, h. Main
Morgan Wm, tin plate wkr, bds 1527 n C
Morgie Moses, tin plate wkr, bds 1812 s H
Morgie Wm, tin plate wkr, bds 1812 s H
Moreland Lafayette, glass wkr, bds 1111 Main
Morris Ella M, domestic, 2012 Main
Morris Wm, glass wkr, bds 2020 Main
Morrison & Boyer (C Z Morrison, A H Boyer), 412 s Anderson
Morrison Charles Z (Morrison & Boyer), h. 1706 s D
Moschell Harry, glass wkr, bds 2022 s A
Moschell Paul, glass wkr, bds 2022 s A
Mosiman Fred, foreman B F Wiley & Co, h. 1814 n C
Motz Fred J, timekpr Diamond Plate Glass Co, h. 503 s Anderson
Mound James, foreman Plate Glass Wks, h. 815 Main
Mound John, glass blower, bds 803 Main
Mount Robert H, policeman, bds 1st e 1911 Main
Moyer Daniel, lab, h. 603 n 15th
Moyer Ferd, carp, bds 1350 s A
Moyer Rev Henry H, h. 1916 s G
Moyer Rev Z C, h. 1722 s H
Mullen Fred, cigar maker, bds 408 s Anderson
Mullen Ida, dressmkr, wks 312 s Anderson, rms 2527 s A
Murch Leonard L, carp, h. 1410 s G
Murdock Francis, lab, h. 2538 n B
Murphy Bernhard, lab, h. 1803 n D
Murphy Charles, lab, h. 1803 n D
Murphy Christopher, lab, h. 1803 n D
Murphy Francis, lab, h. 1803 n D
Murphy George, plumber, J M Livingston, bds Erie House
Murphy Margaret, teacher, St Joseph's Parochial School, bds 607 s Anderson
Murphy Sylvester, glass blower, bds 730 n Boulevard
Murray George, tin plate wkr, h. 1718 s H
Musser Albert, lab, bds 1st s I
Mussleman Harvey, clk, 201 s Anderson, h. 2021 s A
Myerley Thomas J, lab, h. 1818 n B
Myers Alexander K, china, glass and queensware, toys and holiday goods, 209 s Anderson, h. 1400 s G
Myers Alvin A, glass wkr, h. 1621 Main
Myers & Dickerson (G W Myers and Wm H Dickerson), proprs The Boston House, 1531 and 1533 s A
Myers George W (Myers & Dickerson), h. Boston House
Myres Noah, stonemason, h. 1604 n F

JOHN O. MILLER'S For FINE WATCH REPAIRING and DIAMOND SETTING.

3 N. Meridian, - - - ANDERSON, IND.

N

Nading Elmer, glass wkr, bds 1522 s A
Nagel Frederick, glass blower, h. 413 n 7th
Nagel Charles E, gatherer, h, 413 n 7th
Nagel Catherine E, wid, h. 413 n 7th
National Building Loan & Savings Association, Roop & Haynes
    agts, 210½ s Anderson
Nay Acy R, glass wkr, rms 232 n 12th
Nay David, messenger, W U Tel Co, h. 119 n 17th
Nay Nannie, wid, h. 119 n 18th
Nay Wm P, comp, The Elwood Leader, h. 119 n 18th
Nearon Ada E, h. 2320 n C
Nearon Bertha E, student, h. 2320 n C
Nearon Clinton E (Huston & Nearon), h 2320 n C
Nearon Dicy B, h. 2320 n C
Nearon Ezekiel, merchant, h. 2320 n C
Nearon John (Huston & Nearon), h. 2320 n C
Nearon Joseph, farmer, h. 2320 n C
Neely George, A, carp, h. rear 710 n Anderson
Neely Wm H, carp, rear 710 n Anderson, h. same
Neff George, clk, 1521 Main, bds s C
Negley Benj F (Negley Bros), h. 1414 s G
Negley Bros (P L and B F Negley), meat market, 611 s Anderson
Negley Catherine, h. 1414 s G
Negley Philip T (Negley Bros), h. 1414 s G
Nelson, James E, tin plate wkr, h. n e s J and Pan-Handle
Nenninger John, glass wkr, h. 921 n 13th
Nenninger Otilda, domestic, 526 n Boulevard
Nenninger Philip, glass wkr, h. 921 n 13th
Netz John W, lab, h. 1521½ Main
Newcomer G V, physician, secy the Elwood Club, rms 1 and 2
    120½ s Anderson, h. same
Newhouse Cicero, clk, h. 2432 s A
Newkirk Ella J, music teacher, rear 1108 Main, h. same
Newkirk Jennie L, h. rear 1108 Main
Newkirk John M, marble cutter, rear 1108 Main
Niccum George A, glass wkr, h. 1438 n 6th
Niccum James D, glass wkr, h. 1438 n 6th
Niccum Malinda E, wks glass house, h. 1438 n 6th
Niccum Wm F, glass wkr, h. 1438 n 6th
Nichols Ollie, tel opr, P C C & St L Ry, bds 233 n A
Nichols Wm, section hand, h. s s s F bet 13th and 14th
Nickes Julius, glass wkr, h. 2531 n C

WOOLLEY Foundry and Machine Works,
    General Machinery, Heavy and Light Castings, and
    Sheet Iron Work.
    N. W. COR. 14th AND C W. AND M. R. R.

WHEN — The Largest Stock of CLOTHING, HATS, CAPS and Gents' FURNISHING GOODS in ANDERSON.

ELWOOD CITY DIRECTORY.

Niff George, butcher, h. n s L E & W Ry bet 22d and 23d
Niles Sylvie, wid, h. 814 s Anderson
Nipper Wm, lab, bds 1624 n D
Nivison Henry P (Nivison & Weiskopf), bds Stevenson House
Nivison & Weiskopf (H P Nivison and D Weiskopf), bottle factory, cor 26th and s C
Nixon Samuel, clk, 611 s Anderson, h. 2023 n A
Noble Ira, teamster, h. 2402 n B
Noble James, gas fitter, h. 1320 s C
Noble John A, huckster, h. 2401 n B
Noble Sherman, glass wkr, h. 2113 n A
Noble Wm D, teamster, h. 2113 n A
Noftsfer Stephen, carp and contractor, w s n Anderson, h. same
Nokes Amos J, bartender, h. 1726 s G
Nokes Rachel, h. 1726 s G
Norcross Benj O, glass wkr, h. 2511 n A
Norcross Bessie O, h. 2511 n A
Normier John, glass wkr, bds 803 Main
Norris Allen R, clk, 1521 Main, h. 1621 Boulevard
Norris Effie O, h. 112 n 20th
Norris Frank, wks Tin Plate Mill, h. 112 n 20th
Norris James W, fruit stand, 119½ s Anderson, h. 701 s Anderson
Norris Warren, driver, bds 1928 s J
North Andrew (North Bros), h. 1341 s D
North Bros (Chas & Andrew North), meat mkt, 116 s Anderson
North Charles (North Bros), h. 1341 s D
Norton James H, glass wkr, h. w s 10th bet n F and G
Norton Wm R, glass wkr, h. 244 n 7th
Noth Franklin, butcher, h. e s 11th, 2d s s A
Nuding Edward, brickmason, h. 1344 s E
Nuding Henry, student, h. 1821 Main
Nuding Jacob D, carp, h. 1821 Main
Nuding John, glass wkr, h. 1344 s E
Nuding Wm, carp, h. 1821 Main
Nunamaker Charles, glass blower, h. 808 n 11th
Nuzum Charles, clk, 201 s Anderson
Nuzum David P, physician, 1021 Main, h. same
Nuzum George, baker, h. 1401 Main
Nuzum John N, shoemkr, 1530 s A

O

O'Brannon John W, city eng, 1526½ Main, bds Boston House
O'Brien Hugh (O'Brien & Kapphan), h. 1523 Main
O'Brien & Kapphan (H O'Brien, A Kapphan), saloon, 1523 Main

Roop & Haynes Are Agents for FIVE of the BEST BUILDING & LOAN COMPANIES in Indiana.
210½ S. Anderson, - - - - ELWOOD, IND.

Ogel Lisha, glass wkr, bds 819 n 18th
Ogla Andrew T, glass wkr, h. 838 n 11th
Ohio Farmers' Ins Co The, of Le Roy, O, 1534 s A
Oldham Richard, glass wkr, h. 932 s A
Olenhousen Charles, glass blower, bds n w cor 9th and n A
Oliver Reason R, h. n e cor s F and 14th
Oliver Rose N, h. n e cor s F and 14th
Olmstead James B, saloon, 819 n 9th, h. 827 n 11th
Olson Peter P, glass wkr, h. 821 s B
O'Malley Arthur W, glass wkr, h. 925 n 12th
O'Neal Marshall, lab, h. 1520 s G
O'Neill James, gatherer, bds n w cor 10th and n C
O'Neil Elwood, glass wkr, bds 1111 Main
O'Niel Kate, dining room, The Stevenson House, bds same
Orbaugh Emory, gas fitter, wks 213 s Anderson, h. 1341 s B
Osborn A C, clk, 100 s Anderson, h. 2106 s A
Osborn Charles, mess, Citizens' Exchange Bank, h. cor 16th and s E
Osborn Elizabeth, wid, h. 1901 n E
Osborn James, lab, h. n w cor s J and 19th
Osborn John, watchman, Diamond Plate Glass Co, h. s C
Osborn Logan W, carp, h. 1901 n E
Osborn Minnie A, domestic, 115 n 18th
Osborn Theodore, blksmth, wks 1612 Main, h, s E
Osman Henry E, glass wkr, h. n s s J bet 12th and 13th
Oustill Homer, paper carrier, h. 1534 e Main
Overshiner Arthur V, deputy P M, h. s 220 s Anderson
Overshiner James M, P M, pres Elwood N G & O Co, h. 220 s Anderson
Owens Benj, lab, h, 2409 n D
Owen Joseph, glass wkr, bds 1004 n F
Owens Nettie, h 2409 n D
Owens Wallace, lab, h. 2409 n D

P

Pace Clyde, del clk, 212 s Anderson, h. s J
Pace Wm, lab, h. s s s I bet 13th and 14th
Packer G F, laundryman, bds 1111 w Main
Page John, watchman, Diamond Plate Glass Co, h. 1345 s B
Page John R, pres, the First National Bank, res Anderson
Pagan Patrick, rms 1528 Main

Herman F. Willkie, J.P.
COLLECTIONS PROMPTLY MADE.

WHEN—Children's Department
A SPECIAL FEATURE.
Always well Stocked with the LATEST NOVELTIES.

Parish John, plasterer cont, 2422 n A
Parish J A, clk, 110 s Anderson, h. 1820 n C
Parker Mrs Asenath, dressmkr, 1631 s A, h. same
Parker George, glass wkr, bds 1639 Main
Parker George L, lab, h. 1534 n G
Parker Isaac E, fgt clk, P C C & St L, h. 801 n 16th
Parker Mell L, glass wkr, h. 413 n 12th
Parker Marcus E, carp, h. 2409 n B
Parker Perry, h. 633 s 18th
Parker Peter L, lab, h. 2126 n E
Parker Warren, farmer, h. 1631 s A
Parker Wm Q, carp, h. 2120 s A
Parks Albert, carp, h. 1510 n E
Parr Frank M, carp, h. 404 n 6th
Parson & Buroker, painters, 302 s Anderson
Parson C M, clk, 110 s Anderson, h. 416 s Anderson
Parson Frank, clk, 1514 s A, h. 2082 Main
Parson James, h. 1353 s B
Parson Jonathan C, saloon, h. 1201 Main
Parson Joseph, painter, rms 202½ s Anderson
Parson Levi A, lab, h. 1043 n 14th
Parsons Wm E, tailor, wks 113½ s Anderson, h. 314 s 13th
Partlow Samuel, lab, h. 1517 n F
Patrick Rev Francis M, h. 2128 n F
Patterson Celia, clk, 204 s Anderson, bds 1527 n B
Patterson Mary, wid, h. 508 s 16th
Pauley James W N (Briggs & Pauley), h. s C
Pearce John M, asst princ High School, h. 1746 s D
Pearson Isaac, carp, bds 213 n Anderson
Peden Katherine, wid, h. 1819 n C
Peed Albert, h. 1831 n C
Peed James L, clk, 1526 Main, h. 1831 n C
Peed Martin E, news depot, 214 s Anderson, h. 1831 n C
Pemire Charles, h. w s 19th bet s F and G
Pence James W, glass wkr, h. 426 n 7th
Pendergrass Wm, carp, bds 803 Main
Pennsylvania Fire Ins Co, of Philadelphia, net surplus $1,804,-134.71, Roop & Haynes agts, 210½ s Anderson
Penticost Albert, lab, bds 1800 n E
Pobernut Ella, chambermaid Boston House, bds same
Perkins Walter O, eng, h. 2002 n C
Perry Aaron, brickmason, h. e s 22d bet s M and N
Perry Albert C, glass wkr, h. 411 n 8th
Perry David, glass wkr, bds 417 n 7th
Perry Harry, glass wkr, bds 417 n 7th

John L. Lindskoog, Fine Tailoring in Suits and Pants. An examination solicited. A FIT GUARANTEED.
H. H. Block, N. E. Cor. Church and Harrison, ALEXANDRIA, IND.

Perry Lewis, tin plate wkr, h. e s 22d bet s M and N
Perry Thomas F, brickmason, h. 2000 s A
Perry Wm, h. 2000 s A
Perry George H, dining room, Boston House, bds same
Perry Mrs Maggie, cook Boston House, bds same
Pertee Wright, lab, h 1005 s B
Peters Charles, glass wkr, h. 2016 Main
Peters Mrs Kate, wid, cor 11th and n C
Peterson Leonard V. carp, h. 2304 n A
Phare James W, teamster, h. 615 s 17th
Philippe James, lab, bds e s 26th bet s A and B
Philippe John, lab, bds e s 26th bet s A and B
Phillips Adelia, teacher, bds 1809 Main
Phillips Eva, teacher, bds 1809 Main
Phillips Marion E. hatter, clothier and furnisher, 115 s Anderson, h. 1102 s Anderson
Phillips Samuel, lab, bds 2401 n B
Phillips Scott, teamster, bds 2010 n A
Philpoth Lewis W, clk, h. 2120 n E
Pickard D E, carp, rms 1631 s A
Pierce Harrison, mach, h. 2130 n E
Pierce John, glass blower, bds 1009 n 10th
Piercy Nana, glass wkr, bds 1829 s C
Pierson Mary, wid, h. n w cor 10th and n C
Piggott Michael, glass wkr, bds 428 n 9th
Piles Samuel, glass wkr, bds 2129 n A
Pilkie John, glass wkr, bds 431 n 9th
Pippin Anna, wid, h. 2121 n A
Pippin Joseph, glass wkr, h. 2121 n A
Pippin Simeon F, glass teaser, h. 737 Main
Pittsburg Saloon & Restaurant The, D C Bowser propr, 113 s Anderson
Pittsburg, Cincinnati, Chicago & St Louis Fgt and Pass Station, J E Kirkpatrick agt, s e cor s A and P C C & St L track
Placick Wm A, lab, h. 1614 Main
Plackes Burt, wks Elwood Steam Laundry, bds 1111 Main
Plowman Eugene, grocery, n e cor 10th and n C, h. 240 n 12th
Pluff Harry, packer, bds 710 n Anderson
Pool Alta M, domestic, 1522 s A
Popp John J, glass wkr, h. 905 n 12th
Porter George, well digger, h. 1913 s N
Porter Joseph, lab, h. s s a J bet 12th and 13th
Posten Amos, plasterer, h. 2122 n C
Poston Nancy A, wid, h. 2390 n E
Powell John, brick mason, bds e s 23d bet s M and N

INSURE WITH JACKSON & BURR, Latch string always out and light in the window, until the last man's **INSURED.**
69½ N. Meridian, - - - ANDERSON, IND.

Powell Thomas, lab, h. 2315 Main
Powell Thomas, tin plate wkr, bds 800 s 18th
Prall George R, tinner, h. 1809 n D
Pratt James, teamster, h. 215 n 13th
Presbyterian Church, s e cor 18th and A
Preston W. D, treas Diamond Plate Glass Co
Prier Stephen, plumber, h. 1021 n 17th
Prue Charles, eng, bds 1332 s A
Pugh Robert A, carp, h. 2301 n E
Pumler Charles, tailor, bds 1008 s Anderson
Pumphrey Joseph S, carp, h. 2316 n D
Pursall Harry, glass cutter, h. n w cor 13th and n C

Q

Quinn Cicero E, glass wkr, h. 1629 n F

R

Rader James K, glass wkr, h. 2022 s A
Rader Wm, glass wkr, h. 2022 s A
Ramey Quieren, glass wkr, h. s w cor 3d and n F
Randall David F, carp, h. 1203 n 9th
Raney Mary E, h. 1414 s G
Range James, glass wkr, bds 426 n 10th
Range John T, plasterer, h, 2207 s A
Ratcliff Virgil, lather, bds 426 n 10th
Ravenscroft Samuel, drayman, 108 s Anderson, h. 1309 n D
Reagan Nicholas, glass blower, rms 2113 Main
Reamer Winfield S, potmkr, h. 2311 Main
Reardon James, glass blower, rms 2113 Main
Rebuck Schiles, lather, bds 1603 s D
Record Isaac, eng, Elwood Water Works, h. 1701 e Boulevard
Record Walter G, clk, 115 s Anderson, h. 1701 e Boulevard
Rector Wesley, glass wkr, bds 2020 Main
Redd George, farmer, h. n s s D bet Anderson and 13th
Redd John, baker, rms 1505½ Main
Redenbough Edward, glass blower, h. 408 n Boulevard
Redenbough George W, glass blower, h. 827 n 12th
Redenbough Jacob, h. 827 n 12th
Redenbough Samuel J, glass blower, h. 1324 n 9th
Redwine Charles, carp, bds 847 n 12th
Redwine John A, glass wkr, h. 1053 n 14th
Reed Jacob, wks heading factory, bds 1643 s A
Reed Thomas, brick mason, h. 1821 s B

George B. Epperson, Carriage Paints and Varnishes A Specialty.
89 E. 9th St., - - - - ANDERSON, IND.

Reeder Anna E, h. 1411 s E
Reeder Cynthia, wid, h. 1933 Main
Reeder James, lab, h. 1411 s E
Reeder Wm J, carp, h. 941 n 13th
Reel Luther, glass wkr, bds 426 n 11th
Reese George E, glass wkr, h. 731 n 14th
Reeves Nora E, clk, bds 1115 Main
Rehner Albert, h. 240 n 7th
Rehner Ena, h. 240 n 7th
Rehner Frederick, glass wkr, h. 240 n 7th
Rehner Maxwell, h. 240 n 7th
Rehner Richard, glass wkr, h. 232 n 7th
Reid John, lab, bds 1604 Main
Reid Seward C (The Elwood Heading Co), h. Hartford City, Ind
Reidenbauch Wm, teamster, h. 2030 s N
Reifel Elizabeth, h. 1821 e Boulevard
Reigel Daniel W, carp, h. w s L E & W Ry bet 22d and 23d
Reilius John, heater, bds 1700 s D
Reinhart Fredrick, glass wkr, bds 515 Main
Reinhart George, glass wkr, h. 906 s A
Reinhart Jacob, glass wkr, h. 906 s A
Reish John, clk, h. 1805 n K
Reynolds Charles L, mach hand, h. 1612 s E
Reynolds F M, clk, 112 s Anderson, h. 1344 s C
Reynolds Lizzie E, clk, h 1612 s D
Reynolds Wm D, plasterer, h. 2013 n F
Rhoads James K, gas fitter, h. e s 11th, 3d s n C
Rhoads Louis, glass wkr, bds 825 n 9th
Rhodes Wm, lab, h. 2307 n E
Rice Theodore W, musician, bds 408 s Anderson
Rice Walter, rms s s s J bet 14th and Anderson
Rich Wm M, carp, h. 2404 s A
Richards John, supt Tin Plate Wks, h. n w cor s O and 23d
Richards Thomas, tin plate wkr, bds w s 24th bet s N and O
Richards Wm J, iron wkr, bds n w cor s O and 23d
Richards W O, del clk, 1532 Main, h. 2019 n A
Richardson Wm, glass blower, h. 1318 n 9th
Richey Thomas, lab, h. 211 n 19th
Richie Charles, painter, bds 2019 n A
Richie Wm, painter, bds 2019 n A
Richter Bertha E, h. n s s I bet 14th and Anderson
Richter Ernest, teamster, h. n s s I bet 14th and Anderson
Richter Lena, clk, h. n s s I bet 14th and Anderson
Ricker Charles, glass wkr, bds 426 n 7th
Ricker John, glass wkr, h. 430 n 7th

J. T. Knowland & Son, WHOLESALE PLUMBERS and Gas Fitters' Supplies
111 N. Main St., ANDERSON, IND. 'Phone 30.

E. RUMMEL. S. P. RUMMEL.

RUMMEL BROS.

Manufacturers of and Dealers in

FINE CIGARS.

1857 South A Street, ELWOOD, IND.

Riebe Ada, h. 620 s 18th
Riebe Augustus T, glass wkr, h. 1107 n F
Riebe Ernestine, clk, 1517 Main
Riegle Henry, glass wkr, bds 925 n 12th
Riffe George A, wks Starkey's Brick Works, h. 812 s B
Rigby John, glass wkr, h. 723 n 14th
Riggle Anninta, h. 1914 s H
Riker Albert, carp, h. 611 n 15th
Riker George, h. 611 n 15th
Riley Charles, h. n e cor 13th and n C
Riley Edward, glass wkr, rms 1524 Main
Riley Lee, lab, bds 211 n 11th
Ring Mrs Catherine, wid, h. 1933 Main
Ring Elijah, trav sales, h. 2315 n A
Ring Mrs Mary, dressmkr, 2315 n A, h. same
Ringo J L, physician, Hands' Block, e Main, h. 1523 n C.
Ripperger Conrad, bartender, rear 112 s Anderson, h. 1610 n D
Ritler James, lab, h. 1352 s B
Ritler John, farmer, h. 414 n 14th
Roach Ward L, justice of peace, h. 1346 s D
Roberts James, carp, h. 1925 s A
Roberts John, lab, bds 1802 s B
Roberts Mrs Phœbe A, wid, h. 1925 s A
Roberts Wm T, skimmer, h. 1824 n C
Robertson Frank, lab, bds 1829 s M
Robeson Wm S, harness mkr, wks 1524 s A, h. 1009 n 17th
Robey Oscar H, clk, h. 221 n 12th
Robinson Cora M, clk, h. 2022 s B
Robinson George A, glass wkr, h. 407 n 9th
Robinson James, glass wkr, bds 735 n 14th
Robinson Wm C, carp, h. 2022 s B
Robinson Wm C, glass wkr, h. 1301 n D

JOHN O. MILLER, ELEVEN YEARS' EXPERIENCE in Watchmaking. Finisher six years in Elgin & Springfield Watch Factories.
I GUARANTEE MY WORK 3 N. Meridian, ANDERSON, IND.

iefer's Brick Works, Jno T Rodefer, prop, n e c Main and 27th
efer, John F, prop Elwood Window Glass Fact, h. 2718 Main
  Augustus, carp, 1911 n A, h. same
;ers D H, trav sales, h. 1336 s B
;ers Emma, domestic, 1519 n B
;ers Thomas, glass wkr, h. 1017 s A
en Alexander, glass wkr, h. s w cor 2d and n F
en Joseph, glass wkr, h. s w cor 2d and n F
ninger Clarence C, farmer, h. 2135 n D
ninger Frank, lab, bds 2019 s B
oinger Isaac J, lab, h. 2135 n D
oney Elias, glass wkr. h. 1530 s B
oney M Jane, student, h. 1530 s B
oney Theresa, dressmkr, h. 1530 s B
oney Wm, flagman, h. 1530 s B
p & Haynes (I N Roop and George E Haynes), real estate,
  loans and ins, 210½ s Anderson (see left bottom lines)
p Isaac N (Roop & Haynes), notary public, h. 2317 s A
op Maggie, h. 2317 s A
p Oscar P, real estate, loans and ins, 1527½ Main, h. 2317 s A
ie Frank, merchant, rms 2122 Main
enthal Samuel, clk, 120 s Anderson, h. 1519 n B
enthal Simon, druggist, 105 s Anderson, h. 708 s Anderson
is Alfred H, lab, h. 1818 s B
is Charles H, clk, h. e s 11th, 2d s n F
is Charles, barrel and keg hoop mnfr, s w cor 22d and s K, h.
  1401 s G
is David, hostler, wks 1600 s A, bds s B
:h Charles H, clk, 212 s Anderson
:herhan Thomas, glass wkr, h. 737 n 14th
:t C, secy and treas Geo A Macbeth Co, res Pittsburg, Pa
wland Clara E, h. 1527 n C
wland Mrs Lucy, boarding, 1527 n C, h same
y John, glass wkr, h. s s s I bet. 13th and 14th
yal Ins Co, of Liverpool, 1527½ Main
burb Robert, mgr Bottle Works, rms 2025 Main
chey Eugene E, painter, h. 1723 e Boulevard
derman Wm, gatherer, bds 736 n Boulevard
nmel Brothers (Ephraim and Samuel Rummel), cigar mnfrs,
  1357 s A (see adv)
nmel Ephraim (Rummel Bros), h. 1419 s E
nmel Samuel (Rummel Bros), h. s H
ndell Minnie, teacher, 1st grade, 2d ward bldg, bds 1900 Main
nyon George E, beer agt, h. 2008 s A
ssell Clinton, tin plate wkr, bds 1315 s A

WOOLLEY Foundry and Machine Works.
Manufacturers of Clay Working Machinery, Boiler
Makers, and General Machinists.
N. W. COR. 14th AND C. W. AND M. R. R.

WHEN —Manufacturers of— **CLOTHING,**
—And Jobbers in—
HATS AND MEN'S FURNISHINGS.

Rutledge Thomas, glass wkr, rms 1830 Main
Ryan Charles, glass blower, bds 1504 n D
Ryan Mrs Millie, h. 1538 s B
Ryan Richard R, painter, h. 417 n 9th
Ryan Thomas J, brakeman, h 1538 s B
Ryan Wm, tin plate wkr, bds e s 22d bet s M and N
Rybolt Elizabeth F, wid, h. 115 n 21st
Rybolt Wm O, brick mason, h. 115 n 21st

S

Sachse Andrew, glass wkr, h. 1008 n F
Sachse George, glass wkr, h. 1008 n F
Sachse Henry, glass wkr, h. 1008 n F
Sachse James A, glass wkr, h. 1008 n F
Sachse Wm J, glass blower, h. 1019 n 17th
Sampson Wm D, wks Rodefer's
Samuels Gilbert T, harness mkr, wks 1524 s A, h. 1818 Main
Samuels John, section hand, h 1618 s D
Samuels John, carp, h. 1814 s A
Samuels Nancy J, wid, h. 1328 s C
Sandberg Amanda, dressmkr, bds 404 n 9th
Sapp Andrew J, clk, 611 s Anderson
Sarver Charles W, glass wkr, bds 800 n 11th
Schaeffer Edgar W (Schaeffer & Martin), bds 1111 w Main
Schaeffer & Martin (Edgar W Schaeffer, Joseph V Martin), 1422 Main
Scheidler Elizabeth, wid, h. 807 Main.
Schnaitter Frank, carp, bds 2129 n A
Schnasse George Jr (G Schnasse Jr & Co), h. 1807 s B
Schnasse G Jr & Co (George Schnasse Jr, Charles F Segelke), lumber, lath and shingles, cor n B and 13th (see adv)
Schofield George K (Schofield & Jacobs), bds s A
Schofield & Jacobs (George K Schofield, James M Jacobs), carriages, 302 s Anderson
Scholl Henry, glass wkr, bds 1013 Main
Schreck John, butcher, Greulich Bros
Schrinker Robert, glass blower, bds 851 n 11th
Schroth John F, glass blower, h. w s 4th bet n E and F
Schudsinsky Herman, gatherer, bds 835 n 12th
Schuler Berton A, painter, h. 2326 n D
Schutkovske David, brick wkr, bds 1812 s G
Schutkovske John, teamster, h. 1812 s G
Schwab Carl, lab, bds 803 Main

Place Your Real Estate and **FARM PROPERTY** in the Hands of **ROOP & HAYNES,**
AND BE SURE OF QUICK RETURNS.
210½ S. Anderson, - - - - ELWOOD, IND.

MONEY TO BUILD WITH PROCURED WITHIN 15 DAYS. Robinson & Glassco, Loan, Real Estate & Insurance agents
Room 9 "When" Building, ANDERSON, IND.

G. Schnasse, Jr., & Co.
—RETAIL—
❖ LUMBER. ❖
PLATE GLASS ADD.
Corner North B and 18th Sts., ELWOOD, IND.

Schwab Frank, lab, bds 808 Main
Scott Charles G, carp, h. 2324 n C
Scott Mont C, lab, h. 2324 n C
Scott Wm H, bookpr, bds 408 s Anderson
Scott Wm M, lab, h. n s I bet 14th and Anderson
Scribner Charles, glass wkr, h. n s 4th bet n E and F
Scrivner Wm, glass wkr, h. 224 n 7th
See M M, Plate Glass Shaving Parlor, 1427 w Main. h. 800 n 16th
Seeley Richard E, butcher, bds 810 n 11th
Segars Josie, domestic, 1401 s E
Segelke Charles F (G Schnasse Jr & Co), res La Crosse, Wis
Seiberling A G, asst treas Diamond P G Co, res Kokomo, Ind
Seiberling M, gen'l mgr, Diamond P G Co, res Kokomo, Ind
Sellers Homer, glass blower, bds 1602 s D
Seright Stella J, h. 2500 Main
Seward Arthur L, carp, h. 1800 n E
Seward David V, carp, h. 2586 s A
Seward Freeman, carp, h. 1800 n F
Seymour Henry D, secy and treas Elwood Land Co, bds Stevenson House
Shaf Michael, glass blower, bds n w cor 10th and n C
Shafer Anselm, saloon, 526 n Boulevard, h same
Shafer Clinton, glass wkr, h. 420 n 11th
Shafer Sebastian, glass wkr, bds 526 n Boulevard
Shaffer Edward, propr laundry. bds 1111 Main
Shaffer Francis, wid, h. 814 s 18th
Shakespear Ada, clk, h. 1528 n A
Shannon Wm, iron wkr, bds 1925 s J
Sharnell Mary P, h. cor 11th and n C
Sharnell Ombrus, glass wkr, h. cor 11th and n C
Shatzler Charles, glass wkr, bds 825 n 9th
Shaw Frank (G L Shaw & Son), h. 1531 Main

Neal & Willkie, ATTORNEYS AT LAW. We will attend to your legal business promptly, and charge you no exhorbitant fees.
MECHANICS LIENS A SPECIALTY. CALL AND SEE US, ETC

WHEN—Originators of the One Price System
IN SELLING CLOTHING.
FAIR AND SQUARE DEALINGS WITH ALL.

Shaw George L (G L Shaw & Son), h. 1120 s A
Shaw G L & Son (G L and Frank Shaw), saloon, 1522 Main
Shaw James L, drayman, h. 1420 Main
Shaw James R, butcher, h. 1361 s B
Shaw Wm (S Todd & Co), bds 1610 n E
Shaw Zettie F, wid, h. 2108 n A
Shay John, glass wkr, h. 819 n 13th
Shay Thomas W, glass wkr, bds 417 n 14th
Shay Wm, glass blower, bds 481 n 9th
Shearer Joseph, glass blower, bds 948 n 12th
Sheek Stella, wid, h. 1924 n B
Shell Burt, hod carrier, bds 2311 n C
Shell John, lab, h. 2023 s B
Shephard Henry M, plumber, rms 1528 Main
Sherry John H, wagon mkr, wks 1612 Main, bds 1521½ Main
Shetsinger Joseph, gatherer, bds 526 n Boulevard
Shetterly John H, clk, 1525 Main, h. 2418 s C
Shipley Robert, contractor, 1531 s J, h. same
Shipley Grant, lab, h. 1514 n G
Shively Frank, carp, h. 2008 Main
Shively Louis D, pres Elwood Machine Works, h. 1601 s F
Shook Judson, clk, h. 409 n 9th
Shore & Caylor (M L Shore and Walter Caylor), blacksmiths, horseshoers and wagon makers, 111 s 16th
Shore Martin L (Shore & Caylor), h. 1808 n D
Shore Thomas A, lab, h. 2019 s B
Shores Albert, glass wkr, h. 404 n 12th
Shores Nancy, wid, h. 404 n 12th
Shores Stephen, glass wkr, h. 404 n 12th
Shores Walter L, porter, Stevenson House, h. 324 s 13th
Short Edward J, glass packer, h. 216 n 7th
Short Wm J, glass packer, bds 216 n 7th
Shuh Joseph, glass wkr, bds 807 n 11th
Shuh Louis, glass wkr, h. 807 n 11th
Sidwell Andis M, jeweler, h. 2311 s A
Sidwell Mandon, jeweler, 200 s Anderson, h. 2311 s A
Siegwerth John, glass wkr, bds 2531 n A
Sifournant August, glass wkr, bds s w cor 11th and n C
Sigler Bert V, h. 305 s Anderson
Sigler Daniel, physician and surgeon, also treas Elwood N G & O Co, 513 s Anderson, h. 305 s Anderson
Silence Nathan, lab, h. n s L E & W Ry bet 20th and 21st
Sillenberger Albert, gatherer, bds 730 n Boulevard
Silvey James R, carp, h. 2315 Main
Silvey Charles, wks Rodefer's Brick Wks, h. 2323 n C

John L. Lindskoog, Leads in the Merchant Tailoring Line English and French Worsteds, Imported, always in stock.
210½ Not buy until you have seen them.
N. E. Cor. Church and Harrison,   -   -   ALEXANDRIA, IND.

ons Wm L, clk, 121 s Anderson
nops Thomas, teamster, bds 1602 s D
)kins Sallie A, h. 2009 Main
)son Harry, glass wkr, bds 1303 s D
)son James B, glass wkr, bds 1303 s D
n Wright, watchman, bds 1329 s C
Edward, gatherer, bds 812 n 11th
L Ada, h. 1622 Main
Thomas S, grocery, 1620 Main, h. 1622 Main
er Mnfg Co, Cox & Daugherty agents, 1356 s A
Elsie L, glass wkr, h. 6th, 1st n n F
e Elbert A, painter, h. 2326 n D
Lincoln A, hostler, h. 1512 s B
on Wm, glass blower, bds 414 n 14th
1 Anna A, h. 912 n Anderson
1 Isaac G, glass blower, h. 904 n 13th
1 Robert H, glass blower, h. 912 n Anderson
1 Martha J, wid, h. 912 n Anderson
es George, glass wkr, bds 1053 n 14th
l Herman G, glass wkr, h. 810 s Anderson
l Jennie, teacher, bds s D bet Anderson and 14th
zer Ephraim, glass wkr, h. 403 n 9th
h Adam H, glass wkr, h. 1435 n 7th
h Alexander, glass wkr, h. 1000 s A
h Alfred P, glass wkr, h. 1429 n 7th
h Alonzo, hoop mkr, h. 1931 s K
h Alta L, bookpr, 108 s Anderson, h. 1520 n D
h Arthur, glass wkr, rms 1221 n D
h Arthur, hoop mkr, h. 1931 s K
h Belle, h. 1912 s B
h & Berry (W H Smith and C J Berry), furniture, carpets, pictures and frames, undertaking, 114 s Anderson
h Bridget, wid, h. 216 n 12th
h B Frank, lab, h. 1533 Main
h Curtis W, grocer, h. 118 n 16th
h Cynthia, h. 2009 n D
1 D, lab, h. 1807 n C
h Edmond, watchman, h. 2506 n A
h Edward R, lab, h. 1912 s B
h Effie, comp, h. 16th
h Francis M, lab, h. 2506 n A
h Frank, wks Rodefer's Brick Wks, h. n s n B

RE BROS., ICE CREAM, WHOLESALE MANUFACTURERS AND DEALERS IN OYSTERS IN SEASON. *Telephone* 513 Nichol Ave., ANDERSON, IND.

erson Foundry and Machine Works, Manufacturers of **BRICK AND TILE MACHINES, SAW MILLS, ETC**
Jackson Street, 'Phone 53. ANDERSON, IND.

Jackson & Burr Do the Largest INSURANCE Business. Insure in the good old Companies they represent.

69½ N. Meridian, - - ANDERSON, IND.

ELWOOD CITY DIRECTORY.

ELWOOD DAILY CALL

A SPLENDID LOCAL PAPER.

WILL. J. SPRUCE, - - Editor and Proprietor,

ELWOOD, INDIANA.

ONLY **$5.00** PER YEAR. *Finest Grade of Job Printing.*

Smith Frank, glass blower, bds 1610 n E
Smith Frank, heading wkr, bds 1713 s F
Smith George, carp, h. e s 22d bet s N and O
Smith Harry, glass wkr, rms 1017 s A
Smith Harvey H, lab, h. 612½ s Anderson
Smith Henry, lab, h. 23 n D
Smith Howard, grocer, h. 118 n 16th
Smith James, glass wkr, h. 1518 n B
Smith James P, wks Rodefer's Brick Wks
Smith Jesse E, teamster, h. 2506 n A
Smith John, blacksmith, bds 909 n 13th
Smith John C, bartender, 113 s Anderson, h. 216 n 12th
Smith John F, glass wkr, h. 222 n 7th
Smith John L, glass blower, bds 900 n Anderson
Smith John P, glass wkr, bds 2529 n A
Smith John T, carpet weaver, 1931 s K, h. same
Smith John W K, painter, bds 1312 n D
Smith Joseph, lab, h. 1928 s N
Smith Levi F, carp, h. n s of s D bet s Anderson and 13th
Smith Lilbern, h. 1645 s B
Smith May R, comp, h. 118 n 16th
Smith Michael F, glass wkr, h. 417 n 14th
Smith Milton H, teamster, h. 2506 n A
Smith Newton, glass wkr, bds 426 n 11th
Smith Noah, glass wkr, bds 426 n 11th
Smith Omer, lab, bds 420 n 16th
Smith Perry, glass wkr, bds 1303 s D
Smith Thomas M, real estate agent, h. 1520 n D
Smith Wm, plumber, bds 1013 Main
Smith Wm, lab, h. 216 n 12th
Smith Wm H, carp, h. rear 1020 Main
Smith Wm H, grocer, 1526 Main, h. 118 n 16th

George B. Epperson, Contractor and Builder of Felt and Gravel ROOFING.

39 E. 9th St., - - ANDERSON, IND.

Smith W H (Smith & Berry), h. 1309 s A
Smith Wm H M, job printer, The Elwood Leader, rms Boulevard
Smitzmesser Andrew, h. 123 n 13th
Snelson Edward, clk, h. 1352 s B
Snelson Frank, barber, h. 1352 s B
Snelson Mathias, clk, h. 1352 s B
Snelson Walter, butcher, h. 1920 s N
Snider Alice, h. 2511 n D
Snider Jefferson, lab, h. 2511 n D
Snider John R, h. 2511 n D
Snider Wm H, farmer, h. 2511 n D
Snively Henry H, drugs, watches, clocks, jewelry and musical instruments, 112 s Anderson, h. 1415 s E
Snively John F, teacher, h. 1633 n A
Snively Samuel (Garrett & Snively), 1633 n B
Snodgrass Rev Charles W, h. 1630 n F
Snodgrass John, teamster, h. n e cor 11th and s C
Snodgrass Thetus T, lab, h. 622 s 16th
Snoddy Emma, teacher, bds 1809 Main
Snow Flora E, wid, h. 2009 Main
Snyder Frederick, glass wkr, bds 2418 n B
Snyder John A, glass wkr, h. 1309 s D
Snyder John H, delivery clk, h. 1329 s A
Snyder Joseph, glass blower, bds 851 n 11th
Solomon Wm, lab, h. 1332 s B
Southern Ohio Loan & Trust Co, of Cincinnati, O, Roop & Haynes, 210½ s Anderson
Spahr Douglas, drayman, h. 1924 n F
Spahr John H, drayman, h. 2026 n F
Spain Christopher, glass blower, h. 203 n 13th
Spain Mrs Ellen, dressmkr, 203 n 13th, h. same
Spencer Alonzo, carp, bds n e cor 13th and n C
Spigel George, teamster, h. 749 n 14th
Spira Charles, glass wkr, bds 921 n 13th
Spooner Wm, glass wkr, bds 1609 n C
Sprong Charles, lab, h. w s 10th bet n F and G
Sprong Clinton E, glass wkr, h. w s 10th bet n F and G
Sprong W A, attorney, 120½ s Anderson, h. 1351 s C
Spruce Will J, editor and propr The Elwood Daily Call, 118½ s Anderson, bds 1350 s A (see adv)
St Clair John, glass blower, h. n w cor 2d and n F
St Joseph's Catholic Church, Rev B Biegel pastor, 1st e 1320 s A
St Joseph's Parochial School, Rev B Biegel supt, 1st e 1320 s A
Staaford Enoch, mgr Tin Plate Wks, rms 118 n 19th
Stacker John, molder, rms 1528 Main

HUGH FISHER, Manufacturer Screen Doors and Windows all sizes. Furniture repairing a specialty.
198 and 200 N. Milton St.,
ANDERSON, IND.

Stafford David, bill agt, h. s w cor s F and 14th
Stafford Rev Thomas L, h. w s 25th bet s A and B
Stage Francis M, stone mason, h. 1603 n F
Stage Wm, lab, h. 1603 n F
Stager John, glass wkr, rms 1017 s A
Staggs Ella, clk, 201 s Anderson
Stahl John, glass cutter, h. 1332 n 9th
Stahl Wm J, lab, h. 2116 n A
Staker John, molder, bds 1802 s B
Staker Lottie, comp, The Elwood Press, h. 1934 Main
Staley E H (Mellette & Staley), h. Frankfort, Ind
Stam Alonzo (Hamilton & Stam), h. 2528 s A
Stamback Jasper, carp, h. 1359 s B
Stamback Ora, eng hostler, bds 1359 s B
Stanford Thomas, tin plate wkr, bds 1812 s H
Stanger Wm O, glass wkr, h. 236 n 6th
Stanley LaRue, clk, 201 s Anderson, bds 1800 s G
Stansberry Lewis, lab, h. 2127 n D
Stanton James, shoemkr, bds 1643 s A
Star Bakery, D Well propr, 118 s Anderson
Starkey Alonzo L, brickmkr, bds 900 s A
Starkey Francis P, mgr W U Tel Co, h. 825 Main
Starkey George, brakeman, h. 806 s 17th
Starkey Ida, dressmkr, wks 1517 Main
Starkey Tobias, propr Brick Works
Starkey Wm K, carpet weaver, 806 s 17th, h. same
Starkey Wm S, plasterer, h. 1524 n C
Starkey Williard C, h. 900 s A
Stayton Belle, h. 1923 s A
Stayton Hill, hostler, wks 116 s 16th, h. 1923 s A
Steel John, wks Brick Works, b. 936 n 13th
Stein Lewis, lab, h 2517 s B
Sterrett Wm, painter, bds 1821 e Boulevard
Stephenson F, ship clk, Geo A Macbeth & Co
Stevens Albert, bookpr, h. 2012 n Main
Stevens Edwin, genl mngr, The American T P Co, h. 2012 Main
Stevens Henry, glass wkr, bds 1053 n 14th
Stevens Samuel, glass wkr, h. 1217 s A
Stevenson Andrew J, propr The Stevenson House, res same
Stevenson Fred A, ship clk, bds The Stevenson House
Stevenson House The, A J Stevenson propr, rates $2.00 per day, 1615 s A
Stewart Charles A, livery, 112 s 16th, bds 800 s 17th
Stewart Felix, packer, bds 710 n Anderson
Stewart Lucy, wid, h 800 s 17th

tewart Major A, carp, bds 1520 n D
tieglitz Louis, glass blower, h. 407 n 10th
tilwell Frank E, captain and driver, Elwood Fire Co, h. 1644 s B
tilwell Idel, tailoress, h. 1644 s B
tilwell Jessie, clk, 100 s Anderson, h. 1644 s B
tilwell Parthena, wid, h. 1644 s B
:inchfield John P, tailor, wks 113½ s Anderson, bds Erie House
tineback George W, street cont, h. n w cor 14th and n C
tokes Anchor M, tailoress, h. 1620 s E
tokes Andrew H, carp, h. 1303 s D
tokes Charles W, cooper, h. 1620 s E
tokes Elias G, carp, h. 1620 s E
tokes Emory O, switchman, h. 1303 s D
tokes Frank M, brick mason, h. 1308 s B
tokes, Glaspy & Co (J Stokes, M Glaspy and G W Bourdon), plumbers, 213 s Anderson
:okes James A (Stokes, Glaspy & Co), h. 1514 s D
:one John, lab, bds 825 Main
:ookey Myrtle, clk, 201 s Anderson
:orrey Matthew B, glass worker, h 2517 n A
:oute Daniel W, h. 620 s Anderson
:range Jesse, h. n w cor s N and 23d
:ratton James, carp, bds n w cor s A and 19th
:rauss Harry, clothier, rms 2113 Main
:uckey Charles E, lab, h. 2211 s B
:uckey Wm H, carp, h. 2525 s B
:udebaker George, lab, bds 211 n 13th
:udebaker James, lab, h. 15 s I
:ull Joseph J, carp, bds 2013 n F
:garman Louis, barber, h. 1520 s B
:it Simon, wks Brick Wks, h. 2519 s A
:mmers Alexander, glass wkr, h. 2111 n B
:mmers James, glass wkr, bds 426 n 10th
:mmers Rosa, domestic, Boston House
:tles Alexander, carp, bds 847 n 12th
:tton Louis E, glass wkr, h. 1522 n B
:tton Matilda, wid, h. 1522 n B
:tton Omer, glass wkr, h. 1517 n C
van Asa F, grocer, 404 n 9th, h. same
vunfelt Victor (Lawson & Swanfelt), h. 405 n 10th
veeney Frank, lab, bds 1621 Main
vift Benj F, carp, h. 208 s 11th
vift Wm, glass wkr, bds 233 n 12th
vihart Samuel W, barber shop, 1516 s A, h. 2217 s B

WOOLLEY FOUNDRY AND MACHINE WORKS,
Engineers, Founders and Machinists
N. W. Cor. 14th and C. W. and M. R. R.

WHEN — THE — **Anderson Clothiers & Hatters.**
☞ ONE PRICE TO ALL.

T

Tarlton Charles S, secy The American T P Co, h. 503 Anderson.
Tarpy John, saloon, 428 n 9th, h. same
Tarpy Kate, h. 428 n 9th
Tarpy Patrick, bartender, 428 n 9th, h. same
Taylor Bros (C I and H H Taylor), hardware, &c, 108 Anderson
Taylor Calvin M, tinner, h. 2310 n A
Taylor Chester I (Taylor Bros), h. 1532 n A
Taylor Dora, wid, h. 2310 n A
Taylor Edward, lab, bds 1534 n C
Taylor Edward E, grocer, 1532 Main, h. same
Taylor Ella N, h. 1532 n A
Taylor Henry H (Taylor Bros), h. 1602 n B
Taylor Herbert, clk, 1526 Main
Taylor Lora, clk, 1529 Main, h. 1602 s B
Taylor Lucinda, wid, h. 1532 n A
Taylor Wm, glass wkr, bds 2531 n A
Teffer Joseph, glass blower, bds 216 n 7th
Tetrick Nora, h. 1918 n D
Tetrick Wm H, carp, h. 1918 n D
Thayer George W B, carp, h. 2312 s B
Thayer John D, carp, h. 2312 s B
Thoma Joseph, glass blower, h. 234 n Boulevard
Thomas Enoch G, millwright, h. 1605 Main
Thomas Hiram F, boarding, 1809 s I, h. same
Thomas Ida M, h. 1605 Main
Thomas John, tin plate wkr, bds w s 24th
Thomas L O, barber, wks n w cor Anderson and s A, h. 2203 s A
Thomas Mack, blksmith, h. 2200 s B
Thomas Philip, tin plate wkr, bds w s 24th
Thomas Samuel, lab, h. 2127 n E
Thomas Thomas, tin plate wkr, bds n w cor s N and 23d
Thompkins Elbert, lab, h. 1302 s C
Thompkins Isaac, cemetery sexton, h. 1302 s C
Thompson Charles R, teamster, h. 2002 n A
Thompson Le Roy, business mgr The Elwood Press, bds 1934 Main
Thornton Lulu, h. 405 n 12th
Thornton Margaret, wid, h. 405 n 12th
Thornton Michael, glass wkr, h. 405 n 12th
Thornton Patrick, glass wkr, h. 952 n 12th
Thornton Thomas, glass wkr, h. 729 n 14th
Thorp Mattie, bds 2737 s A
Thorp Wm L, watchman, h. 2d w 2741 Main

Roop & Haynes, Real Estate,
LOANS AND INSURANCE.
210½ S. Anderson, • • • ELWOOD, IND.

brift I May, domestic, 1706 s D.
burman Thomas, lab, h. 1815 s A
hurston John M, glass wkr, bds 2020 s A
inder John H, glass wkr, h. e s 9th bet n A and C
ipton James L, lab, bds 404 n 6th
odd Eli, painter, h. 1801 n C
odd Elias, bookpr, 1533 s B, h. 1926 Main
odd Leroy, clk, h. 1512 n C
odd May, h. 1512 n C
odd Sylvester (S Todd & Co), h. 1512 n C
odd S & Co (S Todd and Wm Shaw), carprs, 105½ s Anderson
oll Bessie, domestic, 104½ n 16th
ompkins Carrie L, domestic, 1301 n D
ompkins David, glass wkr, h. 1305 s C
ompkins Edward, section foreman, h. n s s I bet 13th and 14th
ompkins Wm, carp, h. 308 s 13th
oms Edgar, eng, bds 1610 n E
oner George E, comp, The Elwood Press, h. 1327 s A
ousey Wm, carp, h. 2014 s B
ower Anna, wks Glass Factory, h. w s 10th bet n H and I
abue George F, glass wkr, h. 800 s 1 th
rader & Collins (M D Trader and Edwin Collins), barber shop, 1520 s A
rader Marcus D (Trader & Collins), h 1602 s E
aster Wm H H, teacher, h. 2027 s B
owbridge Charles H, blksmith, h. 1088 n 14th
ill Wm, clk, 201 s Anderson, bds 1610 s E
ill Wm G, teacher, rms 1612 s D
irley Cora L, stenographer, Elwood Land Co, h. 220 n 12th
irney Joseph, glass wkr, h. 1101 n F
itrow John W, lab, h. 2515 n D
ittle Theodore, glass wkr, h. 2426 n A
rner Dora, music teacher, 801 s 17th
rner Elmer E, real estate and ins, 105½ s Anderson, h. 801 s 17th
rner Harry, h 801 s 17th
rner John, trav sales, h. 801 s 16th
rner Mary, stenographer, h. 801 s 17th
rrell Joseph, mach, bds 1802 s B

U

ebele Joseph, tin plate wkr, h. 1816 s H
etz Samuel, carpenter, 1010 s Anderson, h. same
en Anna, teacher, bds n s s I, bet 14th and s Anderson
nphrus Wesley, lab, bds 500 n 19th

WHEN—YOUR MEASURE TAKEN, AND *SUITS OR OVERCOATS* MADE TO ORDER.

Underwood Charles E, driver, h. 1620 Main
Underwood John L, city police, h. 2201 s A
Underwriters Ins Co of New York, 1527½ Main
U S Express Co, B & O Express, P P Byrne agt, 112 s Anderson
United States Saving and Investment Co, Roop & Haynes, agts, 210½ s Anderson
United States Saving & Loan Association of St Paul, Minn, 1510 Main
Utrick Wm, iron worker, bds 907 s Anderson

V

Van Buskerk Wm, painter, h. 1813 n D
Vance John, brick mason, h. s s s I bet 12th and 13th
Vandoren Mulford, gas and steam fitter, 405 s Anderson, h. 1519 e Boulevard
Vanhorn Alphonse E, carp, h. 945 n 13th
Vanhorn George N, glass wkr, h. 1320 n 9th
Vannatta Hezekiah R, h. 2008 s A
Vannatta Ida B, milliner, 100 s Anderson, h. 2008 s A
Vannatta Jonas, puddler, h. 1911 s A
Vannatta Matthew M, puddler, h. 2008 s A
Vanness Andrew J, h. 2321 s A
Vanness Belle, h. 2321 s A
Vanness Mary E, h. 2321 s A
Van Netter Susan, wid, h. 1930 n D
Vanscoy Robert, lab, h. 1614 Main
Van Valkinburg Myron E, h. 1339 s C
Van Valkinburg Oscar B, house mover, h. 1339 s C
Vaughn Arthur, teamster, h. 1924 s J
Vaughn Eunice, wid, h. 1924 s J
Vaughn Flora C, h. 1924 s J
Vaughn Oscar S, glass wkr, h. 425 n 9th
Vawter L T, clk, 208 s Anderson, h. 1912 Main
Vencill John E, carp, h. 1310 s D
Venerables Mrs Hettie, domestic, w s s I bet 14 and Anderson
Vennekens Victor, glass wkr, bds 2123 n C
Vermillion Jesse, brick wkr, bds 1332 s A
Vetter Louis, glass wkr, h. 835 n 11th
Vexelberger Frank, glass wkr, h. 937 n 12th
Vincent J M, clk, n w cor Anderson and s A, h. 608 s Anderson
Vins Miley N, carp, h. s w cor 11th and n H
Vinson Elisha, eng, h. 1928 s G
Vinson Melvill, painter, h. 1924 s G
Vinyard James S, glass wkr, h. 403 n 9th

John L. Lindskoog, Fashionable MERCHANT TAILOR. First-Class Work and Fit GUARANTEED.
H. H. H. Block, N. E. Cor. Church and Harrison, ALEXANDRIA, IND.

WM. J. DOVE, Insures against loss by Fire, Cyclone, Accident and Death.
NEELEY BLOCK. 61½ N. Meridian, ANDERSON, IND.

W

Wagaman Henry, glass wkr, bds 515 Main
Wagner Augustus, glass wkr, bds 807 Main
Wagner Charles, driver, rms 1802 s A
Wagner Daniel, glass wkr, h. 1020 s B
Wagner Henry P, glass wkr, h. 2d s cor 4th and n A
Wagner John, glass blower, bds 851 n 11th
Wagner Otto, glass wkr, bds 1008 n F
Wagner Wm, glass blower, bds n w cor 9th and n A
Wagnerer Amazon, painter, bds 1312 n D
Waits Mrs France, h. 202½ s Anderson
Waler Frank, bartender, bds 1522 s A
Walk Florence, glass wkr, h. rear 1020 Main
Walker Augustus, glass wkr, h. n w cor 3d and n F
Walker Benton, glass wkr, h. n w cor 3d and n F
Walker Laura, teacher, bds 194 s F
Walkup Mary, teacher, bds 1914 s H
Wallace Mrs Ada, dressmkr, 2124 Main, h. same
Wallace Andrew, glass wkr, h. 2d e n e cor s F and 14th
Wallace Hugh A, glass wkr, h. 2124 Main
Wallace James A, lab, h. 1616 n D
Wallace Lillie, h. 1616 n D
Wallace Wm L, hostler, h. 1582 s A
Walser Charles E, glass wkr, h. 416 n 7th
Walsh Edward, molder, bds 1350 s A
Walsh James R, teamster, h. 2742 n E
Walsh Philip, glass wkr, bds 428 n 9th
Walsh Thomas H, teamster, h. 2742 n E
Walsh Wm J, lab, h. 2742 n E
Walter Adelot, glass wkr, bds 943 n 12th
Waltman Frank, carp, h. e s 9th bet n A and C
Waltz Clinton J, glass wkr, bds 1013 Main
Wann Ira J, musician, h. s w cor 20th and s A
Wann Jessie, clk, 100 s Anderson, h. 1608 n C
Wann Mahalia, wid, h. 1815 Main
Wann Mary E, wid, h. n w cor 20th and s A
Ward John P, glass blower, h. 911 n 14th
Ward Joshua B, lab, h. 2024 n D
Ward Michael, glass blower, bds s s n C, 1st w Anderson
Wardwell John, molder, bds 1808 s B
Warfield Edward, glass wkr, h. 932 n 12th
Warfield Edward, bartender, h. 819 n 9th
Warner Burt, glass wkr, bds s I
Warner Egburt, gas well driller, h. 1900 s G

Anderson Foundry and Machine Works, Manufacturers of Portable and Stationary **Steam Engines.**
N. JACKSON STREET, ANDERSON, IND. Phone 53.

WHITE RIVER DAIRY, 513 Nichol Avenue, ANDERSON, IND. Telephone 220.

LARMORE BROS., Proprietors, also Manufacturers and Wholesale Dealers in **Ice Cream and Oysters in Season.**

Is Your Property Insured? If not, CALL AT ONCE on **JACKSON & BURR,**
69½ N. Meridian, - - ANDERSON, IND.

→| D. WELL, |←
Star Bakery, CONFECTIONERY, CIGARS AND TOBACCO.
ELWOOD, INDIANA.

Warner Harvey, lather, bds 426 n 11th
Warner Jethero L, lab, h. 1321 s F
Warner John, tool dresser, bds 1900 s G
Warner John, glass wkr, h. 1049 n 14th
Warner Ora E, teamster, h. w s n Anderson
Warner Sylvester J, lab, h. 1321 s F
Warner W W, lather, bds 426 n 11th
Warseller Wm, gatherer, bds 710 n Anderson
Waterhous George C, glass wkr, h. 406 n 7th
Watkins Wm A, clk, 1514 s A, h. 2125 n C
Watkins Wm L, tin plate wkr, bds 1527 n C
Watkinson John, glass wkr, h. 418 n 8th
Watson Elcy P, lab, h. 1909 n E
Watson George, teamster, bds 2329 n B
Watson Jennie, wid, h. 2007 s B
Watson Joseph L, h. 1808 n A
Watson Joshua, foreman, h. 1528 n A
Watson Matilda A, wid, h. 1808 n A
Watson Washington J, glass wkr, h. 2101 n A
Wayland Frank, bartender, rms 202½ s Anderson
Waymire John S, h. 200 n B
Webb Alonzo E (Webb & Ferguson), h 324 s 13th
Webb Elmer T, clk, h. 1926 n A
Webb Emsley, restaurant, 1519 Main, h. 1926 n A
Webb & Ferguson (A Webb, S Ferguson), barber shop, 1516 Main
Webb Nathan, glass wkr, h. 1917 n A
Webb Nelson, wks Rodefer's Brick Wks, h. 2605 s A
Webb N Florence, cook, 1519 Main, h. 1926 n A
Webb Wm, lab, h. 2600 s A
Webb W Riley, clk, 1519 Main, h. 1926 n A
Webber James, tin plate wkr, h. 1520 e Boulevard
Weber Charles, lab, bds 803 Main
Weddell Nettie, h. 1302 n D
Weddel Thomas, lab, h. 1911 n B
Weikel Catherine, dressmkr, wks 2301 n A
Weisenberger Philip, glass wkr, h. n e cor 3d and n E
Weisjohn Edward, tin plate wkr, h. s w cor 12th and n D
Weisjohn Martha S, h. s w cor 12th and n D
Weiskopf Dennis (Nivison & Weiskopf), h. Cincinnati, O

George B. Epperson, Paints, Oils, Varnishes and Painters' Supplies.
39 E. 9th St., - - ANDERSON, IND.

ich James, wks Rodefer's Brick Wks
ich Reuben J, wks Rodefer's Brick Wks
iku Elizabeth, wid, h. 2121 n A
ll Altha, h. 1324 s B
l **David**, propr Star Bakery, also groceries and confectioneries,
    118 s Anderson, h. 1324 s B (see adv)
ll James M, h. 1805 s A
ll Peter, h. 1701 s F
ilbrook Frederick, wks Elwood Planing Mill, h. 608 s 17th
lls Charles C, glass wkr, h. 410 n 7th
lsh Michael, contractor, rms 1528 Main
lsh T J, cigar mkr, rms 1528 Main
nce Jacob, glass wkr, rms 1830 Main
nz Jacob, glass wkr, bds 232 n 7th
nsel Mrs Deborah, boarding house, 812 n 11th, h. same
rking Blanche, h. 635 s Anderson
rking Bros (D O, J E and M O Werking), grocers, 1408 n H
rking David O (Werking Bros), h. 1915 n E
rking John E (Werking Bros), h. 1915 n E
rking Joseph, carp, h. 635 s Anderson
rking Martin O (Werking Bros), h. 1915 n E
rking Myrtle, h. 1915 n E
rking Wm M, carp, 1915 n E, h. same
rline Charles, glass blower, bds 730 n Boulevard
rren Alexander, gatherer, bds 413 n 7th
rtz Edward, bartender, 1522 Main
st Alexander, glass wkr, bds 1515 n B
st Milton, lab, h. 1st e 1538 s B
stcott David, teaser, h. 2507 n A
stcott Richard, tin plate wkr, bds n w cor s N and 23d
stern Union Tel Co, F P Starkey mgr, n w cor Main & Anderson
arton Flora, teacher, h. 1900 Main
eeler Huston, lab, h. n e cor s N and 23d
eeler Jane, wid, h. n e cor s N and 23d
eeler Marcus, glass blower, bds s a n C, 1st n Anderson
eeler Minnie, h. 1524 n C
iner Frederick, glass wkr, bds e s 10th bet n A and C
itaker Mrs Amanda, dressmkr, 1621 Main, h. same
itaker James H, lab, h. 2008 Main
itaker James (Whitaker & Miller), h. 1621 Main
itaker John T, teamster, h. w s 8th bet n K and L
itaker & Miller (Jas Whitaker & Edward Miller), 1621 Main
ittaker Wm H, photogrepher, 1506 Main, h. 1504 n D
hitcomb Wm P, carp, h. 1108 s A
hite & Co (E White, J V Martin), real estate, 108½ s Anderson

J. T. Knowland & Son, Brass & Iron, Steam, Gas and Water Goods.
111 N. Main St., ANDERSON, IND. 'Phone 30.

White Edward, lab, h. 1520 n G
White Exum (White & Co), h. 1111 Main
White Ida B, h. 1111 Main
White James, lab, h. 2108 n F
White Michael, saloon, n w cor 9th and n C, h. same
White Sando, barber, wks 1516 s A, h. 1938 Main
Whitfield Frederick, glass blower, h. 429 n 9th
Whiteman Ida, wid, h. 2001 s A
Whiteman Lewis, clk, 117 s Anderson, h. 1901 s A
Whitney Benj D, real estate, h. 1626 n B
Whitson Jesse J, h. 2701 Main
Wiggins Augustus H, shoemkr, 1512½ Main, h. 1625 s A
Wilburn George W, lab, h. 2118 n C
Wiles Wm, lather, bds 1604 Main
Wiley Albert E (Wiley & Miller), bds 1522 s A
Wiley Benj F (Wiley & Co), bds 1350 s A
Wiley B F & Co (B F and W T Wiley), dry goods, etc, 100 and 102 s Anderson, cor Main
Wiley Edith, cashier, B F Wiley & Co, bds 1814 n C
Wiley & Miller (A E Wiley and A Miller), blksmiths, 1522 s A
Wiley W T (B F Wiley & Co), bds Stevenson Hotel
Wilgus George, cooper, h. 2129 n C
Wilhelm John, gatherer, bds 835 n 12th
Wilkinson Charles, carp, bds 819 n 13th
Wilkinson Edward A, glass wkr, h. 1232 n 10th
Willkie H F (Deal & Willkie), also justice of the peace, h. 1902 s A
Williams Albert, glass blower, h. n w cor 11th and n F
Williams A A, merchant tailor, 213½ s Anderson, h. 1335 s B
Williams Christopher D, painter, 1713 e Boulevard, h. same
Williams Dennis, tin plate wkr, bds n e cor s n and 22d
Williams Elza R, lab, 1511 Main, h. 1901 Main
Williams Eugene, painter, bds 1610 n E
Williams Harmon, glass wkr, bds 1639 Main
Williams Harry, tin plate wkr, bds n e cor s N and 23d
Williams Israel, glass wkr, h. 2020 Main
Williams Julius, painter, bds 1610 n E
Williams John, tin plate wkr, h. w s 24th bet s N and O
Williams Mary A, wid, h. 1718 e Boulevard
Williams Thomas, lab, bds 2304 n A
Williams Thomas, tin plate wkr, bds 800 s 18th
Williamson Albert, lab, h. 2613 s A
Williamson Charles O, glass blower, bds 1504 n D
Willets Beecher, genl delivery clk, postoffice, h. 1352 s C
Willetts Co The, Geo A Macbeth pres, C Rott secy and treas, Jesse Willetts supt, mnfrs glass house pots

John O. Miller, Dealer in WATCHES, CLOCKS & JEWELRY, SILVERWARE and OPTICAL GOODS.
3 N. Meridian, - - - ANDERSON, IND.

letts Jesse, supt The Willetts Co, h. n Anderson
letts Jesse Jr, pot mkr, h. 918 n Anderson
letts Joseph V, pot mkr, bds 918 n Anderson
lis Bertha, h. 2035 n F
lis Cora V, h. 2035 n F
lis Marcus R, lab, h. 2035 n F
lis Pearl E, stenographer, 201 s Anderson, bds 1608 s E
son Allen B, bookpr, Elwood Planing Mill Co, h. 1822 Main
son Charles, plasterer, bds 1812 s H
son Charles E, painter, bds 408 s Anderson
son Everett, h. 1115 n C
son George, carp, h. 2526 Main
son George F, carp, h. 2010 n A
son Harry, glass wkr, h. 1013 s A
son Henry, h. 1626 n D
son Jacob C, teamster, h. 1608 s A
son Jane, h. 218 n Anderson
son John, flagman, s A street crossing, h. 911 s Anderson
son Richard, saloon, h. 1801 s B
son Wm, carp, h. 1115 n C
iebrenner Daniel, wood wkr, h. 814 s Anderson
ies Theodore, hostler, 1819 s A, h. 1321 s A
istel Jacob, gatherer, bds 804 n 11th
istel Joseph, glass blower, h. 859 n 11th
istel Philip H, glass blower, h. 804 n 11th
iters Anna M, clk, 103 s Anderson, bds 1528 n 4th
iters Arthur J (P Kuntz Lumber Co), bds Boston House
ie Columbus S, lab, h. 1614 s A
ie Jesse, shoemkr, 1612 s A, h. 1614 s A
ie Martin C, lab, bds 803 Main
iner Frank, lab, bds s s L E & W R y bet 23d and 24th
ising George, lab, h. 2335 n B
:men Edward, glass wkr, bds 803 Main
:tcaniper Frederick W, carp, h. 2415 s A
lf Frederick, glass wkr, h. 236 n 7th
lf Moses J, h. 908 s Anderson
lf John, glass wkr, h. cor 2nd and n A
lverton Alonzo, pressman, The Elwood Daily Call, h. 416 n A
lverton Arthur H, carp, h. 214 n 13th
lverton Kate, stenographer, h. 416 n 12th
lverton Vincent, shoemkr, wks 1530 s A, h. 416 n 12th
od Clinton, hod carrier, bds 1117 s A
od David S, carp, h. 1925 n D
od Flora E, domestic, 1620 s E
od Wm, teamster, bds 1926 Main

WOOLLEY Foundry and Machine Works,
Designers and Manufacturers of **Heavy Machinery, Engines, Boilers and Rolling Mill Work.**
N. W Cor. 14th and C. W. and M. R. R.

WHEN—The Most Reliable CLOTHING House
✴ IN ANDERSON. ✴
PRICES ALWAYS THE LOWEST.

Woodruff Howe, foreman, The Elwood Press, h. Main
Woods Hugh D, glass blower, bds 900 n Anderson
Woods James C, brickmason, h. 2326 n A
Woods John, glass wkr, bds 417 n 7th
Woods Joshua, carp, h. 1915 s A
Woods Thomas, glass wkr, h. 817 n 13th
Workins Edward, hod carrier, bds 2404 s A
Worley Nettie, wid, h. 2108 n E
Worley Stephen M, glass wkr, h w s 3d bet n F and G
Worley Wm, gas fitter, wks 1604 s A, bds 612 n 16th
Wortman Henry, teamster, bds 1329 s C
Wortz Edwin, bartender, bds 1800 n E
Wray Samuel F, carp, h n w cor s I and 14th
Wright Emma wid, h. s C, 2 w Anderson
Wright Jane, wid, h. 1723 e Boulevard
Wright John S, glass wkr. h. 1600 s H
Wright Julia A, wid, h. 1314 s C
Wright Laura, dressmkr, 1631 s A, bds same
Wylie A, blksmth, rms 1644 s B
Wylie Edward, glass wkr, bds 825 n 9th

Y

Yagel Charles, glass blower, h. 837 n 11th
Yelvington Asa P, bench hand, h. 1615 s D
Yelvington Rob, comp, bds 1615 s D
York Emma, h. 2334 n C
York Esther, wid, h. 2334 n C
York Hattie, h. 2334 n C
Young Benj F, painter, h. 1302 n D
Young Christ, glass blower, bds n w cor 10th and n C
Young Claude, h. 1328 s C
Young Edith P, h. 1302 n D
Young Henry, glass blower, bds 401 n 9th
Young Theodore F, painter, h. 1302 n D
Young Wm R, painter, h. 1302 n D
Youngman Theodore, glass blower, h. 411 n 7th
Younken Clinton, lather, bds 426 n 10th
Younkins Oscar, glass wkr, bds 232 n 7th

Z

Zears Albert, gatherer, bds 526 n Boulevard
Zeke Newton, lab, bds 2400 s A
Zentmyer Joseph, hod carrier, bds 2022 s A
Zerface Wm G, real estate, loans and ins, 1510 Main, h. 2429 n A

Insure with ROOP & HAYNES,
IN THE STANDARD COMPANIES THEY REPRESENT.
210½ S. Anderson, — — — — — ELWOOD, IND

Robinson & Glasseo, Real Estate, Loans and Insurance. Building and Loan money procured in 15 days.
Room 9 "When" Building, - ANDERSON, IND.

ELWOOD, INDIANA,
Classified Business Directory.
1893--'94.

Agricultural Implements.
Loring F M, 1514½ Main
Rrith John, 20 s Anderson
Carting & Co, 1509-11 Main
Taylor Bros, 108 s Anderson

Architects.
Inan John, 2131 s J

Attorneys-at-Law.
rmfield O A, 1526½ Main
Behymer Bros, 118½ s Anderson
Brown Rudolph, 104½ s Anderson
Deal & Willkie, 120½ s Anderson
Greenlee C M, 202½ s Anderson
Griffin & Broadbent, 105½ s Anderson
Jaynes Geo E, 210½ s Anderson

Auctioneers.
Dean Z T, 1516½ s A

Bakeries.
Star Bakery, 118 s Anderson.

Banks.
First National Bank, The, n w cor Main and Anderson

Barber Shops.
Barnes Bros, 216 s Anderson
Icher & Maddock, n w cor Anderson and s A
McCord & Cox, 1512 s A
Lee M M, 142 w Main
Swihart Sam'l W, 1516 s A
Trader & Collins, 1520 s A
Webb & Ferguson, 1516 Main

Barrel Heading Mfgrs.
Elwood Heading Co, The, s w cor 19th and s B

Beer Agents.
Hamm Philip, rear 819 s Anderson

Blacksmiths.
Hamilton & Stam, 150 n B
Hopper & Hutchison, 1612 Main
Shore & Caylor, 111 s 16th
Wiley & Miller, 1522 s A

Boarding Houses.
Bingaman Belle, 2118 s A
Brenner Samuel, 1522 s A
Brobst C, 426 n 11th
Brown Wm, 1515 n B
Desfayes Ernest, 825 n 9th
Dickover Mrs L J, 1392 s A
Gorman Mrs Lizzie, 1009 n 10th
Harrell Mrs Mary F, 426 n 10th
Harris Mrs Martha, 885 n 12th
Hunt Mrs Ellen, 720 n Anderson
Jenner Moses G, 1912 s A
Lee Mrs Sarah, 1013 Main
Metsker Cornelius, 803 Main
Peterson Leonard V, 2304 n A
Rowland Mrs Lucy, 1527 n C
Thomas Hiram F, 1809 s I
Wensel Mrs Deborah, 812 n 11th

Books and Stationery.
Finch W A & Co, 200 s Anderson
Green E E, n w cor Anderson & s A

Boots and Shoes.
(RETAIL).
Goldnamer E & Co, 103 s Anderson and 1507 Main
Hand F B & Co, 1529 Main
Hupp & Conner, 107 s Anderson
Kraus J & Co, 120 s Anderson
Leeson R L, 201-3-7 s Anderson
Levy D & Co, 127 s Anderson
Phillips M E, 115 s Anderson
Wiley B F & Co, 100 s Anderson

Boot and Shoe Makers.
Buchanan John, 1538 Main
Stanton James, 1504 s A
Wiggins A H, 1512½ Main
Wise Jesse, 1612 s A

Deal & Willkie, have placed 85 loans in six months, Farm loans at 6%. All parties desiring to secure loans
WILL SAVE MONEY BY CALLING ON US.

J. P. CONDO & SON, FURNITURE DEALERS, ESTABLISHED 1857. We have the largest stock, latest styles, latest designs, sold on EASY WEEKLY PAYMENTS. ALEXANDRIA, IND.

WHEN — The Only Retail Clothiers
In the State of Indiana
That Manufacture their OWN CLOTHING.

Bottlers.
Elwood Bottling Works, rear 319 s Anderson

Brick Contractors.
Long Henry M, 120 n 13th
Lyst John, 2021 Main
Whitaker & Miller, 1621 Main

Brick Works.
Starkey Tobias, cor s E and s 8th
Rodefer Jno T, n e cor Main & 27th

Butter Dealers.
Carson Kit, 1528 s A

Carpenters, Contractors and Builders.
Besch Jacob, w s n Anderson
Clayball Howard, 2540 n C
Coxen Emanuel, 1510 n E
Duncan Joseph, 223 n 16th
Maddock Thomas R, 1921 Main
Neely Wm H, rear 710 n Anderson
Noftsker Stephen, w s n Anderson
Roe Augustus, 1911 n A
Todd S & Co, 105½ s Anderson
Utz Samuel, 1010 s Anderson
Working Wm M, 1915 n E

Carpets, Oil Cloth, &c.
Goldnamer E & Co, 103 s Anderson and 1507 Main
Leeson R L, 201-3-7 s Anderson
Smith & Berry, 114 s Anderson

Carpet Weavers.
James Mrs Sarah, rear 1926 n A
Smith John T, 1931 s K
Starkey Wm K, 806 s 17th

Carriage Dealers.
Boving F M, 1514½ Main
Frith John, 208 s Anderson.
Harting & Co, 1509 and 1511 Main
Schofield & Jacobs, 302 s Anderson

China, Glass and Queensware.
Elliott H B, 125 s Anderson
Leeson R L, 201-3-7 s Anderson
Myers A K, 209 s Anderson
Smith W H, 1526 Main
Wiley B F & Co, 100 s Anderson

Cigars and Tobacco.
WHOLESALE AND MNFRS.
Bond George H, 115½ s Anderson
Ferguson L & Co, 1704 s D
Rummel Bros, 157 s A
RETAIL.
Andres Bros, 1530 Main
Binford & Binford, 111 s Anderson
Carson Kit, 1528 s A
Everhart A L, 1514 Main
Gillespie & Carr, 121 s Anderson
Huston & Nearon, 1514 s A
Webb E, 1519 Main

Clothing.
Kraus J & Co, 120 s Anderson
Leeson R L, 201-3-7 s Anderson
Levy Emanuel, 202 s Anderson
Phillips M E, 115 s Anderson
Wiley B F & Co, 100 s Anderson

Commission Merchants.
Horne R H Produce Co The, 113 n 16th

Confectioners.
Andres Bros, 1530 Main
Everhart A L, 1514 Main
Ferguson L & Co, 1704 s D
Gillespie & Carr, 121 s Anderson
Huston & Nearon, 1514 s A
Mahan Charles, 212 s Anderson
Webb E, 1519 Main
Well David, 118 s Anderson

Dentists.
Browne H M, 120½ s Anderson
Harrold D C, 202½ s Andersod

Doors, Sash and Blinds.
Bauer & Finan, 2123 to 2131 s J
Heffner, Geo W & Lewis, 1538 s B
Kuntz P Lumber Co, rear 1534 s A
Schnasse G Jr & Co, cor n B & 13th

Dressmakers.
Adair Mrs E R, 1320 s B
Allen Lydia, 1814 s A
Clement Mrs Barbara, 2301 n A
Clifford Lena J, w s 11th, 1st s n F
Dugan Mrs Anna A, 1517 Main
Forcum Jane, cor 12th and n A
Jessup Mrs Mary F, 801 s 16th
LaRue Cora, 1812 s H
Parker Mrs A, 1631 s A
Ring Mrs Mary, 2315 n A
Sandberg Amanda, 314 s Anderson

John L. Lindskoog, The Leading Tailor of Alexandria.
All the Latest Novelties in Suitings and Trouserings.
H. H. H. Block, N. E. Cor. Church and Harrison, ALEXANDRIA, IND.

I. J. DOVE — Can give you choice in 20 of the oldest and best Insurance Companies represented. Note this fact when placing your insurance.

EELEY BLOCK.   61½ N. Meridian, ANDERSON, IND.

ELWOOD CITY DIRECTORY.   85

ARMORE BROS., 513 Nichol Avenue, ANDERSON, IND. Telephone 220. Will deliver you your ICE CREAM, OYSTERS AND MILK any place in the city, and guarantee first-class goods.

Irs Elles, 203 n 13th
Mrs Ada, 2124 Main
er Mrs Amanda, 1621 Main

Druggists.
1510 Main
A & Co, 200 s Anderson
E, n w cor Anderson & s A
F M, 104 s Anderson
al S, 105 s Anderson
H H, 112 s Anderson

Dry Goods.
O & Co, 204 s Anderson
206 s Anderson
er E & Co, 103 s Anderson
07 Main
J 1527 Main
L, 201-3-7 s Anderson
1620 Main
F & Co, 100 and 102 s An-

lectric Light Co.
Electric Light and Power
7 n 16th

celsior Factories.
and Goddard, Junc, L E & Pan Handle tracks.

ress Companies.
xpress Co, 104 s Anderson
ress Co, B & O Express,
nderson

Feed Mills.
eorge W, 1504 n B

lour and Feed.
Goode, 1513 Main

Flour Mills.
louring Mills, 817 s An-
Goode, 1513 Main

Foundries.
(CASTINGS).
ron Wks, n e cor 22d & s J

Furniture.
H, 1534 Main
Finan, 2123 to 2131 s J
Pauley, 1401 Main
nstallment Co The, 1525-
Berry, 114 s Anderson

Gas Companies.
Citizens' Gas & Mining Co, w s Anderson, opp n A
Elwood Natural Gas & Oil Co, 201 s Anderson

Gas Well Supplies.
Elwood Iron Wks, n e cor 22d & s J

Gents' Furnishing Goods.
Goldnamer E & Co, 107 s Anderson and 1507 Main
Hand F B & Co, 1529 Main
Kraus J & Co, 20 s Anderson
Leeson R L, 201-3-7 s Anderson
Phillips M E, 115 s Anderson

Glass Mnfrs.
(BOTTLE).
Nivison & Weiskopf, cor 26th & s C
(LAMP CHIMNEY).
McCloy W R Glass Co, w e n J
(PLATE).
Diamond Plate Glass Co, cor 9th and n E

Grain Elevators and Dealers.
Harting & Co, 1509-11 Main
Jay Grain Co The, 401 s Anderson
Kidwell & Goode, 1513 Main

Grocers.
Brobst C, 424 n 11th
Brown John R, 2401 s M
Cox Charles, 1512 Main
Duncan Joseph W, n s L E & W Ry bet 23d and 24th
Knotts David C, 2216 s B
Leeson R L, 201-3-7 s Anderson
Linville Martin W, 613 s Anderson
Lorah Andrew, 1508 Main
McMahan Thomas, 819 n 11th
Mahan Charles, 212 s Anderson
Mason & Bull, 2122 Main
Metsker Cornelius, 803 Main
Morrison & Boyer, 412 s Anderson
Plowman Eugene, n e cor 10th and n C
Sims T S, 1620 Main
Smith W H, 1526 Main
Swan A F. 404 n 9th
Taylor E E, 1532 Main
Well David, 118 s Anderson
Werking Bros, 1408 n H
Wiley B F & Co, 100 s Anderson

on Foundry and Machine Works, Manufacturers of BOILERS, Steam Heaters, Castings, and General Machinery.
CKSON STREET, ANDERSON, IND.   'Phone 53.

Jackson & Burr Represent the Largest Lines and the Strongest INSURANCE Companies.
69½ N. Meridian, - - - ANDERSON, IND.

86 ELWOOD CITY DIRECTORY.

Hardware.
Frith John, 208 s Anderson
Leeson R L, 201-3 and 7 s Anderson
Taylor Bros, 108 s Anderson

Harness and Saddlery.
Austin C M & Bro, 1524 s A
Lee Wm, 119 s Anderson

Hats and Caps.
Leeson R L, 201-3 and 7 s Anderson
Phillips M E, 115 s Anderson
Wiley B F & Co, 100 s Anderson

Hotels.
Boston House, The, 1531 and 1533 s A
Erie Hotel, 408 s Anderson
Stevenson House, The, 1615 s A

Ice Companies.
Elwood Crystal Ice Co, s w cor Anderson and n F

Incubator and Brooder Mfgrs.
Garrett & Snively, 111 n Anderson

Insurance Agents.
(ACCIDENT.)
Behymer J & Co, 118½ s Anderson
(FIRE.)
Behymer J & Co, 118½ s Anderson
Deal & Willkie, 120½ s Anderson
Elwood Real Estate Co, 1534 s A
Hupp G W, 105½ s Anderson
Roop & Haynes, 210½ s Anderson
Roop Oscar, P, 1527½ Main
White & Co, 108½ s Anderson
Zerface W G, 1510 Main

Justice of the Peace.
Willkie H F, 120½ s Anderson

Laundry.
Elwood Steam Laundry, 1422 Main

Lime and Cement.
Heffner Geo W & Lewis, 1583 s B

Livery, Feed and Sales Stables.
Clymer R H & Son, 1600 s A
Dunlap A J, 1624 s A
Elliott J H, 1819 s A
Stewart Charles A, 112 s 16th

Loans.
Behymer J & Co, 118½ s Anderson
Deal & Willkie, 120½ s Anderson
Heller J C, 120½ s Anderson
Roop & Haynes, 210½ s Anderson
Roop Oscar, 1527½ Main
White & Co, 108½ s Anderson

Lumber, Lath and Shingles.
Bauer & Finan, 2123 to 2181 s J
Elwood Planing Mill Co, cor C and Pan Handle R R
Heffner Geo W & Lewis, 1533 s B
Kuntz P, Lumber Co, rear 1534 s A
Schnasse G Jr & Co, cor n B & 13th

Machine Shops.
Elwood Iron Wks, n e cor 22d & s J
Elwood Machine Works, 209 n 16th

Meat Markets.
Baker A J, 128 s Anderson
Beck Vallorous, 2507 n D
Cramer John, 1521 Main
Greulich Bros, e end Main
Knotts David C, 2216 s B
Lawson & Swanfelt, 408 n 10th
Lorah Andrew, 1508 Main
Montgomery I W, 117 s Anderson
Negley Bros, 611 s Anderson
North Bros, 116 s Anderson

Merchant Tailors.
Kessler D, 206½ s Anderson
Klueh C, 114½ s Anderson
Kranz E F, 104½ s Anderson
Williams C A, 213½ s Anderson

Milliners.
Buchanan Sophia, 1529 Main
Dugan Mrs Anna A, 1517 Main
Hand F B & Co, 1529 Main
Heck Alice, 1418 Main
Miller B F, 312 s Anderson
Wiley B F & Co, 100 s Anderson

Mining Companies.
Citizens' Gas & Mining Co, w s Anderson opp n A

Music Teachers.
Tyner Dora, 301 s 17th
Newkirk Ella J, rear 1108 Main

George B. Epperson, Contractor & Builder of Concrete Side Walks.
89 E. 9th St., - - ANDERSON, IND.

ALEXANDRIA CITY DIRECTORY

ALPHABETICAL LIST OF NAMES.

A

ott Mrs Alice, dress mkr, h Clinton
ott George W, saloon and restaurant, w Washington, h. same
ott John, h. Clinton
ott Lee R, bartender, h. w Washington
ott Mamie G, h. w Washington
ott Norve E, bartender, bds w Washington
ott Silas B, barber shop, n Harrison, h. Clinton
rnathey Mary, domestic, Madison
ms John, carp, bds s West
a Fire Ins. Co, of Hartford Conn, H J Leonard, agt, s s Washington, 3d e Canal
right Charles, glass wkr, bds McLeod's add
right Earl W, teacher, h. n e cor Canal and Berry
right Rev P J, pastor M E Church, h. n e cor Canal & Berry
rich Charles, hod carrier, h. n Canal
ridge Frank, ship clk, h. n Canal
ridge Marion, lab, h. n Canal
xander Dennis, lab, bds w Washington
xandria Bank, U C Vermillion & Co, proprs, Harlan & Phillips Block
xandria Brass Band, n w cor Harrison and Church
xandria Co The, A A Arthur, pres, C T Doxey v-pres, Chas Meriwether secy and treas, Land and Gas Development Co, n e cor Church and West
xandria Flour Mills, Browning & Co proprs, cor Canal and L E & W Ry
xandria Hotel, G W Garst propr, w Church

WOOLLEY Foundry and Machine Works,
General Machinery, Heavy and Light Castings, and Sheet Iron Work.
N. W. COR. 14th AND C W. AND M. R. R.

WHEN—The Largest Stock of CLOTHING, HATS, CAPS and Gents' FURNISHING GOODS in ANDERSON.

ALEXANDRIA INVESTMET CO.

Originators & Controlers

The Star Development

OF THE GREAT INDIANA GAS BELT.
ALEXANDRIA, - , INDIANA.

Alexandria Investment Co, G W Arthur pres, H W Ralph secy. and treas, managers and controlers of 3,000 lots on the four sides of Alexandria, Ind, n e cor Church and West (see adv, also side lines)

Alexandria Land & Gas Co, C T Doxey pres, E P Schlater secy, George Nichol treas, Frank K Peirce resident mgr, e s Harrison nr Church

Alexandria Laundry, Hezekiah C Thompson, n Harrison

Alexandria Loan Association, John S Shannon secy, s w cor Washington and Harrison

Alexandria Lodge No. 335 K of P, instituted Oct 28, 1891, meets every Tuesday night at K P Hall

Alexandria Marble and Granite Works, J F Brenaman, propr, e Church (see adv)

Alexandria Oar Factory, J W Neily propr, n e Harrison

Alexandria Stone Quarry, Nathan Booth propr, ¼ mile s w Big 4

Alexandria Stone Quarry, L C Nicoson propr, w e Washington opp Plate Glass Works, h. n Harrison

Alexandria Sun The, Moore & Meyer pubs, West near Church

Alexandria Times The, T N French editor and manager, established 1878, n w cor Harrison and John

Alexandria Window Glass Co The, Heer, Booth & Co proprs, Henry W Heer secy

Allan Florence, domestic, Kent House.

Allen Lynly, well driller, h. Clinton

Allen R W (McLead & Allen), h. n s 1st bet Pugh and Ross

Allen Wilson, h. Fairview and Adams

Allen Wright, clk, rms e Pickard

American Fire Ins Co, of Philadelphia, Clinton & Hughes agts, rms 7 and 8 cor Church and Harrison

Roop & Haynes Are Agents for FIVE of the BEST BUILDING & LOAN COMPANIES in Indiana.
210½ S. Anderson, - - - - ELWOOD, IND

Robinson & Glassco, Room 9 "When" Building, ANDERSON, IND.

xandria Marble & Granite Works
J. E. BRENAMAN, Propr.
XANDRIA, - - - INDIANA.

rson Axle, glass wkr, bds s West
ll Amelia N, h. n e cor 6th and Shelby
ll Grace E, h. n e cor 6th and Shelby
ll Jennie, h. w Church
ll John, glass blower, h. w Church
ll Mrs Mary, boarding, n e cor 6th and Shelby, h. same
egate Edward, clk, M Kelly & Co, h. e Berry
trong Raymond, glass wkr, bds s Wayne
trong Thornton W (Swindell & Armstrong), bds s e cor John and West
tt Milton W, watchman, h. Canal
ld James, carp, bds Clinton
d John G, lather, bds w Madison
ld Mollie, domestic, George House
ir **Alexander A**, pres The Alexandria Co, h. Harrogate, Tenn
ir **G W**, pres Alexandria Investment Co, rms n e cor Church and West
ir Harry, glass wkr, bds w Monroe
ir John, glass blower, h. cor Adams and Fairview ave
ison George, glass wkr, bds w Washington
ison John, glass blower, bds w Washington
ison Thomas, glass wkr, bds w Washington
Life Ins Co, The, of Indianapolis, s e cor Harrison and Church

B

nan Jacob, brickmason, bds s Wayne
Henry, h. Curve
Rosetta, h. n Harrison
Wesley K, ins agt, n w cor Harrison and Church
B, Alexandria Bank, h. Indianapolis
Charles, gas fitter, bds George House
John, glass wkr, bds Riverview
Julia, h. Madison

erman F. Willkie, J. P.
COLLECTIONS PROMPTLY MADE.

P. CONDO & SON, The oldest FURNITURE dealers and UNDERTAKERS in the County. ESTABLISHED 1856. ALEXANDRIA, IND.

WHEN—Children's Department
A SPECIAL FEATURE.
Always well Stocked with the LATEST NOVELTIES.

W. H. BIRELEY, —THE— Druggist and Stationer,
A Full Line of CHOICE CONFECTIONERY, FOREIGN AND DOMESTIC CIGARS.

W. Washington near Harrison St., - ALEXANDRIA, IND.

Baker Lafayette, eng, bds George House
Baker Lee J, barber, rms e Pickard
Baker Wm T (Harrison & Baker), rms s w cor Harrison and Washington
Ball John W, lab, h. Van Buren
Ball Ora E, clk, bds n e cor Berry and West
Barker George, carp, bds 3d
Bardeau Louis, flatner, bds s w cor Black and Berry
Barido Emil, glass wkr, h. n Canal
Barnett R, lab, rms e Washington
Barrett A A, clk M Kelly & Co, h. s Harrison
Barth James, glass blower, h. w Church
Barth Lewis, glass blower, h. w Church
Batholomew John, shoemkr, bds cor Berry and John
Barton Minnie B, h. s Wayne
Bauhee John, glass wkr, bds w Pickard
Baumberger, h. cor Canal and John
Baylor Benj, yd clk L E & W, bds s West
Beach Wm, glass wkr, bds w Madison
Beck John, glass wkr, bds Riverview
Becknell Mrs Alice, h. w Washington
Becknell Francis M, lab, h. 5th
Becknell Josie, domestic, Clinton
Beeson Jesse E (Miller Bros Co), also atty-at-law and princ high school, h. s e cor Pickard & Lincoln ave
Beidler Conrad R, miller, h. s Black
Bell Mertie, h. n Harrison
Belt Edward, carp, h. w John
Benedict J, saloon, agt Terre Haute Brewing Co, h. w Washington
Benefiel Austin, carp, h. w John
Bennett James, carp, h. e Washington
Bensinger Christopher, glass wkr, bds s West
Bentine Fred, barber, wks n Harrison, bds Commercial Hotel
Bentine James, barber, bds Commercial Hotel
Bernard Minnie, dining room, St Elmo Hotel
Bernard Mrs Matilda, cook, St Elmo Hotel
Bertsche Anthony, harness & saddlery, n Harrison, h. cor Church and Wayne

John L. Lindskoog,
Fine Tailoring in Suits and Pants. An examination solicited. A FIT GUARANTEED.
H. H. H. Block, N. E. Cor. Church and Harrison, ALEXANDRIA, IND.

WHEN—Children's Department
A SPECIAL FEATURE.
Always well Stocked with the LATEST NOVELTIES.

W. H. BIRELEY, —THE— *Druggist and Stationer,*
A Full Line of CHOICE CONFECTIONERY, FOREIGN AND DOMESTIC CIGARS.
W. Washington near Harrison St., - ALEXANDRIA, IND.

Baker Lafayette, eng, bds George House
Baker Lee J, barber, rms e Pickard
Baker Wm T (Harrison & Baker), rms s w cor Harrison and Washington
Ball John W, lab, h. Van Buren
Ball Ora E, clk, bds n e cor Berry and West
Barker George, carp, bds 3d
Bardeau Louis, flatner, bds s w cor Black and Berry
Barido Emil, glass wkr, h. n Canal
Barnett R, lab, rms e Washington
Barrett A A, clk M Kelly & Co, h. s Harrison
Barth James, glass blower, h. w Church
Barth Lewis, glass blower, h. w Church
Batholomew John, shoemkr, bds cor Berry and John
Barton Minnie B, h. s Wayne
Bauhee John, glass wkr, bds w Pickard
Baumberger, h. cor Canal and John
Baylor Benj, yd clk L E & W, bds s West
Beach Wm, glass wkr, bds w Madison
Beck John, glass wkr, bds Riverview
Becknell Mrs Alice, h. w Washington
Becknell Francis M, lab, h. 5th
Becknell Josie, domestic, Clinton
Beeson Jesse E (Miller Bros Co), also atty-at-law and princ high school, h. s e cor Pickard & Lincoln ave
Beidler Conrad R, miller, h. s Black
Bell Mertie, h. n Harrison
Belt Edward, carp, h. w John
Benedict J, saloon, agt Terre Haute Brewing Co, h. w Washington
Benefiel Austin, carp, h. w John
Bennett James, carp, h. e Washington
Bensinger Christopher, glass wkr, bds s West
Bentine Fred, barber, wks n Harrison, bds Commercial Hotel
Bentine James, barber, bds Commercial Hotel
Bernard Minnie, dining room, St Elmo Hotel
Bernard Mrs Matilda, cook, St Elmo Hotel
Bertsche Anthony, harness & saddlery, n Harrison, h. cor Church and Wayne

John L. Lindskoog, Fine Tailoring in Suits and Pants. An examination solicited. A FIT GUARANTEED.
H. H. H. Block, N. E. Cor. Church and Harrison, ALEXANDRIA, IND.

WM. J. DOVE — Is Agent for National Home Building and Loan Ass'n of Bloomington, Ill. You can get all the money you want on short notice
NEELEY BLOCK.   61½ N. Meridian, ANDERSON, IND.

ALEXANDRIA CITY DIRECTORY.   93

rtsche Daisy, h. cor Church and Wayne
rtsche Ralph H, clk, h. cor Church and Wayne
nkley Howard C (Manlove & Binkley), h. s Black
nley Mark, hod carrier, bds n e cor Canal and Church
nson Elizabeth, wid, h. McLeod's add
dson Wm, lab, h. McLeod's add
:eley J Fred, drug clk, Washington, h. Berry
:eley Wm H, druggist and news dealer, Washington, b. Berry (see adv)
sell George, brickmason, bds s Black
ick Dora, domestic, e Church
ick James, bartender, h. w Church
ick Louisa, teacher, bds n Canal
ick Milton, glass wkr, h. w Washington
ick Wm W, h. s West
ickstone Georgia, wid, h. n Harrison
iir David, physician, h. Riverview
iir Orr, glass wkr, h. Riverview
iir Otis, clk, h. Riverview
om Fred J, clk, rms s Canal
ie Barnett, painter, h. Madison
ie John, carp, bds Madison
iton-Ferd, packer, h. West add
mberger Phillip M, clk, h. cor Canal and John
mberger Mrs P M, milliner, s Canal, h. cor Canal and John
okter Flora, domestic, s Harrison
oth Nathan (Heer, Booth & Co), rms s e cor Washington and Canal
rright Mrs Ella, h. Madison
:kins Jacob, butcher, bds Madison
werman Lundy L, carp and contractor, h. e Pickard
wers John, lab, bds w Washington
wman Eli, carp, bds Madison
wman Frank, carp, bds s Harrison
/er Wm, glass wkr, bds w Munroe
/les J W, stonemason, bds w John
.ndon S J, propr Commercial Hotel, n s Church, e of Harrison
.atz Fritz, stonemason, bds s e cor John and West
dley James, glass wkr, bds w Washington
mbel David, lab, h. Van Buren
nnon James F, glass wkr, h. w Munroe
nnum Joseph G (The Brannum Lumber Co), bds Kent House

derson Foundry and Machine Works, REPAIRS and Job Work of all Kinds A SPECIALTY.
'PHONE 58.
3 N. Jackson Street, - - - ANDERSON, IND.

TELEPHONE LARMORE BROS: for your ICE CREAM, MILK AND OYSTERS, and he sure of prompt delivery and first-class goods. 513 Nichol Ave., ANDERSON, IND. TELEPHONE 220.

INSURE WITH JACKSON & BURR. 69½ N. Meridian, - - ANDERSON, IND. Latch string always out and light in the window, until the last man's INSURED.

94 ALEXANDRIA CITY DIRECTORY.

BRUNSWICK BAR,

H. P. WILLIAMS, Propr. Choicest Wines, Beer, Liquors and Cigars in the city. Milwaukee Beer on Tap. Brunswick-Balke Billiard and Pool Tables. N. Harrison St., ALEXANDRIA, IND.

Brannum Lumber Co The (P Kuntz, F L Mercer, W S and J G Brannum), lumber, lath & shingles, s w cor Curve & Berry (see adv)
Brannum Wm S (The Brannum Lumber Co), h. Hartford City, Ind
Branson C, stenographer, h. n Canal
Branson Ethel, h. n Canal
Branson Hettie, wid, h. n Canal
Brasher Florence C, h. s Black
Brasher Mary, wid, h. s Black
Brattain Augustus E (Brattain Bros), h. Scott's add
Brattain Bros (A E and J C F Brattain), plumbers, gas and steam fitters, e s Wayne bet Church and Washington
Brattain John C F (Brattain Bros), h. s Black
Brattain Wm M, plumber, Brattain Bros, h. Scott's add
Bratton John C F (Bratton & Davis)
Bratton & Davis (J C F Bratton and E Davis), saloon, s w cor Harrison and Church
Brecker Joseph, lab, bds w Washington
Brenaman J F, propr, Alexandria Marble and Granite Works, e Church, h. s Black
Brink Adelbert C (Walker & Co.), also notary Public, bds s West
Brodrich Wm, glass wkr, rms w Madison
Bronder Jacob, glass wkr, bds w Pickard
Bronder Wm, glass wkr, bds w Pickard
Brooks Edwin D, gas well driller, h. s Harrision
Broombaugh Sol, carp, h. w John
Brown Arthur C, contractor and painter w John, h. same
Brown Charles, lab, h. Madison
Brown Ella M, clk, bds n e cor Berry and West
Brown George, glass wkr, bds Riverview
Brown George, well driller, h. s Harrison
Brown George W, drayman, h. C W & M Ry
Brown James, glass blower, bds George House
Brown Jessie, lab, h. junc L E & W and Big 4
Brown Mary E, h. n Harrison
Brown Peter, glass packer, h. n Harrison
Brown Lurnee, stone mason, h. n Harrison
Brown Wm T, glass packer, h. n Harrison
Browning Anthony S, mgr Browning & Co, h. Berry

George B. Epperson, Carriage Paints and Varnishes A Specialty.
39 E. 9th St., • • • • ANDERSON, IND.

THE BRANNUM LUMBER CO.
Lumber, Lath, Shingles, Flooring,
Siding, Sash, Doors and Blinds,

And the East Lake Finish of Southern Long Leaf Yellow Pine,

S. W. Cor. Berry and Curve Sts., - ALEXANDRIA, IND.

Browning Clara (Browning & Co), h. Berry
Browning & Co (M A and C Browning), proprs Alexandria Flour Mills, cor Canal and L E & W
Browning Mary A (Browning & Co), h. Berry
Browning Wm E, miller, Browning & Co, h. Berry
Browman Charles, glass wkr, h. w John
Brumbaugh Aretta, dressmkr, h. s e cor Berry and Curve
Brumbaugh Daniel, carp, h. s e cor Berry and Curve
Brumbaugh L R Frank, teamster, h. s e cor Berry and Curve
Brunswick Bar The, H P Williams propr, saloon, billiards and pool, n Harrison (see adv)
Brush George A, agt U S Ex Co and W U Tel Co, rms s e cor Washington and Canal
Bryant Bradford, stone cutter, h. s Black
Bucher Nicholas, glass wkr, bds w Pickard
Burk Joseph, street cont, rms s e cor Pickard and Canal
Burkhardt Effie J, bookpr, M Kelly & Co, h. cor Pickard & Canal
Burkhart Oneida L, h. s e cor Canal and Pickard
Burkhart Washington, farmer, h. s e cor Canal and Pickard
Burnett John, carp, bds Madison
Burt John, glass wkr, h. w Church
Butler John, brick mason, bds n Canal

C

Cahall Dainty M, h. e John
Cahall W H, paiter cont, h. e John
Cain George, glass wkr, bds w John
Call Mary, wid, h. Berry
Callaban John, bartender, bds n Harrison
Callaway Beniah T, prest Commercial Bank, h. Elwood, Ind
Callaway Henry C, v-prest Commercial Bank, h. Elwood, Ind

Novelty Works, 198 AND 200 N. MILTON ST. ANDERSON, IND.
HUGH FISHER, Propr., manufacturer and dealer in Step Ladders, Garden Wheelbarrows, Screen Doors and Windows, Picture Frames, etc.

PALACE PHARMACY, Anderson, Ind. FOR FINE GOODS OF ALL KINDS IN THEIR LINE.

J. T. Knowland & Son, WHOLESALE PLUMBERS *and Gas Fitters' Supplies*
111 N. Main St., ANDERSON, IND. 'Phone 30.

ALEXANDRIA CITY DIRECTORY.

M. E. CLAYTON,
—DEALER IN—
Staple & Fancy Groceries
Queensware and Glassware a Specialty.

ALEXANDRIA. - - - - - **INDIANA.**

Callaway John, glass wkr, h. w Washington
Campbell John, stone mason, h. Clinton
Campfield A G, treas The Phillips Land & Gas Co, h. Richmond, Ind
Canfield Albert H, carp, bds Canal
Canfield E B, oysters and confectionery, w Church, h. s Canal
Canfield Morton, hod carrier, n Canal
Cannon Emma, domestic, St. Elmo Hotel
Cannon Sadie, domestic, St. Elmo Hotel
Carey Charles, carp, h. Madison
Carey Henry, gatherer, bds s w cor Black and Berry
Carter Cora, domestic, s w cor West and Water
Carter Fannie, comp the Times, h. s Pickard
Carter John, lab, h. w Canal
Carter Leva, cook, bds n Harrison
Cartwright C C (Cartwright & Headington Co), h Portland, Ind
Cartwright Charles, bus line, office cor Harrison and Washington, h. e Church
Cartwright Fred, tobacco and cigars, n Harrison, h. s Black
Cartwright & Headington Co The, C F Headington pres, J S Davis v-pres, W E C Spade secy and treas, C C Cartwright, dry goods, clothing, etc, Harrison
Cartwright Retta, wid, h. s Black
Cartwright Washington, teamster, h. e Church
Carr Jack, glass blower, rms e Church
Carver A C, county prosecutor, h. w Washington
Carver David K, real estate and notary pub, h. w Church
Carver Levi, well driver, h. w Church
Carver Wm, h. w Washington
Carver Wm J, h. w Washington
Casey Thomas, glass wkr, bds n Canal
Cash ———, stonemason, h. Clinton
Cassell Samuel, h. cor Wayne and Washington
Cassel Sherman, glass wkr, h. s Wayne
Catey Stace C, teamster, h. e Washington

JOHN O. MILLER, ELEVEN YEARS' EXPERIENCE in Watchmaking. Finisher six years in Elgin & Springfield Watch Factories.
I GUARANTEE MY WORK. 3 N. Meridian, ANDERSON, IND.

)R FINE FURNITURE do not fail to call on **MUNCHHOF** the Leading **FURNITURE DEALER.**
40 and 42 East Eighth St., - - ANDERSON, IND.

CLINTON & HUGHES,

il Estate, Loan & Insurance Agents.
Real Estate bought and sold on Commission.
PROMPT LOANS GUARANTEED, IF TITLE IS GOOD.

ot Payment of Losses. Largest Agency. Largest Business. Largest ined Assets of Companies. Strangers are cordially invited to make fice headquarters while in the city. Stationery furnished free.

s 7 & 8, New Opera House Block, - - ALEXANDRIA, IND.

y Florence, boarding, e Washington
, Wm, lab, h. e Washington
in Clayton, farmer, h. n Canal
in Frank, farmer, h. n Canal
in Levi, clk, h. n Canal
ness Edward B (Chamness & Rizer), h. cor Church & West
ness & Rizer (Edward B Chamness, L A Rizer), attys-at-law and notaries, room 5, Harlan & Phillips' Block, n e cor Harrison and Washington
lin Polly, wid, h. n Harrison
man S C, carp, h. e Pickard
ers Mrs Belle, h. John
ers John, carp, h. n West
tian Church, Rev Moore pastor, s e cor Berry and West
ty Patrick, glass wkr, bds w Pickard
hill C W, tinware, roofing, etc, w Washington, h. cor West and Church
hill Mrs Laura, housekpr, n Harrison
hill M, stenograpr, Clinton & Hughes, h. cor Church & West
& St L R R Pass & Fgt Statn, F W Torrance, agt, w e Church
James C, glass blower, h. n w cor Canal and Washington
F, carp cont and yd master C C C & St L R R, h. w John
Georgiana, h. w John
on Frank B, grocer, h. n s John
on **M E**, groceries, queensware and glassware, e s Harrison, ; P O, h. n s John, 2 w Canal (see adv)
Francis, glass wkr, h. w Church
Mamie, h. w Church
nger Zacharia, glass wks, h. s Wayne
John, carp, bds s Black
n **Eugene O** (Clinton & Hughes), h. n e cor Canal and John
n **& Hughes** (E O Clinton & W I Hughes), real estate, loan and insurance agents, rms 7 and 8 cor Church and Harrison (see adv)

OOLLEY Foundry and Machine Works.
Manufacturers of Clay Working Machinery, Boiler Makers, and General Machinists.
N. W. COR. 14th AND C. W. AND M. R. R.

WHEN—CLOTHING,

—Manufacturers of—
—And Jobbers in—

HATS AND MEN'S FURNISHINGS.

Cling Henry, lather, bds s w cor Berry and Curve
Clinton & Hughes (E O Clinton and W I Hughes), real estate, loan and ins agts, s w cor Washington and Harrison
Cloud James, lab, h. Prosperity Heights
Coffal Susanna, wid, h. w Washington
Coffin Arthur A, student, h. Jefferson
Coffin India E, clk, h. Jefferson
Coffin Oliver F, physician and surgeon, Jefferson, h. same
Coffman Glenn, glass wkr, h. West
Coffman John H, bartender, bds s Black
Coffman J F, carp, h West
Cole Benj F, carp, h. s Black
Cole Laura E, h. n e cor Black and Water
Cole Myran E, h. n e cor Black and Water
Cole Perry P, h. n e cor Black and Water
Commercial Bank, B T Calloway pres, H C Callaway v-pres, S Free cashier, s e cor Washington and Canal
Commercial Hotel, S J Brandon propr, n s Church, e of Harrison
Condo Anna E, clk, Com Bank, h. s w cor Harrison and Berry
Condo John P (J P Condo & Son), h. s w cor Harrison and Berry
Condo Joseph C (J P Condo & Son), h. s w cor Harrison & Berry
Condo J P & Son (J P & J C Condo), furniture, undertakers and arterial embalmers, s s Washington, 2d w Harrison (see right side lines)
Condo Wm W, del clk, h. s Harrison
Connaty Bridget, wid, h. n Harrison
Conner Ada, dressmkr, s w cor Washington & Harrison, h. John
Conner Charles A, carp, h. n Harrison
Conner Wm H, teamster, h. Monroe
Conners John, glass wkr, h. West add
Connor Frank M, oar finisher, h. Lincoln ave
Connor James, plasterer, h. e Washington
Connor James L, supt and genl mgr of Lumber, Oar & Handle Factory, h. n Harrison
Connor Samuel F, oar finisher, bds Lincoln ave
Conroy Harry S, glass blower, h. cor John and West
Conroy James, glass wkr, bds w Madison
Continental Fire Ins Co, of New York, s e cor Harrison & Church
Coplin George, glass wkr, bds w Washington
Coplin John, glass wkr, bds w Washington
Corcoran Thomas, glass wkr, h. Riverview
Corter Rev Wm, pastor Christian Church, h. s Clinton
Covey Charles, teamster, bds Pickard
Covy Morgan (Gooding, Son & Co), h. s Harrison
Cowgill Edwin, canvassing agt, h. w John

Place Your Real Estate **and FARM PROPERTY in the Hands of ROOP & HAYNES,**
AND BE SURE OF QUICK RETURNS.
210½ S. Anderson, - - - - ELWOOD, IND.

MONEY TO BUILD WITH PROCURED WITHIN 15 DAYS. Robinson & Glassco, Loan, Real Estate & Insurance agents
Room 9 "When" Building, - - ANDERSON, IND.

owlie Levi, glass wkr, bds w Pickard
ox Amos J, blacksmith, bds Van Buren
ox Robt V, stone mason, h. w Washington
raig John C, lab, h. Clinton
rail Robert, teamster, bds Curve
ramer Joseph, glass wkr, h. w Pickard
rashee Lenious, teamster, bds Clinton
rawford A B, grocer, h. Church
ree Calvin (Cree & Perry Bros), h. cor Church and Wayne
ree & Perry Bros (C Cree and S S and W R Perry), livery, feed and sale stable, n Canal
restler Orin, plasterer, bds n Harrison
rist Alonzo A, farmer, h. Madison
rist Leander M, farmer, h. Madison
rosby Richard, glass wkr, bds Riverview
ross Mrs Anna, h. s Clinton
rouse John R, glass wkr, h. s Wayne
immins Edward F, clk, n w cor Harrison & Washington, bds same
immings Mrs Anna, h. w Church
immings Charles, h. w Church
immings Eliza, wid, h. w Church
immings Lucien, carp, h. w Church
immings Wm, bartender, n Harrison, h. Church
implin Benj, glass wkr, bds w Pickard
imingham Edward, glass wkr, h. s Harrison
inningham Harry, carp, bds McLeod's add
unningham James, glass wkr, bds w Pickard
unningham John, carp, bds McLeod's add
unningham Luther, lab, bds Curve
inningham Maude, h. s Harrison
irts James, teamster, h. e Washington
itter Ammi R, lumber, rms n w cor Black and Berry
itting Samuel, carp, bds n Canal

D

ile Robert, gatherer, bds s Black
inforth Oda, lab, bds George House
arby Thos, prof of music, also boot and shoe mkr, e Washington, h. s Harrison
arter Sam'l R, teamster, h. s w cor Berry and Curve
augherty Wm H, sewing machines, w Washington, h. Lincoln
avenport Mrs Joanna, trimmer, h. n w cor Harrison and Monroe
avenport Chas W, oar finisher, h. n w cor Harrison and Monroe
avenport Maud E, clk, bds n w cor Harrison and Monroe
avis E E (Storkey & Davis), bds n e cor Canal and Church

eal & Willkie, **ATTORNEYS AT LAW.** We will attend to your legal business promptly, and charge you no exhorbitant fees.
MECHANICS LIENS A SPECIALTY. CALL AND SEE US.

J. P. CONDO & SON, WILL SELL YOU FURNITURE ON EASY WEEKLY PAYMENTS. ESTABLISHED 1856. ALEXANDRIA, IND.

WHEN—Originators of the **One Price System**
IN SELLING CLOTHING.
FAIR AND SQUARE DEALINGS WITH ALL.

Davis Eugene (Bratton & Davis), h. Anderson, Ind
Davis F Jennie, h. Madison
Davis James S, The Cartwright & Headington Co, h. s w cor Berry and West
Davis Reece T, carp, bds Lincoln ave
Deadman Erastus, teamster, h. Clinton
DeLong Benj, carp, h. Clinton
Demmel Fredrick, glass wkr, h. w Pickard
DeMoss Louis, carp, bds Madison
DePauw C W (The W C DePauw Co), h. New Albany, Ind
DePauw N T, pres DePauw Plate Glass Co, h. New Albany, Ind
DePauw Plate Glass Co (N T DePauw pres, C T Doxey v-pres, W D Keyes secy and treas, L L Pierce supt, w end Washington
DePauw W C Window Glass Co The, N T DePauw pres, C W DePauw v-pres, George F Penn secy, one mile e on L E & W Ry
DeTour Jacques, supt, bds e John
Detro Wesley cont plasterer, bds s e cor John and West
DeVoll John, tailor, wks Harrison, bds Commercial Hotel
DeWitt & DeWitt (T H & J W), feather renovators, s Harrison
Dickey Edgar L (Pugh & Dickey), h. n w cor Black and Water
Diederichs Reinhold O, glass wkr, bds w Washington
Dillon John, finisher, h. West add
Dixon Anna M, h. w Washington
Doan Lester, lab, h. Clinton
Doan Mrs L, wid, h. Clinton
Doan Sylvester, lab, h. Clinton
Doans Frank, bookpr, h. s Harrison
Dobson Henry, lab, h. cor Wayne and Berry
Doerr Peter C, brick mason, h. 6th
Donahoo Laura, h. 4th
Donnell Mrs Fannie L, milliner, s Canal, rms w Washington
Dorsey Samuel O (S O Dorsey & Co), rms s e cor John & Canal
Dorsey S O & Co (S O Dorsey and J B Wood), dry goods, boots, shoes, &c, Church
Dowler Hiram, teamster, h. w Washington
Downey M H, civil eng, rm 4, n e cor Harrison and Washington, h. e Madison
Downs Claude, lab, h. Berry
Downs James M, mgr, s w cor Harrison and Church, rms same

John L. Lindskoog, Leads in the Merchant Tailoring Line English and French Worsteds, imported, always in stock.
Do not buy until you have seen them.
I. H. H. Block, N. E. Cor. Church and Harrison, - - ALEXANDRIA, IND.

n Nelson, hod carrier, bds n Harrison
Charles T, v-pres The Alexandria Company, h. Anderson, Ind
Henry, glass wkr, bds s West
Fred D (Hallisy & Drake), rms n e cor Canal and Berry
avid, eng, h. w Madison
ı John H, carp, b. McLeod's add
ı Samuel, shoemkr, w Pickard, h. same
n Fred, glass wkr, bds s w cor Berry and Curve
ı.Fred, blksmith, Gipe & Mullen, h. e Washington
ohn F, cigars and news stand, s Canal, bds s West
Thomas A, glass wkr, bds s West

E

Mary, rms n Harrison
l, tinner, bds St Elmo Hotel
Mack D, carp, bds 4th
Wm E, carp, h. 3d
James, lab, bds Van Buren
s Evan E, teacher, h. n Canal
ın Frank, glass wkr, bds w Madison
Wm, builder and cont, s Harrison, h. same
rood Clayton, lab, h. Prosperity Heights
bds w Washington
ınie, dressmkr, h. Clinton
ı Fred, photographer, n Harrison, rms Church
ı Helen, h. e Church
Alonzo, teamster, h. n Jackson
John, teamster, h. n Jackson
Frank, glass wkr, bds s Clinton
ı Charles, lab, bds. w Washington
ı Mary A, domestic, s Black
le Loan and Investment Association of Bloomington, Ills., s e cor Washington and West

F

ırry Mrs R A, domestic, Kent House
rank O, bartender, h. w Washington
John, teamster, h. e Washington
Mary, widow, h. e Washington

Jackson & Burr Do the Largest INSURANCE Business. Insure in the good old Companies they represent.
69½ N. Meridian, - - ANDERSON, IND.

102   ALEXANDRIA CITY DIRECTORY.

Fauver & Mathews (U G Fauver & A L Mathews), grocers and bakers, meat market, w Washington (see adv.)
Fauver Ulysess G (Fauver and Mathews), h. w Church
Fenimore Joseph, saloon, e s Harrison, h. country
Fenimore Sallie, h. Wayne
Fenimore Waldo, city marshal, h..Wayne
Fergus Ambrose, carp, h. n Canal
Fiedlei Edward, glass wkr, h. w Pickard
Fields Frank, carp, bds n Harrison
Fields Ida L, bookpr, h. n Harrison
Fields Nina, domestic, e Washington
Fieser Sebastian, glass wkr, h. Fairview ave
Finch Athol, h. n Harrison
Finch Edith, h. Lincoln
Finch Jubal A, h. Lincoln
Finch Paul, barber, h. n Canal
Finch O M, barber, n Harrison, bds same
Finch Wm O, blacksmith, n Harrison, h. n Canal
Finey Samantha, dressmkr, h. Commercial House
Fink Elias, h. n Canal
Fink John A, carp, h. w Washington
Fink Roberta M, h. w Washington
Finton Marion, stone mason h. Berry
Fireman's Fund Ins Co of California, Clinton & Hughes agts, rms 7 and 8, cor Church and Harrison
Firestone Freeman, carp, h. Riverview
Firestone Lewis, packer, h. West add
Fitzgerald Michael, glass wkr, h. w Pickard.
Fitzgerald Wm, glass wkr, bds w Pickard
Flaningan Patrick, lab, bds s Black
Flecker Charles, glass blower, h. West add
Foland James, lab, h. w Canal
Foley John, teamster, h. s e cor Black and Washington
Ford Charles, stone mason, bds w John
Foster J P, teamster, h. West add
Fox Catharine, wid, h. West add
Fox Cyrus, glass wkr, h. Clinton
Fox George, lab, h. 3d
Fox John, farmer, h. w Pickard
Fox Markus, teamster, h. 3d
Fox Mary, wid, h. 3d
Fox Mollie, domestic, w Washington
Fox Robert, bds George House
Franks Simon, carp, h. s Clinton
Frazie Wm, stone mason, h. n Canal

George B. Epperson, Contractor and Builder of Felt and Gravel R O O F I N G.
39 E. 9th St.,   •   •   ANDERSON, IND.

John Donnelly, The Real Estate Dealer of Anderson. If you wish to buy, sell or rent, call at 10 E. 10 St., ANDERSON, IND.

ALEXANDRIA CITY DIRECTORY. 103

U. S. FAUVER.   A. L. MATHEWS.

FAUVER & MATHEWS,
✻ Grocers and Bakers. ✻

Dealers in STAPLE AND FANCY GROCERIES, FRESH & SALT MEATS, CANNED GOODS, Etc.

—STORES:—

W. Washington & west end Broadway Sts.,   -   ALEXANDRIA, IND.

Free Cyrus, glass wkr, rms w Church
Free Olie, music teacher, w Church, h. same
Free Randolph, h. w Church
Free Sylvanus, cashier Commercial Bank, also Hier, Booth & Co, rms s e cor Washington and Canal
Freestone Aaron M, eng, h. McLeod's add
Freestone Elmira C, h. McLeod's add
Freestone Wm J, stone cutter, h. McLeod's add
French Arthur G (Times Publishing Co), h. n Harrison
French Thomas N (Times Publishing Co), h. n Harrison
French Walter E (Times Publishing Co), h. Anderson, Ind
Freyberger Harry, glass wkr, bds w Pickard
Friddle Wm, glass wkr, bds s West
Fritz Nancy, wid, h. s West
Fry Ernest, watchman, bds w Washington
Frymuth Frank, brick wkr, h. 6th
Fulton Adam, lab, h. n Harrison
Fulton Bros (Joseph, jr, and Wm A Fulton), hardware, etc, w Washington
Fulton Joseph, jr, (Fulton Bros,) h. n Canal
Fulton Wm A (Fulton Bros), h. Anderson, Ind
Funk Joseph, brickmason, bds s Black
Funk Noah, brickmason, bds s Black
Furrow, M H, lab, bds Commercial Hotel

G

Gale Oscar R, glass wkr, h Riverview
Gale Richard R, h. Riverview
Gall Wm T, glass wkr, bds w Washington
Gamble J S, teacher, n w cor Washington & West, h. Lincoln ave
Gardner Thomas, finisher, bds George House

HUGH FISHER, Manufacturer **Screen Doors and Windows** all sizes. Furniture repairing a specialty.
198 and 200 N. Milton St., ANDERSON, IND.

BUCK, BRICKLEY & CO., THE LEADING DRUGGISTS, Cor. Ninth and Meridian Streets, ANDERSON, IND.

J. T. Knowland & Son, SANITARY PLUMBERS. Gas and Steam Fitters.
111 N. Main St., ANDERSON, IND. 'Phone 30.

Garr Wm, glass wkr, bds n Canal
Garrett Callie, domestic, n e cor Church and Canal
Garrison Wm C, glass wkr, h. Riverview
Garst George W, propr Alexandria Hotel, h. same
Gause Milo B, carp, h. Madison
Gehring Jacob, glass wkr, h. n Curve
Gehring Joseph, glass blower, h. s Black
Gehring Louisa, h. s Black
Geiger Addison, oar finisher, h. Madison
George A W, carp, h. George House
George House, Mrs M A George propr, cor Fairview ave & Adams
George M E, propr George House, cor Fairview ave and Adams
German American Ins Co, of New York, Clinton & Hughes agts, rms 7 and 8, cor Church and Harrison
Germania Fire Ins Co, of New York, s e cor Harrison & Church
Gerrard Wm, glass wkr, bds w Washington
Gerrard Wm R, clk, s Harrison, bds cor Berry and John
Gettel Thomas, clk, Harrison, h. Lincoln
Gilbride James, glass wkr, bds w Pickard
Gillett George F, livery, h. Washington
Gipe Charles H (Gipe & Mullen), h. s Harrison
Gipe George, carp, h. Van Buren
Gipe Jacob, carp and builder, h. s w cor Harrison and Pickard
Gipe & Mullen (Charles H Gipe, Thomas W Mullen), blacksmiths, carriage dealers, Washington near Harrison
Gipe Ulysess S, carp, h. s w cor Harrison & Pickard
Goggins James, glass wkr, h. w Madison
Goggins Thomas, glass wkr, h. w Madison
Golder Elias, carp, h. n e cor Pickard and Canal
Gooding John E (Gooding, Son & Co), h. Madison
Gooding, Son & Co (J E and W M Gooding and Morgan Covy), meat market, West near Church
Gooding Wm M (Gooding, Son & Co), h. Madisonville
Goodwin Alexander, carp, bds s West
Gordon Albert, grain elevator and commission, C C C & I track cor John, h. Church
Gordon Frank, grain dealer, h. n w cor Church and Canal
Gordon Lewis, barber, h. w Washington
Gosling Joseph, glass wkr, bds 4th
Gosling Thomas, glass wkr, h. 4th
Gott J R, h. George House
Goulden Elisha, glass wkr, bds w Black
Graham Frank, plasterer, bds McLeod's add
Graham John A, saloon, n Harrison, h. s w cor Washington and West (see adv)

John O. Miller, Practical Watchmaker & Jeweler. Eleven Years' Experience in the Manufacturing of Watches.
3 N. Meridian, - - - ANDERSON, IND.

OHN A. GRAHAM,
✳ ✳ SALOON. ✳ ✳
Wine, Beer, Liquors and Cigars. The Coolest Beer and Best Liquors in the City.

Harrison St., - ALEXANDRIA, IND.

ham Richard M, lab, h. s Black
nt George, drayman, h. Berry
y Harvey, glass wkr, bds s w cor Black and Berry
y Henry, pot mkr, bds s w cor Black and Berry
y Ida, domestic, s Canal
y Leander, glass wkr, h. Clinton
en Frank, well digger, h. Prosperity Heights
en Joseph, glass wkr, bds w Washington
er Charles, lab, bds Van Buren
er Clinton, lab, bds Van Buren
er G W, lab, h. w Washington
gory Wm, watchman, bds s s Clinton
iner Charles, glass wkr, h. Clinton
iner Elizabeth, h. s Clinton
iner Pembroke, glass wkr, h s Clinton
ler John L, grocer, Harrison, bds e Pickard
fin John, glass wkr, h. w Church
fith Ira, cook, n Harrison
fith Omar, stonemason, h. Berry
fy Wm, carp, h. West
nes Charles C, tinner, h. s e cor Canal and John
nes James W, clk Harrison, h. Berry
nes Samuel C, tinner, h. s e cor Canal & John
idell Effa C, student, h. Canal
idell James A, carp and builder, Canal, h. same
zle Albert, stone mason, h. s Clinton
om Clemmont L, carp, h. s w cor Harrison and Pickard
wler Henry, glass wkr, bds s West
rd Benj F, lab, h. s West
rd Charles, painter, h. Clinton
rd Charles E, clk, h. s West
rin Thornton L, dry goods, clothing, etc, s w cor Harrison and Washington, h. n e cor West and Berry

H

John, lab, bds George House
ord Sallie, domestic, w Washington
Alden S, clk, h. n Harrison
Charles M, h. Garfield

OOLLEY FOUNDRY AND MACHINE WORKS,
Engineers, Founders and Machinists
N. W. Cor. 14th and C. W. and M. R. R.

WHEN ——THE—— Anderson Clothiers & Hatters.

☛ ONE PRICE TO ALL.

⇒❦FRANK HETTMANSPERGER,❧⇐
DAILY MEAT MARKET.
Dealer in FRESH AND SALT MEATS, BOLOGNAS, &c.
Lard and Tallow. Also dealer in HIDES. North side Church east of Harrison.

Hall Mortimer, teamster, h. Madison
Hall Wm I, real estate, loan and insurance agent and notary public, rear Commercial Bank, cor Washington and West, h. w Washington
Hall Wm S, hardware and queensware, Harrison, h. same
Hallan Arthur E, bank, h. cor Lincoln ave and John
Hallisy & Drake (L S Hallisy and F D Drake), merchant tailors, Harrison
Hallisy Louis S (Hallisy & Drake), h. Curve
Hamilton Isaac, glass wkr, rms s e cor Canal and Pickard
Hammer George, carp, bds Madison
Hammond A M, carp, h. Clinton
Hanes Leander F, tile mkr, h. w Washington
Hanley Wm H, teamster, h. Pickard
Hanmore Cora H, clk, h. John
Hanmore Mrs Maria, dressmkr, w John, h. same
Hanmore Thomas, section hand, h. w John
Hannah Robert H, h. n w cor Harrison and Berry
Hardesty David L, mgr and genl agt The Phillips Land and Gas Co, bds Kent House
Hardesty George A, mgr and genl agt The Phillips Land & Gas Co, bds Kent House
Harlan A E, Alexandria Bank, h. cor Lincoln ave and John
Harlan Charles, h. cor Lincoln ave and John
Harmess Len, glass wkr, bds n Harrison
Harper Oscar, carp, bds Commercial Hotel
Harris Birdie, tailoress, h. s West
Harris Jennie, rms n Harrison
Harris Lillie, h. Lincoln ave
Harrison Albert, hod carrier, bds John
Harrison Thomas, glass wkr, h. West add
Harrison Wm, glass wkr, h. Madison
Harrington Lee, glass wkr, bds s West
Hartford Fire Ins Co, of Hartford, Conn, s e cor Harrison & Church
Hartman Amos, glass wkr, h. w Madison
Hartman John, glass wkr, bds s Wayne
Hartman Peter, glass wkr, h. w Pickard
Hartzel John, painter, h. w Pickard
Havens Frederick, glass wkr, bds s Clinton

Roop & Haynes, Real Estate,
LOANS AND INSURANCE.
210½ S. Anderson, • • • ELWOOD, IND.

✣ W. I. HALL, ✣
Real Estate, Loan & Insurance Agt., Notary Public.
Special Attention Given to Private Investments.
Office in rear Commercial Bank, S. E. Cor Washington & West Sts., ALEXANDRIA, IND.

Hawk Charles, clk, e Church, h. West
Haworth Charles, lab, bds w Church
Hayden George, lab, h. Madison
Hayden James, lab, h. e Washington
Hayden Sarah, wid, h. Madison
Hayes Harry, foreman, The L Glass Co
Hayes Ryne, glass wkr, bds Riverview
Haywood Bert, carp, bds Commercial Hotel
Hays Mrs Harry, h. cor Wayne and Washington
Hays Harry G, cont, h. cor Wayne and Washington
Hays John, glass wkr, bds-Riverview
Headington Charles F, pres The Cartwright & Headington Co, h. Portland, Ind
Heer Henry W, secy Alex Window Glass Co, h. s w cor West and Water
Heiblig Jacob, carp, h. w John
Hellum Charles, carp, bds 4th
Henshaw Frank R, clk, h. e Church
Henshaw Fred R, teacher, h. e Church
Henshaw Seth B Jr, brickmason, h. e Church
Henshaw S B, merchant, h. e Church
Heritage C F, Alexandria Bank, h. e Church
Henley L J, jeweler, n e cor Harrison and Washington, h. John
Herendeen Newton, teamster, bds w Washington
Hershey Harry, h. w Madison
Hermansperger Charles, boarding, n w cor West & Berry, h. same
Hermansperger Frank, daily meat market, e Church, h. West (see adv)
High School, J E Beeson prin, s w cor Washington and Canal
Hitt Albert, glass wkr, bds w Madison
Holle John, pipe wkr, bds George House
Hoover John, lab, h. Riverview
Hoover Mary E, h. Riverview
Hoover Samuel M, carp, h. Riverview
Hoover Wm, lab, h. Riverview
Horn Jesse, driver, h. Riverview
Horn Robert D, transfer and express line, s e cor Canal and Washington, h. Riverview
Hornick Hosea F, tinware and roofing, s Canal, h. same

Hall & Willkie,
We will write your Insurance in none but Standard Companies; All parties are treated alike, no cut-rates and no wildcat Insurance.
REAL ESTATE AND NOTARY PUBLICS.

P. CONDO & SON, FURNITURE, UNDERTAKERS and EMBALMERS, ESTABLISHED 1856. ALEXANDRIA, IND.

Hodson Charles, glass wkr, bds n Curve
Holfin Washington, lab, bds n Canal
Hollaway Leonard, lab, h. n West
Hollowell Emmet, glass wkr, h. n Canal
Holmes Anna, domestic, s West
Holmes Edward, mach, bds George House
Hoover Charles L, lumber dealer, h. n w cor Canal and Berry
Hoover G S (Hoover & Irish), h. n w cor Canal and Berry
Hoover & Irish (G S Hoover and J M Irish), saw mill, n e West
Hoover James, lab, h. Berry
Hoover Mary, wid, h. n w cor Canal and Berry
Hopkins Thaddeus, glass wkr, rms w Church
Horn ——, carp, bds s Black
Houston Charles, teamster, h. Clinton
Houston Truman, brickmason, h. Clinton
Houston Oscar, lab, h. Clinton
Howard Leander M, saloon, billiards and pool, n Harrison, h. s w Berry and Canal (see adv)
Howard Samuel, drayman, h. cor Church and Clinton
Howenstein Wm, glass wkr, h. w Washington
Hubbard John, real estate, rms West
Hughes Addie M, dressmkr, h. cor Church and Canal
Hughes John W, carp and builder, h. s w cor Black and Berry
Hughes Joseph, lab, rms n Harrison
Hughes Joseph L (Hughes & Moreland), h. Clinton
Hughes & Moreland (J L Hughes and W F Moreland), carriage dealers, s Canal
Hughes Vada L, clk, Harrison, h. cor Church and Canal
Hughes Walter I (Clinton & Hughes), h. Black
Hughes W T R, groceries, e Church, h. country
Hull W Gilder, lime, plaster, &c, room 4, n e cor Harrison and Washington, h. West
Humble Benj, glass wkr, h. w Church
Humphrey Samuel C, carp, h. w Madison
Humphrey Wm, carp, h. w Madison
Huntzleman Charles, glass wkr, bds 3d
Hupp DeWit C, justice, Harlan & Phillips Blk, h. Scott's add
Hurlock Ellen, bookpr, The Brannum Lumber Co, h. Black
Hurst Edward, carp, bds w Washington
Hurst Mack, carp, bds w Washington
Hutchins Dennison, lab, h. s Harrison
Hutt Lizzie E, dressmkr, e Church, h. same
Hutt Wm, carp, h. e Church

M. J. DOVE, Insures against loss by Fire, Cyclone, Accident and Death.
NEELEY BLOCK. 61½ N. Meridian, ANDERSON, IND.

ALEXANDRIA CITY DIRECTORY. 109

✢ L. M. HOWARD, ✢
—DEALER IN—
Wine, Beer, Liquors, Imported and Domestic Cigars.
BILLIARDS AND POOL.
arrison St., - - - - ALEXANDRIA, IND.

WHITE RIVER DAIRY, 513 Nichol Avenue, Telephone 220. ANDERSON, IND.

I

ts George, tie contractor, n Harrison, h. same
ts Jesse, painter, h. n Harrison
ts John, plasterer, h. n Harrison
ts Rebecca, widow, h. n Harrison
ana Brick Oven Works, C T Doxey, propr, Wm Piner, supt, ¼ s on Mich Div Big 4
ana **Mutual Building and Loan Association,** H J Leonard, secy and treas, w Washington
w Horace, clk, h. cor Pickard and Canal
w Jas E, physician, w Washington, h. cor Pickard and Canal
w Wm, barber, h. cor Pickard and Canal
rance Co of North America of Philadelphia, Clinton & Hughes, agts, rms 7 and 8 cor Church and Harrison
J M (Hoover & Irish), h. Sullivan add

J

son Alma, h. e John
son John, carp, h. e Washington
bs Max, clothing, e s Harrison, h. Findlay, O
bson Saml, mgr, Max Jacobs, bds cor Harrison and Washington
es H May, domestic, s w cor West and Berry
ies Emma, h. n West
ies John, plasterer, h. n West
ins Joseph, glass wkr, bds w Pickard
ison Alice, domestic, s w cor Canal and Berry
ison Charles, brickmason, bds w Madison
ison Charles, saloon, w Washington, h same
ison Felix, drayman, bds s Wayne
ison Nancy, domestic, Commercial Hotel
ison Ritta, h. John
ison Wilcher, lab, h. John
es Alex E, city marshal, h. e Pickard
es Beatrice, teacher, h. e John
es Edward, glass wkr, bds 3d

LARMORE BROS., Proprietors, and Wholesale Dealers in **Ice Cream and Oysters in Season.** also Manufacturers

lerson Foundry and Machine Works, Manufacturers of Portable and Stationary **Steam Engines.**
N. JACKSON STREET, ANDERSON, IND. Phone 53.

Is Your Property Insured? If not, CALL AT ONCE on **JACKSON & BURR,**
69½ N. Meridian, - - ANDERSON, IND.

110 ALEXANDRIA CITY DIRECTORY.

Kent House,
D. H. KENT, Propr.
The only FIRST-CLASS HOUSE In the City.
S. W. Cor. Canal and Church, - - ALEXANDRIA, IND.

Jones Erie, plasterer, h. w Washington
Jones George, glass wkr, bds n Curve
Jones Jane C, wid, h. Church
Jones Marshall, blacksmith, h. w Madison
Jones Rev Richard C, h. s West
Jones & Sheffield (V C Jones and A K Sheffield), plumbers and gas fitters, w Washington
Jones Thomas H, cont and builder, h. s West
Jones Valentine C, (Jones & Sheffield), h. Church
Jones Walter M, asst P M, h. n Canal
Jones Wm, plasterer, h. w Washington
Judson Thomas M, bookpr The Lippincott Glass Co, h. w John

K

Kapp George, glass blower, h. w Washington
Kapp John, glass blower, h. w Washington
Kapp Wm, glass blower, h. w Washington
Kauffeld Louis, glass wkr, h. w Pickard
Kauffeld Wm, glass wkr, h. w John
Kauffman Claud, lather, bds n West
Kaufman George, lab, bds n West
Kaylor Daniel, clk, h. West add
Keck Christ, gatherer, h. West add
Keefer Alice, domestic, n e cor Berry and West
Keller Clara, bookpr, h. cor John and West
Keller Lena, h. cor John and West
Keller Lorenzo D (McNees, Keller & Co), h. cor John and West
Kelley Daniel, glass wkr, h. w Monroe
Kelley George S, saloon, billiards and pool, n Harrison (see adv)
Kelley Harry, glass wkr, h. w Monroe
Kelly M & Co, groceries, e s n Harrison, h. e Washington
Kelly Wm, grocer, h. e Washington
Kemp Benj, lather, h. Clinton
Kendall Daniel, glass wkr, h. n West
Kennedy Henry, lab, h. Clinton
Kent Cora, h. Kent House
Kent David H, propr Kent House, h. same

George B. Epperson, Paints, Oils, Varnishes and Painters' Supplies.
89 E. 9th St., - - ANDERSON, IND.

n Donnelly will sell your property, and insure quick returns. Place your business in his hands.
1st 10th Street, - ANDERSON, IND.

ALEXANDRIA CITY DIRECTORY. 111

GEO. S. KELLEY,
—DEALER IN—
ce Wines & Liquors, for the Retail Trade.
BEST LINE OF CIGARS IN THE CITY.
rison St., ... ALEXANDRIA, IND.

larry A, clk Kent House, h. same
louse, D H Kent, propr, s w cor Church & Canal (see adv)
Maud, h. Kent House
r Lloyd E, carp, h. w Washington
Frank, cook, h. Madison
George, glass wkr, bds w Church
Robert, glass wkr, bds w Church
r Aaron, clk, h. River ave
W D, secy & treas De Pauw P G Co, res New Albany, Ind
Vm, glass blower, h. w Church
Douglass, teamster, h. Curve
N Z, dentist, bds Commercial Hotel
urg James W, teamster, h. n w cor Berry and Curve
Anthony, glass wkr, h. w Canal
an John B, drayman, h. n West
Jacob, bartender, h. cor Pickard
George L, cigar mnfr, w Washington, h. Church
l Josiah W, clothing renovator, n Harrison, h. same
rank, glass wkr, rms w Madison
' Hall, w s Harrison 2d n Berry
Edgar M, propr St Elmo Hotel, res same
August, glass wkr, h. w Monroe
Peter (The Brannum Lumber Co), h. Chicago, Ill

L

Erie & Western Fgt and Pass Station, C G McFarland agt, s e cor Black and L E & W track
ohn Q, painter cont, h. cor Harrison and John
, boots and shoes, bds s Black
J Edward (Alexandria Investment Co), rms n e cor Church and West
nce Frank, glass blower, bds s w cor Black and Berry
nce Jacob, glass blower, h. s Wayne
nce Wm T, brick cont, h. s w cor John and Canal
n Lizzie, cook, n w cor Harrison & Washington, bds same
Bros (J S and J W Layne), boots and shoes, n Harrison
James S (Layne Bros), rms n Harrison

URE FRAMES of sizes and prices at Hugh Fisher's Novelty Works,
d 200 N. Milton St., - - - ANDERSON, IND.

J. T. Knowland & Son, Brass & Iron, Steam, Gas and Water Goods.
111 N. Main St., ANDERSON, IND. 'Phone 30.

Layne Josephus W (Layne Bros), h. Evansville, Ind
Leach John, plasterer, h. Lincoln ave
Leach Philip, plasterer, h. Madison
Leadbetter Dempsy, lab, h. s Wayne
Leaver Wm, photographer, rms n Harrison
Lederer David B, glass blower, bds s West
Lee ——, barber, rms e Pickard
Lee George W, carp, h. n Harrison
Leeson Wm B, teamster, h. w John
Lemair Louis, genl supt The W C DePauw Co Glass Factory
Lemons Allen, gas well driller, bds 4th
Leonard Harvey J, real estate, loan and insurance agt, s s Washington 3d e Canal, h. w John
Lester Frank, glass wkr, rms w Madison
Lewis Horace, carp, bds s West
Lewis John H, surveyor, h. w Madison
Lewis Melville C, carp, h. n Harrison
Ley Frank, glass wkr, bds w Pickard
Libler Val, glass wkr, h. w Pickard
Lily George A, glass wkr, bds Curve
Lily Wm H, glass wkr
Lindemood John, carp, bds Canal
Lindermuth George W, bartender, St Elmo Hotel, bds same
Lindskoog John L, merchant tailor, H H H Blk, n e cor Church and Harrison, h. e s Lincoln ave nr John (see left bottom lines)
Line Benajah A, physn, n w cor Harrison & Church, h. s Pickard
Line Della, music teacher, h. s Pickard
Line Edgar D, printer, h. s Pickard
Line Otho F, comp, The Alexandria Sun, h. s Pickard
Lines Joseph F, carp, h. w Church
Lippincott Glass Co The, W J Lippincott pres, J Evans Lippincott secy and treas, w Washington
Lippincott J Evans, secy and treas The L G Co, bds e John
Lippincott Wm J, pres The L G Co, h. Cincinnati, O
Lipps Wm H, painter, h. n e cor Church and Canal
Livengood Caddie E, trimmer, rms w Washington
Lloyd's Plate Glass Ins Co, of New York, Clinton & Hughes agts, rms 7 and 8, cor Church and Harrison
Londer Daniel, brick mason, bds Commercial Hotel
Long Mrs Emil, wid, h w John
Long Harry, glass blower, h. West add
Long Irvin, wks Oar Factory, bds n w cor Harrison & Monroe
Lowery D L, barber shop, n Harrison, h. same
Lowery Frank, carp, h. n w cor Harrison and Pickard

John O. Miller, Dealer in WATCHES, CLOCKS & JEWELRY, SILVERWARE and OPTICAL GOODS.
3 N. Meridian, - - - ANDERSON, IND.

A. Munchhof & Bros. Undertakers and Funeral Directors and Practical Embalmers. Office and Warerooms,
phones 189, 24 and 51.   No. 98 N. Main St., ANDERSON, IND.
OFFICE OPEN DAY AND NIGHT.

HARVEY J. LEONARD,
ary Public, Real Estate and Insurance Agent.
S. S. Washington, 3d E. Canal, ALEXANDRIA, IND.

ery Mattie A, wid, h. s West
ber, Oar & Handle Factory, Joseph W Neily propr, James L Connor supt and genl mgr, n e cor n Canal & Monroe
 Walter, glass wkr, bds w Washington
rger Mrs Sarah K, h. s West
r Walter, glass wkr, bds s Wayne
s Fred, glass wkr, bds w Washington
s Wm, glass wkr, bds w Washington
er Charles, glass wkr, bds w Pickard

M^c

onn Joseph, section boss, h. Clinton
oy Katie, domestic, n w cor Harrison and Washington
ray ——, real estate, bds e Church
uen Wm A, barber, h. w Washington
uthel George, glass wkr, bds 3d
aniel Elmer, lab, bds s West
ermit Myram, saw mill, h. s e cor Black and Church
lgott James, tailor, bds Commercial Hotel
rland Charles G, tkt and fgt agt L E & W Ry, h. John
eorge John, contractor and builder, s Clinton, h. same
eorge John, meat market, s Canal
nnis James, brick mason, h. Madison
wan Edward, glass wkr, h. w Madison
aw Brittana, wid, h. n Harrison
e John, plasterer, h. n West
own Michael, plasterer, bds McLeod's add
own Wm, plasterer, bds McLeod's add
wen Belle, domestic, s w cor Black and Berry
wn Cynthia E, h. s West
wn Jasper N, lab, h. s West
wn Ruth A, wid, h. s West
wn Thomas, h. 4th
wn W Arthur, glass wkr, h. s West
ughlin Arthur N, clk, h. s Harrison
d & Allen (H McLead and R W Allen), druggists and chemists, s e cor Church and Harrison

OOLLEY Foundry and Machine Works,
Designers and Manufacturers of **Heavy Machinery, Engines,** Boilers and Rolling Mill Work.

J. S. STUART, "THE FLORIST," Cut Flowers and Floral Work a specialty
99 to 111 W. 3d.   Telephone 79.   ANDERSON, IND

WHEN—The Most Reliable CLOTHING House
※ IN ANDERSON. ※
PRICES ALWAYS THE LOWEST.

McLead Herbert (McLead & Allen), rms n w cor Canal & Church
McMann Michael F, glass wkr, h. Monroe
McMurtrie Archie, glass wkr, h. w Washington
McMurtrie Joseph, mgr The L Glass Co, h. w Washington
McNeal Albert, glass wkr, bds George House
McNeary Cassius, clk, h. n w cor Harrison and Pickard
McNees Andrew H (McNees, Keller & Co), h. s Black
McNees Blanche N, h. s Black
McNees Harvey A (McNees, Keller & Co), h. John
McNees, Keller & Co (H A & A H McNees and L D Keller), lumber and planing mill, w Washington
McRea J M, real estate, rms e John

M

Mabbitt Wm, teamster, h. Riverview
Macy George, plasterer, bds McLeod's add
Magill Maggie, milliner, h. e Washington
Malone Harry, glass wkr, bds w Madison
Malone John W, brick cont, h. cor Wayne
Manchester Fire Ins Co, of England, Clinton & Hughes agts, rms 7 and 8, cor Church and Harrison
Manley Thomas, glass wkr, h. w Church
Manlove & Binkley (G H Manlove & H C Binkley), hardware, stoves, tinware, mantels, grates, paints, oils and window glass, w s Harrison opp postoffice (see adv)
Manlove G H (Manlove & Binkley), rms w Washington
Maple Nelson, lab, h. 5th
Markle S E, carp, h. Lincoln ave
Marlette Oscar, lab, h. Lincoln ave
Marley Joseph J, timber buyer, h. s West
Martin John, painter, bds Commercial Hotel
Martin Warwick, trav sales, The L G Co, bds e John
Martin Wm, stone mason, bds w Monroe
Mason John E, stone cutter, h. McLeod's add
Mason John H, stone cutter, h. McLeod's add
Mason Oscar A, clk, h. n Harrison
Mathews Andrew J, grocer, h. w Washington
Mathews Anna L (Fauver & Mathews), h. w Washington
Mathews Joseph A, clk, h. w Washington
Matthes Henry C, butcher, rms cor Wayne and Church
Matthes Mrs H C, rms cor Wayne and Church
Mattox Jasper, lab, bds w Washington
Matz Phillip, glass wkr, bds w Washington
Maxwell Bernard, glass wkr, bds Riverview

Insure with ROOP & HAYNES,
IN THE STANDARD COMPANIES THEY REPRESENT.

MANLOVE & BINKLEY,
――― DEALERS IN ―――
ware, Tinware, Stoves, Paints, Oils, Varnishes,
Lime, Window Glass and Mantels.
Hardware a Specialty. W. S. Harrison, Opp. Post-office, ALEXANDRIA, IND.

Vm H, school teacher, h. Lincoln ave
.rd Barney, contractor, h. Clinton
.rd Wm, stone mason, h. Clinton
er Levi, glass wkr, h. s Wayne
r **Fielding L** (The Brannum Lumber Co), h. Chicago, Ill
en Wm S, grocer, w Washington, h. s Black
nan M, glass blower, rms e Church
ether **Charles**, secy and treas, The Alexandria Co, h. Louisville, Ky
Thomas, eng, h. w Pickard
f Catherine, wid, h. w Washington
hurch, n w cor John and West
Charles, glass wkr, h. w Monroe
Charles F (Moore & Meyer), h. West near Church
Henry, glass wkr, bds w Monroe
Bros & Co (W W & R P Miller & J E Beeson), real estate and loans, Opera House Blk, s e cor Harrison and Church
Cora, dressmkr, h. Clinton
Harry, glass wkr, rms w Madison
Louis, glass wkr, bds s w cor John and West
Martha A, wid, h. Lincoln ave
Mary, wid, h. n Curve
Michael, glass wkr, bds w Madison
Mortimer, clk, bds n Canal
Peter, glass wkr, bds w Madison
Robert, carp, h. w John
Ryneldo P (Miller Bros & Co), h. s w cor Pickard and Walnut
Wm W (Miller Bros & Co), h. s e cor Pickard and Lincoln ave
Marguerite, stenographer, The Lippincott Glass Co, h. n w cor West and Water
ukee Mechanics Ins Co, of Milwaukee, s e cor Harrison and Church
ll Charles' hod carrier, bds n Harrison
y Albert, cooper, h. e Washington
y L L (L L Mobley & Co), h. 1 mile north
y L L & Co, farm impts, n Church 5th e Harrison

l & Willkie, have placed 85 loans in six months, Farm loans at 6%. All parties desiring to secure loans
WILL SAVE MONEY BY CALLING ON US.

Mobley Theodore, carp, h. n Harrison
Moninger Frank E, blksmith, h. Clinton
Montimer Alfred, glass wkr, bds s Wayne
Montross Romeo, glass wkr, bds n Curve
Mood Ollie O, music teacher, McLeod's add, h. same
Moody Charles, barber, h. McLeod's add
Moody Ebenezer T, carp, h. McLeod's add
Moore Charles, teamster, h. Canal
Moore Judson P (Moore & Meyer), editor The Alexandria Sun, h. West nr Church (see adv)
Moore & Meyer (Judson P Moore and Charles F Meyer), publishers The Alexandria Sun, West nr Church (see adv)
Moreland Wm F (Hughes & Moreland), h. w Berry
Morgan E, painter, bds n w cor West and Berry
Morgan Walter, carp, h. Clinton
Morian Wm, glass wkr, bds w Pickard
Morris Frank R, clk, C M Clayton, h. e John
Morrison Eroin, carp, h. s Clinton
Morrison Samuel, carp, h. s Clinton
Mugfor Richard, glass wkr, bds w Madison
Mulcahy Joseph, glass wkr, bds w Madison
Mullen Thomas W (Gipe & Mullen), h. n Harrison
Munger John K, street sprinkler, h. n West
Muthert Clara M, domestic, Kent House
Myers Charles, glass blower, bds w Church
Myers Wm, carp and cont, bds n e cor Canal and Church

N

Naily John, glass wkr, bds w Monroe
National Fire Ins Co, of Hartford, Conn, s e cor Harrison & Church
National Loan & Saving Association, of Indianapolis, Clinton & Hughes agts, rms 7 and 8, cor Church and Harrison
Necessity Lodge No 222, I O O F, instituted, meets every Thursday evening at I O O F Hall
Neff Abraham D, plasterer, h. Madison
Neff Bertha J, music teacher, Madison, h. same
Neff Charles O, carp, h. s Harrison
Neily Joseph W, propr Alexandria Oar Factory, h. Baltimore, Md
Nelson Oscar, glass engraver, rms s e cor Canal and Pickard
Newman Horace, carp, bds s Wayne
Newton Julia, h. w Church
New York Plate Glass Ins Co, of New York, s e cor Washington and West
Nicholson James N, clk, n Harrison, rms same

WM. J. DOVE
NEELEY BLOCK.

Can give you choice in 20 of the oldest and best Insurance Companies represented. Note this fact when placing your insurance.
61½ N. Meridian, ANDERSON, IND.

ALEXANDRIA CITY DIRECTORY.   117

THE ALEXANDRIA SUN,
INDEPENDENT WEEKLY.

MOORE & MEYER, Publishers.

FINE · JOB · PRINTING.

COME TO US FOR YOUR
Business Cards, Letter Heads, Note Heads,
Envelopes, Posters, Etc.

ESTIMATES ON ALL KINDS OF PRINTING.

West Street, ALEXANDRIA, IND.

Nicoson L C, propr Alexandria Stone Quarries, h. n Harrison
Nicoson Mary L, h. n Harrison
Nisley George, glass wkr, bds Riverview
Noble Charles W, life ins, h. n Canal
Noble Clarence, carp, bds n Canal
Noble Jacob, carp, h. s Canal
Noonan James, glass wkr, bds s Wayne
Noonan Michael, lab, h. West add
Noonan Patrick, lab, h. West add
Norris Gilbert F, painter, h. w Church
Norris Margaret, wid, h. w Church
Norris Oscar E, tel opr, h. w Church
North John D, carp, bds n w cor West & Berry
Northwestern Masonic Aid Assn, s e cor Harrison and Church
Northwestern National Fire Ins Co, of Milwaukee, Clinton & Hughes agts, rms 7 and 8, s e cor Church and Harrison
Norton Fred, tinner, bds St Elmo Hotel
Nuzum T M, supt public schools, s w cor Washington & Canal

O

Obrien James, hostler, h. e Church
Bryant Mary, h. w Pickard
Bryant Nathan, h. w Pickard
Bryant Wm, quarryman, h. Canal

Anderson Foundry and Machine Works, Manufacturers of BOILERS, Steam Heaters, Castings,
5 N. JACKSON STREET,   *Phone 53.*
ANDERSON, IND.   and General Machinery.

LARMORE BROS.
813 Nichol Avenue, ANDERSON, IND.
Telephone 220.

Will deliver you your ICE CREAM, OYSTERS AND MILK any place in the city, and guarantee first-class goods.

Jackson & Burr Represent the Largest Lines and the Strongest INSURANCE Companies.

69½ N. Meridian, ANDERSON, IND.

Odd Fellows' Cemetery, s e cor s Clinton and 4th
Odd Fellows' Mutual Aid and Accident Association, of Piqua, O, Clinton & Hughes agts, rms 7 & 8, cor Church & Harrison
Offbaugh David, glass wkr, bds Riverview
O'Harra Edward E, plumber, bds s Black
O'Hara John, plasterer, bds s Black
O'Hara Thomas J, stone mason; h. Madison
Ohio Farmers' Ins Co, of Le Roy, O, s e cor Washington & West
Oiler Jacob, stone mason, bds w Monroe
Olsen Charles G, glass wkr, h. w Church
O'Neil John, carp, bds George House
Orient Ins Co, of Hartford Conn, s e cor Washington & West
Otto Anthony E, physn & surgeon, n Harrison, h. same
Overshott Joseph, brick wkr, bds 8th
Owen A T, tel opr, C C C & St L Ry, h. e Church & Clinton
Owens Stephen, carpet weaver, h. n Canal

P

Paddock Wm W, real estate, cor Church & Harrison, bds Pickard
Painter Albert V, student, h. n Harrison
Painter Alfred M, secy The Phillips Land & Gas Co, h. n Harrison
Painter Bessie, h. n Harrison
Painter Harry W, stone cutter, h. n Harrison
Painter Jessie, h. n Harrison
Painter Paron P, contractor and builder, n Harrison, h. same
Palmer Charles E, meat market, e s Harrison, h. n Harrison
Palmer Dora, clk, bds n Harrison
Park Boyd S, furniture and undertaker, s e cor Canal and Church
Parsons Jonathan W, real estate, s w cor Washington & Harrison
Patterson Benj G, restaurant, n Harrison, h. same
Patton John, lab, rms n Harrison
Pauley Scott, watches, clocks and jewelry, w s Harrison 3d n Washington, rms same (see adv)
Paynter H D, atty-at-law, e s Harrison near Church, h. Odd Fellows Bldg
Peck Osmon, glass wkr, bds s Wayne
Peirce Frank K, mgr The Alexandria Land & Gas Co, h. s Canal
Penn George F (The W C DePauw Co), h. New Albany
Penticost Philip, glass wkr, h. Riverview
Perry Amos M, clk, bds McLeod's add
Perry Andrew J, physician, h. Tyler
Perry Benj F, carp, h. n West
Perry Daisy, h. cor Washington and Wayne
Perry Emma, h. cor Washington and Wayne

George B. Epperson, Contractor & Builder of Concrete Side Walks.

39 E. 9th St., ANDERSON, IND.

Real Estate Exchange does a general Real Estate business. The finest lots in the world for sale or trade at our office.
10 East 10th Street, - ANDERSON, IND.

ALEXANDRIA CITY DIRECTORY. 119

SCOTT PAULEY,
—DEALER IN—
Diamonds, Watches, Clocks, Jewelry,
NOTIONS AND FANCY GOODS.
W. S. Harrison, 3d N. Washington, - ALEXANDRIA, IND.

Perry Margaret, wid, h. cor Church and West
Perry Newton A, clk, bds s e cor Canal and Pickard
Perry Samuel S (Cree & Perry Bros), h. Washington
Perry Solomon, hotel, s e cor Wayne and Washington, h. same
Perry Wm, glass wkr, h. 4th
Perry Wm C, tool dresser, h. s Harrison
Perry W Riley (Cree & Perry Bros), h. Church
Phœnix Fire Ins Co, of Brooklyn, s e cor Harrison and Church
Phillips Benj, lab, bds n Harrison
Phillips Ernest, clk, h. Alexandria pike
Phillips Frank, turner, bds s e cor John and West
Phillips Land & Gas Co The, I P Watts pres, A M Painter secy, A G Campfield treas, s e cor Washington and Canal, up stairs (see front paster)
Phillips Marion, stone mason, h. Berry
Phillips Marion E, barber shop, s w cor Harrison and Church, h. Elwood, Ind
Phillips Samuel G, bookpr, h. n w cor Harrison and Berry
Phillips Wm F, barber, rms Berry
Pickard Amanda, wid, h. Clinton
Pickard Sallie A, h. e John
Pickard Thomas J, constable, h. e John
Pierce L L, supt De Pauw P G Co, rms cor Church and Wayne
Pierce Stephen, glass wkr, bds 3d
Pierson Andrew, brick mason, bds s Wayne
Pierson Chester D, farmer, h. s Harrison
Piner Wm, supt Ind Brick Oven Wks, bds 6th
Plackard W E, foreman, De Pauw P G Co, h. w Washington
Polm Frank S, lab, h. Curve
Porter Scott S, carp, bds Lincoln ave
Potts J M, wagon mkr, bds s Black
Powell R F, restaurant, w Washington, h. same
Presbyterian Church, cor Harrison and Washington
Prince Foy, glass blower, bds w Church
Public School Building, J S Gamble prin, cor Washington & West
Pugh & Dickey (J W Pugh & E L Dickey), druggists, Harrison
Pugh John, teamster, bds w Washington
Pugh Joseph W, physician (Pugh & Dickey), h. s e cor Harrison and Pickard

Pugh Fisher's Novelty Works! Jig and Scroll Saw Work in all the latest designs and patterns. Call and examine my work.
198 and 200 N. Milton St., ANDERSON IND.

Buck, Brickley & Co., Anderson, Ind.,

THE LEADING DRUGGISTS, FINE WALL PAPER AND DECORATIONS.

J. T. Knowland & Son, MAKERS AND DESIGNERS OF **NATURAL GAS Fixtures and Fittings**
111 N. Main St., ANDERSON, IND. 'Phone 30.

RUBLE { The Shoe Man, The Shoe Maker, The Shoe Repairer.

Pugh Juliet, h. s e cor Pickard and Harrison
Pugh Robert, drayman, h. n w cor Water and Curve
Pyle Jesse D, blksmith, bds Washington
Pyle & Stewart (W A Pyle & A Stewart), barber shop, n Harrison
Pyle Wm A (Pyle & Stewart), rms cor Church and Berry

Q

Queen Ins Co, of New York, Clinton & Hughes agts, rms 7 and 8, cor Church and Harrison
Quick Oliver M, clk, h. e John
Quick & Tomlinson (V C Quick, Al Tomlinson), dry goods, n e cor Harrison & Church
Quick V C (Quick & Tomlinson), h. e John
Quinn Wm, carp, bds s West

R

Radel Maggie, h. s e cor Black and Washington
Ralph H W, secy and treas Alexandria Investment Co, h. Louisville, Ky
Raulton N H, civil eng, bds Commercial Hotel
Ray Frank, lather, h. e Washington
Ray John, lather, h. e Washington
Ray Robert, eng, h. n Jackson
Raybould John, glass wkr, h. w Washington
Reaves Edwin, school teacher, h. Pickard
Reaves Sarah C, wid, h. Lincoln ave
Reed Newton, pipe fitter, rms e Washington
Reed Sterling, carp, h. n Harrison
Reed Wm, glass wkr, bds w Pickard
Reese Jennie, clk, bds w John
Reese John T, farmer, h. s Wayne
Reese J T, sewing machines, w Washington
Reid Budd C, dentist, s w cor Harrison & Washington, h. n w cor Berry & Black
Reid Robert, teamster, bds w Washington
Reide Wm, glass wkr, bds w Monroe

JOHN O. MILLER'S For FINE WATCH REPAIRING and DIAMOND SETTING.

A. Munchhof, LEADING FURNITURE DEALER, Nos. 40 and 42 E.8th St., ANDERSON, IND. Largest Stock to select from, and always lowest **CASH PRICES.** Watch our show windows.

ynolds Charles, cont roofer, bds s West
inehart Elmer, glass wkr, bds w Pickard
:hardson James R, lab, h. n West
:hardson Jane, wid, h. n West
:hardson Simeon, plasterer, h. n West
:hardson Thomas, glass wkr, bds w Church
:hman Samuel W, carp, h. s Wayne
:hter John B, glass wkr, h Berry
ler G P, physician and surgeon, w Washington, rms same
:erd Joseph, bartender, bds n Harrison
ig Theodore, glass wkr. h. w Washington
sler Joseph, brick mason, w Monroe
er **Leonidas A,** (Chamness & Rizer), h. Riverside
ibins Clair, waiter, bds n Harrison
ibins John, painter, bds w Monroe
ibins Ward B, clk, L E & W, h. e Berry
erts Amos E, butcher, h. Madison
erts Edward, carp, bds 4th
erts Wm, lab, h. n Curve
inson & Baker (E C Robinson, W T Baker), druggists and
    dealers in toilet articles, books, stationery, etc., Harlan
    & Phillips Block, Harrison
inson Erastus C (Robinson & Baker), h. n Harrison
inson Louis, carp, bds 4th
ckwell Harry W, brick layer, bds s w cor John and Canal
ers Harriet B, widow, h. Madison
ers James R, mgr, s w cor Harrison and Church, rms Berry
ers Peter, lab, bds w Madison
ers Wilber E, h. Madison
S F, asst agt C C C & St L R R, bds Commercial Hotel
nberg Jacob, glass wkr, bds w Pickard
nberger Albert, glass wkr, bds w Washington
Emma, h. s Wayne
Herman, drug clk, Harrison
James D, glass wkr, h. s Wayne
Sarah J, widow, h. s Wayne
:opf George, baker, bds w Washington
Charles, hardware, w Washington
Charles, glass wkr, bds s Wayne
Elmer E, boots and shoes, s Harrison, h. same (see adv)
: Samuel, h. s w cor West and Berry
an Atlantis, real estate, also township trustee, w Church,
    h. n Canal
an Ira, farmer, h. n Canal
an James F, physician, h. Berry

'OOLLEY Foundry and Machine Works,
    General Machinery, Heavy and Light Castings, and
    Sheet Iron Work.
    N. W. COR. 14th AND C W. AND M. R. R.

WHEN—The Largest Stock of CLOTHING, HATS, CAPS. and Gents' FURNISHING GOODS in ANDERSON.

ALEXANDRIA CITY DIRECTORY.

SCHOLL & SCHATZ, BAKERS
AND DEALERS IN Fine Confectionery, Fruits, Nuts, Etc.
East Church, - - ALEXANDRIA, IND.

Runyan Lethie, dressmkr, n Canal, h. same
Runyan Olive, domestic, w Washington
Ruper Fred, restaurant, h. e Washington
Ruppert Godfrey (Stockton & Ruppert), h. n Washington
Ryan Matthew, glass wkr, bds w Monroe
Rynehart James E, real estate dealer, w Madison, h. same

S

Sapp Lizzie, domestic, cor Wayne and Washington
Saxon LeRoy, drayman, h. s Wayne
Sayers Jesse, glass wkr, bds s Wayne
Schaefer Augustus R, physician, h. n e cor Washington & West
Schatz Rudolph (Scholl & Schatz), h. e Church
Scholl James (Scholl & Schatz), h. e Church
Scholl & Schatz (James Scholl and Rudolph Schatz), bakers, e Church nr Harrison (see adv)
Schwalm John H, bds w Washington
Schwinn Nathan, h. w Washington
Schwinn Noah W, clk, h. w Washington
Scott Benj, painter, h. w Monroe
Scott Carrie, h. s West
Scott Emery, clk, L L Mobley & Co, h. 1 mile north
Scott Ida M, h. s West
Scott James P, grocer, n w cor West and L E & W Ry, h. same
Scott Wm F, groceries, near West opp L E & W Ry, h. same
Sertell Joseph, saloon, w Washington, h. cor Monroe
Shafer John H, glass wkr, bds w Washington
Shane James, glass wkr, h. 8d
Shannon John S, atty-at-law and notary public, s w cor Washington and Harrison, bds e Church (see adv)
Sharman W J, glass blower, bds George House
Sharp T R, ins agt, bds Commercial Hotel
Shaw Douglas, carp, h. n e cor Washington and Black
Shaw Frank, teamster, bds Canal
Shawgo George, carp, bds n Harrison
Sheffield Arthur K (Jones & Sheffield), h. e Washington
Sheffield Charles E, plumber, h. e Washington
Sheffield John, draughtsman, rms cor Lincoln ave and John

Roop & Haynes Are Agents for FIVE of the BEST BUILDING & LOAN COMPANIES in Indiana.
210½ S. Anderson, - - - - ELWOOD, IND.

To Buy or Sell Real Estate, To procure money to build with promptly, for Insurance or Loans, Call on Robinson & Glassco, Room 9 "When" Building, ANDERSON, IND.

JOHN S. SHANNON,
Attorney-at-Law and Notary Public.

Collections a Specialty. S. W. Cor. Harrison and Washington Sts., ALEXANDRIA, IND.

Shelly Samuel, driver
Shepard Peter, clk; h. cor Berry and Wayne
Sherman Bertha, h. Clinton
Sherry Peter, gas well driller, bds 4th
Shetterly John, carp, h. Clinton
Shevlin John, glass wkr, bds Berry
Shipley Milton H, teamster, h. e Washington
Shirk Christian, jeweler, w Washington, h. s Black
Shook Clyde, lab, h. Clinton
Shook Jesse, teamster, bds n West
Shroad Mellard, stone mason, bds w John
Shroyer Milton, plasterer, h. Riverview
Shuman David, glass wkr, h. Riverview
Simison Allie, domestic, s Black
Simmons Richard, lab, bds Madison
Simpson Edward, lab, bds George House
Slippers Levi, plasterer, bds n Harrison
Smalley Lucinda, domestic, John
Smalley Richard, hostler, h. Washington
Smelser James S, livery, e Washington, h. e Church
Smith Edward, box mkr, h. cor Clinton and Church
Smith John, glass wkr, bds w Monroe
Smith John F, foreman, Nicoson's Stone Quarry, h. s Wayne
Smith Martha, bds cor Church and Clinton
Smith Mary, wid, h. s w cor Washington and Black
Smith Phillip, brick mason, bds n w cor West and Berry
Smith Richard, glass blower, bds w Church
Smith Sadie, h. s w cor Black and Washington
Smith Wm, glass wkr, bds s West
Smithwick Ollie, agt The Indiana Brewing Co, storage rooms, John and C C C & St. L Ry
Snider Frank, butcher, bds n w cor West and Berry
Snyder Nellie, h. w Washington
Sorden George, glass blower, h. n s e Church
Spade Charles, glass wkr, h. w Monroe
Spade Elizabeth, h. w Madison
Spade Ellery, dry goods, h. Berry
Spade Frederick, glass blower, rms e Church

Herman F. Willkie, J. P.
COLLECTIONS PROMPTLY MADE.

WHEN—Children's Department
A SPECIAL FEATURE.
Always well Stocked with the **LATEST NOVELTIES**.

124 ALEXANDRIA CITY DIRECTORY.

L. STOOKEY. E. E. DAVIS.

STOOKEY & DAVIS,
Furniture Dealers, Undertakers & Embalmers.
FURNITURE SOLD ON EASY PAYMENTS.
Herr Block, W. Washington St., ALEXANDRIA, IND.

ST. ELMO HOTEL,
E. M. KOONTZ, Proprietor.
The Leading Hotel of the City. Commodious Sample Rooms for use of Commercial Travelers. Fine Bar attached. Choice Wine, Beer, Liquors and Cigars. W. Harrison St., ALEXANDRIA, IND.

Spade George, glass wkr, h. w Madison
Spade Henry, glass blower, h. w Washington
Spade Wm E C, secy and treas, The Cartwright & Headington Co, h. Berry
Spence Thomas, farmer, h. n Canal
Sprong Emory, clk, h. w Washington
St Elmo Hotel, E M Koontz propr, n Harrison (see adv)
Standard Life and Accident Insurance Co, of Detroit, Clinton & Hughes agts, rms 7 and 8, cor Church and Harrison
Stanley Frank, teamster, h. s Wayne
Stanley Lillian, h. s Wayne
Stanley Mary E, h. s Wayne
Stanley Thomas, well digger, h. s Wayne
Starkey Adam, plasterer, bds McLeod's add
Starr Wm, teamster, bds n Church
Steinour Clinton, carp, h. w John
Steinour Daniel, contractor and builder, w John
Stephens Grant, mach, h. w Madison
Stevens Ella M, h. n Canal
Stevens Willis C, carp, h. n Canal
Steward Thomas, carp, bds w Monroe
Stewart Adrian (Pyle & Stewart)
Stewart Harry, lab, h. n Canal
Stewart John H, hod carrier, h e s C C C & St L Ry
Stillwell Thomas S, bookpr, Ind Brick Oven Wks, h. 7th
Stiner John, glass wkr, bds s Black
Stiner Peter, glass wkr, bds s Black
Stinson Wm F, flour and feed, cor Canal and Pickard, bds same
Stockton J R, h. e Washington
Stockton & Ruppert (W E Stockton and G F Ruppert), restaurant, e s Harrison
Stockton W E (Stockton & Ruppert), h. John and Canal
Stokes Wm J, glass wkr, bds w Washington

John L. Lindskoog, Fine Tailoring in Suits and Pants. An examination solicited. A FIT GUARANTEED.
H. H. H. Block, N. E. Cor. Church and Harrison, ALEXANDRIA, IND.

WM. J. DOVE Is Agent for National Home Building and Loan Ass'n of Bloomington, Ill You can get all the money you want on short notice
NEELEY BLOCK. 61½ N. Meridian, ANDERSON, IND.

ALEXANDRIA CITY DIRECTORY. 125

W. A. SWINDELL, *Attorney-at-Law.*   T. W. ARMSTRONG.

SWINDELL & ARMSTRONG,

Real Estate, Loan and Insurance.

Office, Room 11, Harlan & Phillips Block, Corner Harrison and Washington Streets,

ALEXANDRIA, - - - - **INDIANA.**

Stookey & Davis (L Stookey and E E Davis), furniture dealers, undertakers and embalmers, w Washington (see adv)
Stookey Lincoln (Stookey & Davis)
Strauss Louis M, physician and surgeon, Opera House Blk, s e cor Harrison and Church, h. Madison
Strieby Ella, wid, h. West add
Strickler Joseph, glass wkr, bds w Pickard
Stroud Daniel, lab, h. Junc L E & W and Big 4
Stroud George, lab, h. Junc L E & W and Big 4
Stroud Hattie, domestic, s Black
Stroud Ira, lab, h. w Washington
Stroud Joshlin, lab, h. w Canal
Strud Isaac, farmer, h. w Washington
Stultz J H, carp contractor, h. cor Lincoln ave and John
Stultz Lewis, painter, rms West
Sullivan Andrew T (Sullivan Land Co), h. n Canal
Sullivan Daniel, bartender, s w cor Harrison & Church, rms same
Sullivan Land Co (T W and A T Sullivan), w Church
Sullivan Matthew, glass wkr, bds w Pickard
Sullivan O H, physician, bds St Elmo Hotel
Sullivan Thomas W (Sullivan Land Co), h. Lincoln ave
Sun Ins Co, of London, Eng, Clinton & Hughes agts, rms 7 and 8, cor Church and Harrison
Surber John, brick mason, rms s e cor Canal and John
Sutton Arthur G, bookpr, Walker & Co, h. s West
Sutton Elmer, lab, h. Curve
Sutton Henry, contractor and builder, h. s West
Suttonwright Clyde, brick mason, bds s Black
Swindell Anna, wid, h. Riverview
Swindell & Armstrong (W A Swindell, Thornton W Armstrong), real estate dealers, room 11, Harlan & Phillips Block, n e cor Harrison and Washington (see adv)

Anderson Foundry and Machine Works, REPAIRS and Job Work of all Kinds A SPECIALTY.
'PHONE 53.
265 N. Jackson Street, - - - ANDERSON, IND.

TELEPHONE LARMORE BROS. 518 Nichol Ave., TELEPHONE 220. ANDERSON, IND. for your **ICE CREAM, MILK AND OYSTERS,** and be sure of prompt delivery and first-class goods.

INSURE WITH **JACKSON & BURR**, Latch string always out and light in the window, until the last man's INSURED.
69½ N. Meridian, - - ANDERSON, IND.

126 ALEXANDRIA CITY DIRECTORY.

✳ N. E. TOMLINSON, ✳
Fancy & Staple Groceries, and Confectioner.
Fancy Candies, Fruits and Nuts, CIGARS, TOBACCO, &c.
ALEXANDRIA, - - - INDIANA.

Swindell Charles R, head sawyer, h. Riverview
Swindell David, plasterer, h. Riverview
Swindell Edward T, clk, h. s Wayne
Swindell Emma, h. s w cor Black and Water
Swindell Mattie R, h. s w cor Black and Water
Swindell Norris, lab, h. s Wayne
Swindell W A (Swindell & Armstrong), also attorney-at-law and collections, room 11, Harlan & Phillips Blk, h. s w cor Black and Water
Swinn Lee, hostler, rms n Canal
Swisher Frank E, tel opr, L E & W, bds s West
Switz Herman, saloon, w Washington

T

Tarpening Charles A, bartender, bds w Washington
Taughinbaugh A C, attorney-at-law, notary public and collection agency, legal business promptly attended to, collections a specialty, room 9, Harlan & Phillips Block, n e cor Harrison and Washington, h. Riverview
Taylor Alta, h. n Harrison
Thomas Albert, carp, bds n Canal
Thomas Arden, carp, bds n Canal
Thomas E E, milliner, e Washington
Thomas S M, h. e Washington
Thomas Willis, glass wkr, bds w Monroe
Thompson Albert, bartender, h. Canal
Thompson Frank, glass wkr, bds w Pickard
Thompson Hezekiah C, laundry man, h. n Harrison
Thompson James, lab, h. Canal
Thompson Louis, glass worker, bds s Wayne
Thompson Maud, h. n Harrison
Thompson Perry, glass wkr, bds w Pickard
Thompson Rena F, h. Canal
Thompson Rosa, wid, h. Canal
Thornburg Wm, eng, bds e Pickard
Times Publishing Co (T N, W E & A G French), n w cor Harrison and John

George B. Epperson, Carriage Paints and Varnishes A Specialty.
89 E. 9th St., - - - - ANDERSON, IND.

mmons Charles A, tel opr, W U T Co, bds Kent House
zzard James H, harness mkr, bds n e cor Church and Canal
mlinson Albert D (Quick & Tomlinson), h. n Harrison
mlinson Catharine, wid, h. n Harrison
mlinson James, teamster, h. s Harrison
mlinson Joseph M, post master, h. West
mlinson N E, grocer, confectioner, fancy candies, fruits and nuts, cigars and tobacco, e s Harrison, n of Church, h. n Harrison (see adv)
mlinson Walter A, clk, h. n Harrison
rrance F W, agt, C C C & St L Ry
cker James, glass wkr, bds s West
llis Charles, stone mason, bds s e cor John and West
rgie Wm, glass wkr, bds w John
riggs John W, real estate, n w cor Church and Harrison, rms Madison

U

derhill Lorn, machinist, h. Clinton
derhill Sylvester, glass wkr, h Clinton
derwriters Ins Co of New York, s e cor Washington and West
ted States Express Co, G A Brush, agt, s. e cor Canal and Washington
ion Mutual Building & Loan Ass'n of Indianapolis, Clinton & Hughes, agts, rms 7 and 8 cor Church and Harrison
:hold Joseph, glass wkr, bds w Madison

V

1 Camp Frank, cont, bds s Black
daman I Allie, domestic, s Black
ner James, glass wkr, bds s Wayne
ighn John, brick mason, bds George House
ighn Mary J, domestic, George House
million Jesse, glass wkr, h. Curve
million U C, Alexandria Bank, h. 3 miles s e
million U C & Co (U C Vermillion, D B Baker, S E Young, A E Harlan, C F Heritage), proprs Alexandria Bank
non E G, stone quarries, w e Washington, h. Anderson, Ind
son Edward, painter, rms West
son J E, clk, M Kelly & Co, h. cor Canal and Pickard
son Walter, painter, rms West

J. T. Knowland & Son, WHOLESALE PLUMBERS *and Gas Fitters' Supplies*
111 N. Main St., ANDERSON, IND. 'Phone 30.

W

Wadkins Mrs Hattie, h. w Washington
Wakefield ———, brick mason, bds n e cor Church and Canal
Walker & Co (E M Walker, A C Brink), attorneys and notaries and real estate brokers, rms 4, 5 and 7, Harlan & Phillips Blk, over Alexandria Bank, n e cor Harrison & Washington
Walker Eugene M (Walker & Co), h. s West
Walker James, brickmkr, h. 8th
Walker Mary J, wid, h. s West
Walker Walter, hod carrier, bds s Clinton
Wall Marion, sawyer, bds Canal
Wall Wm, carp, bds Canal
Walling Mark E, bartender, rms n Harrison
Walters Henry, brick mason, bds s Black
Walton John, glass wkr, bds w John
Ward Albert, brick mason, h. w Monroe
Ward Wm G, brick mason, h. w Monroe
Warner ———, rms n Harrison
Wasson Lottie, h. s West
Watkins Mrs Hattie J, trimmer, h. w Washington
Watson John, glass wkr, bds Riverview
Watts Isaiah P, pres The Phillips Land & Gas Co, rms s e cor Washington and Canal (up stairs)
Webster David, plasterer, h. Monroe
Weed Wm, glass wkr, h. s Harrison
Wellinger Louis D, glass wkr, h. n Canal
Wellman H B, sign painter, bds e Pickard
Wellman Wm W, sign painter, bds e Pickard
Wells Charles, barber, bds Clinton,
Wells James, lab, rms e Washington
Wensell Louis, glass wkr, bds w Monroe
Wert Charles M, baker, wks Scholl & Schatz, h. e Church
Western Union Telegraph Co, G A Brush mgr, s e cor Canal and Washington
Westlake Wm, glass wkr, h. w Washington
Whetstone Grace, h. Berry
Whetstone Mrs Mary, h. Berry
White Jennie, domestic, s e cor Washington and Black
White John, glass wkr, bds w Church
Whitesides Elbridge, mgr s w cor Washington and Canal, bds Kent House
Whitesides Nort, hatter, clothier and furnisher, s w cor Washington and Canal, h. Franklin, Ind

JOHN O. MILLER, ELEVEN YEARS' EXPERIENCE in Watchmaking. Finisher six years in Elgin & Springfield Watch Factories.
GUARANTEE MY WORK. 3 N. Meridian, ANDERSON, IND.

Viesenmyer Henry, glass wkr, bds w Monroe
Viesenmyer John, glass wkr, bds w Monroe
Viggins John S, restaurant, n w cor Harrison and Washington
    h. same
Viley Richard, brick mason, bds e Pickard
Villiams Birdie B, h. n Harrison
Villiams Carrie, h. n Anderson
Villiams Hiram P, propr The Brunswick Bar, h. same
Villiams John, real estate, h. e Church
Villiams John B, teamster, h. e Church
Villiams Katie, widow, h. n w cor John and Canal
Villiams Thomas C, wks Alexandria Laundry, bds n Harrison
Villiams Wm, clk, h. n Harrison
Villiamson David, carp, h. n Canal
Vilson Charles, brick mkr, h. 6th
Vilson John, stone mason, bds w Monroe
Vilson Le Roy, glass wkr, h. w Church
Vilson Omer G, brick mkr, h. 6th
Vilson Thomas, glass wrk, bds w Pickard
Vilson Thomas H, shoe mkr, h. w Church
Vilson Zachariah, brick mkr, h. 7th
Vinkleman Albert, glass wkr, bds Riverview
Vinks John, brick mason, h. w Monroe
Visenberger George, glass wkr, bds s West
Visner Frank, well driller, bds s Harrison
Volf Powell, hod carrier, bds n e cor Canal and Church
Vood John B (S O Dorsey & Co), h Garfield
Vood Marion, carp, bds George House
Vood Vinnie, clk, h Madison
Voodcock Nellie, wid, h. Madison
Voods Lottie, domestic, Church
Voods Thomas, student, h. w Church
Voods Thomas, real estate, bds Church
Vorman Frank, lab, bds n Canal
Vright Calvin B, wood wkr, h. n e cor Berry and Curve
Vright John W, wood wkr, h. n e cor Berry and Curve
Vycoff Henry, carp, bds Madison

Y

Young Cyrus M, farmer, h. n Harrison
Young Edward, h. s Canal
Young George W, teamster, h. Canal
Young S E, Alexandria Bank, h. Canal
Young Charles M, harness wkr, rms n Harrison

TOWNS AND VILLAGES IN MADISON COUNTY

ALFONTE, in Green Township, is located on the C C C & I Railway, 13 miles south-west of Anderson, the county seat. Population, 80.

Alfonte Curtis
Amick Henry
Collins W N
Cummins J S, genl store
Fort Gabriel
Helms A H
Hiding Wm
Huston O
Manifold Bros, genl store
Manifold John C
Manifold W W
Modlin J P, blksmith
Olvey Alfred
Randall Bros, grain dealers
Randall P H
Randall W P
Russell Wm
Ridenour Frank
Ridenour Isaac
Smethers John

CHESTERFIELD, a village on the C C C & I Railway, in Union Township, is 5 miles east of Anderson. Population, 160. ANDREW J. CORNELIUS, P. M.

Arbuckle J, barber
Biddinger Ed, peddler
Biddinger John, retired
Bromenburg Fred, farmer
Carpenter George, lab
Cartwright Ira, lab
Cartwright Joseph, carp
Cornelius Andrew J, genl store also postmaster
Foster Frank, photographer
Gold Anson, lab
Gold Jacob, mgr brick works
Gold James, farmer
Gold Wm, brick works
Hahn John, brick mkr
Hall R C, gardener
Herrick Q, Medium
Highmiller Henry, carp
House H V, lab
Isenogle Samuel, lab
Jones L, lab
Kennedy Pat, blksmith
Laurance Wm, teamster
Lenard Rev Irwin
Lowrey D, lab
McCashlin Henry, lab
McGriff Allen, teamster
McGriff Quincy, lab
McGriff Thomas, retired
Makepeace Q A, retired
Minear James, carp
Nelson Benj, brick mkr
Pierce Cornelius, farmer
Quinn John, lab
Rennington Saml, band teacher
Rinker Jacob, farmer
Sherrer Newton, teamster
Shiner L, lab
Shriner Marion, eng
Stineman Fred, stockdealer
Suton Henry, brick mkr
Thompson Jno, supt R N Gas Co
Trimble James, retired
Trimble Robt, saloon
Trublood Charles, teacher
Trublood Ferd, lab
Trublood W T, genl store
Vosbinder Murdoch, plasterer
Wandell W S, carp
Wilson Walter, bricklayer

Anderson, the county seat. U.S. express. Population 180. HOWILL, postmaster.
Allen Alkana, G A R vet
Benedict Benj, lab
Bowers Frank, lab
Bowers John, lab
Bowers Thomas, lab
Bowers Wm, lab
Denney Abel, lab
Ebert J D, physician
Etchison Berry, lab
Etchison Frank, lab
Etchison John, lab
Etchison Joseph, lab
Etchison Robert, lab
Etchison Riley, miller
Etchison Wm, lab
Gisse Adam, carp
Griffin Samuel, lab
Hodge Emanuel, lab
Howell A G, postmaster, also mgr W J B Luther general store
Johnson Milton, lab
Jones Charlie, lab
Kellog Elvin, lab
Ferry James, shoemkr
Reed Wm, lab
Remington A
Richter John, lumber dealer
Robeson T A, dentist
Shaw John, lab
Ivey Charles, lab
Ivey Joseph, lab
Amison Alex, lab
Amison Theo, lab
Stone Joseph, lab
Stroud Joshua, lab
Welborn J A, blacksmith
Welborn Mell, lab
Williams Thomas, grocer

La Pelle on the Midland R R is the nearest shipping station. Population, 315.
Bodenhorn C & Son, genl store
Cook Daniel, physician
Farmer Isaac, barber
Fisher Homer, carp
Fisher Stephen, justice
Hacker James, blksmith
Hiney John, blksmith
Horton L L, teacher
Markle R R, wagon mkr
Markle & Leonard, saw mills
Moreland M A, express agt
Myrick E S, druggist
Presser H & Son, saw mill
Wochstetter C, shoe mkr

FLORIDA, a post village in Lafayette Township, on the C, St L & P Ry, is four miles north of Anderson. Population, 100. SPENCER G BEVELHIMER, P. M.

Ashby George, teamster
Avery Edward, wks saw mill
Avery Jane, wid
Badger Benjamin, lab
Badger Charles, wks Saw Mill
Badger Leora
Badger Mansel, lab
Barnes Wm H, Pan-Handle R R and Adams Expres agt and general store
Beaman Duey, teamster
Bevelhimer & Co, Spencer G and Thomas M Bevelhimer, grocery and notions
Bevelhimer George W
Bevelhimer Spencer G (Bevelhimer & Co), grain elevator, also postmaster

Beal & Willkie, **ATTORNEYS AT LAW.** We will attend to your legal business promptly, and charge you no exhorbitant fees.
MECHANICS LIENS A SPECIALTY. CALL AND SEE US.

WHEN —Originators of the One Price System
IN SELLING CLOTHING.
FAIR AND SQUARE DEALINGS WITH ALL.

132 MADISON CO. DIRECTORY.

Bevelheimer Thomas M (Bevelheimer & Co)
Clem Jesse, farmer
Custer Mabel G, teacher
Davis John R, carp
Golding Sarah, wid
Gooding Albert, wks saw mill
Gooding Sallie
Gooding Sylvester, lab
Guisinger John S, physician
Hill John W, wks saw mill
Jenkins Ike, clk
Jones D, student
Jones John L, farmer
Jones Walter, student
Keal Charles, lab
Kirk Alvin, farmer
Kirk Sylvester, farmer
Oldman Wm A, wks saw mill
Parson John P, blacksmith
Roadcap Henry, farmer
Ross Luella, domestic
Sturges Richard, lab
Thomas Alva J (Thomas Bros)
Thomas Bros (Alva J & Jesse V Thomas), saw mill and tile factory (see adv)
Thomas Jesse V (Thomas Bros)
Vanmeter Isaac N, physician
Vanmeter Mary

FRANKTON, on the C St L & P R R, is an incorporated town of over 700 inhabitants; it is in Pipe Creek Township, 10 miles northwest of Anderson. BENJ. F. DAVIS, P. M.

Aikman Ocea, domestic
Alexander Jasper, farmer
Alexander Luris, lab
Andris Edward, glass blower
Andris Octavie G, dressmkr
Armfield Emsley, pat med agt
Barrett Feste, glass blower
Baum F W (Baum & Pingel)
Baum & Pingel (Fletcher W Baum & Samuel Pingel), blksmiths and wagon shop
Beason Otta
Beason Peter, farmer
Beck Jessie, wid
Beck Joseph H, meat market
Beeson Trenulius
Bernard Ernest, glass blower
Bittner Elvin D, prin Frankton Schools
Blake Ora S, wks restaurant
Blake Wm R, restaurant and confectioner
Blodgett Milton J, pres & mgr Clyd Window Glass Co
Braddock James (Braddock & Lineberry
Braddock & Lineberry (James Braddock, Addison Lineberry), fence mnfrs
Braddock Wm J, timber dealer
Bradley David D, carp
Bradley Wm H, meat market
Branun Joseph, teamster
Bratton Jonas, clk
Brown Wm, plasterer
Burke Wm, gas fitter
Cadwell John F, tinner
Call John
Callahan Andy, lab
Callahan Charles L, lab
Campbell George N
Campbell Joseph C, carp
Campbell Mantie L, musician
Campbell Ocea A, p o clk
Campbell T J, propr saw mill
Campbell Wm (Hockman & Campbell)
Campbell Wm, livery stable
Cannaday Cora B, student
Cannaday David
Carlton Wm, well digger
Carothers Robert, gatherer

John L. Lindskoog,
Do not buy until you have seen them.
H. H. H. Block, N. E. Cor. Church and Harrison

Leads in the Merchant Tailoring Line English and French Worsteds, Imported, always in stock.

WM. J. DOVE, Real Estate, Loans and Insurance,
NEELEY BLOCK. 61½ N. Meridian, ANDERSON, IND.

MADISON CO. DIRECTORY. 133

ALVA J. THOMAS.   JESSE V. THOMAS.

THOMAS BROTHERS,
SAW MILL, and dealers in LUMBER.
Also Drain and Tile Factory.
FLORIDA,   INDIANA.

Carpenter Rev G W, pastor M E Church
Carter Elmer, teacher
Castor Louis, section foreman
Charles Henry J, glass blower
Christian Church, Collins pastor, cor Church and Maple
Clyde Window Glass Co, Milton J Blodgett pres, Frederick Dussler secy, John Lus treas
Cochran Wm, carp
Coverston Dollie, tel opr
Coverston John W, physician
Cox Matthew, city marshal
Cranmer Russell R, hardware and harness
Cripe Thomas B, glass wkr
Davis Benj F (Davis & Niswonger), also postmaster
Davis Gertrude
Davis & Niswonger (Benj F Davis and Jesse S Niswonger), hardware
Davis Rose A, clk p o
Davis Wm L, miller
Deaton Archibald, lab
Deaton John N, lnb
Deaton Nancy
Derville Julius, glass teaser
Dussler Frederick, glass cutter
Dwiggins John W (Urmston, Hurst & Dwiggins)
Dwiggins Joseph S, restaurant
Dwiggins Lincoln H, painter
Dwiggins Rufus, teamster
Ellison Wm D J, shoe mkr
Eppard John W, clk
Eppard Marion, carp

Ernest Joseph E, blksmith
Etchison Albert, bartender
Etchison Francis M, glass wkr
Etchison Isaac G, saloon
Etchison Ollie
Farlow Ella E
Farlow James M, attorney
Farlow Micajah S, lab
Folan John W, deputy recorder
Folan Marwell, tel opr
Frankton Bnk, Cornelius Quick pres, David O'French cashr, Wm H H Quick asst cashr
Frankton Nat Gas & Oil Company, Perry Jones pres, John A Howard secy, A Wise treas
French David O, cashr C Quick & Co Bank
French Mary J, wid
French Wm J, physician
Funkhouser Cora B
Funkhouser Mary A
Funkhouser Wm H, lab
Gadway Wm, gatherer
Gibson Flora E, domestic
Gibson Perry E, lab
Gibson Solomon, carp
Girton Isaac N, lab
Gooding J, stone & gravel dealer
Goosens Hector, glass flatner
Gorman Mattie E, dressmkr
Grand View Hotel, F Z Moreland propr
Granger Rebecca, wid
Granger Charles M, lab
Granger Wm, glass wkr
Greulich Reynold, butcher
Hackett Thomas, glass cutter

Anderson Foundry and Machine Works, Manufacturers of **BRICK AND TILE MA-**
65 N. Jackson Street.   'Phone 53.

Jackson & Burr Do the Largest INSURANCE Business. Insure in the good old Companies they represent.
69½ N. Meridian, - - ANDERSON, IND.

134 MADISON CO. DIRECTORY.

Grandview Hotel, Rates $2.00 per Day
F. Z. Moreland, Propr.
FRANKTON, IND.

Hagerety George A, glass wkr
Hardcastle John R, glass wkr
Harrison Ella, teacher
Hedley Amos
Hicks Hugh (Spencer & Hicks)
Hiser Wm, carp
Hitchens Edmond F, engineer
Hockman Bessie
Hockman Clyde
Hockman & Campbell (Solomon J Hockman and Wm Campbell), dry goods and groceries
Hockman Solomon J (Hockman & Campbell
Hodge Manervia, wid
Hogan Thomas, glass flatner
Holland Wm, glass wkr
Hosier Mary C, wid
Howard John A, real estate agt
Howland Charles H, gatherer
Hughes John F, glass wkr
Hughes Martin L, lab
Hughes Wm H, glass wkr
Hurst A D (Urmston, Hurst & Dwiggins)
Jackley Charles T, glass wkr
Jackley Christian, glass blower
James Alfred, lab
James Frank, lab
James Roey, lab
Jarrell John, glass wkr
Johnson Otto T, glass wkr
Jones George, mach
Jones Melvin, wks planing mill
Jones Perry, saw and planing mill and lumber yard (see adv)
Jones Thomas, wks planing mill

Keaster James B, lab
Kemp Edward A, editor The Frankton Leader
Kiddel John B
Kiddel Mary J
Kime Charles, glass blower
King Benj, carp
King David, drayman
King Elizabeth, wid
King Frank M, carp
King Heaton H, teacher
King Henry H, teacher
King Margaret L
Knotts Wm H, lab
Laden Kate
Laden Thomas, lab
Laub Wm H, carp
Laudig A, wks planing mill
Lambiot Augustus
Lambiot Fredrick, glass blower
Langley Percy, glass wkr
Langston Isaac, janitor, Frankton Schools
Laning Wm, hostler
Lankaster Isaac, carp
Laub F M, wks planing mill
Layne Joseph D, barber
Layne Logan A, barber
Layden Malinda, wid
Legg A H, impl & buggies
Lenington Eli M, lab
Liggett Chas H, agt Pan Handle Ry Co and Adams Exp Co
Liggett Phoebe, wid
Lineberry A, propr fence factory
Little Elizabeth, wid
Lord Robert, gatherer
Ludlow Cora, domestic
Lux J, treas Window Glass Co

George B. Epperson, Contractor and Builder of Felt and Gravel ROOFING.
39 E. 9th St., - - ANDERSON, IND.

)hn Donnelly, The Real Estate Dealer of Anderson. If you wish to buy, or rent, call at 10 E. 10 St., ANDERSON, IND.

MADISON CO. DIRECTORY. 135

ERRY JONES, MANUFACTURER OF AND DEALER IN Hardwood Lumber, Hard and Soft Pine, Doors, Sash, Glass, Shingles, Lath, Lime, Hair, Plaster Paris, Etc.

FRANKTON, IND.

:auley Samuel, lab
:ord Charles F, teamster
:ord John L, farmer
:ord Mollie R
)aniel John R, baker
)aniel Mrs J R, millinery
)aniel Vinie M, milliner
bott Wm, carp
:el H A, livery stable
)n Adam, teamster
)n Casper, lab
)n Wm E, teamster
ose Frank, lab
Church, Rev J B Carpenter
)astor, Church & Walnut
:r Mrs Meverva, dressmkr
ick Anthony
James T, watchman
Jane, wid
·e Amanda J
·e Jonathan
·e Joseph A, teamster
land F. Z, propr Grand View Hotel (see adv)
is Estella
is John, glass wkr
is Presley, teaser
Thomas D, grocer
Anna, domestic
)erry Jacob, farmer
vanger Jesse, hardware
Amos, bartender
Joseph S, cabinet mkr
man Joseph, glass blower
man Joseph Jr, glass wkr
man Paul, gatherer
igh Phœbe

Ornamental Lawn Fence Co,
 A D Hurst pres, h. Pipe
 Creek Township
Orr & Campbell (Martin V Orr,
 Thomas J Campbell and
 George W Campbell), saw
 mill
Orr Martin V (Orr & Campbell)
Parkison John W, lab
Parkison Malin D, lab
Parkison Sarah L
Phillips John W, teamster
Phillips Walter G, clk
Phil Augustus, pot mkr
Pingel Samuel (Baum & Pingel)
Powers Cynthia, wid
Powers Kate
Pugh Joseph (Pugh & Runyan)
Pugh & Runyan (Josehh E
 Pugh, Wm A Runyan),
 saloon
Quear Joseph H, plasterer
Quick Lavina, wid
Quick Nellie C
Quick Wm H H, baker
Reason James, lab
Richwine Gideon
Rigsby Calvin B, lab
Rigsby Jasper N, lab
Rigsby Milliard F, lab
Rigsbp Samuel T, teamster
Riley L Alonzo, clk
Riley Margaret E, widow
Ring James J, real estate, building and loan and notary public (see adv p. 136)
Ring John, teamster

BUCK, BRICKLEY & CO., THE LEADING DRUGGISTS, Cor. Ninth and Meridian Streets, ANDERSON, IND.

GH FISHER, Manufacturer Screen Doors and Windows all sizes. Furniture repairing a specialty
8 and 200 N. Milton St.,
ANDERSON, IND.

J. T. Knowland & Son, SANITARY PLUMBERS, Gas and Steam Fitters.
111 N. Main St., ANDERSON, IND. 'Phone 30.

⇾J. J. RING,⇽
Notary Public, Real Estate and Building and Loan Agent,
FRANKTON, IND.

Ring Mary E, wid
Ring Oliver F, lab
Roach Louisa, wid
Rummel Benj F, plasterer and contractor
Runyan W A (Pugh & Runyan)
Sckell Andrew J, drug store
Scott Alice M, teacher
Scrackangast A P, carp & cont
Scrackangast Elizabeth, wid
Scrackangast Thomas F, carp
Scrackangast Wm, carp
Sharp John, farmer
Shaw Albin, bartender
Shaw Thomas J, saloon
Shell Andrew J, druggist
Shetterly James, teamster
Shields Louis, gatherer
Shirley James W, glass wkr
Shoemaker S B, general store
Sigler Albert R. teacher
Sigler Cynthia J, clk
Sigler Frank, farmer
Sigler George W, druggist
Sigler Joseph E, teacher
Silvey Anthony, teamster
Smelser Jacob
Smelser Solomon, glass wkr
Smith Charles, glass blower
Smith Elmer C, notary public and ins agt
Smith Jacob C, boarding house
Smith Wm, lab
Spencer Charles E, glass wkr
Spencer Henry E (Spencer & Hicks)
Spencer & Hicks (H E Spencer and H I Hicks), blacksmith shop
Steele John, glass wkr
Steffy Erasmus, teamster
Stuart Joseph L, lab
Sutton Jonathan, carp
Swarts Agnes, wid
Swarts Barn J, trav sales
Swarts Charles R, carp
Tash Jordan, glass wkr
Taylor Tilman, lab
Tesh Ulysses E, druggist
Thorpe Louis, carp
Thorpe Josiah, teamster
Timmons Milton J, lab
Timmons Orville, lab
Todd Mahalia, wid
Towsend Eliza A, wid
Urmston Augustus G (Augustus G Urmston & Son)
Urmston Augustus G & Son (Augustus G Urmston and Le Roy Urmston), flour mills
Urmston, Hurst & Dwiggins (Le Roy Urmston, A D Hurst and John W Dwiggins), Ornamental Lawn Fence Factory, s Washington
Urmston Le Roy (Augustus G Urmston & Son, and Urmston, Hurst & Dwiggins)
Urmston & Son, Gas Co and retail gas supplies
Vincen Edgar B, saloon
Wallace Isaac N, carp
Wallace John L, drayman
Wapel Wm, clk
Waymere Hattie J, domestic
Weary Charles, glass blower

John O. Miller, Practical Watchmaker & Jeweler. Eleven Years' Experience in the Manufacturing of Watches.
3 N. Meridian, - - - - ANDERSON, IND.

A. Munchhof & Bros. Undertakers and Funeral Directors and Practical Embalmers. Office and Warerooms,
lephones 189, 24 and 51. No: 98 N. Main St., ANDERSON, IND.
OFFICE OPEN DAY AND NIGHT.

MADISON CO. DIRECTORY. 137

'arker & Kirkman, DEALERS IN DryGoods, Notions, Boots and Shoes, Domestic and Fancy Groceries, and ?erything kept in a first-class general merchandise store.
GILMAN, IND.

/eaver Frank, lab
/eaver Martha A, wid
/ebb Minor, miller
/ebb Wm, jeweler and barber
/ebb Wilson M, farmer
/elsh Belle, wid
/illiams Josiah, plasterer
/ise Jennie, teacner
/oodyard H, wks saw mill
/right C R, physician, also city clerk
/right Eli, glass wkr

ILMAN, a small village in Monroe Township, is on the L E & W R R, 14 miles ortheast of Anderson. Population, 75. J. M. WILLIAMS, P. M.

:ennet George, teamster
:ollins A M, lab
:ollins Frank, lab
)unn Thos, tel opr, L E & W Ry
'linn Ed, lab
[arrison Maley, teamster
[iatt Ed, teamster
ackson Frank, teamster
ackson James, lab
.irkman John P, notary public
:oon Samuel, lab
:oon Wm, lab
.acy Frank, teamster
lorgan J M, carp
lorgan J W, physician
lorgan Walter, carp
arker & Kirkman, genl store
.utledge E, stock dealer
hearer M, druggist
hockly David, teamster
idall A, blacksmith

Stout C, lab
Stout L, lab
Williams J M, postmaster

HALFORD, Hamilton Station, in Jackson Township, is 5½ miles from Anderson, the nearest shipping point. Population, 65. W. H. BENEFIEL, P. M.

Anshutz Oliver, farmer
Ashby Daniel, lab
Ashby James, carp
Ashby John, ret
Benefiel George, lab
Benefiel Jonathan, lab
Benefiel Wm H, postmaster
Bricker Cyrus, lab
Brown James, lab
Busby A S, farmer
Busby John M, agent
Busby J V, stock dealer
Busby Silas, retired
Cannon George, farmer
Coy George, farmer
Coy John, farmer
Coy Luther, farmer
Coy Matthew, farmer
Coy Seth, stock dealer
Cunningham George, farmer
Cunningham James, carp
Davis James, lab
Eppesly Peter, machine agt
Kemp Daniel W, saw mill
Kessling Charles, farmer
Moore Cornelius, farmer
Morrison Rev James F
Penisten Frank, lab
Perry Aaron, carp

WOOLLEY FOUNDRY AND MACHINE WORKS,
Engineers, Founders and Machinists
N. W. Cor. 14th and C. W. and M. R. R.

J. S. STUART, "THE FLORIST", DEALER IN PLANTS, ROSES and BULBS, ANDERSON, IND.
99 to 111 W. 3d. Telephone 78.

WHEN—Anderson Clothiers & Hatters.
☞ ONE PRICE TO ALL.

JAMES W. HECKER,
Practical Blacksmith and Horseshoer,
REPAIR WORK A SPECIALTY,
Railroad Street, - - LAPEL, IND.

Perry Henry, machine agt
Perry Thomas, lab
Rector Jackson, farmer
Rector Melvin, lab
Rector Wm, farmer
Robinett Charles, teamster
Robinett George, farmer
Robinett Milton, lab
Ryan N, farmer
White B F, farmer
White James
Young James M, farmer
Young Matthew, farmer

JOHNSON'S CROSSING is a station on the Midland R R, in Stony Creek Township, 6 miles west of Anderson. Population, 25. E. J. HASKINS, general store and P. M.

LAPEL, a village in Stony Creek Township, on the Midland R R, is 9 miles west of Anderson. U S Express, W U Telgraph. Population, 200.

Adams Express Co, P W Russel agt, cor Railroad and C & L E
Aldred Edward, lab
Aldred Frank L, barber, h. Railroad
Aldred G, carp
Aldred G Jr, teacher
Aldred Robert K (Conrad, Wright & Co), h. Anderson Pike
Anshutz John, lab

Armstrong James M P, general store, cor Main and C & S E Ry, h. Main
Baker M A (Rambo & Baker), h. Noblesville, Ind
Barrett Charles E, genl store, Main, h. same
Bennett H F, watches, clocks, etc, Main, h. Meridian
Barret James, genl store
Bartholomew S, carp
Beach Bailey, lab
Bird George E (Huffman & Bird), h. cor Elm and Mindian
Bothes Frederick, livery
Boyce Rev J
Bradley Patrick, cont
Brattain Albert, lab
Busby Wade P, general store, Main, h. same

Chicago & Southeastern Pass & Fgt Station, P W Russell agt, cor Railroad and C & S E track
Calder A, lab
Conner James, lab
Conner Richard, lab
Conrad David (Conrad, Wright & Co), pres The Lapel Natural Gas & Oil Co, h. Anderson Pike
Conrad, Wright & Co (D Conrad, G W Wright and R K Aldred), mnfrs gas regulators, Main
Daley James, contractor
DeWitt B, lab

Roop & Haynes, Real Estate, LOANS AND INSURANCE,
210½ S. Anderson, - - - ELWOOD, IND.

Robinson & Glassco, Real Estate, Loan and Insurance Agents, room 9 "When" Building Agents Fidelity Building and Savings Union.
ANDERSON, IND.

MADISON CO. DIRECTORY. 139

P. N. INGALLS,
DEALER IN HIGH GRADE
PIANOS, ORGANS AND SEWING MACHINES,
ould be pleased to leave any of my goods in your own home for trial. I am 14 years in e trade, and think I know good goods. Send a postal card for prices, etc. Goods delivered any part of the country. P. N. INGALLS, Lapel, Ind.

yer Robt, meat market, Main, h. same
dwards John, plumber
isher Homer, carp
isher Stephen E (Sears & Fisher), h. Avenue
isher Will, farmer
orbes U S, lab
ord Bros (Geo & John Ford), livery stable, Main
ord Geo (Ford Bros), bds Main
ord Jno (Ford Bros), bds Main
ord L E, sawyer
oss C, ed and propr The Lapel Dispatch, h. Woodward
raham John J, physician and grocer, Main, h. same
ross E, lab
ross Martin, lab
ross Walter, lab
winn W R, barber shop, Railroad, h. Fishersburg, Ind
ecker James W, blksmith & horse shoer, Railroad, h. Fishersburg, Ind
awkins J A, restaurant and bakerp, Railroad, h. same
oobler Frank, carp
orton L L, teacher
uffman & Bird (W J Huffman & G E Bird), hrdware, Main
uffman E G, treas The Lapel N G & O Co
uffman Wm J (Huffman & Bird), h. Main
unter Wm R, photog, Main
Igalls P N, pianos, organs and sewing machines
arret Ed, carp

Jones J M, physn, Main, h. same
Klepper Nelson W, druggist, Main, h. same
Klepper Mrs N W, milliner, Main, h. same
Lapel Dispatch The, C Goss ed and propr, cor Main and C S E Ry
Lapel Elevators, Woodward Bros proprs, cor Main and C & S E Ry
Lapel Natural Gas and Oil Co The, David Conrad pres, E G Huffman treas, J R Woodward secy
Lee Luther (Lee & Shetterly), h. Main
Lee & Shetterly (L Lee and O C Shetterly), grain & feed, cor Ave and C & S E Ry
Leggett Al, platserer
Leggett David, plasterer
Leggett John, plasterer
Lloyd Levi W, bartender, h. Wright's add
McCarthy John C, furniture & undertaking, Main, h. same
McCarthy J Charles, wagon mkr, Main, h. same
McKinsie Ed, plasterer
McKinster George T, hotel and restaurant, Main, h. same (see adv p. 140)
Mericle Edward J, veterinary surgeon, Main, h. Avenue
Miller Claude, lab
Mills Mrs Mahala, saloon, Avenue, h. Anderson, Ind
Montgomery R, painter

Deal & Willkie, We will write your Insurance in none but Standard Companies; All parties are treated alike, no cut-rates and no wildcat Insurance.
REAL ESTATE AND NOTARY PUBLICS.

J. P. CONDO & SON, FURNITURE, UNDERTAKERS and EMBALMERS, ESTABLISHED 1856. ALEXANDRIA, IND.

WHEN—YOUR MEASURE TAKEN, AND *SUITS OR OVERCOATS* MADE TO ORDER.

Estimates Furnished on Application. **ALEXANDRIA, IND.**

140 MADISON CO. DIRECTORY.

McKINSTER HOUSE,
GEORGE T. McKINSTER, Propr.

The only First-Class Hotel in the City.

SPECIAL ACCOMMODATIONS FOR THE TRAVELING PUBLIC. RESTAURANT ATTACHED.

MAIN STREET, LAPEL, IND.

W. Washington St.,

Moore J Rollin, physician and dentist, Main, h. same
Morris Isaac N, barber shop, Main, h. Pearl
Post Office, W H Walker, postmaster, cor Main and C & S E Ry
Rambo & Baker (E R Rambo & M A Baker), heading mfgrs, cor Avenue and C & S E Ry
Rambo Edwin R (Rambo & Baker), h. Pendleton Pike
Ray Frank, lab
Reddick W, teamster
Ridgway Solomon C, bartender, h. Railroad
Rubart Wm W, wagon mkr, Railroad
Russel James M, harness, Main
Russell P Wilson, agt C & S E, Adams Exp and W U Tel, h. Meridian
Ryan David, drayman
Ryan N, lab
Sears & Fisher (J W Sears and S E Fisher), blacksmiths, Main
Sears Jas W (Sears & Fisher), h. Main
Sears Wm, hostler
Shafer C, lab
Shetterly Oliver C (Lee & Shetterly), h. Main
Sinder Wm, saloon, Railroad, h. same
Snell John, grocer, also boarding, Main, h. same
Snider D, sect boss, C & S E Ry

Tinker Daniel A, livery, feed & sale stable, Railroad opp C & S E Station, h. Railroad (see adv)
Walker Sarah E, milliner and dressmkr, Main, h. same
Walker Wm H, P M, h. Maple
Walksletter Cris, harness mkr
Western UnionTelegraph Office, P W Russell mgr, cor Railroad and C & S E
Williams Isaac, carp
Williams James (Woodward Bros & Co), h. Avenue
Williams J R, saw mill
Wilson Geo, hostler, h. Walnut
Wilson Robert, carp
Woodward Arthur R, bookpr, h. Maple
Woodward Bros (James R and Wm Woodward), proprs Lapel Elevator & dealers in grain, cor Main & C & S E (see adv)
Woodward Bros & Co (M, J R and Wm Woodward and James Williams), saw and planing mill and lumber dealers,cor Main & C & S E
Woodward James R (Woodward Bros, also Woodward Bros & Co), h. Maple
Woodward Missouri (Woodward Bros & Co), h. Woodward
Woodward Wm (Woodward Bros, also Woodward Bros & Co), h. cor 2d and Woodward

JUNES & SHEFFIELD, PLUMBERS AND GAS FITTERS.

John L. Lindskoog, Fashionable MERCHANT TAILOR.
First-Class Work and Fit GUARANTEED.

H. H. H. Block, N. E. Cor. Church and Harrison, ALEXANDRIA, IND.

At the Mammoth New Livery Barn near Depot, Lapel, Ind.
Special Attention Given to Traveling Men,
opposite C. and S. E. Pass. Station, - - - - LAPEL, IND.

R. WOODWARD. WILL WOODWARD.

WOODWARD BROTHERS,
Proprietors LAPEL ELEVATOR, And Dealers in Grain,
Hard and Soft Wood Lumber, Lath, Shingles and Mill Work.
r. Main and C. & S. E. Ry. - - - - LAPEL, IND.

right George W (Conrad, Wright & Co), h. Main
right R C, lab

LEISURE, 21 miles north of Anderson and 6 north of Elwood, its banking and shipping point. Population, . A. L. Hiatt, P. M.
esler B F, blksmith

LINWOOD, a village in Lafayette Township, 6 miles north of Anderson on the C W R R. Population, 125. J. U. томаs, P. M.

den James H, wks saw mill
exander W E, timber dealer
ll Wm A, blacksmith
iristian Church, Thomas Stafford pastor
aig Minnie B
irling F, section foreman
nahoo Stephen E, teamster
scus Ferris, teamster
sher George, section hand
plinger Martha J, wid
plinger Nathan D, eng
rk Wm, farmer
Gill P M (Thomas & McGill)
Kee Charles M, teamster
y John C, school teacher
ynard Richard, teamster

Parker Joseph E
Parker Lydia A, wid
Patker Susan V
Pence Alexander, genl store
Pence Mary J, dressmkr
Pine Joseph, lab
Riggs Charles E, physician
Riggs Esom M, wks saw mill
Shaw James H, teamster
Shaw Samuel, carp
Simpson Harry, grain thresher
Stanley Joseph, carp
Stansberry David, lab
Stansberry Emma A
Taylor Sarah, wid
Thomas Alonzo, horseman
Thomas Hulda, wid
Thomas John U (Thomas & McGill), postmaster
Thomas & McGill genl store. P O
Thomas Martha
Thomas Samuel, wks saw mill
Van Dyke Wm W, blksmith
Williams Wm, carp

MARKLEVILLE, in Adams Township, is 11 miles southeast of Anderson, and is 7 miles southeast of Pendleton on the C C C & St L R R, its nearest shipping point. Population, 125. S. F. HARDY, P. M.
Aultman Manor, barber

Anderson Foundry and Machine Works, Manufacturers of Portable and Stationary
N. JACKSON STREET, Phone 53. Steam Engines.
ANDERSON, IND.

Is Your Property Insured? If not, CALL AT ONCE on **JACKSON & BURR,**
69½ N. Meridian, - - ANDERSON, IND.

142 MADISON CO. DIRECTORY.

Barrett B B, agt
Blake James, livery
Blake Martha, wid
Borain Loyal, farmer
Brofman C, lab
Chaphan John, teacher
Clevenger Charles, teacher
Cochran Wm, genl store
Collier Grant, farmer
Cooper Cynthia, wid
Craig Joseph, carp
Cranford Joseph, teamster
Crummins Wm, painter
Dunlap Alonzo, shoe mkr
Evans James, retired farmer
Evans John, retired farmer
Fattic A W, drugs
Forts Alonzo, blacksmith
Forts M, blacksmith
Frampton Charles, teacher
Fussell B L, physician
Greenlee Emma, milliner
Greenlae L G, shoe mkr
Hammer Cora
Hammer John, retired farmer
Hardy Charles M, student
Hardy S F, general store
Hardy W H, clk
Harlin Louis, teamster
Honnimer P L, teamster
Hudson Don, barber
Hunter Lincoln, lab
Huston Frank, saw mill
Huston Harry, carp
Huston James H, hotel
Huston John L, hostler
Huston Otho, mason
Jestes Charles, farmer
Johnson & Miller, saloon
Judd Chas, grocer
Judd John D, blksmith
Leaky A, clk
Lewis Eliza, wid
Lewis U A & Co, grain elevator
McCallister C A, butcher

McCormack J, lab
McCullough A L, carp
McCurdy Wm, harness mkr
McCurdy Wm Jr, lab
Manzy W S, teacher
Markle Betty, milliner
Markle Hannah, wid
Muterspan Wm, lab
Newman Wm, lab
Noland Samuel, retired farmer
Peele Orval, station agt
Peele W, agt C C C & St L Ry
Peters Mrs Mary, dressmkr
Petro B L, physician
Richardson John R, teacher
Rosenfield H P, clk
Senard Aaron, lab
Seward Loveless
Seward O H, teacher
Seward Wm, townp supervisor
Varner John
Walker L, butcher
Younkin John, hostler
Younkin Roscoe, carp

MYERS is situated 7 miles west of Anderson, the county seat and banking location. R. W. TAYLOR, P. M.

Ashby Isophene, wid
Ashton Jacob, farmer
Clark Alfred, farmer
Clauser Frank, farmer
Clauser John, farmer
Coy Henry, farmer
Davis James W, farmer
Davis John H, farmer
Doyle Charles, farmer
Doyle James, farmer
Funk Timothy
Holder Nathan, farmer
Hoosier Lemuel
Hoosier Peter, farmer
Hoosier Philip, farmer
Humes Lewis, farmer

George B. Epperson, Paints, Oils, Varnishes and Painters' Supplies.
39 E. 9th St., - - ANDERSON, IND.

Donnelly
10th Street,   -   ANDERSON, IND.

will sell your property, and insure quick returns. Place your business in his hands.

MADISON CO. DIRECTORY.   143

Plackard — DEALER IN —
Dry Goods, Notions, Boots and Shoes,
GROCERIES and HARDWARE,
o——Everything kept in a General Store.——o

ORESTES, INDIANA.

g Elias, farmer	French Charles, lab
sse, farmer	Jackson J L, lab
seph, farmer	Johnson James, carp
Wm, farmer	Johnson Joseph, lab
Moses, farmer	Johnson Wm, lab
amuel, farmer	Laycock M V, lab
Absolem, farmer	McDermott M, saw mill
Dow	McMahan J R, carp
George, farmer	McMahan Marshall, tel opr
c, farmer	McMahan S C, carp
Noah, farmer	McMahan S S, plumber
Wm, farmer	McMahan W S, carp
Jacob, farmer	Miller Henry, lab
sper, farmer	Moyer G W, cooper
bert W, postmaster	Osborn J J, blksmith
rocer	**Plackard E S**, general store and
John, farmer	and postmaster (see adv)
uel, farmer	Plackard M, merchant
	Plackard Thomas, carp
, a village in Monroe	Powell J M, brick and tile wks
ship, is 15 miles south	Richardson W E, blksmith
derson, on the C E &	Robinson J, grain dealer
nd 3 miles west of	Russell James, merchant
. Population, 100.	Shaw Wm, carp
car, carpenter	White John, lab
, barber	
3, druggist	**OVID**, a village in Adams
arles, drug clk	Township, 7 miles south of
), clk	Anderson, the nearest ship-
eon, lab	ping point. Population, 215.
K, poultry	Adams Amos, lab
m, lab	Ashby Benj, lab
, lab	Begley Hugh, stock
lva, lab	Brock Abraham, lab
rant, lab	Brock John, lab
George, carp	Carmany Wm & Son, carps
acob, lab	Clark Eph, mail carrier
les, lab	Clark Sam, lab

FRAMES of and prices at **Hugh Fisher's Novelty Works,**
10 N. Milton St.,   -   -   -   ANDERSON, IND.

J. T. Knowland & Son, Brass & Iron, Steam, Gas and Water Goods.
111 N. Main St., ANDERSON, IND. 'Phone 30.

144   MADISON. CO. DIRECTORY.

Clem Jacob, carp
Clem Phillip, farmer
Clem Sam, lab
Davis Jeff, plasterer
Dodge Wm, tailor
Forney Jacob, retired farmer
Forney John, farmer
Fort Charles, lab
Gray Charles, lab
Gray John, farmer
Gray Lewis, carp
Gray Sam, stock
Guinn H, lab
Jackson George, painter
Krall John L, farmer
Letten Wm, lab
McCray Joseph, carp
Moneyhun Isaac, merchant
Moneyhun J P, farmer
Muncy John, carp
Porter Irwin, poultry
Rumler Wm & Son, blksmith
Scott Wm, farmer
Stohler Frank, eng
Taylor Charles, teamster
Wood Charles, plumber
Wood John M, blksmith
Wood J E, house mover

DERKINSVILLE is situated 12 miles west of Anderson, the county seat and banking location. Population, 600. REUBEN NEESE, P. M.

Adair Wm, saw mill, h. Washington
Albright Mrs Alexander, wid, h. Water
Albright J. merchant, h. Water
Alexander Mrs Elizabeth, boarding, Washington, h. same
Alexander Louis, farmer, h. Washington
Applegate Jackson. h. Water

Applegate James B, druggist, h. Washington
Applegate Wm, h. Water
Armstrong F, h. Washington
Farrer Flora, h. Water
Farrer Sarah, wid, h. Water
Barnett Ida
Barnett Lydia, wid, h. Washington
Barnett Sarah, h. Washington
Bauner Jno, lab, h. Washington
Bauner George, blksmith, h. Washington
Beckley J, teamster, h. Mulberry
Beckley John, lab, h. Mulberry
Beckley Moses, lab, h. Mulberry
Branch Charles, U S mail carrier, h. Mulberry
Chatman Marion, lab
Chesney S, carp, h. Mulberry
Cole Mary, wid, h. Water
Cook Milton M, dentist, Washington, h. same
Cook Samantha, wid, h. Washington
Cooper Robert H, butcher, h. Mulberry
Copper Benj, barber
Davis A J, merchant, h. Water
Davis Elizabeth, general store, Water, h. same
Davis John M, clk, h. Water
Davis Laura M, clk, h. Water
Dean Thomas A (Dean & Willits), also genl blksmith, h. Water
Dean & Willits (T A Dean and H M Willits), druggists, stationers & fancy grocers, Meridian
Diven Charles E, physician, Washington, h. same
Downham Albert, teamster, h. Washington

John O. Miller, Dealer in WATCHES, CLOCKS & JEWELRY, SILVERWARE and OPTICAL GOODS.
3 N. Meridian,   -   -   -   ANDERSON, IND.

ers. Office and Warerooms,
ephones 189, 24 and 51.   No. 98 N. Main St., ANDERSON, IND.
OFFICE OPEN DAY AND NIGHT.

MADISON CO. DIRECTORY.   145

:AN & WILLITS, **D**RUGGISTS AND STATIONERS,
Meridian Street,   Dealers in Toilet Articles, Fancy
:RKINSVILLE, IND.   Groceries, Cigars, Tobacco, Wines, Liquors, etc.

wnhan Henry, lab, h. Washington
er Ida, wid, h. Water
glish Zapporah, wid, h. Washington
ıler Charles, h. Washington
ıler John, shoemkr & boarding, Washington, h. same
ıler Lousis, h. Washington
ıler Walter, h. Washington
rretson Mary, wid, h. Water
rretson Wm M, physician, Water, h. same
rrison Daisy M, h. Washington
rrison Nancy, wid, h. Washington
od Joseph, lab, h. Mulberry
ay Alvin, teamster, h. Washington
ıll Caleb, teamster, h. Water
ıyes J E, saloon and billiards
:nn Elvira, wid, h. Mulberry
:nn Oscar (Neese & Henn), h. Mulberry
ll Wm, fruit tree agt
nkle Charles, township trustee, h. Mulberry
)ugham John S, physician, Water, h. ¼ mile w town
ınson Reeves, h. Water
ınson Wm, h. Mulberry
ırtz J, carp, h. Washington
ırtz Samuel, h. Washington
ırtz Wm, h. Washington
ırtz Wm Jr, h. Washington
/nett Jennie, teacher, bds Washington

Lacy Rev Frank M, pastor M E Church, h. Washington
Lannes W, merchant, h. Washington
Lannes J, carp, h. Washington
Lee Jane, wid, h. Water
Lennis Wm, groceries & meats, cor Meridian and Washington, h. Washington
Leward Albert, h. Mulberry
Leward Robert L, brick mnfr, h. Mulberry
McClintock J, h Washington
McClintock Mrs Mary E, h. Water
Methodist Episcopal Church, Rev Frank M Lacy pastor, Mulberry
Miller Alonzo, h. Water
Miller Ellen, wid, h. Water
Miller Solomon, tmstr, h. Washington
Miller Wm, clk, h. Washington
Neese & Henn (R Neese, O Henn), genl store, Water
Neese J Emory, farmer, bds Washington
Neese Reuben (Neese & Henn), also P M, h. Washington
Neese Wm, carp, h. Washington
Neese Wm S, carp, h. Mulberry
Perkins Mrs James, wid, h. Water
Pogue J Milton, supt public school, h. Water
Rich George, lab
Rich Peter, lab, h. Mulberry
Roller John, lab, h. Water

WOOLLEY Foundry and Machine Works,
Designers and Manufacturers of Heavy Machinery, Engines, Boilers and Rolling Mill Work.
N. W Cor. 14th and C. W. and M. R. R.

WHEN — The Most Reliable CLOTHING House
✳ IN ANDERSON. ✳
PRICES ALWAYS THE LOWEST.

L. EDWARD ALEXANDER,
PHYSICIAN AND SURGEON,
Office over No. 1 Commercial Block E. State. - Res. E. S. Main, near State.

PENDLETON; IND.

Ryan John, feed and agrcl imp, Water, h. Washington
Schuyler Mfs Jacob, wid
Truitt James, h. Water
United Brethren Church, Washington
Wall Mrs Julia, dressmaker, Water, h. same
Whitehead John, lab, h. Washington
Whitehead Sarah, wid, h. Washington
Whitehead Thomas, h. Washington
Wier John, lab, h. Mulberry
Wier Jos, lab, h. Washington
Willits Horatio M (Dean & Willits), h. Water
Wyatt George W, clk
Young Nathan, h. Water
Young Thomas, h. Water
Zeller Jacob, h. Water
Zeller Matilda, wid, h. Water

ENDLETON is situated on the Big 4 R R; 8 miles from Anderson, the county seat, has e bank, W U Tel Office and nerican Express. Population, 00. CHARLES CADDY, P. M.

:na Insurance Co of Hartford, Goodrich & Burdette agts
ıan Andrew R, lab
ıan Benj F, grain, seed, etc
ıan Frederick B, clk
ıan Olive I
ıan Water H, clk
n E D, supt public school

Allen James S, carp
Alexander L Edward, physician and surgeon, 1 Commercial Blk, e State (up stairs), h. n Main
American Exp, L E Ireland agt
Anderson Josie
Atkins Elizabeth, wid
Bailey Leon O, treas The Pendleton G T & P Wks
Baker Andrew, glass wkr
Baker Charles E, lab
Baker James T, barber
Baker Lizzie M
Baker Melvina T, wid
Baker Wm A, eng
Banks Adam, glass wkr
Barrett Dave, farmer
Base David, gatherer
Beck Robert R, barber shop
Beck Sophia, wid
Bellette George, glass blower
Biser Adam, lab
Biser Dora I
Biser James M, lab
Biser Ripley E, lab
Bodakar Charles, glass blower
Bond Eli, farmer
Bond Jeremiah A, sect hand
Bond Sarah, wid
Boone Sarah J, wid
Boright A, glass wkr
Bowden Lillie E
Bowsman Benj F, millwright
Bowsman Harry O, millwright
Bowsman Mary E
Branson T Swain (Swain, Branson & Co)

sure with **ROOP & HAYNES,**
IN THE STANDARD COMPANIES THEY REPRESENT.
; S. Anderson, - - - - - - ELWOOD, IND.

)inson & Glassco, Real Estate, Loans and Insurance. Building and Loan money procured in 15 days.
m 9 "When" Building, - ANDERSON, IND.

ain Mort, lab
gh Mary, wid
/n Charles, glass wkr
/n David M, real estate
/n Eva, trimmer
/n Isaac S, box mkr
/n John, blksmith
vn Laura R, teacher
vn Mary, wid
vn Nellie
vn Samuel, glass wkr
vn Water, glass wkr
vn W E (Taylor & Brown)
vnbeck F, wood carver
vnbeck Mrs F M, wid
vnbeck Orlando W, physician, secy and genl mgr The Pendleton N G Co, Illinois ave
int George, lab
int Sarah, wid
int Wm C, blksmith
George, gatherer
dy Kate L, domestic
dette Wm C (Goodrich & Burdette), bds s Tariff
dsall John W, glass cutter
ns Thomas E, millwright
nette Saristine, teaser
dy Charles, postmaster, h. n w cor State and John
dy Mrs Mary E, asst P M
n Joseph W, carpet weaver
lihan Patrick, lab
npbell Edwin W, news agt
npbell Geo W, grocer and news dealer
roll Abraham
ter Chester G, carp
ter Wm M, carp
e Arthur H, lab
e John N, comp
/ell John, glass blower
itral Union Telephone Co

Chaming Wm S, physician and surgeon
Chapman Eliza, wid
Chapman Erastus O
Chapman Melvin, carp
Chapman Wm, carp
Clark Albert J, clk
Clark Charles, lab
Clark Daaid S, boarding
Clark Edward J, lab
Clark Harry O, clk
Clark Mary E, wid
Clark Reuben, gatherer
Clark Walter S, glass cutter
Cleveland, Cincinnati, Chicago & St Louis Pass and Fgt Station, L E Ireland agt
Cliff Charles M, glass wkr
Cliff Samuel H, glass blower
Cocayne Benj, wagon mkr
Cocayne Mary E, teacher
Coffman F A, trav sales
Coffman John P, stone quarries
Coffman Samuel L
Cole David B, candy mkr
Cole George W, mnfr confectr, also grocer
Cole Inez V, stenographer
Cole Wellington, merchant
Collins Newton, carp
Collis Enos W, jeweler
Commercial Hotel, Elijah Munsey propr
Cook A W, township trustee
Cook Harlie E, drug clk
Cook John W, physician and surgeon
Cook Margaret wid
Cook Morton, lab
Cook Ossian H, physician and surgeon
Cook Ward
Copper Ezra W flatner
Copper John, carp
Cottrell John H, lab

:al & Willkie, have placed 85 loans in six months, Farm loans at 6%. All parties desiring to secure loans
WILL SAVE MONEY BY CALLING ON US.

WHEN—The Only Retail Clothiers
In the State of Indiana
That Manufacture their OWN CLOTHING.

148   MADISON CO. DIRECTORY.

→ **H. B. CRAVEN,** ←
—DEALER IN—
Drugs, Medicines, Chemicals, Toilet Articles,
Soap, Perfumes, Patent Medicines, etc.
East State Street.   **CIGARS.**   PENDLETON, IND.

Cottrell Nancy, wid
Cottrell Thomas, carp
Cox Russell, glass cutter
Crabs John, glass cutter
Crabs John Jr, glass wkr
Crady John H, lab
Crady Thomas, teamster
Cratty D B, secy Ind W G Co
Craven Alice A
Craven Harvey B, druggist and stationer, e State, h. s Tariff (see adv)
Craven Jessie F
Craven Leah, wid
Crosley Corydon W, hostler
Crosley D Webster, lab
Crosley E B (Crosley & Thrall)
Crosley Mary, wid
Crosley & Thrall (E B Crosley & G G Thrall), grocers
Crosley Wm H, lab
Crosley W F, mgr P R M Co
Crouse Mary, wid
Culp John H
Culp Walter, gatherer
Cummins Eldon, lab
Dagrave Arthur, gatherer
Dagrave Gaspard, glass blower
Danes George, blksmith
Davenport Emma, wid
Davis Alice
Davis Lydia A, wid
Davis M Lizzie
Davis Stephen A, glass wkr
Delph Lafayette, well driller
Deming Harry, glass wkr
Deming House, S J Deming propr
Dennis Joseph M, glass wkr

Detraz Bros (E R, Frank and C A Detraz), planing mill and lumber dealers
Detraz C A (Detraz Bros)
Detraz Eugene R (Detraz Bros)
Detraz Frank (Detraz Bros)
Dickinson C, glass wkr
Dickinson Louis, glass wkr
Dickinson Thomas D, carp
Drake George S, watch mkr
Ellington Chalmus G, glass wkr
Eminger Conrad
Eminger C Harry, blksmith
Eminger Ira D, blksmith
Eminger Wm D, novelty store
Fanning Joseph T, secy The Pendleton G T & P Wks
Fate Henry, baker
Felix Peter, glass wkr
Fireman's Fund Ins Co, of California, Goodrich & Burford Mrs Rena, housekeeper
Ford Frank O, teacher
Foust Henry, glass wkr
Fox Alfred E, glass blower
Fox David, glass blower
Frampton Anna M
Frampton Sarah B, wid
Frampton Wm C, wagon mkr
Franck George, glass blower
Franck Phillip, glass blower
Frank Bruce, bartender
Franklin Coral E, druggist and stationer, paints and oils
French Elizabeth, wid
Fussell Charles R, livery, feed and sale stable
Fuqua Anna M, wid

John L. Lindskoog, The Leading Tailor of Alexandria. All the Latest Novelties in Suitings and Trouserings.
H. H. H. Block, N. E. Cor. Church and Harrison, ALEXANDRIA, IND.

M. J. DOVE — Can give you choice in 20 of the oldest and best Insurance Companies represented. Note this fact when placing your insurance.
NEELEY BLOCK. 61½ N. Meridian, ANDERSON, IND.

MADISON CO. DIRECTORY. 149

GOODRICH & BURDETTE,

REAL ESTATE DEALERS,

Insurance and Collecting Agents,

E. State Street, opposite Post-Office,

PENDLETON, IND.

---

bler Louis, lehrsman
bler Valentine, glass wkr
llagher Frank J, bartender
rretson Mary A, wid
spard Frank, gatherer
orge Cora D
orge Julia A, boarding
orge Matthew, teamster
orge Nancy, wid
orge Wm, carp
orge Wm, bartender
ermania Fire Ins Co, of N Y, Goodrich & Burdette agts
bbons Kate, wid
bbons Nellie M
lathart Frederick, saloon
lathart Jno A W, stone mason
oe Edgar H, glass flatner
odrich & Burdette (C E Goodrich & W C Burdette), real estate and ins, e State opp postoffice (see adv)
odrich CharlesE (Goodrich & Burdette), h. 2 miles w city
oodrich Lulu M, clk
oul George, miller
oul Henry, lab
raul George W, glass wkr
riffith M Anna, dressmkr
riffith M Lora, dressmkr
riffith Wm, glass wkr

Guptill Robert G, genl mgr The Pendleton G T & P Wks
Hair Addah B
Hair Charles L (The M A Teague Map Co)
Hair Emma
Hair Stephenson, drayman
Hallowell Edward E (Hallowell & Sons)
Hallowell G (Hallowell & Sons)
Hallowell Kirk M (Hallowell & Sons)
Hallowell & Sons (G, E E & K M Hallowell), meat market
Handley Albert E, painter
Harden Oscar
Hardman James W
Hardman W Frank, snapper
Hardy C Sumner, glass wkr
Hardy Thomas M (Pendleton Banking Co)
Harper Charles W, tel opr
Harris E L
Haupt Lizzie, wid
Hayes Edith, domestic
Headley George, mgr Indiana W G Co
Hedrick Charles W, glass wkr
Helim Mrs, wid
Henderson J Oscar, pres The Pendleton G T & P Wks
Henry Jules, glass blower

LARMORE BROS. 513 Nichol Avenue, ANDERSON, IND. Telephone 220. Will deliver you any place in the city, and guarantee first-class goods. **ICE CREAM, OYSTERS AND MILK**

Anderson Foundry and Machine Works, Manufacturers of BOILERS, Steam Heaters, Castings, and General Machinery.
165 N. JACKSON STREET, 'Phone 53. ANDERSON, IND.

Jackson & Burr Represent the Largest Lines and the Strongest INSURANCE Companies.
69½ N. Meridian, - - - ANDERSON, IND.

150 MADISON CO. DIRECTORY.

M. L. JORDAN,
Hardware, Stoves, Cutlery and Tinware
GAS FIXTURES, HUNTERS' SUPPLIES;
Room No. 3 Union Block, - - - PENDLETON, IND.

Hite Henry, saw mill
Hite Jesse, bartender
Hoffman Henry, glass blower
Home Ins Co, of New York,
  Goodrich & Burdette agts
Hoopes J M (Thrall & Hoopes)
Huff Edward N, carp
Huff J Warner, teamster
Hull Jessie, domestic
Hunt H F, princ High School
Hunter Samuel, gatherer
I O O F Hall, e State
Indiana Window Glass Co, F B
  Wilkinson pres and treas,
  D B Cratty secy, George
  Headley mgr
Insurance Co of North America,
  Goodrich & Burdette agts
Ireland Albert S, harness mkr
Ireland Alonzo E, agt C C C &
  St L and American Exp
Ireland Anna P
Ireland Benj A, plumber
Ireland David A
Ireland Edward R, clk
Ireland Mrs Fannie L, opr, C C
  C & St L R R
Ireland George A, harness
Ireland Harry L, tinner
Ireland John L, blksmith
Ireland Joseph O
Ireland L E, agt Big 4 R R
Ireland Walter T, glass wkr
Irish Ira, farmer
Irish Sarah F, wid
Jackson Cassius C (Jackson & Jackson)
Jackson Frank P (Jackson & Jackson)

Jackson Griffith
Jackson & Jackson (F P & C C Jackson), grocers & bakers
Jackson O Wm, teacher
Jackson Samuel, teamster
Janney N Chapline
Janney Jonas
Jewell W S, v-pres The Pendleton G T & P Wks
Johnston John D, shoemkr
Jones Bros (G H & J P Jones), grocers
Jones Edward, gatherer
Jones Emma J, wid
Jones George H (Jones Bros)
Jones Jane, wid
Jones John P (Jones Bros)
Jones Kate
Jordan Henry, clk
Jordan Melvin L, hardware, stoves, tinware, etc, rm 3, Union Blk, e State (see adv)
Kahle Harry F, secy and mgr The Pendleton W G Co
Kahle Samuel
Kaufelt Harry, master teaser
Keesling Cornelius B, furniture and undertaker
Keilholz Julia
Kellum John M, photographer
King Louis, painter
Kirkman Elisha
Klarr Jacob, barber
Kline Joseph, glass wkr
Knight George, glass wkr
Knight Richard, glass blower
Knight Ruth E
Knight Thomas, glass blower
K of P Hall, e State

George B. Epperson, Contractor & Builder of Concrete Side Walks.
39 E. 9th St., - - ANDERSON, IND.

Real Estate Exchange — does a general Real Estate business. The finest lots in the world for sale or trade at our office.
10 East 10th Street, - ANDERSON, IND.

W. H. LEWIS.   H. F. LEWIS.

✢ LEWIS ✢ BROS., ✢

—AND DEALERS IN— DRUGGISTS,   No. 5 Commercial Block, E. State Street.

Books, Stationery, Wall Paper, Paints, Notions, Etc.   PENDLETON, IND.

Konegar Leonard, glass wkr
Kuhns Arabella
Kuhns John
Kulp John W, glass blower
Kuntz Henry, farmer
Lackey Otto, saloon
Lackey Sarah, wid
Laing Fannie, wid
Lay Jacob Jr
Levering Charles, section hand
Lewark Amy E
Lewark Clara E
Lewark John W, horse breeder
Lewis Albert G, farmer
Lewis Bros (W H and H F Lewis), druggists, books, stationery, wall paper, etc, 5 Commercial Blk, e State (see adv)
Lewis Eliza A
Lewis Eugene J, carriage pntr
Lewis Horace F (Lewis Bros)
Lewis John J, well driller
Lewis Joseph W
Lewis Lydia A, wid
Lewis M Martha, wid
Lewis Nathan, carp
Lewis Thomas, glass wkr
Lewis Walter H (Lewis Bros)
Liggs Edith, wid
Lois Clinton, gatherer
Long Ross O, merchant
Longenecker Geo P, shoemkr
Longtof Wm, gatherer
Loy George lab
Loy Jacob
Lukens Mary L, wid
Lukens Wm I, teamster
McCabe Edith B
McCabe Emma J
McCabe Rebecca, wid
McCabe Theodore, lab
McCarty Alonzo, painter
McCarty Howard C, comp
McCarty Samuel A, restaurant
McCoy Rev Jasper I, pastor M E Church, h. s e cor West and High
McGriff Wm, painter
McIntire L Mattie
McIntire Robert E, gatherer
McKee Samuel, policeman
McShane Mrs Flora M
McSane Lawrence E, comp
Madden Barney, glass wkr
Madison Lodge No 44, F & A M, e State
Manifold Eddy R, clk
Manifold Martha A, wid
Manning John C, atty-at-law
Mannon Elijah, baker
Mannon Fulton, baker
Mannon Wm T
Martin Herbert, glass wkr
Masonic Hall, e State
Maul Corry, glass wkr
Maul George K, brick layer
Methodist Episcopal Church
Middlehurst Edward, gatherer
Middlehurst Geo, glass blower
Middlehurst Thos, glass blower
Mingle Albert, glass wkr
Mingle Henry W, saloon
Mingle Jane
Mingle Wm H, glass wkr
Mitchell Thompson G

Hugh Fisher's Novelty Works | Jig and Scroll Saw Work in all the latest designs and patterns. Call and examine my work.
198 and 200 N. Milton St., ✢ ANDERSON IND. ✢

Buck, Brickley & Co., Anderson, Ind. — THE LEADING FINE WALL PAPER AND DECORATIONS DRUGGISTS.

J. T. Knowland & Son, MAKERS AND DESIGNERS OF **NATURAL GAS Fixtures and Fittings.**
111 N. Main St., ANDERSON, IND. 'Phone 30.

MADISON CO. DIRECTORY.

Morris Aaron (Pendleton Banking Co)
Morris Wm F, asst cashier Pendleton Banking Co
Morton Adeline
Moulden Harry, painter
Moulden Susan, wid
Mourey E, Commercial Hotel
Mullica Thomas, flatner
Mullica Wm S, flatner
Murphy Robert A, glass wkr
Neibreacht Chas H, barber shop
Nicklous Wm, glass wkr
Nicholson George B, painter
Noble Charles, glass blower
Noble Minnie
North British & Mercantile Ins Co, of England, Goodrich & Burdette agts
Oldham A W (Oldham & Co)
Oldham & Co (A W, G A and F T Oldham), meat market
Oldham F T (Oldham & Co)
Oldham G A (Oldham & Co)
Oldham Joseph, butcher
Parker Samuel, gatherer
Parsons Sarah, wid
Patterson Bessie
Patterson John, plasterer
Patterson J T, merchant tailor
Patterson Lillie F
Patterson Mollie A
Patterson Reuben, wood turner
Pavey Bertha M
Pavey Dawie J, lab
Pavy George W
Pavy Nannie
Pendleton Banking Co (E P Rogers, T M Hardy and A Morris)
Pendleton Glass, Tube & Pipe Wks The, J O Henderson pres, W S Jewell v-pres, J T Fanning secy, L O Bailey treas, R G Guptill genl mgr
Pendleton Loan Association The, W H Lewis pres, W E Brown secy, W F Morris treas
Pendleton Natural Gas Co, B F Aiman pres, G W Campbell treas, O W Brownback secy
Pendleton Republican The, Joe N Taylor editor and propr, e State (see adv)
Pendleton Roller Mill Co, W F Crosley mgr
Pendleton Social Club, W F Morris secy
Pendleton Window Glass Co The, G A Phipps pres, B F Aiman v-pres, H F Kahle secy and mgr, E P Rogers treas
Pense Newton F, druggist
Pettigrew Jesse, plasterer
Pettigrew Oliver, plasterer
Phipps Geo A, pres The Pendleton W G Co
Phœnix Fire Ins Co of Brooklyn, Goodrich & Burdette agents
Phœnix Fire Ins Co of Hartford, Goodrich & Burdette agts
Post Office, Charles Caddy P M, e State
Price George H, lab
Public School, E D Allen supt
Pyke Elizabeth, wid
Pyke Fannie C
Pyke Lulu M
Randolph George, gatherer
Rhinehamer Cyrus L, lab
Rhinehamer Wm, watchman
Riffle Albert, section boss
Rinewalt Emma A
Rinewalt Isaac P, shoemaker
Roberts Catherine C, wid
Roberts Howard, ins agt
Rockenfield Mrs Deborah, wid

JOHN O. MILLER'S For FINE WATCH REPAIRING and DIAMOND SETTING.
N. Meridian, - - - ANDERSON, IND.

J. A. Munchhof, LEADING FURNITURE DEALER, Nos. 40 and 42 E. 8th St., ANDERSON, IND. Largest Stock to select from, and always the lowest CASH PRICES. Watch our show windows.

MADISON CO. DIRECTORY. 153

→❦G. W. STURM,❧←
DEALER IN ALL KINDS OF
Agricultural Implements, Wagons and Buggies.
A FULL STOCK ALWAYS ON HAND.
N. Tariff Street, - - PENDLETON, IND.

Rodnam John, glass wkr
Rogers Benjamin
Rogers Elijah P (Pendleton Bnkg Co), treas The Pendleton W Glass Co
Rogers J J (Rogers & Thomas)
Rogers Joseph M, carp
Rogers Lizzie S, wid
Rogers Mame
Rogers Reba W, physician
Rogers & Thomas (J J Rogers & S F Thomas), genl store
Rolen Thomas R, carp
Royal Insurance Co of England, Goodrich & Burdette
Sablon Francis, glass wkr
Savage Charles A, carp
Savage Henson H, stone mason
Schneider Carl, glass cutter
Scott Carrie, milliner
Scott Rebecca, wid
Seelbach L, glass blower
Seward Alonzo, lab
Sexton John R, city marshal
Shad George, snapper
Sharp Barney, well driller
Shepherd Isaac N, glass blower
Shield John Jr, glass wkr
Shield John Sr, glass wkr
Sicilian Lodge No 234, K of P, meets Tuesday night
Siffrin Joseph, glass wkr
Silver Arthur, clk
Silver Charles H, carp
Silver H L (J R Silver & Son)
Silver J R (J R Silver & Son)
Silver John F, stone mason
Silver J R & Son (J R & H L Silver), dry goods, &c
Silver Wm G, lab
Slight Joseph, gatherer
Smethers James H, well driller
Smethers Linnie B
Smith Hiram, lab
Smith Watson, carp
Smithwait Asa, lab
Spear Jesse, del clk
Spear Joel, lab
Springfield F & M Ins Co, Goodrich & Burdette agts
Staggs John C, carp
Steele James, gatherer
Stephenson Bertha J
Stephenson Essie
Stephenson Josephine, wid
Stewart Wm T, glass blower
Stidham Joseph E, carp
Stone Frank L, physician
Sturm George W, agricultural implements, wagons, carriages, n Tariff, h. w State (see adv)
Swain, Branson & Co (E H & E B Swain and T S Branson), hardware
Swain Elwood B (Swain, Branson & Co)
Swain E Howard (Swain, Branson & Co)
Taylor Albert B, grain and feed
Taylor & Brown (J B Taylor & W E Brown), lumber
Taylor Jacob C, stock dealer
Taylor J B (Taylor & Brown)
Taylor Jesse E, ice dealer
Taylor Joe N, editor and propr The Pendleton Republican, h. cor Taylor and Franklin

J. S. STUART, THE FLORIST, Wholesale and Retail Plants, Bulbs, and Cut Flowers, 99 to 111 W. 3d, ANDERSON, IND. Telephone 73.

WOOLLEY Foundry and Machine Works, General Machinery, Heavy and Light Castings, and Sheet Iron Work.
N. W. COR. 14th AND C W. AND M. R. R.

WHEN — The Largest Stock of CLOTHING, HATS, CAPS and Gents' FURNISHING GOODS in ANDERSON.

THOMAS G. WELCH,
BARBER SHOP, Dealer in CIGARS AND TOBACCO,
E. State Street, Opposite Masonic Hall,
PENDLETON, IND.

Taylor John R
Taylor John W, mgr Todd & Co
Taylor Louisa A, wid
Taylor Melvina M, wid
Taylor M Ward, clk
Taylor Samuel
Taylor W Grant, farmer
Teague Augustus H
Teague Ercie A, tel opr
Teague Harry B, clk
Teague Martin A, mchnt tailor
Teague Merrill A (The M A Teague Map Co)
Teague Mettie
Teague The M A Map Co (M A Teague and C L Hair)
Teague Wm
Teague Wm A, glass wkr
Teague Wm T, tailor
Teeters Charles, glass wkr
Thomas Oliver H, dentist
Thomas R Frank, clk
Thomas S F (Rogers & Thomas)
Thompson Kate B, teacher
Thrall G G (Crosley & Thrall)
Thrall & Hoopes (L H Thrall & J M Hoopes), shoes
Thrall Lincoln H (Thrall & own John H, glass cutter
Todd J & Co, J W Taylor mgr, dry goods, notions, etc
Todd Miles, merchant
Truitt Wm E, clk
Tyler Frank S
Underwriters' Ins Co, of N Y, Goodrich & Burdette agts
Universalist Church, cor Main and Water
Van Aman Ella M
Van Aman Geo B, glass cutter
Van Aman Wm L, glass cutter
Walker Charles
Walker Edward, hostler
Walker Hervey, lab
Walker John, stone mason
Walker Nettie
Walters John, glass blower
Walter Wm, livery stable
Watson Mrs Casandra, wid
Weiford Jacob, carp
Weile Godfrey
Welch Mrs Sarah, milliner
Welch Thomas G, barber shop, cigars and tobacco, e State opp Masonic Hall, h. s Main (see adv)
Western Ins Co, of Toronto, Goodrich & Burdette agts
White B, brick and tile mnfr
White Frank, well driller
White Hannah, wid
White Robert, watchman
White Wilson, lab
Whitford Wm, clk
Whitley E D, lime, cement, etc
Widener Robert S, drayman
Wildridge Ralph, clk
Wilkinson Frank B, pres Indiana W G Co
Williams Charles, flatner
Williams Eliza, wid
Williams Florence, dressmkr
Williams Frederick C, flatner
Williams John D, glass wkr
Williams Robert B, carp
Windell James B, painter

Oop & Haynes
Are Agents for FIVE of the BEST BUILDING & LOAN COMPANIES in Indiana.

9½ S. Anderson, - - - - ELWOOD, IND.

To Buy or Sell Real Estate, To procure money to build with promptly, for Insurance or Loans, Call on **Robinson & Glassco,** Room 9 "When" Building, ANDERSON, IND.

MADISON CO. DIRECTORY. 155

L. F. BEAR,
Satisfaction Guaranteed to Patrons.
SUMMITVILLE, IND.

NEW LIVERY STABLE.
Neat Rigs, Good Horses, and Reasonable Price.

Windell John A, physician
Windell Volney C, clk
Windell Thomas
Wiseman Jessie
Witmer M Bell, wid
Wittebort Arthur, snapper
Wittebort Emil, glass blower
Wittebort John B, glass blower
Wood Cornelius, glass wkr
Wood Esther, wid
Woods Joseph, lab
Woolverton David, brick layer
Worrall Izella B, milliner
Wynant Wm G, trav sales
Wynn Mary A, wid

SUMMITVILLE, in Van Buren Township, 18 miles north of Anderson, nearest bank, Fairmount, U S Express, W U Tel. Population, 1,000.

Abdon Albert, saloon
Abraham Isaac, tailor
Abraham Jacob, merchant tailor
Adams Erse P
Albright Rev P G, pastor M E Church
Allen Emma F
Allen Jesse, head sawyer
Allen Joseph A, farmer
Allen Joseph O, cashier Summitville Bank, and treas Summitville Brick Co, h. s Main
Allen Willard, lab
Andrews Silas
Athan Oscar
Ball & Ochiltree (R E Ball & T F Ochiltree), grocery

Ball R E (Ball & Ochiltree)
Barton Albert, engineer
Barton Frederick, lab
Barton George, lab
Barton George, brick mason
Barton Henry O, city marshal
Barton John, lab
Barton Marshall, brick mason
Barton Minnie
Bear Litel F, livery, feed and sale stable, e s s Main, h. same (see adv)
Beck Joseph, glass wkr
Beeson Frank, lab
Beeson Joseph, clk
Beeson Wm G, bartender
Beeson Wm S, attorney-at-law
Black Enoch E, hardware
Black Samuel G, clk
Blose Mary, wid
Blose Mahlon, trav sales
Boes Charles E
Bookout Charles A, real estate
Bookout John F, painter
Bookout Wm, clk
Bowers Wm J
Brady Eliza, wid
Brown Frank drug clk
Brown Henry
Burns Louis, lab
Burnwell John, painter
Burnwell Otto F, painter
Calloway Wm (Calloway & Co
Caplinger Charles A
Caplinger Emma J
Carr Frank
Carr Harvey
Cartwright Arden, carp

J. P. CONDO & SON, The oldest FURNITURE dealers and UNDERTAKERS in the County. ESTABLISHED 1856. ALEXANDRIA, IND.

Herman F. Willkie, J. P.
COLLECTIONS PROMPTLY MADE.

WHEN — Children's Department
A SPECIAL FEATURE.
Always well Stocked with the **LATEST NOVELTIES.**

156   MADISON CO., DIRECTORY.

W. C. FEAR & CO. LUMBER AND FENCE.
Frame Stuff and Fence a Specialty.
SUMMITVILLE, IND.
WRITE US FOR PRICES.

Central Lamp Co The, C A Sieglen & Co proprs
Chapman Charles C, lab
Charles F Williams (Williams & Swallow)
Christian Church, Rev Harry I Riggs pastor, e Walnut
Christopher Charles, lab
Christopher Edward
Christopher Thomas, lab
Clark Benj H, section foreman
Clark Henry, saloon
Clark James, harness mkr
Clark Maggie
Clark Thomas J, physician
Clark Wm H, bartender
Coffin James D, carp
Coffman Pratt S, plumber
Collins Effie, domestic
Connily W, boot & shoe repairng
Conody Wm, shoemkr
Continous Tank Glass Factory, J B Rhodes & Co proprs
Cook Minerva, wid
Cowgills Samuel C, propr D T Wks, also v-pres Summitville Brick Co
Craig Moses
Cran Commodore
Cranfield Luther
Crowell Henry (Crowell & Plackard)
Crowell & Plackard (H Crowell and J. Plackard), furniture
Curr Herbert, carp
Curr Sarah J, wid
Custer Wm, blacksmith
Davis Andrew J (Davis & Son)
Davis & Son (A J and T B), stoves and tinware
Davis T B (Davis & Son)
Davis Sadie
Dawdy James, photographer
Dickey Miles A, tile mkr
Diltz Carrie, lab
Diltz John T, clk
Duncan Harvey B
Duncan Lemuel S
Duncan Mary A, wid
Dunlap John
Dunlap Noah
Edwards Wm F, lawyer
Elkworth John D, lab
Elkworth John, lab
Ellis Charles D, plasterer
Etchison Charles, lab
Farmer Benson, eng
Farmer Frank M, lime, cement
Farmer Greenburg, lab
Farmer James, lab
Farmer Nancy, wid
Faucett R D, druggist & paint
Faucett Wm, farmer
Fear & Co (Wm C and John P Fear), lumber and fence mnfrs, w s s Main (see adv)
Fear George P, teamster
Fear John P, real estate, loan, insurance & notary public, also Fear & Co, w s s Main, h. Monroe Township
Fear Wm C (Fear & Co); h. w s Main
Felton James, restaurant
Fennimore Matthews, eng
Fesler Charles, livery

John L. Lindskoog,
Fine Tailoring in Suits and Pants. An examination solicited. A FIT GUARANTEED.
H. H. H. Block, N. E. Cor. Church and Harrison, ALEXANDRIA, IND.

M. J. DOVE
NEELEY BLOCK.   61½ N. Meridian, ANDERSON, IND.

Is Agent for National Home Building and Loan Ass'n of Bloomington, Ill You can get all the money you want on short notice

MADISON CO. DIRECTORY.   157

. M. Hundley, ATTORNEY AT LAW,
Insurance, Real Estate, Loans and Collections given Special Attention.
SUMMITVILLE, IND.

sler Wm G, livery
ght James, carp
nney Alonzo, lab
ame Louis, lab
ilton J F (Gordan & Fulton)
)ble James, lab
)bel John, lab
ırdan **John N** (Gordan & Fulton), also postmaster, h. e Walnut
)rdan & Fulton, grain elevator
)ssett Wm (Love & Gossett)
reen Geo Jr (Painter & Co)
reenawalt Clyde, tailoress
reenawalt Sarah, wid
riffee Oliver, saloon
rubb Lulu C, milliner
annon Elizabeth
annon James, bartender
annon Mary, dressmkr
arris Catherine, wid
azelbaker Samuel, lab
endricks Martin, plasterer
endrickson Emily, wid
endrickson Wm C, restaurant
:inton Joseph S, farmer
:inton Martin, lab
[olmes Frank, lab
[oppes George, lab
[oppes Wm, lab
[oward Homer, student
[oward James, teamster
[oward John J (Painter & Co)
[oward Margaret J, wid
[oward Mary, canvasser
[oward Robert C, supt Summitville Co
[oward Wm (Howard Bros)

Howard Wm A (Painter & Co)
Hundley James M, attorney-at-law, insurance, real estate and loans, e s s Main, h. Van Buren Tp (see adv)
Hundley Jane, wid
Ice Ransom, bartender
Irvin Wm, lab
Jackson Lee, jeweler
Johnson Dora, wid
Johnson Elijah, carp
Johnson Emma, wid
Johnson Isabelle
Judd Frank, baker
Kaufman A R, school teacher
Kaufman Andrew F (A F Kaufman & Co)
Kaufman A F & Co (A F and Pratt Kaufman and Frank Safford), plumbing
Kaufman J M, school teacher
Kaufman Judson, saloon
Kaufman Pratt (A F Kaufman & Co)
King James, harness mkr
King Stephen. harness mkr
Kinley C C, buggies & harness (see adv p 158)
Lamb Jesse T, lab
Leegarde John C, druggist
Louiso Edward W, propr Park Place Hotel
Louiso George P, editor Summitville Wave
Louis J Paul, canvassing agt
Love & Gossett (J Vincent Love and Wm Gossett), grocery and meat market

Anderson Foundry and Machine Works, REPAIRS and Job Work of all Kinds
'PHONE 53.   A SPECIALTY.
265 N. Jackson Street, - - - ANDERSON, IND.

TELEPHONE LARMORE BROS:
518 Nichol Ave., ANDERSON, IND.
TELEPHONE 220.
for your ICE CREAM, MILK AND OYSTERS, and be sure of prompt delivery and first-class goods.

INSURE WITH **JACKSON & BURR.** Latch string always out and light in the window, until the last man's **INSURED.**
69½ N. Meridian, - - ANDERSON, IND.

C. C. KINLEY,

DEALER IN *Buggies, Carts and Carriages,* ALSO A FULL LINE

HARNESS, ROBES AND WHIPS,

East Side Main, South of Mill, - - - - SUMMITVILLE, IND.

Love Vincent (Love & Gossett)
Lumber and Fence Factory, W
 C Fear & Co proprs; s e cor
 Mill and C C C & St L
McCaslin James, teamster
McCoy David, lab
McCune Jasper, lab
McFarland Robert H, hostler
McLaughlin Catherine, wid
McMahon Thomas, tel opr
McNabney Wm J, genl store
 and harness shop
McNabney Wm L, clk
Marshall George, farmer
Marshall Mrs Sarah J, milliner
Maynard Sophia, wid
Maynard Wm, lab
Menifee Reuben, druggist and stationery
Methodist Episcopal Church, P J Albright pstr, e Walnut
Miles Margaret, millinery
Miles Peter W, horseman
Miller George, lab
Miller Wm H, lab
Mohler John C, clk
Mohler Lewis
Monahan Winnie, domestic
Moore Aquilla
Moore Elda I
Moore George W, agent
Moore James K, lab
Morris Alonzo, tile wkr
Morris Ernest, lab
Morris Frank, tile wkr
Morris Wm, carp
Morrison Andrew M, brick mkr
Musick Betsy, wid

Myrick Louis, trav sales
Nation Charles E, atty-at-law
Nelson Charles, lab
Nichols George, plasterer
Nichols Hosea, canvassing agt
Ochiltree T F (Ochiltree & Boll)
Odle James, lab
Olden Wm, lab
Oldfield George, teamster
Oldfield John A, teamster
Oldfield Irain, lab
Paden Catherine M
Painter Eleanor A
Painter Elvestsa D, wid
Painter Geo A (Painter & Co)
Painter Marietta L
Park Place Hotel, Ed W Louiso
Paxson Henry C, plasterer
Payne Albert W, lumber dealer
Peper George P, drayman
Plackard B F (Plackard & Son)
Plackard C F (Plackard & Son)
Plackard Electa
Plackard Elizabeth, milliner
Plackard J (Crowell & Plackard
Plackard Lulu
Plackard & Son (Benj F and Charles F), planing mill
Powley Vern, straw dealer
Price Charles, lab
Price James, carp
Price Monroe, lab
Price Thomas, lab
Price Wm, lab
Pugh Robert A, saloon
Pyle John, blacksmith
Ratliff Sarah, wid
Ray Albert, lab

George B. Epperson, Carriage Paints and Varnishes A Specialty.

19 E. 9th St., - - - - ANDERSON, IND.

Donnelly & Komenger, **BARN.**
48 West 9th St. Telephone 76. ANDERSON, IND.
Fine Horses and Buggies always on hand, at reasonable prices. Driver furnished when required. Also office at John Donnelly's Real Estate Office, 10 E. 10th St. Tel. 166.

MADISON CO. DIRECTORY. 159

SUMMITVILLE BANK,
J. O. ALLEN, CASHIER,

STOCKHOLDERS:
- JAMES JOHNSON, Upland.
- Dr. A. HENLEY, } Fairmount.
- LEVI SCOTT,
- J. A. J. BRUNT, Anderson.
- J. O. ALLEN, Summitville.

Redding Alvin W, lab
Redding John, teamster
Reed Betsy, wid
Rhodes J & B (Rhodes & Co)
Ribelin Jasper, lab
Richardson Lewis, lab
Richer Frederick, lab
Rigg Rev H S, pastor Christian Church, h. e Walnut
Roberts George, lab
Robertson John W., real estate
Robertson Minerva J, wid
Robinson James M, clk
Rasell Ignasius
Rosenbaum Wm A, genl store
Russell John, teamster
Safford Frank (Kaufman & Co)
Safford Hodson, barber
Safford John A, barber
Safford Judson, lab
Safford Martha, wid
Sapp Benj F, clk
Sapp Joseph, bartender
Sapp Louis T, lab
Sapp Wm, lab
Scott Ervin, bookpr
Searle Ernestus P, druggist
Shelley Edward C
Shewalter Grant (Shewalter Stave Co)
Shewalter Mary E (Shewalter Stave Co)
Shewalter Stave Co The, Mary E & G Shewalter proprs
Shipley Lafayette, farmer
Shotts Andrew, lab
Shrader Bessie M

Shrader John E, supt Sigelen & Co's Glass Factory
Shrader Maud E
Shultz Charles S, barber shop
Sieglen C A (Cent'l Lamp Co.)
Simmons Beecher, lab
Simons Hiram, lab
Simons Johanna, lab
Simons Wm H, lather
Slusser Perry, lab
Smith Charles A, barber
Smith Richard J
Smithson Schuyler, carp
Spitzmesser Bernard (Spitzmesser & Todd)
Spitzmesser & Lodd (Bernard Spitzmesser and Harvey Lodd), saloon
Sprung James, lab
Stanley Amanda, domestic
Stanley Andrew, lab
Stanley Oscar R
Stanley Wm L, lab
Starr Matthew
Stilwell Stephen, lab
Stokes John W, carp
Stokes Silas, lab
Stone Albert, lab
Stone Benj, lab
Stone Edgar, teamster
Stone Mattie
Stone Moses, brick mnfr
Stone Wm, brick mkr
Street John, lab
Summitville Bank, Joseph O Allen cashier, w s s Main, incorp. 1891, capital stock $21,000 (see adv.)

Novelty Works,
198 AND 200 N. MILTON ST.
ANDERSON, IND.

HUGH FISHER, Propr., manufacturer and dealer in Step Ladders, Garden Wheelbarrows, Screen Doors and Windows, Picture Frames, etc.

THE PALACE PHARMACY, Anderson, Ind. } FOR FINE GOODS OF ALL KINDS IN THEIR LINE.

J. T. Knowland & Son, WHOLESALE PLUMBERS and Gas Fitters' Supplies
111 N. Main St., ANDERSON, IND. 'Phone 30.

160   MADISON CO. DIRECTORY.

J. M. WILLIAMS, Sec'y.   FACTORIES representing Millions of Dollars.

GAS-CENTER LAND CO., REAL ESTATE DEALERS, SUMMITVILLE, IND.
Owners and Subdividers of City Additions.   *ELEGANT College Grove. Beautiful Park Addition. Bright Star Addition. Immense Manufacturing Addition.*

Summitville Brick Co The, Wm A Howard pres, S Cowgill v-pres, M F Woods secy, Joseph O Allen treas, R C Howard supt
Summitville Wave The, Geo P Louiso editor & publisher
Surrell E P, merchant
Surver E C, lab
Surver Perry, lab
Swain Charles W, carp
Swallow Geo E (Williams & Swallow)
Swallow Joal A, justice of peace
Swallow Joseph
Swallow & Williams (Geo E Swallow & C F Williams), physicians and surgeons
Swaney Oliver
Swindle Alfred, carp
Swisher Geo W, barber shop
Tappan S, tile wkr
Taylor A M, tile mnfr
Teale Philip J, lab
Tellas Wm, tile wkr
Terrel Ransome, lab
Thawley Joseph B, farmer
Thompson Carrie, deputy P M
Thorn Joseph S, saloon
Todd H (Spitzmesser & Todd)
Tomlinson A, tile wkr
Unthank John, tile wkr
Van Winkle C, wks saw mill
Van Winkle Ira, eng saw mill
Van Winkle Wm W, saw mill
Vincent Ezra, carp
Vinson Oscar, tile wkr

Waltz I A, agt C C C & St L
Warner F (Warner & Sons)
Warner M (Warner & Sons)
Warner & Sons (Wm, M and F Warner), genl store
Warner Wm (Warner & Sons)
Webb James N, blksmith
Webster O E, lab
Wesleyan Methodist Church, cor Church and Howard
Wheeler Wm, tile wkr
White Elizabeth, wid
White Frank W, physician
White John D, school teacher
White John W, physician
White Morris, dentist
Whitney Benj, blksmith
Whitney H O, bookpr
Wilkins Wm H, genl store
Williams Charles F, physician
Williams John M, real estate
Williams Leander S, real estate
Wilson Wm, teamster
Window Glass Wks, Calloway & Co proprs
Winn Lewis, tile wkr
Winn Wm, tile wkr
Winslow Wm, farmer
Wood Miles F, justice peace
Woods Alice, domestic
Woods James, tile wkr
Woods M, tile wkr
Worth Josephine, dressmkr
Worth Leroy E, wheelwright
Worth Peter, wagon mkr
Worth Sylvester, tile wkr
Wright Wm, carp

JOHN O. MILLER, ELEVEN YEARS' EXPERIENCE in Watchmaking. Finisher six years in Elgin & Springfield Watch Factories.
I GUARANTEE MY WORK   3 N. Meridian, ANDERSON, IND.

FOR FINE FURNITURE do not fail to call on **MUNCHHOF** the Leading **FURNITURE DEALER.**
Nos. 40 and 42 East Eighth St., - - ANDERSON, IND.

MADISON CO. GAZETTEER. 161

Madison County Gazetteer.

❧1893-4.❦

STATE SENATOR.—Wm. J. Houck.
REPRESENTATIVE.—James M. Farlow.
JOINT REPRESENTATIVE.—Andrew J. Behymer.
JUDGE 24TH JUDICIAL CIRCUIT.—Alfred Ellison.

COUNTY OFFICERS.

AUDITOR.—C. H. Allen.
CLERK.—James J. Netterville.
CORONER.—Charles L. Armstrong.
PROSECUTING ATTORNEY.—Bartlett H. Campbell.
RECORDER.—Daniel W. Black.
SHERIFF.—Wm. W. Van Dyke.
TREASURER.—John R. Page.

COUNTY COMMISSIONERS.—1st District, A. J. Cunningham; 2d District, Henry Bronnenberg; 3d District, R. C. Howard.
MADISON CO. ORPHANS' HOME.—Mrs. Mary Robertson, Matron.
MADISON CO. POOR FARM.—John Kenyon, Superintendent.

TOWNSHIP TRUSTEES.

NAME.	TOWNSHIP.	POST OFFICE.
Adam Forney,	Adams,	Ovid.
T. P. Kelley,	Anderson,	Anderson.
J. W. Sullivan,	Boone,	Rigdon.
M. D. Harmon,	Duck Creek,	Leisure.
A. W. Cook,	Fall Creek,	Pendleton.
P. F. House,	Greene,	Fortville.
C. W. Henkle,	Jackson,	Perkinsville.
T. N. Van Meter,	Lafayette,	Florida.
A. Runyan,	Monroe,	Alexandria.
George E. Noland,	Pipe Creek,	Frankton.
W. A. Curtis,	Richland,	Alexandria.
James Manderson,	Stony Creek	Johnson's Crossing.
Alfred Falkner,	Union,	Chesterfield.
B. F. Plackard,	Van Buren,	Summitville.

WOOLLEY Foundry and Machine Works.
Manufacturers of Clay Working Machinery, Boiler Makers, and General Machinists.
N. W. COR. 14th AND C. W. AND M. R. R.

J. S. STUART, "THE FLORIST," 99 to 111 W. 3d. Tel. 73. Funeral Designs and Plant Decorations Furnished on Short Notice. Anderson, Ind.

WHEN—CLOTHING,
—Manufacturers of—
—And Jobbers in—
HATS AND MEN'S FURNISHINGS.

162   MADISON CO. GAZETTEER.

ADAMS TOWNSHIP.
POST OFFICES.
Anderson, Chesterfield, Markleville, Pendleton.
"A" FOR ACRES.

Adams J, 24 a Chesterfield
Adams Sarah,120 a Summitville
Adamson W, 80 a Middletown
Addison E, 21 a Markleville
Andrews Mary E, 116 a
Ayleshire Sarah, 48 a Ovid
Bachman S M,91 a Greenville,O
Baker L & S, 16 a Ovid
Barnett Benj B, 1 a
Basicker Rachel, 4 a Ovid
Bennett J A, 10 a Markleville
Bennett Wm A, 21 a "
Bensonbower C, 78 a Anderson
Bensonbarger M, 152 a "
Biddle Chas W, 14 a Ovid
Biddle Geo M, 20 a "
Biddle Ida M, 14 a "
Biddle Jerusha A, 14 a "
Biddle John, 34 a
Bills Alfred, 24 a Fortville
Blake B, 29 a Markleville
Blake H, 4 a "
Blake James F, 2 a "
Blake John, 82 a "
Blake Jos P, 108 a "
Blake R M, 80 a "
Booram Allen, 107 a "
Booram Gideon, 360 a Anderson
Booram Jane A, 6 a Markleville
Booram Preston, 18 a "
Boston C E, 102 a Pendleton
Boston Margrat, 80 a "
Bray Archibald I, 146 a Ovid
Bray F M, 115 a Markleville
Bray Mary A, 20 a Ovid
Bray Rachel, 63 a "
Bright Geo, 1 a Markleville
Brock Abraham, 2 a Ovid
Bronnenberg L, 116 a Anderson
Brown Mary, 6 a Ovid
Brumfield E J, 14 a Markleville

Cappie Nancy, 40 a
Carmany W J, 70 a Summitville
Carpenter T, 2 a Markleville
Chambers M J, 101 a Pendleton
Clark Barney, 58 a Anderson
Clark Harriet E, 20 a "
Clark James A, 152 a "
Clark John, 4 a "
Clark Robt H, 55 a "
Clark Samuel, 4 a "
Clem Neoma, 1 a "
Clem Samuel, 1 a
Collier Chas R, 41 a Markleville
Collier Clarissa, 12 a "
Collier John, 165 a "
Collier L M & U G, 2 a "
Collier Margaret Jr, 47 a "
Collier Philip A, 12 a "
Collier Wm L, 1 a "
Combs Leah, 4 a "
Cook Harrison, 70 a "
Cook Jno F, 26 a "
Cookman M J, 51 a Ovid
Coolman Lydia F, 1 a
Cooper E, 65 a Mechanicsburg
Cooper Isaac, 34 a "
Cooper & Lewis, 1 a
Cooper M E, 40 a Mechanicsbg
Cooper Melissa, 36 a "
Cooper V M, 94 a Alexandria
Corbin Jno J, 10 a Markleville
Corwin A,20 a Middletown,N Y
Corwin Jno E, 50 a "
Cory Wilson, 28 a Anderson
Craig Aaron & Mary, 84 a Ovid
Creason George, 5 a Markleville
Creason Michael, 160 a "
Creason Sol, 80 a "
Crim Otis P, 46 a Anderson
Crim O, A & J Daniels,22 a "
Crowell D, 160 a Markleville

Place Your Real Estate and **FARM PROPERTY** in the Hands of
ROOP & HAYNES,
AND BE SURE OF QUICK RETURNS.
210½ S. Anderson, - - - - ELWOOD, IND.

ONEY TO BUILD WITH PROCURED WITHIN 15 DAYS. Robinson & Glassco, Loan, Real Estate & Insurance agents
Room 9 "When" Building, ANDERSON, IND.

MADISON CO. GAZETTEER. 163

well M H, 2 a Markleville
ımins H, 232 a Middletown
ıningham G,48 a Markleville
ıningham S & A J, 81 a Markleville
is Elisha E, 72 a Ovid
is Elwood, 80 a "
ris H M, 80 a Pendleton
ris J C, 108 a Markleville
is J S, 239 a Pendleton
ris Lane, 59 a Elwood
ris Mary M, 15 a Anderson
ris Maxey, 120 a Markleville
ker Emma, 89 a Ovid
ph Ralph W, 22 a "
lge Wm, 1 a
)ert S A, 47 a Markleville
son Allison, 160 a
ıson W & A, 40 a Middletown
ıns Jas, 37 a Markleville
ıns John, 40 a "
ıns Jno & Jas, 3 a "
ıns R C, 51 a "
ter Frederick, 165 a Ovid
d Maria, 26 a Markleville
ney Adam, 24 a Ovid
ney Catharine, 56 a Ovid
ney Jonathan, 25 a "
ıter Andrew J, 26 a "
ıter Lydia A, 82 a "
ı Lucy, 2 a Middletown
ıst Jacob, 1 a Markleville
ınklin C, 82 a "
ınklin John, 108 a "
ınklin M A, 17 a "
lton Mary M, 40 a Ovid
il Wm, 39 a Mechanicsburg
lmore C J & others, 90 a Ovid
more Mary A, 38 a Ovid
ınore Roman, 154 a "
aham A, 120 a Anderson
aham J C, 20 a "
aham J W, 300 a Markleville
ay John, 1 a Ovid
ay Samuel, 135 a Ovid

Gustin Isaac H, 40 a Anderson
Gustin Moses, 40 a "
Gustin Walt, 1 a "
Gwin Nora, 1 a Ovid
Haines Noah C, 20 a Pendleton
Ham Adalaide, 40 a Markleville
Ham Charity, 74 a "
Hammer Charity, 1 a Anderson
Hardman D J, 40 a Markleville
Hardman E & P, 71 a Anderson
Hardman Elizabeth, 80 a ".
Hardman L D, 120 a Markleville
Hardman Peter, 1 a Anderson
Hardy Sol, 70 a Markleville
Hartzell E et al, 20 a Markleville
Hartzel Victoria A, 40 a Ovid
Hays Elanthan, 27 a Markleville
Hays Godfrey (heirs), 40 a
Hays Wm, 13 a Pendleton
Heaton P J, 4 a Markleville
Hess Amos, 27 a Ovid
Hess Samuel (heirs), 2 a Ovid
Hicks Samuel Sr, 65 a "
Hicks Samuel Jr, 2 a "
Hilburt John, 1 a Markleville
Hodson E Jr, 165 a Mechanicsbg
Hodson Isaac N, 160 a "
Hodson John D, 90 a "
Hodson Julia A, 10 a "
Hodson R, 30 a Middletown
Hoel George W, 104 a Ovid
Hoel M V, 42 a Mechanicsburg
Hoel Sophia et al, 40 a "
Hoppas Emily, 40 a Ovid
Hoppas Isaac F, 52 a "
Hoppas Jos, 21 a Anderson
Hoppas Laura, 20 a Ovid
Hoppas M A, 130 a Anderson
Hoppas Sarah, 97 a Ovid
Howard Nancy A, 40 a Ovid
Hull Perry, 59 a Ovid
Hull Wm, 80 a Anderson
Huston Frank, 1 a Markleville
Huston John, 1 a Anderson
James Chas R, 27 a Pendleton

eal & Willkie, ATTORNEYS AT LAW. We will attend to your legal business promptly, and charge you no exhorbitant fees.
MECHANICS LIENS A SPECIALTY. CALL AND SEE US.

J. P. CONDO & SON, WILL SELL YOU FURNITURE ON EASY WEEKLY PAYMENTS, ESTABLISHED 1856. ALEXANDRIA, IND.

WHEN —Originators of the One Price System
IN SELLING CLOTHING.
FAIR AND SQUARE DEALINGS WITH ALL.

MADISON CO. GAZETTEER.

:ster Chas, 32 a Markleville
:ster Nancy J, 12 a "
hnson C, 105 a Wichita, Kas
hnson M A, 10 a Summitville
nes Isaac, 120 a Markleville
rdan Benj, 88 a Anderson
stice J J, 48 a Markleville
istice Marion, 58 a Markleville
istice Wm A, 79 a "
:esling A, 344 a Mechanicsbg
:esling Eli, 10 a "
:esling Geo, 40 a "
:esling Jno R, 79 a Ovid
:esling M, 30 a Mechanicsburg
:esling Robt, 118 a "
:esling Samuel, 260 a "
:ller E E, 120 a Markleville
:ller Geo W, 160 a Pendleton
:ller John H, 33 a Ovid
nnedy M J, 20 a Markleville
nnedy Nora A, 20 a
idle Wm A, 1 a Anderson
inard J K, 100 a Pendleton
iling D C, 40 a Mechanicsbg
ne Peter, 14 a Markleville
ill Albert & wife, 40 a Ovid
ill John L, 40 a Ovid
·cher Henry, 13 a Anderson
·cher Mathias, 83 a "
iky Isaac, 5 a Ovid
:g Frank, 23 a Frankton
vis Abisha, 325 a Anderson
vis Geo C, 110 a Markleville
vis Jas M, 565 a "
vis Stanford, 226 a "
lge N J, 15 a Mchanicsburg
Allister A S, 149 a Anderson
Allister A, 144 a "
Cullough Cynthia, 2 a
Cullough E, 49 a Markleville
Cullough J P, 60 a "
Cullough Mary, 21 a "
Curdy Wm A, 1 a "
Daniel Levi, 1 a
kle Abner, 40 a Ovid

Markle Chas D, 20 a Milner's
Corners
Markle Dewitt, 75 a Markleville
Markle E J & G, 1 a "
Markle J & E, 65 a "
Markle J F & L, 1 a "
Markle Samuel, 122 a "
Markleville Nat Gas Co "
Mauzy C, 24 a Markleville
Mauzy James F, 80 a "
Mauzy Silas R, 135 a "
Mauzy Wm S, 1 a "
Miller Lydia, 134 a Anderson
Millikin Thomas, 71 a Elwood
Mitchell Chas, 58 a Markleville
Mitchell Samuel, 124 a Ovid
Moneyhen J P, 92 a "
Morris A A, 2 a Summitville
Muncy John H, 1 a Ovid
Muterspaugh F D, 1 a Anderson
Noland J E, 20 a Markleville
Noland Wm, 120 a Chesterfield
Olinger W, 50 a Mechanicsburg
Padgett C (et al), 50 a Marklev.
Padgett F, 30 a Markleville
Palmer C R, 29 a "
Palmer Wm L, 25 a Elwood
Pearson Jesse, 20 a "
Pendleton J, 120 a Mechanicsbg
Poindexter R E, 120 a Indianapolis
Poor A, 80 a Mechanicsburg
Poor George, 20 a Anderson
Poor Lillian, 20 a "
Poor Lorenzo, 40 a "
Poor Oliver, 20 a "
Prigg E, 16 a Mechanicsburg
Prigg Parker L, 40 a "
Prigg Wm H, 80 a "
Probasco H, 167 a Cincinnati, O
Rank Wm, 1 a Florida
Rector Eliah J, 18 a Anderson
Rector Isaac, 17 a Ovid
Rector Joseph, 123 a Ovid
Rector Lundy, 19 a "

hn L. Lindskoog,
Leads in the Merchant Tailoring Line
English and French Worsteds, imported, always in stock.

Do not buy until you have seen them.
H. Block, N. E. Cor. Church and Harrison, - - ALEXANDRIA, IND.

WM. J. DOVE, Real Estate, Loans and Insurance, 61½ N. Meridian,
NEELEY BLOCK.   ANDERSON, IND.

MADISON CO. GAZETTEER.   165

Rector Mary E, 80 a Anderson
Rector T, 1 a Mechanicsburg
Reger A. 165 a Pendleton
Reger L D Jr, 40 a Ovid
Reger L D Sr, 234 a "
Reger M, 158 a Markleville
Reynolds Adalasta, 7 a Ovid
Richardson A, 1 a Anderson
Rittenour E, 244 a Mechanicsbg
Rittenour G & E W, 40 a "
Rittenour Jas M, 110 a Ovid
Rittenour W H, 110 a Anderson
Roberts E, 32 a Pendleton
Rogers Sarah A, 80 a Pendleton
Rosenfield J A, 50 a Markleville
Sanders Elizabeth, 44 a Ovid
Schlater E, 40 a Anderson
Scott Elizabeth, 95 a Ovid
Scott Lydia, 39 a Ovid
Sebrell G T, 80 a Markleville
Sebrell G & J A, 44 a "
Seward Aaron D, 1 a "
Seward Loveless, 1 a "
Shafer J & J, 40 a Anderson
Sheets Susanna, 1 a Ovid
Shelton John, 125 a Markleville
Shiner Mary E, 2 a
Shock Noah, 66 a Anderson
Slaughter J, 120 a Markleville
Slaughter J H, 10 a "
Small Jas M, 186 a "
Small Melissa, 44 a Anderson
Sparks John W, 2 a "
Stant Charles W, 1 a
Stephens T J and Mary M, lots, Anderson
Stickler W Jr, 60 a Markleville
Stinson Isom, 147 a Anderson
Stinson Jas A, 105 a "
Stinson Jno and wife, 38 a Ovid
Stohler Abram, 80 a Ovid
Stohler George, 60 a "
Stohler Henry, 75 a "
Stohler John, 20 a "
Stohler Samuel, 38 a "

Sullivan Mary A, 40 a Ovid
Sullivan M and Jas, 105 a Ovid
Swartz Zimri, 10 a
Thompson N E, 15 a Noblesville
Titus Charles, 71 a Markleville
Titus Clara K, 64 a "
Titus Elizabeth, 67 a "
Titus John S, 140 a "
Titus J R, 56 a "
Titus L M, 94 a Markleville
Titus Nora A, 70 a "
Titus Susan M, 60 a "
Trueblood Edwin, 299 a Ovid
Trueblood W N, 10 a Anderson
Vanduyn Isaac, 40 a
Vanhorn L A, 8 a Warrington
Van Winkle Aletha A, 58 a Mechanicsburg
Van Winkle Charles C, 90 a Mechanicsburg
Van Winkle George J, 73 a Mechnnicsburg
Van Winkle H G, 32 a Mechanicsburg
Varner John, 2 a Markleville
Vestal L C, 20 a Anderson
Walker A, 22 a Markleville
Walker Solon, 320 a "
Waltz Elizabeth, 33 a Anderson
Weeks J, 25 a Mechanicsburg
West W H & Mary E, 80 a Markleville
Whetsel A J, 13 a Markleville
Whetsel Wm, 20 a Anderson
Williams A H, 71 a Markleville
Williams Francis M, 101 a Ovid
Williams J (et al), 4 a Marklev
Williams Katie, 5 a "
Williams M A, 100 a Anderson
Williams M F & C, 1 a Dundee
Wilson A E, 239 a Markleville
Wilson N C, 80 a "
Windell C W, 170 a Ovid
Windell J B, 8 a Ovid

Anderson Foundry and Machine Works, Manufacturers of **BRICK AND TILE MA-**
265 N. Jackson Street,   Phone 53.
ANDERSON, IND.   **CHINES, SAW MILLS, ETC.**

Jackson & Burr Do the Largest INSURANCE Business. Insure in the good old Companies they represent.

69½ N. Meridian, - - ANDERSON, IND.

MADISON CO. GAZETTEER.

Windell L F, 40 a Pendleton
Windell Seth, 46 a Ovid
Windell Thomas, 160 a Ovid
Winehart & Franklin, 251 a
Winehart Martin, 80 a
Younkin S, 1 a Markleville

ANDERSON TOWNSHIP.

POST OFFICE.

Anderson.

"A" FOR ACRES.

Adams David A & Anna T, lots
Adams John, 40 a
Allen Gertrude, 80 a
Allen Isaac, 3 a
Allen Patrick, 30 a
Allen Samuel, 44 a
Badgley Charles A, 14 a
adgley Francis, 56 a
adgley John, 22 a
adgley Mary, 10 a
aer Louis, 108 a
arnes John, 1 a
atty George E, 1 a
echler Sacob, 92 a
eson John & Caroline, 117 a
gin John F, lots
ll Alexander, 38 a
nnett Adelia, lots
ckbam Chas & Nancy, 1 a
ick McFarland, 268 a
icklidge H J, 213 a
ike Margaret L, 80 a
nd David P, 7 a
yer Edward H, 15 a
yer Evaline, 50 a
dbury C E, 10 a
nson (heirs), 13 a
nnenberg Michael, 80 a
wer W H, 1 a
wer Leander, 3 a
wn Elizabeth, 1 a
wn Francis M, 70 a
wn Hamilton, 39 a
wn Henry T, 60 a
wn James R, 71 a
wn Martin J, 60 a
Brown Wm A, 69 a
Brundage R N, lots
Burke Margaret, T J & Jos, 111 a
Burner Florence, 4 a
Burner John, 40 a
Burton Benj F, lots
Cain Cassandria, 80 a
Cain Christopher, 50 a
Cain Christopher & Rhoda, 50 a
Cain Joseph R, 90 a
Canady H (et al), 3 a
Cather Emma I, 2 a
Clark Francis, 80 a
Clark Leander, 80 a
Clark Mary E, 20 a
Clarke Courtland, 50 a
Clem Daniel, 6 a
Clem Jacob A, 1 a
Clem Jeremiah, 88 a
Clem Mary E, 1 a
Clemens Joseph B, 1 a
Clevenger Sarah, 14 a
Clifford Benj, 15 a
Clifford Sallie, lots
Collis Franklin, 1 a
Comer Elizabeth, 1 a
Conner Nancy, 45 a
Corwin Elvira J, 260 a
Cory Wilson, 280 a
Craycraft Zadoc, 165 a
Cridge Robert, 160 a
Crim Wm, 86 a
Cullipher W H, 40 a
Davis Albert C, 75 a
Davis Ann, 16 a
Davis Anna, 13 a

George B. Epperson, Contractor and Builder of Felt and Gravel ROOFING.

89 E. 9th St., □ □ ANDERSON, IND.

...of Anderson. If you wish to buy, sell or rent, call at 10 E. 10 St., ANDERSON, IND.

MADISON CO. GAZETTEER, 167

Davis Charles, 20 a
Davis Jas and Florence, 8 a
Davis Levi, 8 a
Davis Maria C, 60 a
Davis Matilda E, 8 a
Davis Wm P, 27 a
Delawter Eli F, 2 a
Denny James H, 30 a
Dillon David W, 80 a
Eads J W and Amanda, 8 a
Eby Jacob, 200 a
Edwards Wm (heirs), 80 a
Eggman Elizabeth, 40 a
Eggman Ezekiel, 20 a
Eggman George F, 100 a
Eggman John W, 80 a
Eggman Sarah A, 80 a
Farmer Charles, 22 a
Farmer Edgar, 1 a
Fisher Granville C, 58 a
Forkner James M, 7 a
Forkner John L, 80 a
Forkner Madison, 20 a
Forrey George C, 96 a
Free Nathaniel, 58 a
Gale Dora, 10 a
Globe Mnfg Co, 1 a
Goodykoontz Daniel, 278 a
Gray Mary O, 13 a
Groff Joseph, 616 a
Harless Elizabeth, 1 a
Hamell Elizabath, 80 a
Hamell Eliza and Wm, 5 a
Hamell Wm & Elizabeth, 5 a
Harmer Andrew, 65 a
Harmeson Levi A, 287 a
Harmeson Nancy, 17 a
Harmeson Sarah & Luella, 18 a
Harmeson Thomas J, 187 a
Harmeson Wm, 39 a
Harpold Emaline, 2 a
Harpold D K, 80 a
Harpold Samuel F, 60 a
Harrison John A, 133 a
Hartley Joseph H, 78 a

Hartman George W, 1 a
Hartzel Joseph (heirs), 160 a
Hawkins Elizabeth (et al), 5 a
Henry C L (et al), 2 a
Hickey John, 80 a
Hicks Eli H, 4 a
Holder Joseph, 3 a
Hollingsworth James M, 1 a
Hollingsworth Mary E, 1 a
Hoppas Alfred Jr, 7 a
Hoppas Daniel Sr, 40 a
Hoppas Francis M, 104 a
Hoppas Isaac Jr, 61 a
Hoppas Jacob, 184 a
Hopper John H, 24 a
Horn L, Mary & Susan Boone, 5 a
Howard Tilghman, 129 a
Hughel Mathias B, 309 a
Hughel Samuel, 215 a
Hughel S and T F, 20 a
Humphrey F M, 1 a
Huntsinger Mary E, 24 a
Jackson Emma, 20 a
Jarrett Wm J, 2 a
Johnson Charles, 80 a
Johnson Nora R, 100 a
Johnson N P and R J, 40 a
Johnson Rebecca, 76 a
Johnston John, 63 a
Jones Charles F, 1 a
Julius Peter, 40 a
Kemp Nancy A, 94 a
Kenton John and Della, 1 a
Kimerling George, 45 a
Kindle Brasselton, 80 a
Kindle Maria J, 13 a
Kirkpatrick D B, 34 a
Krugler Rena, 8 a
Krugler Wm, 20 a
Langley Mary E, 63 a
Langley Thomas C, 72 a
Landes Sarah, 7 a
Lasure Eliza, 106 a
Latshaw Elizabeth, 50 a
Lee Daniel, 80 a

HUGH FISHER, Manufacturer **Screen Doors and Windows** all sizes. Furniture repairing a specialty.
198 and 200 N. Milton St.,
ANDERSON, IND.

BUCK, BRICKLEY & CO., THE LEADING DRUGGISTS, Cor. Ninth and Meridian Streets, ANDERSON, IND.

J. T. Knowland & Son, SANITARY PLUMBERS, Gas and Steam Fitters.
111 N. Main St., ANDERSON, IND. 'Phone 80.

Lee Francis, 120 a
Lemon Absolom, 45 a
Lemon Isabell, 14 a
Lemon Milton, 1 a
Lininger Wm H, 1 a
Logan John, 80 a
Longfellow James E, 120 a
Longfellow J R, 47 a
Lout Nancy E, 23 a
Lowman Ezra, 108 a
Lynch George, 1 a
McCarty Angeline O, 18 a
McCarty Itham V, 2 a
McCarty Joel, 17 a
McCord Samuel, 74 a
McClelland C P. 30 a
McCullough C K, 6 a
McCullough N C, 796 a
McCullough Thomas, 280 a
McFarland R W, 184 a
McGraw Margaret, 21 a
McKay Maria J, 40 a
McNatt Hattie M, 26 a
McNew Mary J, 2 a
Malady Martin, 45 a
Malone E (heirs), 160 a
Maloney Wm, 4 a
Martin Jacob & Elizabeth, 40 a
Martin Levi, 4 a
Martin Susanna, 18 a
Minnick James A, 2 a
Minor John L, 1 a
Morris Isaac, 38 a
Morris John and Elizabeth, 40 a
Morris T J and wife, 80 a
Moss Leroy F, 160 a
Moss Sanford and wife, 230 a
Myers Frank, 12 a
Myers George, 12 a
Myers Samuel, 166 a
Newton Wm, 40 a
Noland Athalia, 5 a
Orbaugh Sampson, 40 a
Parker Maria, 140 a
Parson L B, 21 a

Patterson Mark & Rebecca, 8 a
Payne James, 45 a
Peacock John, 4 a
Pence Joseph A, 137 a
Pence Wm and wife, 40 a
Penniston Francis, 1 a
Perkins John, 80 a
Perkins Sylvester, 40 a
Pittsford Isaac, 13 a
Poindexter Emily, 18 a
Poor Phœbe, 85 a
Puffenbarger Elias, 22 a
Puffenbarger Obediah, 34 a
Rector Beverly, 1 a
Rector Daniel, 80 a
Rector Jacob, 40 a
Rector Nancy A, 15 a
Rhodes B, 80 a
Rhodes Daniel, 73 a
Richardson Catharine, 7 a
Richmond John, 2 a
Riggs Daniel, 80 a
Riggs Isdell, 40 a
Ring Clara M, 40 a
Roadcap Elda, 3 a
Robins James, 2 a
Robertson Mary C, 23 a
Ruddell John M, 14 a
Sansberry J W, 476 a
Sarrah Arretta E, 1 a
Scott Winfield, 57 a
Seward Catharine, 4 a
Seybert Harvey, 170 a
Seybert J Monroe, 40 a
Seybert L D (heirs), 81 a
Seybert Sylvester H, 80 a
Shaul Laura, 80 a
Shephard Robert C, 314 a
Sheets Barbara, 80 a
Sheets Emma, 1 a
Shinkle Phoebe C, 1 a
Shirk Frederick, 40 a
Shock Noah, 82 a
Showlts M E, 3 a
Sikes Elzy, 4 a

John O. Miller, Practical Watchmaker & Jeweler. Eleven Years' Experience in the Manufacturing of Watches.
3 N. Meridian, - - - ANDERSON, IND.

A. Munchhof & Bros. Undertakers and Funeral Directors and Practical Embalmers. Office and Warerooms, Telephones 189, 24 and 51. **No. 98 N. Main St., ANDERSON, IND.** OFFICE OPEN DAY AND NIGHT.

impson John, 40 a
kinner Nancy C, 1 a
mear John S, 40 a
mith Emily M, 8 a
mith Isaac N, 3 a
mith L J and Joseph, 1 a
omerville F M, 3 a
tanley J H, 80 a
tanley Meredith Sr, 103 a
tanley M J, 328 a
tanley Nancy J & M, 40 a
tanley Rhoda, 13 a
tephens Martha, 67 a
tephenson Sallie, 33 a
tewart James W, 19 a
tewart J M B, 86 a
tinson Isom, 69 a
tinson Sarah, 33 a
trout Charles E, 4 a
ummerville John, 120 a
appen David, 20 a
appen Elizabeth D, 1 a
appen Hezekiah, 20 a
appen Wm, 20 a
eneyke Malinda, 1 a
hornburg Richard, 289 a
immons Martin, 27 a
ranbarger O W, 24 a
ress Charles D, 9 a

Troxal A, 40 a
Van Buskirk Daniel, 15 a
Van Buskirk Frank, 14 a
Van Buskirk John, 13 a
Van Buskirk Mary J, 45 a
Van Buskirk, 40 a
Vandevender Isabelle, 26 a
Vandevender Mary M, 120 a
Vandevender Minnie K, 48 a
Vandevender Wm, 4 a
Vandevender Wm A, 59 a
Waggy Evaline, 35 a
Waggy Henry, 187 a
Wallace Maurice, 7 a
Watkins James M, 2 a
Watkins Mary M, 20 a
Webb James L, 1 a
Weir Jesse D, 2 a
Weisman Malinda, 24 a
Wertz Daniel, 160 a
Wertz Joseph W, 40 a
Whetstone Lunis, 98 a
Whippo Amanda K, 160 a
Whittinger Jerry, 240 a
Williams John W, 1 a
Wilson Elizabeth, 40 a
Wilson Wm M, 31 a
Wood John, 1 a
Wynant Adam, 60 a

BOONE TOWNSHIP.

POST OFFICES.

Alexandria, Anderson, Elwood, Fairmount, Frankton, Orestes, Rigdon, Summitville.

"A" FOR ACRES.

rmstrong C, 44 a Anderson
rmstrong J, 20 a Summitville
rmstrong M, 80 a   "
sken Mary C, 80 a Alexandria
ustin Sarah A, 40 a   "
aker Wm T, 45 a Pendleton
all Robt E, 84 a Summitville
all Wm, 156 a   "
ear Emma, 29 a   "
ear George, 15 a   "

Bebout B J, 80 a Elwood
Beeson A, 160 a Summitville
Beeson F, 24 a   "
Beeson I J, 70 a   "
Beeson J W, 40 a   "
Beeson M M, 24 a   "
Beeson Viola, 24 a Summitville
Beeson Wm, 42 a   "
Beeson Wm S, 40 a   "
Bingamon Sarah, 40 a Elwood

J. S. STUART, THE FLORIST, DEALER IN PLANTS, ROSES and BULBS, 99 to 111 W. 3d. Telephone 78. ANDERSON, IND.

WOOLLEY FOUNDRY AND MACHINE WORKS,
Engineers, Founders and Machinists
N. W. Cor. 14th and C. W. and M. R. R.

WHEN—THE—**Anderson Clothiers & Hatters.**

☞ ONE PRICE TO ALL.

170 MADISON CO. GAZETTEER.

Bird Wm L, 56 a Elwood
Black Wm D, 40 a   "
Blades S J, 20 a Summitville
Blake E A & Jas, 60 a   "
Broites Julia, 40 a   "
Brown Joseph, 50 a Rigdon
Brunt A J, 400 a Anderson
Brunt Nancy, 80 a Summitville
Butler Jesse W, 80 a   "
Byram & Cornelius, 49 a
Call Caroline, 80 a Summitville
Call John W, 350 a Elwood
Canup Thos L, 2 a, Summitville
Campbell Eliza, 36 a Rigdon
Campbell Emily, 11 a   "
Campbell J, 80 a Summitville
Campbell M I, 40 a Rigdon
Campbell M E, 7 a Summitville
Carpenter Selvina, 22 a Rigdon
Carter Mary M, 85 a Orestes
Carver George, 103 a   "
Carver Lewis K, 40 a   "
Cartwright W, 200 a Summitville
Chalfant Ann, 80 a Elwood
Chaplin Asbury, 216 a Anderson
Chaplin Jesse, 40 a Orestes
Christopher E, 30 a Summitville
Clark America, 16 a   "
Clark W H, 10 a   "
Cochran Geo W, 113 a Elwood
Cochran W M, 80 a Summitville
Collis Matilda, 32 a Rigdon
Corwin Alvira J, 80 a
Cox James, 15 a Summitville
Cramer T H, 20 a   "
Cullen P D & L A, 79 a Summitville
Cunningham D, 40 a Rigdon
Custer C J, 10 a Anderson
Custer John W, 1 a Summitville
Davis E E, 22 a Anderson
Davis Lewis, 40 a   "
Davis O C, 9 a Rigdon
Day Lewis E, 30 a Elwood
Deadman T, 40 a Summitville

Dean E, 10 a Summitville
Dial Joseph, 114 a non-res
Dickey James, 127 a Rigdon
Dickey Jasper N, 60 a   "
Dickey John E, 40 a   "
Dickey John M, 40 a   "
Dickey M, 51 a Summitville
Dickey Miles A, 20 a Rigdon
Dickey Sarah M, 80 a   "
Dobson E, 60 a Summitville
Dobson H J, 80 a   "
Dobson J & wife, 20 a   "
Dobson Nora B, 62 a   "
Downs Wm H, 60 a Rigdon
Doyle Mary E, 195 a Anderson
Draper Mattie, 20 a Gilman
Drawhorn E, 1 a Rigdon
Drawhorn Geo, 1 a   "
Eakins E B, 50 a Elwood
Earnest J R, 60 a Summitville
Elsworth W A, 80 a Alexandria
Ertell Chas, 160 a Elwood
Fite Andrew J, 1 a Rigdon
Fite R E & heirs, 19 a Rigdon
Forest Elvira, 39 a Summitville
Forest I D & S H, 72 a Elwood
Free Orizin, 40 a Rigdon
Garder A, 1 a Summitville
Gardner J A, 36 a   "
Garther M, 40 a   "
Gassett E E, 60 a   "
Gassett W A, 20 a   "
Greenlee Andrew, 40 a Orestes
Greenlee P A, 80 a Orestes
Greenlee W, 127 a Summitville
Greenlee Wm A, 40 a   "
Griffee O & M E, 27 a   "
Griffee John, 160 a   "
Ham Benj F, 21 a Anderson
Hamilton O M, 80 a Hackleman
Hammond Ann, 40 a Elwood
Hancock W F (et al), 40 a   "
Hancock Wm T, 32 a Rigdon
Hank J J, 160 a
Harting H B, 80 a Alexandria

Roop & Haynes, Real Estate,
LOANS AND INSURANCE.
210½ S. Anderson, - - ELWOOD, IND.

Robinson & Glassco, Real Estate, Loan and Insurance Agents, room 9 "When" Building Agents Fidelity Building and Savings Union.
ANDERSON, IND.

MADISON CO. GAZETTEER. 171

Harting John D, 53 a Elwood
Heater Sarah, 10 a "
Hedrick Laura, 40 a "
Hiatt Elihue, 80 a Rigdon
Hiatt E A, 60 a "
Hiatt John E, 80 a "
Hiatt Nelson, 1 a "
Hiatt N C & W C, 60 a Rigdon
Hook P (et al), 40 a Elwood
Hosier Lucinda, 80 a "
Housencuster Mary, 44 a "
Howard R C, 229 a Summitv
Hull James C, 60 a Rigdon
Hunt Margaret, 20 a "
Hunt Nathan W, 80 a "
Huston John J, 40 a "
Jeffey Wm, 80 a - "
Jeffries Alvis L, 80 a "
Jenkins O, 170 a Noblesville
Johnson C, 10 a Wichita, Kan
Jones Braxton, 40 a Summitville
Jones Cloah A, 40 a "
Jones Eliza, 80 a Fairmount
Jones Geo M, 40 a Elwood
Jones H & wife, 180 a Anderson
Jones L K, 240 a Summitville
Jones Levi, 126 a Elwood
Jones N, 40 a Summitville
Jones Nora B, 80 a "
Jones Rose E, 60 a "
Jones Saml H, 80 a Fairmount
Kaufman J, 64 a Summitville
Keaton Ambrose, 200 a Rigdon
Keaton Harriet, 70 a "
Keaton James T, 78 a "
Keaton Rebecca, 56 a "
Kerr Sallie J, 40 a Summitville
King M C, 80 a Alexandria
Knopp W B, 80 a Summitville
Lindsay W H, 100 a Fairmount
Little Elizabeth, 1 a Elwood
Livengood A E, 2 a non-res
Long A G & C K,152 a Frankton
Long James M, 140 a non-res
Long Martin, 207 a non-res

Lucas Lina, 6 a non-res
McClain E A, 40 a Summitville
McClain H, 120 a "
McClead Chas, 80 a Orestes
McClead F M, 40 a "
McDermit Mary E & J B, 60 a Summitville
McDermit S, 120 a Summitville
McMaban Enoch, 20 a "
McMahan J E, 5 a Alexandria
McMahan M J, 20 a Orestes
McMahan M, 40 a Summitville
McMahan S S, 60 a Orestes
McMahan T J, 160 a Anderson
McPherson Luke, 10 a Elwood
Main Malinda, 1 a Rigdon
Marley James, 40 a Summitvslle
Marley Jesse, 80 a "
Marley Jesse A, 60 a "
Mathes George, 20 a Anderson
Messmore David, 80 a Rigdon
Metcalf Timothy, 280 a Rigdon
Millikin F M, 94 a New Castle
Millikin Thos B, 20 a Elwood
Moore G W, 80 a Summitville
Moore Jas et al, 280 a "
Moreland T, 150 a Summitville
Moreland W F, 80 a Alexandria
Morgan T B, 50 a Summitville
Morris Jas C, 47 a Rigdon
Myres Mary E & Albert, 120 a Summitville
Neltner F, 58 a Summitville
Noble Elizabeth,40 a Alexandria
Noble James L, 88 a "
Noble John N, 152 a "
Noble M J & W D, 49 a "
O'Brien Patrick, 69 a Elwood
O'Bryant E, 30 a Summitville
O'Bryant S, 80 a "
Overshiner M G, 40 a Orestes
Overshiner M L, 206 a Elwood
Overshiner Sarah, 80 a "
Owens Wm, 37 a Elwood
Paden K (et al), 60 a Summitv

J. P. CONDO & SON, FURNITURE, UNDERTAKERS and EMBALMERS, ESTABLISHED 1856. ALEXANDRIA, IND.

Deal & Willkie, We will write your Insurance in none but Standard Companies; All parties are treated alike, no cut-rates and no wildcat Insurance.
REAL ESTATE AND NOTARY PUBLICS.

WHEN—YOUR MEASURE TAKEN, AND
SUITS OR OVERCOATS
MADE TO ORDER.

172   MADISON CO. GAZETTEER.

Palmer Joseph, 7 a Elwood	Spitzmesser A, 80 a Elwood
Painter W M, 20 a Summitville	Spitzmesser D, 320 a Summitv
Palmer W W, 22 a Elwood	Starr Louisa, 80 a Elwood
Perkins Isaac, 20 a "	Stewart M, 80 a Summitville
Pernod Paul, 40 a Elwood	Sullivan E A, 73 a "
Perry Even H, 10 a Alexandria	Sullivan Jeff, 244 a "
Perry John W, 70 a "	Sullivan T, 79 a "
Peters E H, 402 a Summitville	Sullivan T W, 91 a "
Peters I and R, 40 a "	Summons W, 50 a Alexandria
Pickard Arthur E, 9 a "	Swain C, 40 a Summitville
Pickard A & E, 80 a Alexandria	Swain M L, 10 a "
Reece Geo W, 40 a "	Swain M, 40 a "
Richards J, 20 a Summitville	Tappen E, 80 a "
Rittenhouse Chas, 10 a Elwood	Tharp Amanda, 17 a
Ritter Rozina, 20 a Elwood	Thomas J B, 28 a Pendleton
Robertson M, 40 a Alexandria	Tilman Louisa and Jane, 80 a
Robinson M T, 10 a "	Thurston J, 160 a Summitville
Rose Elizabeth, 9 a "	Tomlinson A, 80 a "
Runyan Hugh, 160 a Rigdon	Tomlinson Wm, 115 a "
Runyan Ira, 181 a Summitville	Tomlinson W, 80 a "
Runyan J F, 104 a Alexandria	Townsend O J, 20 a "
Runyan John, 20 a Summitville	Townsend W L, 80 a "
Runyan M, 20 a Alexandria	Townsend Z, 160 a Rigdon
Schuyler Wm, 40 a Anderson	Trick Benj F, 40 a Elwood
Schwim I & M, 80 a Alexandria	Tuteron D, 16 a Summitville
Setriel M, 120 a Summitville	Vernon Elvin, 60 a "
Shaul M & R, 80 a "	Vernon M, 30 a "
Shields Hester A, 40 a Elwood	Vinson J C, 160 a "
Shipley Adam, 39 a Alexandria	Wann J M and P, 13 a Elwood
Sinks Mary, 545 a Indianapolis	Wells Thos, 57 a Summitville
Smalley A J, 63 a Summitville	Whitely G and L, 80 a "
Smith Micajah, 419 a Rigdon	Young Ellison, 40 a "
Smith Jeremiah V, 40 a "	Young E (et al), 14 a "
Smith M J, 49 a Summitville	Young John, 160 a "
Smith Wm N, 120 a Rigdon	

DUCK CREEK TOWNSHIP.
POST OFFICES.
Brookville, Elwood, Frankton, Leisure, New Castle, Orestes,
Richmond, Rigdon, Summitville.
"A" FOR ACRES.

Abbott J. W, 49 a Elwood	Ball Henry T, 50 a Leisure
Abinathy I, 24 a Anderson	Ball Sarah E, 14 a "
Anderson J W, 40 a Leisure	Barr Mathias, 40 a "
Armfield Amelia, 19 a Elwood	Beeks L and A, 100 a Elwood
Bagley Mary J, 39 a- "	Behymer A J, 1 a "

John L. Lindskoog, Fashionable MERCHANT TAILOR.
First-Class Work and Fit
GUARANTEED.
H. H. H. Block, N. E. Cor. Church and Harrison, ALEXANDRIA, IND.

WM. J. DOVE, Insures against loss by Fire, Cyclone, Accident and Death.
NEELEY BLOCK. 61½ N. Meridian, ANDERSON, IND.

MADISON CO. GAZETTEER. 173

Benedict C C, 42 a Elwood
Bentley N M, 160 a Leisure
Bitner Sarah M, 40 a "
Brown Nealy, '40 a Elwood
Brown Wm C, 16 a Leisure
Bucy Nancy, 26 a Alexandria
Calloway H & Co, 1 a Elwood
Carr Irvin W, 20 a Leisure
Carr Jas R, 20 a Homer
Clary John, 1 a Elwood
Clary Wm, 80 a "
Clymer D H, 200 a Elwood
Clymer Jeff C, 80 a "
Clymer Jas F, 40 a "
Clymer R W, 80 a "
Cole John C, 10 a "
Cole Peter J, 120 a "
Copher J L, 10 a "
Cunningham D E, 10 a Rigdon
Dale Daniel, 80 a Elwood
Daugherty C H, 77 a Elwood
Davis Alexander, 58 a Leisure
Davis Ira, 70 a Elwood
Davis Robert, 80 a "
Deal O F, lot, Richmond
Denny Elijah J, 80 a Elwood
Denny Jasper, 10 a "
Douge Luther, 79 a "
Edgell Marcellus, 69 a "
Edgell W F, 30 a "
Edwards Cyrus A, 10 a Leisure
Erdman Amanda M, 80 a "
Estel Silas & wife, 80 a "
Farr W B, 40 a Leisure
Flemming A, 68 a Elwood
Fleener John W, 80 a Leisure
Fleener Oliver, 80 a Rigdon
Forrest Isaac D, 160 a Elwood
Forrest W F (hrs), 20 a "
Frazier H and M, 40 a "
Frazier John R, 110 a "
Gemmill Andrew, 80 a Rigdon
Glass Hannah E, 13 a Leisure
Glass John, 80 a Elwood
Gifford Geo M, 40 a Elwood

Goins Harriet E, 40 a Elwood
Gray David H, 114 a "
Greenlee H, 30 a Leisure
Griselbach Frank, 10 a Elwood
Gritten F and S, 72 a "
Hains B and L, 20 a Leisure
Hains F W, 60 a Elwood
Haines G F, 10 a "
Hanmon R, 80 a Summitville
Hancher Chas N, 13 a Elwood
Hancher C O (et al), 5 a "
Hancher Hiram, 200 a "
Hanchew Jas R, 40 a "
Hand Elizabeth, 80 a "
Haley Patrick, 40 a Anderson
Harmon John N, 40 a Elwood
Harmon Thos W, 120 a "
Harting Andrew, 68 a "
Harting Geo J, 80 a "
Harting Geo W, 42 a "
Harting H G, 160 a Elwood
Harting Jas H, 152 a "
Harting John D, 160 a "
Harting John H, 50 a "
Harting Margaret A, 74 a "
Harting Wm B, 24 a "
Haugher Orla, 39 a "
Haugher Sarah, 80 a "
Hedrick Eleanor, 79 a "
Heffner & Hupp, 80 a "
Heffner Lewis, 80 a "
Heigh Barbara, 30 a "
Heimlick John, 80 a "
Heron Helen M, 160 a "
Hiatt Arthur S, 1a Leisure
Hiatt Oliver, 40 a "
Hiatt Silas W, 1 a "
Higbee Wm, 200 a Elwood
Hinds Abbie S, 15 a Elwood
Hobb Alfred H, 10 a Leisure
Hoppenwroth F, 157 a Elwood
Hoppenwroth M, 80 a "
Hoppenwroth Wm, 2 a "
Hunt & Murphy, 80 a "
Huston F M, 112 a "

WHITE RIVER DAIRY, 513 Nichol Avenue, Telephone 220. ANDERSON, IND.

LARMORE BROS., Proprietors, also Manufacturers and Wholesale Dealers in **Ice Cream and Oysters in Season.**

Anderson Foundry and Machine Works, Manufacturers of Portable and Stationary **Steam Engines.**
265 N. JACKSON STREET, 'Phone 53. ANDERSON, IND.

Is Your Property Insured? If not, CALL AT ONCE on **JACKSON & BURR,** 69½ N. Meridian, - ANDERSON, IND.

174 MADISON CO. GAZETTEER.

Ismone E and M, 79 a Elwood
Jarrett Mary E, 20 a Alexandria
Johnson C, 220 a Wichita, Kan
Jones Edgar P, 80 a Rigdon
Jones Harriet M, 120 a Elwood
Jones Levi, 40 a Elwood
Jones W R, 160 a Rigdon
Keaton A E, 80 a "
Keaton M W, 80 a "
Knotts Geo W, 30 a Elwood
Knotts N (heirs), 50 a "
Knotts L and J, 40 a Elwood
Knotts Robert, 40 a Leisure
Knotts U B, 120 a Elwood
Krome Mattie, 120 a "
Krome Perry, 80 a "
Kramer Gustave, 320 a "
Lambertson S, 40 a "
Leisure Nathan, 160 a Leisure
Leonard Reuben, 45 a "
Leonard Wm C, 80 a "
Little John, 32 a "
Lyons Lemuel M, 20 a Elwood
McAllister Wm, 20 a Anderson
McClure J, 393 a Brookville
McConnell Jesse, 70 a Rigdon
McIntosh A W, 100 a Elwood
McIntosh I E, 20 a Nevada
McIntosh John J, 38 a Leisure
McLuman J F, 1 a Elwood
McMahan A, 60 a Summitville
Mauring N & wife, 1 a Ridgon
Miller Rachel S, 57 a Leisure
Millikin F M, 40 a New Castle
Millikin Thos B, 40 a Elwood
Minnick A, 160 a Frankton
Minnick Joel M, 120 a Elwood
Moore Jas N, 40 a Rigdon
Moore John W, 10 a Elwood
Moore J and M, 16 a Carthage
Moore Nancy A, 80 a Leisure
Morse Daniel, 31 a Elwood
Morse Wooster, 80 a "
Morris Jas, 40 a Rigdon
Moser Michael, 160 a Elwood

Newhouse L J, 26 a Rushville
Newkirk Wm R, 27 a Rushville
Noble Benj A, 80 a Rigdon
Noble Jonathan, 235 a Rigdon
Noble John H, 80 a Leisure
Noble Perry E, 80 a Rigdon
Noble Phœbe J, 40 a Leisure
Noftsker Wm L, 4 a Elwood
Ogle Wm, 80 a Elwood
Osborn John D, 36 a Orestes
Osborn Joseph, 36 a Orestes
Owens Malissa, 40 a Elwood
Owens Albert D, 153 a "
Owens Joseph, 94 a "
Parson Jonathan, 160 a Rigdon
Patrick & Minnick, 80 a Elw
Peck Sarah C, 200 a Alexandria
Pearson E M. 30 a Elwood
Pearson Rachel, 10 a "
Powell Alonzo, 160 a Frankton
Reddick John B, 30 a Leisure
Reeder Benj, 16 a Elwood
Reeder Elmira, 50 a "
Repperger C, 120 a "
Reybolt E C, 60 a "
Roberts James E, 40 a "
Ross Alice A, 5 a "
Scott A & M, 3 a Leisure
Scott J W, 60 a "
Scott Thos M, 40 a "
Sells Nannie, 160 a "
Shaffer Joseph, 127 a Elwood
Shaffer Wm, 86 a "
Shawhan Malinda, 40 a Leisure
Shay Michael, 20 a Elwood
Shay Patrick 110 a "
Shell Elizabeth M, 20 a "
Shirk Nannie R, 160 a "
Singer Peter, 40 a "
Smelser E C, 20 a Rigdon
Smelser John, 60 a "
Smith M J J & T, 80 a Elwood
Stam Lucinda V, 20 a "
Starkey Sarah, 120 a "
Steel H & S, 98 a Leisure

George B. Epperson, Paints, Oils, Varnishes and Painters' Supplies.

39 E. 9th St., - - ANDERSON, IND.

John Donnelly, 10 East 10th Street, - ANDERSON, IND. will sell your property, and insure quick returns. Place your business in his hands.

MADISON CO. GAZETTEER.   175

Stretcher W W, 60 a Elwood
Stutcher John A, 40 a   "
Petrick Saml H, 80 a Rigdon
Petrick W H (et al), 25 a Leis
Tranbarger David, 20 a Elwood
Trick Benj F, 40 a   "
Tyner Curtis, 13 a   "
Tyner Sarah A, 13 a   "
Vann Jas & Presley, 233 a   "
Vann James M, 80 a   "
Vann Matilda, 40 a   "
Vann Presley, 80 a   "
Vardwell I C, 120 a   "
Vardwell Theodore, 56 a   "
Vardwell & Strader (et al), 11 a Elwood
Varner J W, 80 a Elwood

Waymire A, 60 a Elwood
Waymire Chas, 160 a "
Waymire Jacob, 323 a "
Waymire J S, 40 a   "
Waymire M, 88 a   "
Wickerd M J, 80 a   "
Williams C E, 40 a   "
Williamson M L, 13 a "
Williamson S R, 40 a "
Winder John 40 a   "
Wisler Benj F, 1 a Leisure
Wisler Paris, 25 a   "
Wittkamper F W, 80 a "
Wood Dora, 80 a Elwood
Wright W C, 48 a   "
Young Laura E, 8 a "

FALL CREEK TOWNSHIP.

POST OFFICES.

Alfonte, Anderson, Leisure, Myers, Indianapolis, Pendleton,

"A" FOR ACRES.

nner B F, 528 a Pendleton
nderson A C, 160 a   "
rmstrong I N & S F, 20 a Pendleton
rmstrong N E, 10 a Pendleton
rmstrong S F, 10 a   "
aird C, 17 a Wooster, O
aker Philip, 2 a Pendleton
aker W A, 157 a   "
arnsly E, 28 a   "
arrett D G, 114 a   "
ates H T, 47 a   "
ates S (et al), 71 a   "
enefiel Joel B, 81 a Elwood
lazier J T & M A, 6 a Pendtn
oland Ellen, 80 a Pendleton
oston Benj W, 160 a   "
oston Chas, 73 a   "
oston Eliza A, 1 a   "
oston E & M, 80 a   "
oston Jas G, 210 a   "
oston Margaret, 80 a   "
oston Wm S, 152 a   "

Brickley W P, 160 a Anderson
Bronnenberg F, 223 a   "
Brooks Madison, 100 a   "
Brown C F, 135 a Pendleton
Brown Emma A, 40 a   "
Brown Hannah E, 80 a   "
Brown Isaac, 4 a   "
Brown Simon P, 5 a   "
Bunker Miranda, 59 a   "
Burditt Alex, 113 a   "
Burditt Oliver H. 81 a   "
Burton Jessie E, 28 a   "
Catron David, 80 a   "
Catron Mary J, 20 a   "
Catron Wm D, 80 a   "
Chambers Martha J, 68 a Pendl
Clarke G C, 116 a   "
Clarke M E (et al), 20 a Andrn
Combs A B, 10 a Pendleton
Cook Lydia E, 10 a   "
Cook A W, 82 a   "
Coombs Lewis B, 5 a   "
Copper M, 106 a Pendleton

PICTURE FRAMES of all sizes and prices at Hugh Fisher's Novelty Works, B-t..d 200 N. Milton St., - - - - ANDERSON, IND.

J. T. Knowland & Son, Brass & Iron, Steam, Gas and Water Goods.
111 N. Main St., ANDERSON, IND. 'Phone 30.

Corroll M, 80 a Frankton	George A & L M, 40 a " Pendln
Costello John, 100 a Pendleton	George Wm A, 106 a "
Costello Mary, 120 a Anderson	Gibbons Rodney, 80 a "
Cotterell Nancy, 1 a Pendleton	Gilbert E W, 135 a Anderson
Cotty Wm M, 80 a	Ginn Henrietta, 80 a Pendleton
Coverdale P S 56 a Anderson	Gowl Evaline, 8 a "
Cox A & A, 30 a Pendleton	Gowl John L, 66 a "
Cox Mary E, 39 a "	Gowl John W, 29 a "
Cox Wm. 147 a "	Gowl Mary E, 37 a "
Cranfill Thos M, 3 a "	Gowl Olive A, 21 a "
Crossley D W, 112 a "	Graham R B, 20 a Anderson
Crossley S & E B, 65 a Pndlton	Gray Phoebe, 71 a Pendleton
Crossley Wm F, 49 a Pendleton	Gregory B F, 160 a "
Cullipher J, 100 a "	Gregory Viluna C, 64 a "
Cummins C E, 40 a Middletwn	Guy John, 131 a "
Daniell Charles, 50 a Pendleton	Guy Lorenzo D, 93 a "
Darlington Z, 270 a "	Haines Charles, 5 a "
Davis Bailey, 522 a "	Haines Mary B, 48 a "
Davis Benj F, 73 a "	Haines Noah C, 160 a "
Davis Calvin F, 73 a "	Ham Benj F, 140 a Anderson
Davis John S, 127 a "	Harden Lucinda,160 a Pendleton
Davis Washington, 121 a "	Hardy Thos M, 66 a "
Dille Emma A, 119 a "	Harless E (et al), 84 a Myers
Divin W & J R, 240 a "	Harpold Emaline,14 a Anderson
Dobson Adam, 174 a "	Hays S (heirs), 60 a Pendleton
Dotty Sarah A, 40 a Alfonte	Hays Susan, 20 a "
Downs Isaac, 110 a Pendleton	Hays Wm, 27 a "
Duffey Margaret A, 40 a "	Heacock Jesse, 85 a "
Dunwoody Jesse J, 106 a "	Heiday Mary, 82 a "
Eppert Margaret, 100 a "	Henry Charles L, 382 a "
Fesler Benj P, 127 a Anderson	Hensley Mary M, 110 a "
Fesler Frederick, 137 a "	Hiatt Branson, 33 a "
Fisher Maria J, 80 a Pendleton	Hickey J & Maria, 22 a "
Fisher Mary, 73 a "	Hiney Isabell, 49 a "
Fogarty James, 80 a Anderson	Hodges Edward W, 3 a "
Foust Leonard J, 18 a Pendleton	Hudson Theodore, 80 a "
Fowler James A, 3 a "	Hull John H, 35 a Anderson
Frank George P, 60 a "	Hull Wm, 105 a "
Fussell John S, 5 a "	Huntsinger S A, 40 a Pendleton
Gallagher Mary, 91 a "	Huntsinger W F, 33 a "
Garretson Amos, 120 a "	Hussy J R, 388 a Indianapolis
Garretson H, 106 a Pendleton	Iford Daniel, 160 a Pendleton
Garretson Nathan, 159 a "	Irish Adda K, 52 a "
Gelling R and wife, 31 a "	Isgrigg Daniel, 45 a "
Gelling Richard, 133 a "	Jackson George W, 4 a "

John O. Miller, Dealer in WATCHES, CLOCKS & JEWELRY, SILVERWARE and OPTICAL GOODS.
3 N. Meridian, - - - ANDERSON, IND.

J. A. Munchhof & Bros. Undertakers and Funeral Directors and Practical Embalmers. Office and Warerooms,
Telephones 189, 24 and 51.   No. 98 N. Main St., ANDERSON, IND.
☞ OFFICE OPEN DAY AND NIGHT. ☜

MADISON CO. GAZETTEER.   177

Jackson John, 35 a Pendleton
Jacobs Cassius C, 78 a   "
Jacobs Charles P, 210 a   "
James Charles R, 152 a   "
James Charles R Jr, 5 a   "
James Mary B, 20 a   "
Janney Jonas, 273 a   "
Johnson C, 91 a Wichita, Kan
Jones Jonathan, 119 a Anderson
Jones John D, 20 a Pendleton
Jones Sarah, 39 a   "
Jordan Katharine, 80 a Elwood
Kerr James V, 160 a Pendleton
Keesling Louisa (et al), 151 a Mechanicsburg
Keller Geo W, 160 a Pendleton
Kemper Joel, 77 a Anderson
Kessler J & M, 20 a Pendleton
Kinmamon Conrad, 42 a   "
Kinmamon S (heirs), 61 a   "
Kinard Joseph D, 117 a   "
Kinnard J H, 120 a   "
Kinnard W R, 79 a   "
Koeniger W & C, 1 a Anderson
Kuhns John, 100 a Pendleton
Kuhns Levi A, 80 a   "
Larcher Henry, 47 a Anderson
Larcher Mathias, 63 a   "
Lewis Albert G, 1 a Pendleton
Lewis J B, 69 a   "
Lewis John J, 9 a   "
Lick Zelphia, 46 a   "
Lisey M E, 200 a Indianapolis
Loy David, 100 a Pendleton
Loy Jacob, 80 a   "
Lukens A, 83 a   "
Lukens Elizabeth, 38 a   "
Lukens Jane, 8 a   "
Lukens Lydia, 46 a   "
Lukens Perry, 56 a   "
Lukens Wm A, 60 a   "
Lunsford Sarah J, 21 a   "
McCarty Hannah, 140 a   "
McCarty Ulyses G, 28 a   "
McCarty Wm A, 56 a   "

McGraw John, 80 a Anderson
McKee Samuel, 80 a Pendleton
Marble E F (et al), 160 a   "
Manifold James M, 38 a   "
Manifold J W, 207 a Alfonte
Manning Alice B, 18 a Pendleton
Manning Belena, 2 a   "
Manning Elizabeth, 97 a   "
Manning John E, 56 a   "
Manning Mary, 80 a Pendleton
Manning Robert C. 18 a   "
Martin Frank P, 118 a   "
Michael Jos H, 20 a Anderson
Millikin T M, 6 a New Castle
Mingle George, 40 a Pendleton
Mingle H W, 124 a   "
Mingle Peter, 324 a   "
Mingle Sarah, 1 a   "
Mittank Cyntha F, 80 a   "
Mort Wm, 7 a Pendleton
Nicholson Eva, 43 a Pendleton
Oldham Abner, 120 a   "
Oldham Mary A, 92 a   "
Parsons J B & Mary, 59 a   "
Patterson Martha, 121 a   "
Pavey George W, 141 a   "
Pavey Wm, 104 a   "
Pearson J, 1 a Mechanicsburg
Petty E & G Snell, 20 a Pendleton
Phipps Geo A, 6 a Pendleton
Pine Mary, 88 a Cincinnati, O
Piper Mary A, 80 a Pendleton
Poindexter E, 57 a Anderson
Poindexter R E, 134 a Anderson
Poor Phoebe, 111 a   "
Pritchard N, 200 a Pendleton
Pritchard Sarah, 41 a   "
Props Louisa C, 101 a   "
Quinlan James, 120 a   "
Raines Emily, 15 a   "
Raines H W (heirs), 160 a"
Rash Martha J, 1 a Kansas
Reason Jas H, 80 a Pendleton
Reason Jesse, 70 a   "
Reger Anthony, 80 a   "

J. S. STUART, "THE FLORIST," Cut Flowers and Floral Work a specialty. 99 to 111 W. 3d. Telephone 73. ANDERSON, IND.

WOOLLEY Foundry and Machine Works,
Designers and Manufacturers of **Heavy Machinery, Engines, Boilers and Rolling Mill Work.**
N. W. Cor. 14th and C. W. and M. R. R.

WHEN—The Most Reliable CLOTHING House
✲ IN ANDERSON. ✲
PRICES ALWAYS THE LOWEST.

178 MADISON. CO. GAZETTEER.

Reid John I, 71 a Pendleton
Reynolds E A, 37 a Maxwell
Reynolds Jas A, 120 a "
Rider Sarah E, 67 a Ovid
Riggs W (heirs), 40 a Pendleton
Roberts Edward, 80 a "
Roberts James L, 1 a "
Roberts Kitty A, 40 a "
Roberts Sarah J, 102 a "
Rogers Benj, 81 a "
Rogers George A, 46 a "
Rogers Joseph R, 170 a "
Rogers Levi, 102 a "
Rogers Sarah A, 70 a "
Rogers Sarah D, 34 a "
Scott Alice L, 10 a "
Scott Elsbury, 161 a Alfonte
Scott Evaline, 7 a "
Scott James M, 120 a "
Scott John W, 80 a Leisure
Scott M & others, 10 a Alfonte
Scott M & Haywood, 79 a "
Seybert Elizab'th, 40 a Pendleton
Seybert Margaret, 113 a "
Seybert Wm, 48 a "
Shaffer Wm H, 5 a "
Shaul Della, 10 a "
Shaul Emaline S, 10 a "
Shaul Melvin & Ora, 1 a "
Shaul Solomon, 107 a "
Shaw Levi & Rosa, 94 a "
Shelhorn David W, 40 a "
Shelton Malissa, 1 a "
Shuman H H, 120 a "
Shuman Jehu, 140 a "
Shuman Wm D, 20 a "
Silver Amanda E, 45 a "
Silver James R, 342 a "
Sisson Wm, 120 a "
Smith Wm, 83 a "
Snyder Daniel, 143 a "
Stickler Lewis, 199 a "
Swain Charles E, 160 a "
Swain Jos S, 172 a Pendleton
Swain Samuel, 75 a "
Swain W, 117 a Pendleton
Talbott Angeline, 12 a "
Talbott John T, 50 a "
Talmage Mary J, 33 a Anderson
Taylor A B & J B, 104 a Pendln
Taylor Hattie G, 40 a Pendleton
Taylor Jacob C, 189 a "
Taylor James A, 240 a "
Taylor Jesse B, 1 a "
Taylor Ssmuel A, 1 a "
Taylor U G, 131 a "
Thomas Caroline T, 1 a "
Thomas Jonathan W, 29 a "
Thomas John L, 116 a "
Thornburg Mary, 1 a Anderson
Tillson B B, 146 a Pendleton
Tillson B B & Mary, 33 a "
Tyson C, 70 a Pendleton
Tyson D W, 26 a "
Van Buskirk Nancy E, 105 a
Vernon Abner, 56 a Pendleton
Vernon Edward B, 80 a "
Vestal L C, 60 a Anderson
Watson Hannah, 80 a Pendleton
Whisler George W, 20 a
White B, 26 a Pendleton
Whiteley Alice T, 9 a Pendleton
Widener M J, 80 a "
Wilhoit Thos. 80 a Anderson
Wilkinson W L, 80 a Pendleton
Williams David J, 72 a "
Williams D (et al), 65 a "
Williams Elijah, 221 a "
Williams E A, 40 a Frankton
Williams Jas, 64 a Pendleton
Williams Silas W, 342 a "
Williams S G, 222 a "
Wilson Sarah J, 44 a "
Wiseman J B, 77 a "
Wood Albert C, 160 a "
Woolman I and E, 1 a "

Insure with ROOP & HAYNES,
IN THE STANDARD COMPANIES THEY REPRESENT.
210½ S. Anderson, • • • • • • ELWOOD, IND.

Robinson & Glasseo, Real Estate, Loans and Insurance. Building and Loan money procured in 15 days.
Room 9 "When" Building, - ANDERSON, IND.

Wynant Adam, 2 a Anderson Yost Helen M, 24 a Pendleton
Wynant M M, 4 a Pendleton Zueblin J W, 166 a   "
Wynant S & wife, 21 a   "   Zueblin John E, 9 a   "

GREEN TOWNSHIP.

POST OFFICES.

Alfonte, Anderson, Fishersburg, Fortville, Frankton, Markleville, Nobleville, Pendleton.

"A" FOR ACRES.

Abdon Catherine, 8 a non-res   Day T C & Co, 105 a Ind'apolis
Alfonte W (heirs), 8 a Alfonte Decamp Saml, 80 a Greenfield
Allison Nancy, 81 a Fishersbrg Delawter Julia, 160 a Lapel
Amick Henry, 51 a   "   Denton Saml, 151 a Alfonte
Anderson M J, 50 a Pendleton   Diven C E, 60 a Pendleton
Anderson S I (et al), 30 a "   Doty B & M, 33 a Fortville
Bargus W M, 112 a Fishersbrg   Doty Sarah A, 43 a Alfonte
Bedel Luther, 40 a Pendleton   Doty Thos J, 85 a Fortville
Bells Josephus, 306 a   "   Duffy Wm, 65 a Pendleton
Bell Millard F, 110 a Fortville Dunham Geo, 49 a Lapel
Bennett C and A, 16 a Andersn   Edwards R S, 153 a Fortville
Bennett Wm, 1 a Pendleton   Emery Margaret, 10 a   "
Bennett Wm H, 4 a   "   Everson Amos, 40 a Pendleton
Bixler, Evaline, 6 a Fortville Faussett C E, 1 a Fortville
Bixler John, 56 a Fortville   Faussett Jno K, 127 a Fortville
Bolinger A E, 150 a Pendleton   Faussett R J, 138 a   "
Bolinger Elijah, 60 a   "   Ford Amanda A, 31 a Pendleton
Brattain Emery E, 13 a   "   Ford Eugene L, 32 a   "
Brattain Isaac M, 120 a   "   Ford Martha A, 206 a   "
Brown Calvin F, 64 a   "   Fotout P H, 56 a Fortville
Brown Frank E, 84 a Fortville   Foust J & F, 80 a Pendleton
Burdett J C, 100 a   "   Frey Frederick, 16 a   "
Burk E & L, 120 a Anderson   Gardner A C, 17 a Anderson
Chappel Angeline, 66 a Fortville Gardner Mary A, 60 a Fortville
Clark E & wife, 80 a Pendleton Gascho Jno B, 45 a Noblesville
Clark Edward J, 3 a   "   George Jas M, 30 a Pendleton
Cloush Wm N & M, 60 a   "   George Margaret M, 53 a   "
Cohen Joseph, 17 a Anderson   Ginder George, 40 a Fortville
Cohen Lydia, 64 a   "   Girt Nancy, 36 a   "
Conger Sarah, 5 a Fortville   Glenn E & A, 50 a Pendleton
Cramer Thos, 40 a Pendleton   Goodrich C & E, 145 a   "
Crossley Andrew, 87 a   "   Gowl Henry, 80 a   "
Cummins John S, 5 a Alfonte   Gowl Noah B R, 40 a   "
Davis Addison C, 120 a Fortville Greenlee J K, 30 a   "

Deal & Willkie, have placed 85 loans in six months, Farm loans at 6%. All parties desiring to secure loans
WILL SAVE MONEY BY CALLING ON US.

J. P. CONDO & SON, FURNITURE DEALERS, ESTABLISHED 1856. ALEXANDRIA, IND. We have the largest stock, latest styles, latest designs, sold on EASY WEEKLY PAYMENTS.

WHEN — The Only Retail Clothiers
In the State of Indiana
That Manufacture their OWN CLOTHING.

180   MADISON CO. GAZETTEER.

Greenlee S, 10 a Pendleton
Guinn J H & T, 40 a Fortville
Haas Godfrey, 60 a Pendleton
Haas John G, 70 a   "
Haskell Jno H, 80 a Fortville
Heaton Ross, 129 a   "
Hersberger Howard, 4 a Lapel
Hickey J and M, 156 a Fortville
Hiday Colder, 2 a Alfonte
Hiday Jas W, 50 a Fortville
Hiday Thos E, 144 a   "
Hiday Wm, 55 a   "
House P T, 1 a   "
House Wm R, 99 a   "
Hunter Louisa, 34 a Alfonte
Huston John W, 103 a   "
Huston Jos L, 195 a   "
Hutton S W, 176 a Pendleton
Johnson C, 34 a Wichita Kan
Johnson Emma, 31 a Pendleton
Johnson M & E, 3 a   "
Jones Hiram R, 78 a Alfonte
Jones James T, 200 a   "
Jones Rebecca, 55 a   "
Jones Silas J, 217 a   "
Jones S A D, 37 a   "
Jones Wm A, 40 a   "
Kincaid Amos, 78 a Fortville
Kinnamon Howard, 90 a Florida
Kramer Emma E, 20 a Elwood
Laufer Ann M, 78 a Alfonte
Leonard Wm L, 4 a Leisure
Lewis M M, 85 a Anderson
Losey Mary E, 4 a Indianapolis
Lukens Wm I, 100 a Pendleton
McAdams E, 22 a Alfonte
McCord Jas P, 30 a Frankton
McGuire M and M, 5 a Alfonte
McVey James, 40 a Greenfield
Manifold Jno C, 80 a Alfonte
Manifold W H, 240 a   "
Manifold W W, 81 a   "
Markle M M, 4 a Markleville
Michael H & wife, 1 a Pendleton
Michaels Jonas W, 5 a   "

Miller Belamy J, 40 a Pendleton
Millikin F M, 50 a New Castle
Moon Saml D, 40 a Pendleton
Myers Elizabeth, 60 a Fortville
Nicholson Abram, 286 a   "
Page John R, 144 a Anderson
Passwater W J, 3 a Lapel
Pelkington E, 40 a Fortville
Pettigrew Chas, 55 a Fortville
Pettigrew F M, 5 a   "
Pettigrew G W Jr, 43 a Pendltn
Pettigrew G W Sr, 80 Fortville
Pettigrew Jas M, 78 a Pendleton
Pettigrew John, 160 a   "
Pettigrew Sarah, 80 a   "
Pettigrew Wm C, 80 a Alfonte
Petty, Petty & Cotrell, 60 a
  Pendleton
Pike Lydia, 40 a Pendleton
Pike N T, 20 a   "
Pyle Absolom, 20 a Fortville
Randall P & W, 120 a Alfonte
Randall W P, 89 a   "
Rayner Emma L, 133 a   "
Remler A, 16 a Pendleton
Richards Emily C, 120 a Alfonte
Riggs L & L, 80 a Pendleton
Roberts S J & D, 40 a Alfonte
Rogers & Morris, 210 a Pendleton
Rumler Alex, 17 a   "
Ryan Henry C, 100 a   "
Savage C A, 40 a   "
Scott James M, 154 a   "
Shaul George K, 80 a   "
Shaul O B, 189 a   "
Sherman Hester, 69 a Fortville
Skinner Elijah J, 28 a   "
Smith Branson, 200 a Pendleton
Smith B & C E, 76 a   "
Smith Wm & wife, 200 a   "
Smithers John A, 119 a   "
Smithers Willard, 27 a   "
Springer J F & E, 180 a   "
Stanley Wm, 46 a   "
Stewart Jos C, 15 a Anderson

John L. Lindskoog, The Leading Tailor of Alexandria. All the Latest Novelties in Suitings and Trouserings.

H. H. H. Block, N. E. Cor. Church and Harrison, ALEXANDRIA, IND.

WM. J. DOVE
NEELEY BLOCK.   61½ N. Meridian, ANDERSON, IND.

Can give you choice in 20 of the oldest and best Insurance Companies represented. Note this fact when placing your insurance.

MADISON CO. GAZETTEER.   181

tinson Abraham, 35 a
tinson N E, 78 a Pendleton
:inson W & wife, 35 a "
:ottlemyer H, 11 a Fortville
immers Sarah C, 15 a Lapel
wain Henry, 135 a Alfonte
'lvester Jno H, 80 a Pendleton
'lvester Nora M, 40 a   "
'lvester Wm, 161 a   "
ylor Ethel P, 31 a   "
ylor Jas, 77 a Anderson
ylor Jos (et al), 60 a Pendleton
ylor Leroy C, 40 a   "
eters Milan M, 40 a   "
ıkle Almeda, 16 a   "
ıe David, 34 a Fortville
ick Peter, 40 a Pendleton
lentine James, 66 a "
lentine J H, 13 a Pendleton
ɑ Buskirk, G W, 160 a Fortville

Vanzant I E, 160 a Fortville
Watts Amelia, 31 a   "
Welchel Jno, 66 a   "
Welchel Jno W, 26 a "
Whetsel T, 100 a   "
White Joseph, 80 a Nobleville
White Lydia, 1 a Pendleton
White Reuben P, 113 a Alfonte
White Samuel, 160 a Pendleton
White W (heirs), 160 a "
White Wesley Jr, 183 a "
Williamson B. 404 a   "
Williamson G A, 238 a "
Wilson Jas A, 82 a   "
Wilson Lona E, 17 a   "
Wine Jezriel, 40 a   "
Wise Samuel V, 89 a   "
Wood Amos I, 40 a   "
Yanncy Simeon T, 80 a "
Young Hattie, 56 a   "

JACKSON TOWNSHIP.

POST OFFICES.

Anderson, Halford, Lapel, Pendleton, Perkinsville, Myers.

"A" FOR ACRES.

ıott Jno W, 16 a Halford
erson E A, 80 a Perk'vlle
erson H T, 92 a   "
erson Sam, 20 a Pendleton
ar Peter, 13 a Perkinsville
ar Wm H, 88 a   "
legate A J, 234 a Perk'vlle
ıy Anna M, 1 a Halford
ıy Josephine, 77 a Halford
ıy J M, 1 a Halford
ıy Richard, 52 a Halford
y Wm & R, 53 a   "
James, 153 a Perkinsville
Sarah, 6 a Summitville
with T L, 28 a Perk'ville
with Z, 140 a   "
Henry R, 93 a Lapel
Zerelda, 50 a   "

Bogart J & S, 24 a Perkinsville
Boone J W, 5 a Noblesville
Branch C N, 87 a Anderson
Busby Andrew G, 40 a Lapel
Busby J M, 114 a Fishersburg
Busby Mary A, 56 a Lapel
Cannon Walter & Bessie, 40 a
Cather Robert, 114 a Anderson
Clark Alfred H, 240 a Myers
Clifford A J, 29 a Anderson
Codington W A, 44 a Perk'ville
Cooper Ethelina, 27 a Frankton
Cooper R, 32 a Perkinsville
Cox T C & others, 119 a Elwood
Cox Thos K, 326 a   "
Coy Euphemia, 63 a Halford
Coy Geo W, 80 a   "
Coy John W, 69 a   "

ırson Foundry and Machine Works, Manufacturers of BOILERS, Steam Heaters, Castings, and General Machinery.
JACKSON STREET,   Phone 53.
ANDERSON, IND.

Jackson & Burr Represent the Largest Lines and the Strongest INSURANCE Companies.

69½ N. Meridian, - - - ANDERSON, IND.

182   MADISON CO. GAZETTEER.

Coy Luella, 40 a Halford
Coy Martin L, 53 a   "
Coy Mathew, 360 a   "
Coy N & wife, 40 a   "
Coy Seth T, 80 a   "
Cunningham S, 26 a Marklevlle
Danforth F M, 267 a Perk'ville
Davis Corwin, 39 a Anderson
Davis Jane, 53 a   "
Davis Jesse E, 56 a   "
Davis Nancy, 11 a   "
Davis Chas J, 246 a Myers
DeHority Jas M, 50 a Elwood
Dewitt N H, 90 a Perkinsville
Downham A J, 82 a   "
Downham C, 71 a   "
Downham Jas Jr, 74 a   "
Downham L, 16 a   "
Doyle Abraham, 160 a Myers
Doyle J B & Isabell, 20 a Myers
Dyer Fred, 1 a Perkinsville
Etchison J, 343 a Perkinsville
Etchison Mary, 240 a Frankton
Farlow Jos M, 160 a Frankton
Flowers Mary F, 40 a
Foland T, 120 a Perkinsville
Funk Timothy H, 80 a Myers
Garner Lucy, 23 a Myers
Garretson M A, 70 a Perk'ville
Garretson Wm M, 101 a   "
Gentry Elvin, 300 a   "
Gentry F M, 106 a   "
Gill Geo C, 150 a   "
Goldsberry D, 100 a   "
Goldsberry Jas M, 1 a   "
Gwinn Laben, 40 a Lapel
Hadess Ann, 30 a
Hall Caleb, 1 a Perkinsville
Hanger Samuel M, 78 a
Harless Chas, 34 a Myers
Harless Elizabeth, 70 a Myers
Harless Isabell, 100 a Myers
Harvey C M, 93 a Perkinsville
Harvey H E, 40 a   "
Hays Amanda, 15 a   "

Hays Julia A, 29 a Perkinsville
Heaton S F & P, 40 a Marklevlle
Hem Chris, 2 a Frankton
Hilligoss C, 87 a Henderson
Hilligoss Geo N, 40 a Anderson
Hoover E. 40 a Perkinsville
Hoover W H, 45 a Perkinsville
Hosier Edna, 16 a Myers
Hosier Peter, 134 a Myers
Hozier S E, 120 a Perkinsville
Huffman C, 74 a Perkinsville
Huffman Minard, 10 a Lapel
Huffman Z, 100 a Perkinsville
Huntzinger S. 40 a Pendleton
Johnson Chas, 2 a Wichita Kan
Johnson James, 80 a Anderson
Jones Elijah, 120 a Frankton
Kemp D W, 392 a Halford
Kemp Henry, 320 a   "
Kimmerling Sarah, 26 a Elwood
Knopp Jas M, 80 a Frankton
Knopp Jesse. 25 a   "
Knopp J B, 116 a   "
Lee J Heirs, 1 a Perkinsville
Leever Elmira, 40 a Anderson
Lennis L, 80 a Perkinsville
Lennis W H, 40 a   "
Leonard F & wife, 40 a Leisure
Likens Jacob, 160 a Aroma
Likens Jos, 160 a Myers
Likens M A, 14 a Perkinsville
Likens Wm, 266 a   "
McCarty L, 24 a   "
McCarty L B, 21 a   "
McClintock A P, 140 a   "
McClintock A W, 155 a   "
McClintock D, 240 a   "
McClintock Ira E, 80 a   "
McClintock J, 10 a   "
McClintock L E, 80 a   "
McClintock L, 110 a Halford
McClintock L J, 75 a Perk'ville
McClintock M et al, 80 a   "
McClintock N. 70 a Halford
McClintock O E, 120 a Perk'vlle

George B. Epperson, Contractor & Builder of Concrete Side Walks.

39 E. 9th St.,   -   -   ANDERSON, IND.

...l Estate Exchange does a general Real Estate business. The finest lots in the world for sale or trade at our office.
East 10th Street, - ANDERSON, IND.

intock O & E, 40 a Prkville
lintock O, 123 a "
intock S, 76 a "
intock W E, 79 a, "
rd Aaron, 592 a Frankton
rd. A, 25 a Perkinsville
rd Geo, 23 a Myers
rd Jno R, 160 Frankton
rd Moses, 191 a Myers
rd S T, 46 a Perkinsville
rd Wm, 160 a Frankton
rd W W, 120 a Myers
y T E, 40 a Perkinsville
F Jr, 80 a Perkinsville
ll Wm, 160 a "
er A T, 77 a "
J P, 120 a–Middletown
M E, 17 a Perkinsville
an Thos B, 21 a Elwood
Anna E, 54 a Daleville
Hrs, 17 a Perkinsville
Cornelius, 235 a Halford
W R, 80 a Anderson
Geo W, 167 a Anderson
R, 308 a Perkinsville
Wm, 127 a "
ville J. J. 100 a Anderson
Vm H et al, 120 a Halford
M, 27 a Perkinsville
E J, 40 a Frankton
W B, 160 a Lapel
G W, 25 a Perkinsville
Jackson, 160 a Anderson
S & F, 40 a Anderson
s Eli, 16 a Perkinsville
Thos, 48 a Myers
Tm A, 71 a Perkinsville
nd G, 158 a Frankton
ne Martha J, 1 a Myers
ne Noah, 222 a Frankton
neline, 1 a Perkinsville
t Cynthia, 40 a Myers
t L & G, 52 a Halford
os, 97 a Perkinsville
oah, 110 a Halford

Ryan W P, 70 a Perkinsville
Schingler H, 68 a "
Schuyler Geo W, 85 a "
Smith Asa, 38 a Middletown
Sumpter J R, 55 a College Cor, O
Sharp Jas P, 200 a Frankton
Shell Amanda, 20 a Perkinsville
Shell Flora D, 13 a "
Shell Geo M, 13 a "
Shell Lowell B, 13 a "
Shell Susan, 40 a Frankton
Sheppell E, 20 a Perkinsville
Shetterly Geo L, 60 a Anderson
Shetterly R, 16 a Perkinsville
Shingles Richard, 1 a
Shinkle Mary L, 25 a Anderson
Shively Sam, 187 a Perkinsville
Taylor Mary, 36 a Myers
Todd S & wife et al, 80 a Myers
Todd Sam & Marie, 143 a "
Tooly Jno W, 80 a Lapel
Truett Mary, 80 a
Tuttle Darlin & J Watson, 20 a
Wade N A, 60 a Perkinsville
Wade Wm & N, 32 a "
Wall Julia A, 1 a "
Webb Jacob Jr, 8 a Frankton
Webb Sophia. 24 a Halford
White Benj F, 125 a Halford
Williamson B F, 40 a Perk'ville
Wise Augusta V, 30 a "
Wise Henry A, 71 a "
Wise Jno Sr, 216 a "
Wise Mary J, 81 a "
Wise Nancy, 48 a "
Wise Rachel, 138 a "
Wise Seth, 56 a "
Wise Simeon, 20 a Lapel
Wise Susan, 58 a Perkinsville
Wise Wm H, 58 a "
Wise Wm S & R, 40 a "
Woodward Wm, 13 a Lapel
Wright W T. 105 a Frankton
Zeller M, 97 a Perkinsville

Buck, Brickley & Co., Anderson, Ind.

THE LEADING. DRUGGISTS, FINE WALL PAPER AND DECORATIONS.

Fisher's Novelty Works! Jig and Scroll Saw Work in all the latest designs and patterns. Call and examine my work.
and 200 N. Milton St.,
※ ANDERSON IND. ※

J. T. Knowland & Son, MAKERS AND DESIGNERS OF **NATURAL GAS Fixtures and Fittings**
111 N. Main St., ANDERSON, IND. 'Phone 30.

184 MADISON CO. GAZETTEER

LAFAYETTE TOWNSHIP.

POST OFFICES.

Alexandria, Anderson, Elwood, Florida, Frankton, Halford, Linwood, Myers.

"A" FOR ACRES.

Abercombie Anna M, 20 a
Adams Ephraim, 83 a Florida
Alexander Alvah D, 11 a
Alexander Jas E, 26 a Frankton
Alexander J, Jr, 12 a Frankton
Alexander J R, 10 a Frankton
Alexander W & L, 1 Frankton
Allen Thos, 5 a Frankton
Allison Jno A, 160 a Henry Co
Antrim A E, 5 a Florida
Applegate A, 160 a Rush Co
Armstrong M R, 66 a Anderson
Ashby Jno & H 9 a Halford
Ashton F E, 23 a Frankton
Ashton F G, 90 a "
Ashton Jacob, 60 a "
Ashton J N, 110 a "
Ashton M J, 40 a "
Austin Mary, 40 a Alexandria
Avery Jane, 1 a Florida
Badger Chas, 1 a Anderson
Ballard & McGill, 40 a Linwood
Barnes John, 110 a Anderson
Beal Elmer, 46 a Linwood
Beal Jno, A 66 a "
Beal M A, 68 a "
Beal Nathan, 10 a "
Beeson J & A, 150 a Richmond
Berkenbine E, 71 a Frankton
Berry Robt J, 80 a Linwood
Bevelhimer E J 1 a Anderson
Bevelhimer S, 199 a "
Bevelhimer T & wife, 1 a Florida
Bilby Martha R, 75 a "
Billingsby E, 67 a "
Bixby R, 40 Frankton
Bodkin C M, 15 a Florida
Bodkin G W & C M, 20 a Florida
Bodkin Isiah M, 34 a

Bond H, (Trust) 80 a Non Res
Bowers J A, 40 a Frankton
Brandon A M, 50 a Anderson
Brewer P A, 40 a Linwood
Briggs W J, 40 a Florida
Broderick J, 199 a "
Broderick T, 60 a "
Bronnenberg I, 80 a Frankton
Bronnenberg J, 75 a Anderson
Bronnenberg M, 80 a Frankton
Brown B J, 40 a Florida
Brown C & S, 160 a Florida
Brown E, 25 a Frankton
Brown G W, 199 a Frankton
Brown Samuel, 13 a Frankton
Brown Sam, Jr 3 a "
Brunt J S J, 56 a Anderson
Canaday H & J, 80 a Anderson
Canaday S & W, 120 a Frankt
Cannaday H, 320 a Anderson
Carew M E, 61 a Florida
Carroll M, 38 a Frankton
Carter M L, 40 a Linwood
Cassell E S, 20 a Anderson
Chambers J H, 200 a Anderson
Childers P A 79 a Florida
Christman M, 38 a Myers
Clark G W, 117 a Florida
Clem Jesse A, 60 a "
Clem Mary, 40 a "
Clem P M, 40 a Anderson
Clem Wm H, 56 a Anderson
Clock Henry, 20 a Florida
Closser Amando, 9 a Andeason
Closser J & C. 20 a "
Closser J W, 160 a "
Closser M E, 19 a "
Cloud Henry, 1 a Mon Res
Collins A M, 79 a Florida

JOHN O. MILLER'S For FINE WATCH REPAIRING and DIAMOND SETTING.
3 N. Meridian, - - - ANDERSON, IND.

A. Munchhof, LEADING FURNITURE DEALER, Nos. 40 and 42 E.8th St., ANDERSON, IND. Largest Stock to select from, and always west CASH PRICES. Watch our show windows.

er Amelia, 20 a Florida
er Elizabeth, 80 a Florida
ier James, 20 a Elwood
:llo Michael, 42 a Anderson
in Hugh, 58 a Anderson
Clarissa, 13 a Frankton
Lewis C, 40 a Anderson
; Nancy, 8 a Florida
; Robt, 97 a Linwood
cer Muniford, 80 Florida
; F & M, 40 a Anderson
; Jas W, 82 a Myers
; Jno H, 160 a Anderson
; Jno R, 1 a Florida
; J W et al, 20 a Myers
; Thos J, 19 a
; Wm J, 62 a Anderson
ig Thos, 200 a Florida
ler Elias, 188 a Linwood
or M M, 68 a Anderson
elly J M, 68 a "
hwart R, 20 a "
: Jas B, 110 a Myers
Jas, 18 a Anderson
Joseph F, 140 a Anderson
d A J, 60 a Frankton
d M F, et al, 40 a Frankt
Jno A, 54 a "
Abraham, 115 a Florida
Geo, 40 a "
Harriet, 40 a Elwood
N, 198 a Anderson
eath A, 80 a Anderson
iner M, 60 a Linwood
son D A 147 a Anderson
ing J R 80 a Frankton
ing Jno D, 80 a Frankton
ing Lena, 271 a "
:ndyke E, 38 a Linwood
:nkyke T, 38 a Linwood
inger S A, 35 a Florida
n J Q, 60 a Anderson
n M, 110 a "
ah James, 80 a
:astle E, 13 a Frankton

Harger David C, 40 a Florida
Harless Charles, 25 a Myers
Harless Elizabeth, 80 a Myers
Harless S E, 39 a Pendleton
Harter J H 60 a Anderson
Hartman D, 122 a Anderson
Hartman Jno C, 50 a Anderson
Hartzell J & B, 19 a Myers
Hawkins B G, 40 a Florida
Hays Luther, 39 a Anderson
Henly Mary, 8 a "
Henn C F, 93 94 a Frankton
Henry Chas L, 93 a Anderson
Hilligoss Ed C, 80 a "
Hinchman Jas, 120 a Linwood
Holden Sarah, 40 a Myers
Hollenbeck H, 128 a Linwood
Hosier Emeline, 25 a Elwood
Howard T A, 77 a Anderson
Hughel Elmer, 160 a Florida
Hughel M, 80 a Anderson
Hume Lewis, 56 a Frankston
Hunt J W, 218 a Anderson
Hunt M V, 180 a "
Jarrett Jas, 200 a Myers
Jenkins I N, 6 a Florida
Jenkins & Thompson, 113 a Florida
Johnson C, 98 Wichita Kan
Jones A D & S, 26 a Linwood
Jones H L, 80 a Florida
Jones Jno L, 323 a Florida
Jones Margaret, 80 a Linwood
Keel C B & Ollie, 1 a Florida
Kerr M, 160 a Anderson
Kerr Russell P. 160 a Anderson
Kimmerling Geo, 34 a Frankton
Kimmerling Jennie, 40 a Myers
Kimmerling Nancy A, 40 a "
Kinnamon H M, 150 a Florida
Kinamon Sarah, 1 a "
Kirk Amanda, 120 a Linwood
Kirk G W & N, 120 a "
Kirk Sylvester, 80 a "
Kirtley R & wife, 47 a Frankton

J. S. STUART, THE FLORIST, Wholesale and Retail Plants, Bulbs, and Cut Flowers, 99 to 111 W. 3d, ANDERSON, IND. Telephone 75.

TOOLLEY Foundry and Machine Works,
General Machinery, Heavy and Light Castings, and Sheet Iron Work.
N. W. COR. 14th AND C W. AND M. R. R.

WHEN—The Largest Stock of CLOTHING, HATS, CAPS and Gents' FURNISHING GOODS in ANDERSON.

186 , MADISON CO. GAZETTEER.

Klepper R, 120 a Frankton
Klipter Jno M, 80 a "
Koehler Adam, 173 a Anderson
Koeniger Louisa, 33 a "
Lambert I, 122 a Frankton
Larkin Hanorah, 10 a Florida
Layne Jas, 140 a Evansville
Leaky Jos & R, 5 a Anderson
Leaky Nancy J, 5 a " '
Lee Thos F, 160 a Linwood
Little John, 40 a Florida
Lowe Wm F, 45 a Linwood
McConnell Thos, 40 a Frankton
McCord H V, 50 a "
McCord Syrena, 44 a "
McCord Wm, 80 a "
McCord Wm W, 24 a Myers
McKee C & wife, 1 a Linwood
McNealey Dom, 40 a Anderson
Mahan Elizabeth, 2 a "
Maladay Martin, 40 a "
Marsh Nelson, 38 a Frankton
Mathes Geo, 37 a Anderson
May Clarinda, 37 a Linwood
May Elizabeth, 40 a Frankton
May Isaac N. 42 a Linwood
May John C, 34 a "
May Polly A, 40 a "
May Samuel, 60 a "
Meck John M, 10 a Anderson
Melser Frederic, 78 a Frankton
Melson Frank, 50 a Myers
Menefee E, 20 a Anderson
Merritt Laura E, 10 a Frankton
Michaels Jno, 160 a Florida
Milburn Isaac, 220 a Anderson
Miller Abe, 20 a Frankton
Miller Jno D, 100 a "
Miller Jonathan, 8 a "
Millikan F M, 95 a New Castle
Misner Sarah E, 24 a Anderson
Moneyhun T & T B, 40 a "
Montgomery A, 20 a Frankton
Montgomery J, 80 a "
Moore J C, 131 a "

Moore Jno, 40 a Frankton
Moore Jonathan, 208 a Linwood
Moore Lucinda, 98 a Frankton
Moss Elijah J, 60 a "
Moss Perry J, 100 a "
Newberry M, 6 a "
Oldham Wm, 1 a Pendleton
Orton Jno, 20 a Frankton
Osburn S A, 157 a Florida
Parker M, 60 a Anderson
Parsons Samuel, 50 a Florida
Pence Alex, 1 a Linwood
Perry Samuel, 40 a Frankton
Pierce E Q, 80 a Frankton
Pierce S, 100 a Frankton
Pipher J H, 40 a Florida
Power J, 20 a Franktan
Rains Thos J, 40 a Florida
Rains Zail, 20 a Anderson
Redington M, 55 a Anderson
Retherford J R, 45 a Linwood
Richwine A, 168 a Myers
Rife Daniel, 90 a Florida
Rife Wm H, 30 a Anderson
Rife Jno W, 120 a Frankton
Riley M C, 40 a Frankton
Riley W S, 6 a Florida
Roadcap Henry, 100 a Florida
Robinet Geo, 22 a Myers
Robinet Lorenzo, 22 a Myers
Rogers Edna, 40 a Myers
Reed Henry, 3 a Frankton
Ryan Alice, 15 a Anderson
Ryan J B, 72 a Perkinsville
Ryan Martin, 50 a Halford
Ryan Wm P, 50 a Perkinsville
Samuels A J, 80 a Frankton
Samuel M, 77 a "
Sanger J N, 39 a Florida
Sansberry J W, 136 a Anderson
Scott Amanda J, 40 a Florida
Scott Amos H, 14 a Frankton
Scott A J, 7 a Frankton
Scott B W, 100 a Anderson
Scott Jas N, 60 a Pendleton

Roop & Haynes
210½ S. Anderson,

Are Agents for FIVE of the BEST BUILDING & LOAN COMPANIES in Indiana.

- - - - ELWOOD, IND.

Buy or Sell Real Estate, To procure money to build with promptly, for Insurance or Loans, Call on **Robinson & Glassco,** Room 9 "When" Building, ANDERSON, IND.

MADISON CO. GAZETTEER.   187

rp Jno, 198 a Frankton	Thomas A & J, 4 a "
tterly W. & M, 91 a Frankt	Thomas Cora A. 15 a Florida
er Daniel, 47 a Elwood	Thomas De R, 195 a Linwood
er D. (Heirs) 8 a Frankton	Thomas Jas U, 41 a Florida
er R, Jr 30 a " "	Thomas N, 120 a Noblesville
er R M, Sr 140 a Frankton	Thomas W & A, 20 a Linwood
er T A, 20 a Frankton	Thomas Wm W, 50 a "
er Xantippe. 65 a Frankton	Thompson C H, 147 a Florida
nons Jacob E, 80 a Myers	Thompson G D, 80 a "
nons Jas A, 60 a Myers	Thompson O R, 40 a Linwood
nons J & L, 80 a Summitv	Tharp H, 40 a Frankton
nons W E, 120 a Frankton	Tingley E, 160 a Non res
son H & A, 1 a Anderson	Townsend E & E 95 a Frankton
r Jane, 22 a	Turner M, 180 a "
ser Heban, 100 Frankton	Van Meter I W, 22 h Florida
ser H, 150 a "	Vasbinder Jno, 1 a Anderson
a Alex, 199 a Florida	Vinyard A, 120 a "
a Jno W, 61 a Anderson	Vinyard Maria, 1 a "
a M A, 80 a Alexandria	Waitmon Mary A, 3 a Florida
a Sarah, 40 a "	Walton & Forkner, 40 a Ander-
son J W, 80 a Frankton	son
ey Adda E, 1 a Anderson	Webb Deniza, 13 a Frankton
ey Amanda E, 70 a Myers	Webb Jno W, 26 a "
r Jacob, 115 a Linwood	Webb Minor, 324 a "
Joel D, 60 a Myers	Wesh Josiah C, 120 a non res
ens Geo, 10 a Florida	Willey Chas, 25 a Florida
ens Samuel, 80 a Florida	Williams E A, 240 a Frankton
ell A, 23 a Linwood	Wilson C C, 39 a Linwood
r Jno F, 21 a Frankton	Wilson C C & L, 37 a Linwood
n E A, 80 a Anderson	Wilson John R. 39 a Anderson
a Jno, 40 a "	Wilson Thos, 80 a Linwood
E, 25 a Frankton	Wise Allen P, 55 a Frankton
ild Jno M, 81 a Myers	Woods Victoria, 40 a "
s Alva, 1 a Florida	Young Belle, 5 a "

MONROE TOWNSHIP.

POST OFFICES.

ndria, Fairmount, Gilman, Linwood, Orestes, Indianapolis.

"A" FOR ACRES.

John, 203 a Alexandria	Baker B, 200 a Indianapolis
le Mathew, 11 a "	Baker Hannah, 40 a, Gilman
n C, 100 a Fairmount	Baker Philip & E, 40 a "
W & J, 68 a Alexandria	Baker W F, 219 a "
W H, 40 a Gilman	Ballard Jno R, 20 a Linwood
W K, 1 a Alexandria	Ballard Rebecca, 20 a "

WHEN—Children's Department
A SPECIAL FEATURE.
Always well Stocked with the LATEST NOVELTIES.

188　　　　MADISON CO. GAZETTEER.

Ballard Thomas, 80 a Linwood
Barrett Edward, 1 a Alexandria
Baxter Chas E, 10 a　　"
Baxter Jeremiah, 37 a Orestes
Baxter Thos, 400 a Alexandria
Beatson Jas & E, 50 a　"
Beck Charity, 11 a Frankton
Beck E W, 226 a Alexandria
Beck Jno, 10 a Summitville
Beck Rachel, 105 a Frankton
Beck & W, 160 a Summitville
Bell John & M, 63 a Alexandria
Bell Thos, 80 a　　"
Benefield Wm, 100 a Gilman
Bickham Chas M, 80 Anderson
Biddle Geo, 80 a Alexandria
Black D W, 67 a　　"
Black Franklin, 1 a　"
Black Mary E, 80 a Orestes
Blackledge M, 80 a Anderson
Blake Wm P, 80 a Alexandria
Booth Nathan, 19 a Linwood
Bowers David, 406 a Alexandria
Bowers Jas E, 80 a　"
Bowers Mary, 40 a　"
Boyce Geo W, 20 a Frankton
Bradbern McC, 2 a Alexandria
Bramel Z W, 136 a　"
Bronnenberg J, 141 a Anderson
Bronnenberg S, 107 a Alexand
Brown Caroline, 2 a　"
Brown J F, 11 a Summitville
Brown Nathan, 80 a　"
Brown S P, 200 a　　"
Brunt Jas A J, 310 a Anderson
Buck Jemima, 10 a Alexandria
Buck Mary E, 25 a　"
Buck S H, 139 a Alexandria
Burton Violet, 10 a Alexandria
Burton Violet Jr, 20 a Anderson
Cammack D, 63 a Alexandria
Campfield, Watts & P, 110 a
Carver D K, 488 a Alexandria
Carver Esther J, 1 a Anderson
Carver Geo, 58 a Orestes

Carver Jno, 40 a Gilman
Carver Lorenzo, 199 a Orestes
Carver Sanford H, 2 a Orestes
Carver Wm, 119 a Alexandria
Carver Wm K, 5 a Orestes
Cassell Jas C, 124 a Gilman
Cassell Jno, 60 a Alexandria
Cassell Samuel, 74 a　"
Chaplin Mary, 12 a Alexandria
Childs Oscar E, 2 a Gilman
Cole Laura S, 40 a Orestes
Cole Perry P, 40 a Alexandria
Conner Oliver, 1 a　"
Cook Joel & wife, 3 a Orestes
Cooper M H, 21 a Alexandria
Cooper Wm, 80 a　"
Countryman Sam, 2 a　"
Cox Alice, 11 a　　"
Cox James F, 11 a　"
Cox Mary A, 18 a Summitville
Cree Ada P, 23 a Anderson
Cree Harry & E, 17 a "
Cree Jno M, 119 a Alexandria
Cree Lucian A, 80 a Anderson
Cree Sarah E, 50 a Gilman
Cridge Robt, 80 a Anderson
Cross A P, 58 a Alexandria
Cunningham G, 60 a Marklevlle
Dartee Hiram H, 100 a Gilman
Davault Abram, 69 a Tipton
Davis Amos S, 69 a Anderson
Deadman T, 25 a Summitvillle
Delinger W. H, 25 a Orestes
Denny Elmira, 25 a Anderson
Depauw W C Co, 7 a Alexand
Ditto S, 83 a Summitville
Divin W S, 80 a Anderson
Dobson Mary, 40 a Gilman
Donahoo Thomas H, 76 a
Donnelly J M, 143 a Anderson
Draper Jno W, 80 a Gilman
Draper Jos, 160 a　　"
Draper Martha J, 80 a　"
Draper Peter, 80 a　"
Duncan C J, 28 a Alexandria

John L. Lindskoog,
Fine Tailoring in Suits and Pants. An examination solicited. A FIT GUARANTEED.

I. H. H. Block, N. E. Cor. Church and Harrison, ALEXANDRIA, IND.

WM. J. DOVE
NEELEY BLOCK.

Is Agent for National Home Building and Loan Ass'n of Bloomington, Ill You can get all the money you want on short notice.

61½ N. Meridian, ANDERSON, IND.

MADISON CO. GAZETTEER. 189

Dwiggins E, 27 a Orestes
East James A, 99 a Frankton
Edwards A E, 200 a Alexandria
Ellis Robt G, 60 a Alexandria
Ellis Sarab A, 20 a "
Ellis Wiley, 80 a "
Ellsworth J, 40 a Summitville
Eppard Jno W, 40 Gilman
Eppard Noah, 40 a Gilman
Fennimore M A, 5 a Alexandria
Ferguson Eli T, 40 a "
Ferguson James, 23 a Orestes
Ferguson Robt, 68 a "
Ferguson S, 122 a Alexandria
Ferguson Wm J, 68 a Orestes
Finch W O & M, 1 a Alexandria
Fink Delilah J, 31 a "
Fink Elizabeth, 32 a "
Fink Jno A, 31 a "
Fink J F & E J, 18 a "
Fisher J H, 77 a "
Flood Mary B, 40 a Orestes
Foland Jacob, 40 a Alexandria
Foland Lesta, 4 a "
Fox Jacob, 9 a Frankton
Fox Mary E, 110 a Alexandria
Frazier Jas M, 160 a Gilman
Fuller Jno H, 80 a "
Fuller Mary, 22 a "
Fuller Polk, 168 a "
Fuller W H, 198 a Alexandria
Garrison A H, 21 Anderson
Gooding F M, 14 a Frankton
Gooding Lenox, 60 a "
Gooding M, 52 a Alexandria
Goodman Isaac, 200 a Orestes
Gordon Jas, 351 a Alexandria
Gordon Jas Heirs, 40 a "
Gordon W B et al, 35 a "
Graves Geo H, 80 a "
Gray M E, 80 a "
Gregory Isham A, 73 a Orestes
Griffin Isabell. 48 a Alexandria
Hall Jesse H, 160 a "
Hall Nathan A, 80 a "

Hall Wm I, 41 a Alexandria
Hammond G W, 162 a Gilman
Hamilton Sarah A, 1 a Elwood
Hannah R H, 85 a Alexandria
Hanger W H, 77 a Lapel
Harling H B, 116 a Alexandria
Harris Margaret, 26 a Orestes
Harrison Mary, 50 a Gilman
Harrold A E et al, 1 a Gilman
Hart Samuel, 40 a Alexandria
Hawkins Aaron, 80 a "
Haydon Cora E, 40 a Gilman
Heer Chris, 10 a Alexandria
Heritage H, 240 a "
Heritage W E, 40 a Summitvlle
Hicks G, 48 a Alexandria
Hicks Wm, 128 a "
Hile Nellie, 1 a "
Holford Geo, 1 a "
Hollowell G T, 60 a "
Hollowell H & G, 60 a Alexandri
Hood Richards, 158 a Gilman
Hoop Isaac N, 40 a Alexandria
Hoover Lydia, 40 a "
Howard Wm, 40 a "
Howerton Marion & N, 85 a
Hudson T J, 80 a Alexandria
Hughes Jas, 236 a "
Hughes Jno M, 91 a "
Hughes Robt, 37 a "
Hughes Sarah E, 32 a "
Hughes Thos E, 80 a "
Hughes Wm A, 25 a "
Hussey Jonathan, 157 a Milton
Hustin Wm, 297 a Alexandria
Innis R E & M, 62 a "
Jarrett A, 12 a Alexandria
Jarrett James, 80 a Gilman
Jarrett Lorenia, 73 a "
Jarrett Smith, 47 a Alexandria
Johnson Ambrose, 1 a Orestes
Johnson A L, 40 a "
Johnson C, 24 a Wichita Kan
Johnson E B, 3 a Alexandria
Johnson Paschel Jr, 80 a Gilman

TELEPHONE LARMORE BROS.
513 Nichol Ave., TELEPHONE 220. ANDERSON, IND.
for your ICE CREAM, MILK AND OYSTERS, and be sure of prompt delivery and first-class goods.

Anderson Foundry and Machine Works,
and Job Work of all Kinds **REPAIRS** A SPECIALTY.
'PHONE 53.
265 N. Jackson Street, - - - ANDERSON, IND.

INSURE WITH JACKSON & BURR Latch string always out and light in the window, until the last man's INSURED.
69½ N. Meridian, - - ANDERSON, IND.

190   MADISON CO. GAZETTEER.

Jones Alpha, 131 a Alexandria
Jones I & wife, 51 a Alexandria
Jones James L, 51 a Alfonte
Jones Joel M, 14 a Alexandria
Jones Levoy, 80 a   "
Jones Mary E, 90 a   "
Jones Nora B, 120 a Summitville
Jones Wm E, 14 a Alexandria
Jones W R, 155 a Gilman
Judd Geo W, 156 a Orestes
Keifer Rebecca, 77 a Alexandria
Kelley Cinderella, 1 a Frankton
Kelley Eliza, 4 a Alexandria
Kelley Geo W, 157 a   "
Kelley M D, 80 a   "
King Cynthia, 80 a   "
King Elizabeth, 105 a Frankton
King Jas A, 12 a Orestes
King Wm M, 240 a Alexandria
Kirkman Ann, 2 a
Knotts Jas, 80 a Gilman
Lamb W C, 50 a Orestes
Lambert Chas, 64 a   "
Lane Addison W, 80 a Anderson
Laws Jas, 160 a Anderson
Leach A & wife, 40 a Alexandria
Lee Isaac J W, 320 a "
Lee N A J, 148 a   "
Lee W N, 80 a   "
Lowry Caroline, 81 a Orestes
Lowry David F, 7 a   "
McClead Chas, 214 a   "
McClead Newton, 1 a   "
McKinley R, 60 a Alexandria
McKinney Josiah, 80 a "
McLaughlin A M, 40 a "
McMahan Elijah P, 63 a "
McMahan Jas R, 1 a Orestes
McMahan M M, 4 a   "
McMahan Nathan J, 20 a "
Manning J H, 120 a Alexandria
Markle Ann, 56 a Gilman
Markle J A, 127 a Alexandria
Markle J D Heirs, 160 a "
Markle T B, 80 a Markleville

Martin Jas E, 78 a Orestes
May Nancy J, 50 a Frankton
Maynard A J, 4 a Gilman
Maynard B, 80 a Alexandria
Maynard Elias G, 20 a Gilman
Maynard Geo W Sr, 40 a "
Maynard Jacob, 140 a Anderson
Meredith Arthur E, 42 a
Milburn Alta B, 75 a Gilman
Miller Carrie & Ed, 75 a "
Miller Emeline, 54 a "
Miller Ira F, 59 a   "
Miller Sarah J, 24 a "
Millikin F M, 28 a New Castle
Millikin Thos B, 60 a Elwood
Millspaugh Jno F, 80 a Gilman
Millspaugh M J, 40 a "
Millspaugh M S, 40 a "
Millspaugh Peter B, 159 a "
Mittendorf J, 125 a Alexandria
Mittendorf Jno, 40 a "
Molone H A, 160 a Frankton
Montgomery Sam, 1 a   "
Montgomery S D, 80 a Orestes
Moreland Ida M, 42 a
Morris R H, 80 a Alexandria
Moyer Geo W, 40 a Orestes
Moyer Jno, 40 a   "
Nelson Jno, 30 a Alexandria
Nealis Thos P, 40 a Alexandria
Nicason Nancy J, 100 a "
Noble C, 40 a Alexandria
Noble J & P, 31 a Alexandria
Noble W, 80 a Alexandria
Norris A 120 a Anderson
Norris J & L, 3 a Gilman
O'Bryant D, 108 a Alexandria
O'Bryant Geo, 80 a   "
O'Bryant P, 120 a   "
Osborn J & M, 90 a Orestes
Painter L, 80 a Summitville
Painter N, 140 a Alexandria
Parkhurst J, 47 a   "
Pence E H, 40 a Orestes
Perdue A L, 3 a Alexandria

George B. Epperson, Carriage Paints and Varnishes A Specialty.
9 E. 9th St., - - - - ANDERSON, IND.

Donnelly & Romenger, Livery, Feed and Sale BARN.

48 West 9th St. Telephone 76. ANDERSON, IND.
Fine Horses and Buggies always on hand, at reasonable prices. Driver furnished when required. ☞ Also office at John Donnelly's Real Estate Office, 10 E. 10th St. Tel. 166.

Perry J W, 158 a Alexandria
Perry P, 160 a   "
Perry S B, 28 a   "
Perry W R, 110 a   "
Phillips M, 40 a   "
Pickard J J, 160 a   "
Plackard T L, 1 a Orestes
Porter E, 1 a Orestes
Painter A, 10 a Alexandria
Painter E E, 61 a   "
Peck I E, 80 a Frankton
Peck S E, 40 a Alexandria
Pernod Paul, 40 a Elwood
Perry Mary, 1 a Alexandria
Plackard Marion, 2 a Orestes
Poindexter S, 40 a Alexandria
Poindexter T, 40 a   "
Powell J M, 31 a Anderson
Rathel L, 80 a Summitville
Rathel Leven, 80 a Gilman
Rea Jno, 80 a Frankton
Reavis J F, 78 a Gilman
Reavis Jno F, 2 a Gilman
Redding Caroline, 1 a Orestes
Reed Frank, 80 a Gilman
Reed Nancy A, 12 a Gilman
Reese Addie G, 40 a Alexandria
Reese Jno T, 40 a   "
Reeves Geo W, 77 a   "
Reeves Jas, Sr 51 a Gilman
Reeves Jno M, 60 a   "
Reeves Jordan W, 40 a Gilman
Reeves Mary E, 40 a   "
Ring R A, 6, a Alexandria
Robertson M, 19 a   "
Robinson E, 200 a Alexandria
Robinson Irwin, 41 a   "
Robinson L, 76 a   "
Robinson M T, 22 a   "
Russell James 30 a Orestes
Russell Mary, 3 a   "
Rutledge Enos, 110 a Gilman
Schwim Peter, 161 Alexandria
Scott Dan M, 86 a   "
Scott Wm F, 12 a   "

Shannon J S, 240 a Alexandria
Shaw Elizabeth A, 1 a Orestes
Shaw Wm & M, 42 a   "
Shepherd A, 30 a Alexandria
Shepherd P, 40 a   "
Sherman C E, 40 a   "
Silvey A L, et al 15 a Alexandria
Simmons T, 80 a Summitville
Sisk Sarah, 40 a Gilman
Sisk Theodore, 38 a Gilman
Sloan Jas B, 80 a Alexandria
Smith E A, 40 a   "
Smith E D, 40 a   "
Smith Fannie, 2 a Gilman
Smith Geo H, 507 a Richmond
Smith Isaac, 1 a Anderson
Smith S A, 40 a Gilman
Smith Wm, 50 a   "
Spencer R A, 20 a Centerville
Stapleton C, 68 a Alexandria
Stapleton T, 55 a   "
Starr M A, 120 a   "
Stephenson, G & M, 20 a Gilman
Stephenson M E, 80 a   "
Stephenson W, 21 a Alexandria
Sullivan E, 38 a Alexandria
Summers W, 110 a   "
Swallow J, 40 a Summitville
Swindell J A, 40 a Alexandria
Taylor Wm A, 1 a Elwood
Thomas B, Jr 51 a Alexandria
Thomas Jas, 80 a Gilman
Thomas W J, 39 a Alexandria
Thompson H D, 50 a Anderson
Thurston J, 160 a Summitville
Thurston S, 90 a Alexandria
Tinker D & S, 80 a Alexandria
Tolle L, 48 a Alexandria
Tomlinson N, 160 a Alexandria
Tomlinson W F, 80 a   "
Torbert E & C, 3 a Alexandria
Van Buskirk J, 93 a Gilman
Vannatter N N, 40 a   "
Verbryck M A, 50 a Alexandria
Vermillion U, 443 a   "

Novelty Works,
**198 AND 200 N. MILTON ST.
ANDERSON, IND.**

HUGH FISHER, Propr., manufacturer and dealer in Step Ladders, Garden Wheelbarrows, Screen Doors and Windows, Picture Frames, etc.

THE PALACE PHARMACY, Anderson, Ind. FOR FINE GOODS OF ALL KINDS IN THEIR LINE.

J. T. Knowland & Son, WHOLESALE PLUMBERS and Gas Fitters' Supplies
111 N. Main St., ANDERSON, IND. 'Phone 30.

192   MADISON CO. GAZETTEER.

Vermillion S, 116 a Alexandria
Vernon E G, 51 a Summitville
Vinson C E, 85 a Alexandria
Vinson Elijah, 10 a Rigdon
Vinson J, 108 a Alexandria
Vinson M, 96 a   "
Virgin V, 40 a   "
Wadleigh H M, 20 a Alexandria
Walker J, 160 a   "
Walker Jno M, 160 a   "
Walker M J, 120 a   "
Walker M, 45 a   "
Ward E C, 20 a   "
Watts I & A, 45 a Fortville
Waymire M, 20 a Orestes
Webb J A, 66 a Alexandria
Webster D W, 56 a Halford
Welch J, 40 a Middletown
White Sophia, 50 a Elwood
Wilborn Nancy, 34 a Dundee
Williams I, 25 a Anderson

Wilson A L, 159 a Alexandria
Wilson B & F, 10 a   "
Wilson J L, 80 a   "
Wilson J & W, 40 a   "
Wilson W F, 80 a   "
Windsor D, 80 a   "
Windsor J, 160 a   "
Windsor W W, 80 a   "
Wisehart A, 80 a   "
Wood T M, 107 a   "
Wright J & E, 68 a   "
Wright Jos, 118 a Alexandria
Yeager Jos, 25 a   "
Young Jane & L, 59 a Orestes
Young Leroy, 72 a   "
Young Maria, 159 a   "
Young Mary, 28 a   "
Young Nancy H, 11 a   "
Young Samuel E, 240 a   "
Zimmerman R, 80 a Alexandria
Zimmerman S C, 80 a   "

PIPE CREEK TOWNSHIP.

POST OFFICES.

Alexandria, Anderson, Elwood, Frankton, Dundee, Muncie, Orestes, Peru, Richmond, Summitville.

"A" FOR ACRES.

Allen Jas (et al), 40 a Elwood
Allen Nathan, 43 a Frankton
Alley S & Melissa, 1 a Dundee
Alvey John, 80 a Elwood
Antrim Thomas, 40 a Frankton
Armfield F O & E, 40 a Elwood
Baker George W, 50 a   "
Baldwin Mary, 15 a   "
Beck James M, 40 a Anderson
Beeson Tremelins, 160 a Frankton
Benefield Jno W, 85 a Frankton
Behymer A J, 13 a Elwood
Bird Jas (et al), 5 a Anderson
Bowers J, 2 a Frankton
Bowers Salathiel, 40 a Elwood
Boyden I & L, 185 a   "
Bradley Daniel D, 2 a Frankton

Bronnenberg & Beall, 112 a Anderson
Brown N & S, 120 a Elwood
Brown Mary E, 6 a Anderson
Broyles G W, 126 a Elwood
Broyles Jemison, 41 a Elwood
Broyles Z T, 120   "
Calloway B T, 305 a   "
Calloway John W, 2 a   "
Canaday Nathan, 199 a Frankton
Canaday David, 33 a   "
Carter John C, 139 a Elwood
Chalfant Albert, 80 a Dundee
Chalfant Marion, 104 a Elwood
Chalfant Sarah M, 60 a Dundee
Chalfant Wesley, 219 a Elwood
Canaday Josiah, 206 a   "

JOHN O. MILLER, ELEVEN YEARS' EXPERIENCE in Watchmaking. Finisher six years in Elgin & Springfield Watch Factories.

I GUARANTEE MY WORK   3 N. Meridian, ANDERSON, IND.

Carleton Robt, 80 a Frankton
Clary Sarah, 75 a Elwood
Cochran G W, 80 a . "
Cole Henry J, 124 a "
Cole S & E, 20 a Alexandria
Conner J & Mary, 60 a Elwood
Cooley D F, 60 a Frankton
Cooper Etheline, 33 a Frankton
Cowley Anthony, 28 a Elwood
Cox Elijah, 65 a Frankton
Cox Levi J, 43 a "
Cox Thos D, 1 a "
Cox Wm, 135 a "
Daugherty J H, 20 a Swayzee
Davenport L, 287 a Peru, Ind
Davis Eli, 40 a Muncie
Davis Jesse, 10 a Anderson
Davis John L, 80 a Dundee
Deal O F, 40 a Richmond
DeHority Chas C, 79 a Elwood
DeHority Hannah, 13 a "
DeHority J M, 40 a "
DeHority J M & sons, 40 a "
DeHority J W (heirs), 40 a "
Dipboye J, 37 a Summitville
Dipboye J W, 40 a Elwood
Dixon Mary, 120 a Frankton
Douglass Wm G, 60 a Elwood
Doyle Abraham, 18 a Myers
Drivers J T, 47 a Elwood
Dugan Patrick, 115 a Elwood
Dwiggins Rufus, 52 a Frankton
East James, 66 a "
Ebert Anna, 20 a "
Ebert Eliza A, 40 a "
Ebert Martin L, 54 a "
Ebert Ora E, 3 a "
Ebert Xenia M, 20 a "
Ebert Wm A, 40 a Frankton
Eikenberry Elias, 1 a Elwood
Edwins M K, 161 a Frankton
Etchison Anna, 22 a "
Etchison Henry, 65 a Elwood
Etchison Henry Jr, 60 a "
Etchison J, 107 a Perkinsville

Etchison James, 111 a Anderson
Etchison J K P, 45 a Frankton
Etchison Jesse, 50 a "
Etchison John, 40 a Dundee
Etchison Joshua, 3 a Elwood
Etchison L, 5 a Summitville
Etchison L & R, 1 a "
Etchison M, 30 a Frankton
Etchison Margt, 44 a Frankton
Etchison Mary, 8 a Perkinsville
Etchison Mary A, 22 a Frankton
Etchison Richard, 45 a "
Etchison Stephen, 102 a "
Etchison Stephen Jr, 21 a "
Etchison W (et al), 6 a Elwood
Etchison Wm B, 3 a "
Etchison W B (et al), 102 a "
Faroes Alva, 65 a Elwood
Fender J J & L, 40 a Elwood
Ferguson Robt Sr, 20 a Orestes
Ferguson W J, 20 a "
Fesler Benj F, 60 a Frankton
Fesler David, 82 a "
Fesler John, 28 a "
Filby Printha, 80 a Elwood
Finney Barbara, 1 a "
Fitch Joseph, 40 a "
Fitch Monroe J, 50 a "
Flint Joseph, 30 a Frankton
Forrest Isaac D, 180 a Elwood
Foust Louisa, 80 a Pendleton
Fox Magdaline, 8 a Frankton
Fox Michael, 37 a Elwood
Frazier Benj C, 40 a Frankton
Frazier Jno (heirs), 80 a "
Frazier Oliver B, 417 a Elwood
French David O, 80 a Anderson
French John W, 80 a "
French Mary J, 160 a Frankton
Funkhouser Isaac, 180 a Elwood
Gallagher James, 40 a "
Gallagher Nicy, 25 a "
Gilliam Andrew J, 105 a Elwood
Gillman Thomas O, 30 a "
Gisse Adam, 2 a Elwood

STUART, 'THE FLORIST', 99 to 111 W. 3d. Tel. 73. Furnished on Short Notice. Funeral Designs and Plant Decorations Anderson, Ind.

WOOLLEY Foundry and Machine Works.
Manufacturers of Clay Working Machinery, Boiler Makers, and General Machinists.
N. W. COR. 14th AND C. W. AND M. R. R.

HATS AND MEN'S FURNISHINGS.

Gooding Mary A, 20 a Frankton
Griffee Julia A, 3 a Summitville
Grunger V, 137 a Frankton
Guard E H, 79 a Elwood
Guyer Mary, 10 a Frankton
Hall & Pence, 32 a Elwood
Halsey Thos, 18 a
Hamilton F & M, 90 a Elwood
Hammon E F, 40 a   "
Harbit Francis M, 159 a "
Harpold E, 12 a Anderson
Harpold Susan, 40 a Frankton
Harris J & Mary, 75 a Orestes
Harrison James, 4 a Elwood
Harrison Nathan, 10 a Elwood
Hartley Emma C, 21 a Dundee
Harting H G, 35 a Elwood
Harvey H E, 40 a Perkinsville
Havens Mary A, 40 a Elwood
Hays Wm L, 50 a Frankton
Heck Mary E, 40 a   "
Herbig Henry C, 74 a
Hester John H, 80 a Frankton
Hicks Wm, 80 a   "
Hillis Wm Sr, 80 a   "
Hobbs Viola A, 20 a Elwood
Hodge E & wife, 1 a Frankton
Hodge F M & R, 1 a   "
Hoffman A Z & B E, 40 a "
Hoffman B E, 120 a   "
Hook Jesse & wife, 20 a "
Huffman Jas, 160 a Elwood
Hurst Noah C, 88 a   "
Hurst Wm, 136 a Frankton
Huston Jas E, 40 a Rigdon
ngram Ezekiel, 2 a Elwood
enminger Wm, 40 a
ackson Monroe, 43 a Elwood
arrell E, 43 a Frankton
rrell J (et al), 115 a Elwood
rrell Nancy A, 38 Frankton
ffries Joseph T, 83 a Elwood
be Elijah J, 30 a Frankton
be Francis M, 74 a   "
hnson A L, 40 a Orestes

Johnson Benj, 7 e Richmond
Johnson Franklin, 27 a Dundee
Johnson Laura J, 40 a Elwood
Kellogg Emaline, 25 a Dundee
Kibbey J T, (trustee), 15 a Richmond
Kidder John B, 120 a Frankton
Kidwell Amanda, 160 a Elwood
Kidwell Ira, 12 a Elwood
Kimmerling G, 160 a Frankton
Kimmerling M, 48 a   "
Kimmerling M & A, 33 a Elwood
Kimmerling S E, 24 a Frankton
King B J, 50 a   "
King James A, 30 a   "
King Thos & Eliza, 73 a "
King Washington, 66 a "
Kirtley Robt & wife, 36 "
Kitchen Charles, 48 a "
Kramer Gustave, 5 a Elwood
Lamberson B F, 139 a "
Laycock David, 12 a   "
Legg Albert B, 40 a Frankton
Legg Arthur, 40 a   "
Legg James, 20 a   "
Legg M & W A, 36 a Elwood
Legg Thomas B, 40 a   "
Legg Wm F, 40 a Frankton
Leeson Clara R, 1 a Elwood
Leeson Richard T Jr, 52 a "
Lester Jas & Mary, 40 a "
Likens Ezra M, 80 a Frankton
Lister Sadie, 30 a Elwood
Little John, 86 a Frankton
Little Lydia C, 9 a Frankton
Little Marcus, 98 a   "
Little Mary, 20 a   "
Little Nancy, 53 a   "
Little Robert M, 80 a Elwood
Long Albert, 17 a Frankton
Lowry Martha A, 42 a "
Ludlow Hampton, 75 a Elwood
Luse Wm H, 36 a Elwood
Luther I B, 12 a Frankton

ace Your Real Estate and FARM PROPERTY in the Hands of
ROOP & HAYNES,
AND BE SURE OF QUICK RETURNS.
)½ S. Anderson, - - - - ELWOOD, IND.

MONEY TO BUILD WITH — PROCURED WITHIN 15 DAYS. Robinson & Glasseo, Loan, Real Estate & Insurance agents
Room 9 "When" Building, ANDERSON, IND.

MADISON CO. GAZETTEER. 195

McCauley & Chamness, 113 a Frankton
McCauley Samuel, 40 a Frkton
McClintock C & J, 45 a Prkville
McClintock Rebecca, 44 a "
McGill Nancy M, 25 a Elwood
McWilliams C E, 25 a Frnkton
Manis Carter, 39 a "
Manis Dalzell, 158 a "
Manis Emma B (et al), 14 a "
Markley Rena, 13 a Markleville
Mattox Wm S, 50 a Elwood
May Geo & C, 50 a Frankton
May G W & wife, 16 a "
May June, 60 a "
May Julia (et al), 96 a "
Merrill W J (et al), 160 a Elwood
Miller J P, 301 a Middletown
Miller Perry, 80 a Elwood
Millikan F M, 234 a New Castle
Millikan Thos B, 48 a Elwood
Minnick W R, 80 a Sterling, Kan
Mohler F M, 53 a Elwood
Montgomery J C, 232 a Frankton
Montgomery J L, 80 a "
Moore A M, 240 a Tipton
Moore Elmer, 17 a Frankton
Moore Geo L, 80 a Elwood
Moore Geo M, 120 a Frankton
Moore M & others, 80 a "
Moore Melvina V, 8 a "
Moore M, O & D, 20 a "
Moore Sarah, 6 a "
Moore Sarah A, 80 a "
Morris Mary A, 20 a Elwood
Morris Wm H, 160 a "
Moyer George, 18 a Dundee
Moyer Laben, 40 a "
Myerly Lusetta, 72 a Elwood
Noland E L, 40 a
Noland Geo C, 105 a Frankton
Noland Martha, 40 a "
Noland W A, 143 a "
Norris Levi, 53 a Elwood
Nuding David Sr, 80 a Elwood
Nuding Geo, 65 a Frankton
O'Brien D, 1 a Indianapolis
Odem Ann, 13 a Frankton
Odem Geo, 13 a "
Odem Lewis, 4 a "
Odem L (heirs), 32 a "
Odem Melissa, 34 a "
Orbaugh Abraham, 80 a Elwood
Osborne Thos, 240 a Elwood
Owens Mary A, 40 a Frankton
Owens Nancy E, 7 a "
Pernod Paul, 80 a Elwood
Plackard Marion, 25 a Frankton
Plummer J M & M, 60 a "
Powell Elijah (heirs), 80 a "
Power Alexander, 25 a "
Quick Cornelius, 280 a "
Quick C & W H, 422 a "
Quick and Sharp, 120 a "
Raines Lucinda A, 22 a "
Reason Henry P, 67 a "
Rector Isaac & L, 130 a "
Reed Rosetta, 37 a "
Reeder W R, 31 a Elwood
Redd Geo, 80 "
Richwine Geo, 16 a Frankton
Ring Jas E, 68 a Frankton
Ring Jno C, 64 a Kokomo
Roach Jno M, 19 a Dundee
Roach Louisa, 70 a Frankton
Roach Ward L, 21 a Elwood
Rodefer John F, 33 a Frankton
Rose John B, 33 a Alexandria
Rose Monroe, 3 a "
Ryan Michael, 170 a Anderson
Savage C L, 160 a Elwood
Schell J (heirs), 10 a Frankton
Schell Wm, 70 a "
Seward J, 80 a Chesterfield
Seybert Pauline, 26 a Frankton
Shell Dora & Rosa, "
Shell J & A J, 40 a "
Shell Margaret, 28 a "
Shell Melvin, 13 a Frankton
Shell Morgan, 13 a Frankton

J. P. CONDO & SON, WILL SELL YOU FURNITURE ON EASY WEEKLY PAYMENTS. ESTABLISHED 1856. ALEXANDRIA, IND.

Deal & Willkie, ATTORNEYS AT LAW. We will attend to your legal business promptly, and charge you no exhorbitant fees.
MECHANICS LIENS A SPECIALTY. CALL AND SEE US.

WHEN —Originators of the One Price System
IN SELLING CLOTHING.
FAIR AND SQUARE DEALINGS WITH ALL.

196   MADISON CO. GAZETTEER.

Shell Wolsey, 13 a Frankton
Shetterly Philip, 180 a "
Shipley Geo W, 60 a "
Shipley Jacob, 77 a Elwood
Shipley Luella, 24 a Frankton
Shipley Nelson, 80 a "
Shipley Sarah J, 40 a "
Sigler A J, 74 a Elwood
Sigler Daniel, 120 a Elwood
Sigler Joseph, 8 a Anderson
Silvey James R, 1 a Elwood
Simmons Lula S, 22 a Dundee
Simmons Martha J, 15 a Elwood
Simmons Melvin, 25 a "
Smith Elmer, 38 a Frankton
Smith Cyrena, 25 a "
Smith F W, 52 a Frankton
Smith Geo H, 40 a "
Smith John, 40 a "
Smith Rachel, 30 a "
Smithson X, 77 a "
Spohr Annie B, 27 a Dundee
Spohr Mary A, 26 a . "
Spohr Sabra S, 27 a "
Starkey J B Jr, 134 a Elwood
Starkey Sarah, 40 a Elwood
Stam Sarah S, 14 a "
Starkey Millard C, 42 a non-res
Stefly Erasmus, 69 a Frankton
Stewart Robert, 80 a Elwood
Stoker Riley W, 200 a Frankton
Stone Jas & Anna, 1 a Dundee
Strough D F & wife, 80 a "
Swart Agnes, 100 a Frankton
Taylor Heirs, 80 a "
Tharp M and J, 64 a "
Tharp Perry S. 324 a "
Triford E W, 52 a Elwood
Trump Mary W, 40 a "
Urban Jacob Jr, 19 a "
Urban Jacob Sr, 80 a "

Urmston A G, 240 a Frankton
Van Valpenberg M E, 2 a Elwood
Vermillion J L, 40 a Anderson
Vestal Albert C, 80 a "
Vestal Robt, 40 a Frankton
Vestal W H, 160 a "
Walker Mary E, 38 a Elwood
Waples Wm P, 40 a
Warner Elizabeth, 40 a Elwood
Warner J W, 37 a "
Waymire Jehu, 66 a Frankton
Waymire J S, 280 a Elwood
Waymire M J, 20 a Frankton
Waymire Rudolph, 119 a "
Webb Jacob A, 22 a "
Webb M W, 191 a "
Webb Silas P, 12 a "
Well James M, 157 a "
Welsh J A, 28 a Middletown
White Daniel B, 60 a Elwood
Whiston J J, 8 a Anderson
Wilborn Jas A. 1 a Dundee
Wilborn John, 40 a Frankton
Wilborn Lewis, 80 a Dundee
Wilborn Mary, 1 a Frankton
Wilborn Wm, 80 a Frankton
Williams E K. 80 a Elwood
Willey M B & C, 39 a Frankton
Williams Margaret, 1 a Dundee
Wilson Allen B, 2 a Elwood
Wise Alexander, 318 a Frankton
Wise Michael, 40 a Elwood
Wise W H, 79 a Frankton
Wood Alex S, 160 a Dundee
Wolverton Emma, 92 a Elwood
Wright David, 111 a Frankton
Wright Elmore, 160 a
Wright Keziah, 51 a Elwood
Wright Leroy, 80 a "
Young John, 80 a Frankton

John L. Lindskoog, Leads in the Merchant Tailoring Line. English and French Worsteds, imported, always in stock.

Do not buy until you have seen them.

H. H. H. Block, N. E. Cor. Church and Harrison,   -   -   ALEXANDRIA, IND.

WM. J. DOVE, Real Estate, Loans and Insurance,
NEELEY BLOCK. 61½ N. Meridian, ANDERSON, IND.

MADISON CO. GAZETTEER. 197

RICHMOND TOWNSHIP.

POST OFFICES.

Alexandria, Anderson, Chesterfield, Elwood, Gilman, Linwood.

"A" FOR ACRES.

Adams G E, 240 a Anderson	Croan Susan, 12 a
Armstrong M, 99 a "	Curtis Enos, 31 a Anderson
Babbitt A, 6 a Alexandria	Decker W E & P, 257 a Ovid
Bamis Wm, 40 a Anderson	Dillon James, 82 a Anderson
Beal Alva O, 35 a Linwood	Dillon J, 160 a "
Beal L S, 41 a Linwood	Dillon Jos, 100 a "
Beal Nathan, 8 a Linwood	Donnelly J, 58 a "
Bell Curren, 160 a Anderson	Duncan Alf, 80 a "
Benefiel L W, 40 a Elwood	Duncan E, 80 a Daleville
Benton I W, 176 a Anderson	Dunham J H, 99 a Anderson
Black W, 171 a "	Dunham J B, 54 a "
Blacklidge H J, 90 a "	Eakins E, 67 a "
Blacklidge J M, 89 a "	Eppard F, 170 a "
Blacklidge J J, 120 a "	Eppard Noah, 70 a Gilman
Blacklidge K, 40 a "	Eshelman A, 80 a Anderson
Bodle Fred, 80 a "	Eshelman N 1 a "
Bodle M, 11fi a "	Eshelman S J, 5 a "
Bodle S, 70 a "	Fish C W, 1 a "
Bonner H, 80 a Chestergeld	Fish Ed, 39 a Anderson
Bright V & others, 37 a Lapel	Forkner J M, 225 a "
Brodbent O, 80 a Anderson	Forkner J, 80 a "
Brodbent S, 39 a "	Forkner M, 63 a "
Bonnenberg, 389 a "	Fosnot J H, 55 a Anderson
Bronnenberg F, 80 a "	Fosnot J T, 40 a Chesterfield
Bronnenberg H, 80 a "	Fosnot P, 630 a Anderson
Bronnenberg H, 332 a Anderson	Fosnot S P, 20 a Chesterfield
Bronnenberg J, 337 a "	Fountain G W, 34 a Anderson
Bronnerberg, 110 a Chesterfield	Fountain N, 100 a Gilman
Brunt J A J, 22 a Anderson	Fountain W, 165 a Anderson
Canaday H, 328 a "	Fuller R, 74 a Alexandria
Canaday H, 34 a "	Fuller Wm, 124 a "
Carpenter W, 6 a "	Fuller W H, 27 a "
Chambers C, 89 a Linwood	Funk Jas, Sr 32 a Linwood
Chambers Elijah, 69 a "	Funk Jas N, 4 a "
Chambers G, 119 a Linwood	Funk W H, 50 e Myers
Chambers J, 130 a "	Gardner J C, 80 a Anderson
Cobum C, 20 a Anderson	Garrison D, 175 a "
Conner Levi, 898 a Anderson	Green George 80 a
Croan Jesse, 106 a Iowa	Groendyke E, 6 a Linwood

Anderson Foundry and Machine Works, Manufacturers of **BRICK AND TILE MA-**
255 N. Jackson Street, 'Phone 53. **CHINES, SAW MILLS, ETC.**
ANDERSON, IND.

LARMORE BROS., ICE CREAM, also OYSTERS IN SEASON; —WHOLESALE MANUFACTURERS AND DEALERS IN—
513 Nichol Ave., ANDERSON, IND. | Telephone 220.

Jackson & Burr Do the Largest INSURANCE Business. Insure in the good old Companies they represent.

69½ N. Meridian, - - ANDERSON, IND.

198 MADISON CO. GAZETTEER.

Hancock H, 40 a Anderson
Hancock J L, 19 a "
Hancock J & L, 92 a "
Hancock J T, 129 a "
Hancock M E, 80 a "
Hancock W, 262 a "
Haney J & A, 40 a Yorktown
Hannah S E, 118 a Anderson
Hansley M A, 27 a "
Harney Jones, 80 a "
Hartman C, 20 a Anderson
Hartman Lucinda, 1 a Gilman
Heagy Geo, 75 a Anderson
Heagy Jane E, 203 a Anderson
Heritage Jos, 280 a "
Hitt Ludwell J, heirs 120 a
Holston J A, 80 a Anderson
Holston R, 74 a "
Hunter Sarah, 50 a "
Immel Geo, 80 a "
Immel M & G, 76 a "
Johnson Jno M, 40 a "
Johnson L, 280 a "
Johnson Lewis, 40 a "
Jones A D, 45 a "
ones Caroline, 61 a "
fones F M, 126 a "
[ones Mary E, 80 a "
ones Nancy J, 45 a "
ones P E, 47 a "
ones Silas, 393 a "
^eicher Jas, 80 a "
^ettry Jno, 85 a Graham
^ilgore Albert, 13 a Anderson
^ilgore Frank, 32 a
^ittenger & Schwim, 3 a Anderson
ane Mary, 37 a Anderson
awler James, 298 a "
awler Jas W, 105 a "
awler W F, 100 a "
iws James, 125 a "
^mon Jas, 60 a Gilman
^wis Mollie, 20 a Anderson
cCullough C, 1 a "

Johnson L, 280 a Anderson
McKeown S, 40 a Linwood
Mabbitt Amanda, 26 a Amanda
Mabbitt A, 29 a Gilman
Mabbitt C, 26 a Anderson
Mabbitt G, 30 a "
Mabbitt R, 25 a "
Mabbitt R, et al 15 a "
Mabbitt S J, 74 a "
Mabbitt Wm, 34 a "
Mahoney A J, 19 a "
Manning L C, 10 a Pendleton
Matthews Jno, 414 a Anderson
Matthews J C, 80 a "
Matthews M F, 62 a "
Matthews W L, 57 a "
Maynard B, 69 a Alexandria
Maynard J, 135 a Anderson
Maynard J & J, 2 a Alexandria
Meek Jno A, 26 a "
Meredith F R, 65 a "
Meredith Wm & S C Miller, 75 a
Miller Samuel C, 40 a Gilman
Misner S E, 128 a Anderson
Moore Jno W, 25 a Elwood
Mustard D F, 80 a Anderson
Myers S, 35 a Chesterfield
Nealy Brazil, 40 a Anderson
Neely Hester, 1 a "
Noble B J, 21 a "
Noland Jno, 108 a "
Noland Nora, 57 a "
Peck Jesse, 160 a "
Pence J J, 133, a "
Pence Vesta J, 120 a "
Phillips M, 91 a Alexandria
Pittsford E, 80 a Anderson
Powell A, 57 a "
Preston J V, 1 a "
Quinn A, 80 a Frankton
Rutherford A, 36 a Anderson
Rutherford J, 40 a "
Rutherford R, 80 a "
Rutherford R. 220 a "
Rutherford W, 64 a "

George B. Epperson, Contractor and Builder of Felt and Gravel ROOFING.

39 E. 9th St., - - ANDERSON, IND.

of Anderson. lf you wish to buy,
sell or rent, call at 10 E. 10 St., ANDERSON, IND.

Saunders Jos, 129 a Anderson
Scott B W, 44 a "
Scott Quincy, 40 a "
Scott W A, 40 a "
Shoemaker, J, 7 a Middletown
Shoemaker J R, 64 a "
Sizelors A, 40 a Alexandria
Sloan J M, 49 a Anderson
Smith Sarah 10 a Linwood
Swain Eliza, 40 a Anderson
Swindell Ashley, 36 a Linwood
Stokes W, 80 a Anderson
Summers L, 85 a Alexandria
Tappen D, 100 a Anderson
Tappen Ea, 20 a "
Tappen J, 199 a "
Thumma J & H, 130 a "

Thumma J, 123 a Anderson
Thornburg J, 20 a "
Thornburg T, 243 a "
Thornburg W, 63 a "
Vandevender, Dempsey & Sarah 40 a Anderson
Vandevender M, 24 a Anderson
Vasbinder M, 23 a "
Vermillion A J, 75 a "
Vermillion C, 144 a "
Vermillion E A, 94 a "
Vermillion M, 28 a Chesterfield
Vermillion U, 215 a Anderson
Vinyard R, 50 a "
Waters D, 80 a Chesterfield
Watkins F, 154 a Anderson
Wills Abigail, 1 a "

STONY CREEK TOWNSHIP.

POST OFFICES.

Anderson, Fishersburg, Lapel, Pendleton, Florida, Johnson's Crossing.

"A" FOR ACRES.

Abbott Mary J, 18 a Lapel
Aldred L M, 31 a Fishersburg
Aldred Mahala O, 2 a Lapel
Aldred R K, 41 a Fishersburg
Anderson E S, 100 a "
Anderson James M, 80 a Johnson's Crossing
Anderson John N, 160 a Johnson's Crossing
Anderson Martha, 38 a Johnson's Crossing
Anderson S S, 197 a Johnson's Crossing
Anshutz Philip, 40 a Anderson
Askins Jacob, 40 a Lapel
Baughan John T, 140 a Lapel
Ballinger Rachel & others, 40 a Anderson
Beach Wm B, 1 a Lapel
Bensenbower F, 79 a Anderson
Bensenbower L, 99 a "

Blazer Frank (heirs), 68 a Johnson's Crossing
Blazer J F, 1 a Johnson's Crossg
Bloomer P, 40 a "
Bodenhorn C, 160 a Fishersburg
Bodenhorn J, 80 a "
Bodenhorn S, 86 a Fishersburg
Boone Charles, 20 a Anderson
Bowers Lewis, 80 a "
Bright Emery B, 20 a Lapel
Bright Frank E, 40 a "
Bright Martha E, 40 a "
Bright W and R, 79 a "
Bulen C B, 2 a Johnson's Crossg
Busby Andrew, 80 a Lapel
Busby Clarissa W, 200 a Lapel
Busby F, 80 a Johnson's Crossg
Busby Jonathan, 80 a Lapel
Busby John, 79 a Fishersburg
Busby Walter R, 40 a Lapel
Byrum Susan, 10 a Anderson

HUGH FISHER, Manufacturer **Screen Doors and**
198 and 200 N. Milton St.,   **Windows** all sizes. Furniture re-
ANDERSON, IND.   pairing a specialty.

J. T. Knowland & Son, SANITARY PLUMBERS. *Gas and Steam Fitters.*
111 N. Main St., ANDERSON, IND. 'Phone 30.

200 MADISON CO. GAZETTEER.

Cecil Mary J, 30 a Pendleton
Cecil Richard A, 44 a Pendlton
Collins Geo H, 74 a Florida
Conrad David, 113 a Lapel
Conrad Emma J, 43 a "
Conrad Mathias, 116 a "
Cook Daniel, 1 a Anderson
Coverdale Isaiah, 23 a Lapel
Coverdale Jane A, 40 a "
Cox Benj, 82 a Pendleton
Cragen C, 9 a Fishersburg
Davis Corwin, 9 a Anderson
Davis D B, 83 a Johnson's Cross
Davis Maria, 79 a Anderson
Day S J, 36 a Johnson's Crossg
Day T E, 21 a Indianapolis
Delawter, Jonathan, 132 a Johnson's Crossing
Delawter Levi, 340 a Johnson's Crossing
Delph E, 26 a Johnson's Crossing
Dewitt Barnett, 9 a Fishersburg
Dewitt Jas A, 161 a "
Diven C E, 200 a Pendleton
Dolan Michael, 60 a "
Dunham George, 186 a Lapel
Durant S & G, 40 a Pendleton
Ebert Rosetta, 40 a Anderson
Eggman Ezekiel, 20 a "
Fisher A & Lydia, 38 a Lapel
Fisher Andrew S, 120 a "
Fisher A B (et al), 20 a "
Fisher Charles, 137 a "
Fisher Emera and wife, 1 a
Fisher Hiram D, 80 a Lapel
Fisher Walter (et al), 10 a Lapel
Fisher S E & wife, 1 a "
Fisher S B, 80 a Lapel
Flanagan B, 85 a Anderson
Ford Benj, 19 a Fishersburg
Ford Bowen (et al), 3 a Lapel
Ford James, 6 a Lapel
Ford Leora E, 60 a Lapel
Ford M and W, 158 a Lapel
Gaither A, 40 a Summitville

Gaither Mary A, 78 a Lapel
Garrett Welcome and Margaret, 6 a Johnson's Crossing
Gates Jas S, 80 a Pendleton
Gee Geo, 40 a Anderson
Gilmore G, 80 a Johnson's Crossg
Gilmore J, 20 a "
Givens Jno L, 32 a Pendleton
Gwinn Harvey, 204 a Lapel
Gwinn James, 159 a "
Gwinn Jesse, 80 a Pendleton
Gwinn Laben, 440 a Lapel
Gonce Geo W, 7 a Fishersburg
Graham Henry W, 79 a Lapel
Graham Josephus E, 50 a "
Haas Henry Sr, 119 a Pendleton
Hackelman Geo W, 20 a Johnson's Crossing
Hackelman Mary, 79 a Johnson's Crossing
Hanger Samuel, 249 a Lapel
Hanger Wm, 80 a Lapel
Hart Susan A, 13 a Alexandria
Harless Charles (heirs), 58 a Johnson's Crossing
Harris Wm, 87 a Lapel
Hawkins Elizabeth, 157 a Johnson's Crossing
Heninger B W, 25 a Fishersburg
Huffman C & wife, 79 a Lapel
Huffman W J, 21 a Lapel
Hershbarger J W, 118 a Lapel
Hershbarger Milton, 112 a Lapel
Hickey John, 80 a Anderson
Hickey Patrick, 117 a "
Hilligoss C, 80 a "
Hilligoss Geo N, 80 a "
Huffman Adam, 80 a Lapel
Huffman Edward, 40 a "
Huffman Isaac, 120 a "
Huffman Jasper, 140 a "
Huffman L, 80 a Fishersburg
Huffman M A, 26 a "
Huffman Nimrod, 40 a Lapel
Huffman Philip, 80 a "

John O. Miller, Practical Watchmaker & Jeweler. Eleven Years' Experience in the Manufacturing of Watches.
3 N. Meridian, - - - ANDERSON, IND.

J. A. Munchhof & Bros. Undertakers and Funeral Directors and Practical Embalmers. Office and Wareroom
Telephones 189, 24 and 51. No. 98 N. Main St., ANDERSON, IND
☞ OFFICE OPEN DAY AND NIGHT. ☜

MADISON CO. GAZETTEER. 20

Huntsinger G, 128 a Johnson's Crossing
Huntsinger Israel, 80 a Johnson's Crossing
Huntsinger J, 155 a Anderson
Huntsinger J M, 80 a Pendleton
Huntsinger J N, 80 a Pendleton
Huntsinger Malinda, 60 a Johnson's Crossing
Huntsinger Monroe, 103 a Johnson's Crossing
Huntsinger Noah Sr, 160 a Johnson's Crossing
Huntsinger Noah Jr, 20 a Johnson's Crossing
Huntsinger Samuel, 80 a Johnson's Crossing
Huntsinger W, 118 a Pendleton
Jarrett Laura B, 1 a Gilman
Johnson C, 32 a Wichita, Kan
Johnson John M, 79 a Johnson's Crossing
Johnson J J, 76 a Johnson's Crossing
Johnson N P, 60 a Anderson
Johnson R J Jr, 100 a "
Julian John D, 88 a Lapel
Kellum Sarah, 17 a Anderson
Keffler Lucy A, 10 a Clarksville
Kephart Jas S, 20 a Anderson
Kephart R A, 40 a Anderson
Kynett Wm, 108 a Lapel
Kyle John W, 40 a "
Larimore L A, 104 a Anderson
Lawson Adda A, 20 a Johnson's Crossing
Lawson Albert, 30 a Lapel
Lawson Alfred, 119 a Johnson's Crossing
Lawson Charles S, 80 a Lapel
Lawson Curtis, 239 a "
Lawson Dallas N, 40 a "
Lawson Ernest G, 20 a Johnson's Crossing
Lawson General F, 19 a Johnson's Crossing
Lawson Geo W, 99 a Johnson's Crossing
Lawson L, 25 a Johnson's Crossing
Lawson M & A, 13 a Anderson
Lawson Martha E, 19 a Johnson's Crossing
Lawson R, 24 a Johnson's Cross
Lawson Spencer, 80 a Anderson
Lawson Wm, 140 a Johnson' Crossing
Lawson Wm A, 8 a Johnson' Crossing
Leady John H, 93 a Lapel
Love Anna and Jas, 25 a Johnson's Crossing
Long James W, 240 a Lapel
Lukins G, 40 a Pendleton
Lutz Ferdinand, 120 a Lapel
McClintock A W, 75 a Perkins
McClintock A, 120 a Lapel
McClintock D, 480 a Perkins
McClintock Eliz, 31 a Lapel
McClintock E C, 40 a "
McCullough T, 40 a Anderson
McDoyle Sampson, 80 a Lap
McDole Isaac, 80 a Lapel
Mahoney Michael, 9 a Johnson Crossing
Mahoney Sarah, 28 a Johnson Crossing
Manis Canaday, 80 a Anderson
Manis T, 30 a Johnson's Cross
Martin Almira, 120 a Anderson
Martin W H & M, 12 a "
Milburn Isaac, 400 a "
Miller Jos, 10 a Lapel
Miller Peter, 10 a Elwood
Millikan F M, 32 a New Cas
Moore C H, 5 a Fishersburg
Moore Sarah E, 24 a Lapel
Nicholson Calvin, 70 a "
Norris Elizabeth, 20 a "
Passwater Emily I, 40 a "

WOOLLEY FOUNDRY AND MACHINE WORKS,
Engineers, Founders and Machinis
N. W. Cor. 14th and C. W. and M. R. R.

WHEN — THE — Anderson Clothiers & Hatters.
ONE PRICE TO ALL.

202   MADISON CO. GAZETTEER.

Passwater W J, 157 a Label
Passwater Z F, 40 a   "
Prather Susanah, 42 a Halford
Prather W B, 80 a Halford
Rambo Eddie & L, 1 a Lapel
Reason Nancy J, 8 a Pendleton
Reason W H, 97 a Lapel
Reddick Mary E, 40 a Johnson's Crossing
Reddick Mary & Sol, 15 a Johnson's Crossing
Ridgeway & Lloyd, lots, Lapel
Richwine A, 10 a Anderson
Robinet Elzy, 184 a Anderson
Robinet Samantha, 26 a   "
Roger Amanda & J, 118 a Johnson's Crossing
Schuyler Chas W, 40 a Lapel
Schuyler G W, 101 a Perknville
Schuyler Philip, 40 a Lapel
Sears A (heirs), 40 a   "
Sears Arminta, 40 a Pendleton
Sears G W, 140 a Lapel
Sears Marion, 20 a   "
Sears T M & G W, 80 a Lapel
Sears Union, 61 a Lapel
Sears Wm, 80 a Pendleton
Seybert Jasper H, 8 a Anderson
Shafer P, 66 a Johnson's Crossing
Shaul Jos F, 5 a   "
Shaul Jas M, 60 a   "
Shaul Wm Sr, 40 a   "
Shaul W W, 39 a   "
Shultz S D, 40 a Lapel
Shuman Nimrod, 97 a Pendleton
Shuman S, 16 a Johnson's Crossg
Simmerman J, 102 a Fishersburg
Simmerman N, 26 a   "
Simmerman W G & wife, 135 a Fishersburg
Simpson W, 80 a Anderson
Small James M Jr, 29 a Johnson's Crossing
Small C, 12 a Johnson's Crossing
Smith Mary, 4 a Lapel
Spegal Wm & wife, 20 a Lapel
Steiner Barbara, 40 a Lapel
Stephens E B, 22 a   "
Studley Chas E, 56 a   "
Taylor Jas A, 3 a Anderson
Tayler Rachel, 1 a Lapel
Valentine Alfred, 40 a Lapel
Vine Margaret, 4 a Lapel
Wene Jezreel, 49 a Pendleton
Wene Mary M, 80 a Lapel
White E & J C, 80 a Anderson
White Samuel C, 213 a Lapel
Williams Jas M, 1 a   "
Winton Annis, 9 a   "
Wise Ida M, 41 a   "
Wise D M, C C & E E, 40 a   "
Wiseman Mary (et al), 60 a   "
Wolf Jas G, 142 a Anderson
Wolf W, 80 a Johnson's Crossg
Woodward A O, 80 a Lapel
Woodward Jas R, 80 a   "
Woodward Missouri, 86 a Lapel
Woodward Wm, 261 a   "
Wright Geo, 25 a Lapel
Wright Mary S, 19 a Lapel

UNION TOWNSHIP.
POST OFFICES.

Anderson, Chesterfield, Daleville, Middletown, Mechanicsburg.

"A" FOR ACRES.

Adams Jno, 160 a Anderson
Adamson W, 200 Middletown
Allen Isaac, 80 a Anderson
Ballingall N J, 10 a   "
Bensenbower C, 69 a Anderson
Bensenbower M, 120 a "
Betterton D K, 25 a Chesterfield
Betterton J B, 25 a   "

Roop & Haynes, Real Estate, LOANS AND INSURANCE.
210½ S. Anderson,   -   -   -   ELWOOD, IND.

)binson & Glassco, Real Estate, Loan and Insurance Agents, room 9 "When" Building Agents Fidelity Building and Savings Union.
ANDERSON, IND.

:erton Nancy, 23 a "
le Lucy A, 21 a Daleville
ın berg A H, 60 a "
ın berg C, 146 a Chesterfield
ınenberg F, 530 a Anderson
ınenberg H, 617 a Chesterfield
ınenberg J, 68 a Anderson
ınenberg J M, 100 a Chesterfield
ınenberg M Jr, 201 a Anderson
ınenberg R, 86 a Chesterfield
ınenberg S, 160 a Chesterfield
ınenberg T, 181 a Chesterfield
nenberg W B, 170 a Chesterfield
ɔn I W, 20 a Anderson
enger M I, 4 a Chesterfield
enger Sarah, 80 a "
ıer Abram, 87 a Anderson
elius A J, 2 a Chesterfield
elius L E, 1 a "
rin Alvira J, 224 a N Y
ıer M A, 195 a Chesterfield
n Jno C, 118 a Anderson
pher Isaac, 43 a "
nins H, 240 a Middletown
nins Martha, 25 a "
nins S, 80 a "
nins Wm C, 40 a "
Lewis, 120 a Anderson
oye C C, 80 a Middletown
am V, 48 a Chesterfield
ıy Jno H, 106 a "
B J, 173 a "
Thos S, 78 a "
ıer Alfred, 140 a "
ıer Jas, 100 a "
ıer Wm A, 112 a "
Catherine, 142 a "

Gold Jacob E, 6 a Chesterfield
Gold Lucy R, 104 a "
Good Julia A, 4 a "
Gray Hulda, 4 a Pendleton
Gustin A, 158 a Chesterfield
Gustin Edw, 80 a Middletown
Gustin W J, 80 a Chesterfield
Harter Wm P, 65 a Anderson
Hodson Amos, 15 a Middletown
Hodson Amos O, 6 a "
Hodson Eli, 40 a Mechanicsb'g
Hodson E, 1 a Middletown
Hodson Jno L, 23 a "
Hodson Lucinda, 15 a "
Hodson Lucy L, 6 a "
Hoppas David E, 80 a Anderson
Hoppas J H, 240 a "
Hoppas Mary A, 82 a "
Hoppas Sam & L, 80 a "
Hoppas Wm J, 88 a "
Hughel Marg't A, 193 a "
Hughel Samuel, 142 a "
Hunter Sarah E, 35 a "
Hurley John, 40 a Daleville
Hurley J, 180 a Chesterfield
Ironogle Sol, 42 a "
Jester J M, 100 a Middletown
John Geo, 40 a Anderson
John Thos A, 100 a "
John W F, 179 a "
Keesling D, 80 a Middletown
Keesling & E, 159 a Anderson
Keesling Jno, 180 a Middletown
Larimore Jas, 100 a Anderson
Leathers R A, 20 a Chesterfield
McCarty Lucy, 26 a "
McClanahan, E, 148 a "
McGriff Allen, 1 a "
McGriff C, 80 a Anderson
Makepeace B, 80 a "
Makepeace S H, 141 a Anderson
Miller Max, 12 a Chesterfield
Mills B, 80 a "
Mills Cynthia A, 1 a Daleville
Mills Monroe, 40 a Middletown

ıl & Willkie, We will write your Insurance in none but Standard Companies; All parties are treated alike, no cut-rates and no wildcat Insurance.
REAL ESTATE AND NOTARY PUBLICS.

WHEN—YOUR MEASURE TAKEN, AND *SUITS OR OVERCOATS*
MADE TO ORDER.

204 MADISON CO. GAZETTEER.

Myers A & Mary, 1 a Fortville
Myers Sol, 320 a Chesterfield
Nealy Bazil, 80 a "
Noland Albert, 53 a "
Noland Daniel, 120 a "
Noland Ethel, 40 a "
O'Bryant Martin, 70 a "
Parkenson G W & others, 34 a Anderson
Patterson Jas, 80 a Chesterfield
Pittsford David,120 a Anderson
Pittsford Isaac Jr, 160 a "
Poor Wm, 80 a "
Quinn Jno, 1 a Chesterfield
Quinn Rachel, 1 a "
Rector Henry, 6 a Anderson
Rector Jacob, 40 a "
Rector Martha, 20 a "
Rinker J & P, 1 a Chesterfield
Rinker Samuel, 75 a Daleville
Richardson M, 40 a Anderson
Richardson R, 40 a "
Richardson S R, 79 a Middletown
Richman M L, 40 a Chesterfield
Saunders Jas, 109 a Anderson
Scott W C, 136 a Chesterfield
Seward & Bronnenberg, 5 a Chesterfield

Seward F H, 51 a Chesterfield
Shepherd R C, 40 a Anderson
Simms C A, 53 a Chesterfield
Simms M J, 145 a "
Smith Asa, 15 a Middletown
Smith Lucinda, 91 a Anderson
Smith S C, 40 a Middletown
Snyder Edwin, 80 a Daleville
Stanley I & wife, 1 a Anderson
Stephenson S J, 7 a "
Stinson Jno & M, 40 a "
Stinson Sarah, 6 a "
Stinson Wm & M, 40 a "
Suman John heirs, 265 a
Tappen H C, 80 a Anderson
Tappen Wm, 80 a "
Toops Wm F, 8 a "
Tucker David, 58 a "
Tucker G W, 80 a "
Tucker Laura C, 40 a "
Tucker Stephen, 10 a "
Vasbinder Mary, 14 a "
Wampler J W hrs, 80 a "
Weeks Jennie, 1 a "
Williams E, 82 a "
Wood Sarah, 23 a "
Wood Walter W, 22 a "
Zion Rebecca, 50 a "

VAN BUREN TOWNSHIP.

POST OFFICES.

Alexandria, Bath, O., Elwood, Fairmount, Frankton, Gilman, Indianapolis, Jonesboro, Liberty, New Castle, New Corner, Rigdon, Orestes, Summitville, Wichita.

"A" FOR ACRES.

Adams C R, 1 a Alexandria
Adams M J, 16 a Summitville
Allen Amos G, 80 a Alexandria
Allen C H, 80 a Summitville
Allen Eli E, 40 a Huntington
Allen Geo, 80 a Summitville
Allen Geo W, 80 a "
Allen Harrison, 93 a "
Allen Jno R, 80 a Anderson

Allen Jos O, 80 a Summitville
Allen Reuben, 120 a "
Allen Wm, 30 a "
Allen Wm & Katie, 44 a "
Allman Jno, 28 a Alexandria
Armstrong J,105 a Summitville
Barrett J & wife, 39 a New Corner
Beck Henry, 79 a Summitville

John L. Lindskoog, Fashionable MERCHANT TAILOR.
First-Class Work and Fit GUARANTEED.
H. H. H. Block, N. E. Cor. Church and Harrison, ALEXANDRIA, IND.

WM. J. DOVE, Insures against loss by Fire, Cyclone, Accident and Death.
NEELEY BLOCK.
61½ N. Meridian,
ANDERSON, IND.

WHITE RIVER DAIRY, 513 Nichol Avenue, Telephone 220. ANDERSON, IND.

LARMORE BROS., Proprietors, also Manufacturers and Wholesale Dealers in Ice Cream and Oysters in Season.

MADISON CO. GAZETTEER. 205

Beck John, 80 a Summitvill
Blacklidge M H & E, 80 a "
Bookout M A, 80 a "
Bowers Marg't, 1 a Alexandria
Bramble Z W, 40 a "
Bramble Lavina, 40 a Summitvle
Brown Jno H, 80 a "
Brown L P & wife, 40 a "
Brown Levi P, 40 a "
Brown Sarah, 120 a "
Broyles Hanley, 40 a "
Broyles M & E, 40 a "
Broyles Thos, 210 a "
Butler Mary, 17 a Alexandria
Carmony I, 78 a Summitville
Clark Jno L, 18 a "
Clark Sarah F, 35 a "
Coffin Jas D, 79 a "
Cottrell Jane, 40 a "
Cowgill Sam'l C, 69 a "
Cox Mary A, 29 a "
Cox Mary C, 108 a "
Crabb Nancy A, 14 a Fairmount
Creamer J W, 75 a Summitville
Creamer Simon B, 33 a "
Creamer Thos, 40 a "
Creamer Wm R, 40 a "
Cree Calvin L, 79 a Alexandria
Cree Victory, 80 a Summitville
Creek Martha, 12 a "
Creek Rebecca J, 44 a "
Crouse Mary J, 20 a "
Davis Jas, 80 a "
Davis W H, 80 a "
Day Thos C, 120 a Indianapolis
Dean J & H, 23 a Summitville
Dickenson Calvin, 5 a "
Dickenson David, 18 a "
Dickson Sidney J, 5 a "
Dipboye Jonathan, 128 a "
Ditto Shadrick, 120 a "
Dobson Henry, 40 a "
Dobson Wm, 80 a "
Dorsey Emma J, 31 a "
Draper Martin, 1 a Gilman

Duncan Jno E, 2 a Summitville
Earnest J R, 80 a "
Eccles J S & M, 20 a "
Edmunds Wm, 10 a
Ellsworth Jas, 40 a Summitville
Ellsworth Madison, 160 a "
Farmer Jas & wife, 1 a "
Farmer Spaul, 1 a "
Farmer Uriah, 40 a "
Fennimore Barbara, 51 a "
Fesler Wm G, 52 a Frankton
Flint Peter, 80 a Summitville
Fassett Clarinda, 40 a "
Gardner Jno, 28 a "
George Jno S, 80 a Fairmount
Gordon M E, 80 a Summitville
Hancock Isabel M, 1 a "
Hancock Lemuel, 40 a "
Hand W W & wife, 40 a "
Hand Lydia Ann, 3 a "
Harmon James, 77 a "
Harris Jno W, 100 a "
Harris L S P, 80 a "
Harris Marg't, 80 a "
Harrison J S D, 50 a Fairmount
Heritage A & G, 20 a Summitville
Heritage W E, 433 a Summitville
Hiat Elias, 40 a Fairmount
Himelick A, 60 a Summitville
Himelick Jos, 40 a Bath, Ohio
Hoppas A J, 29 a
Hoppas G W. 33 a Summitville
Howard I, 40 a New Cumberland
Howard I J, 20 a New Cumberland
Howard Nannie, 40 a Elwood
Howard M A, 6 a Summitville
Howard W A & S, 40 a Alex
Hudson E, 17 a Summitville
Hundley J M & wife, 16 a "
Hundley Jane, 80 a
Hussey Jane, 60 a Summitville

Anderson Foundry and Machine Works, Manufacturers of Portable and Stationary **Steam Engines.**
5 N. JACKSON STREET, 'Phone 53.
ANDERSON, IND.

Is Your Property Insured? If not, CALL AT ONCE on **JACKSON & BURR,**
69½ N. Meridian, - - - ANDERSON, IND.

206 MADISON CO. GAZETTEER.

Ice Rebecca, 70 a Summitville
Ice Wm Jr, 22 a "
Inglis Alex, 120 a "
Inglis Chloe J, 23 a "
Inglis Jabes A, 38 a "
Inglis Jno K, 40 a "
Inglis Jno A, 80 a "
Inglis Thos N, 110 a "
Inglis Wm J, 80 a "
Irwin Mary A, 80 a "
Irwin Wm, 7 a "
James E & James 4 a "
James L & Harmon, 5 a "
Johnson C, 28 a Wichita, Kan
Johnson J, 300 a Summitville
Johnson Mary A, 8 a "
Johnson R O, 80 a Fairmount
Johnson W E, 20 a Summitville
Jones David, 60 a Rigdon
ones Eliza, 31 a Summitville
ones F M, 40 a "
ones Henry, 80 a "
ones Lemuel K, 60 a "
ones Nora B, 61 a "
ones Sam H, 151 a Fairmount
ones Wm, 31 a "
iger Jane, 80 a Summitville
irkpatrick,117 a "
atchaw F, 30 a "
atchaw W, 20 a "
each C M, 151 a Fairmount
each E C, 80 a "
ewis E, 1 a Summitville
ewis D, 40 a "
ndsay N, 40 a "
vingston, 20 a "
cIniston C, 3 a "
cMahon E, 80 a "
arley H, 31 a Fairmount
irsh J W, 120 a Summitville
irshall G & wife, 40 a "
rquis L, 6 a "
son Fred, 13 a Fairmount
ynard S, 1 a Summitville
lser C, 40 a "

Miller M A, 1 a Gilman
Miller Wm, 40 a Summitville
Millikan F M, New Castle
Millikan T B, 100 a Elwood
Moore A, 12 a Summitville
Moore M A, 40 a "
Moore T & wife, 40 a "
Morris A, 40 a "
Morris G, 40 a "
Morris M F, 40 a Liberty
Morris Mary, 30 a Elwood
Morris P, 40 a Alexandria
Musick E, 55 a Summitville
Musick I, 17 a "
Myers A, 80 a Jonesboro
Neal Mariah, 10 a Fairmount
Nutt H, 40 a Summitville
Nutt Levi, 40 a "
O'Bryant S, 40 a "
Ogden S, 39 a "
Oldfield, J, 139 a "
Osborn W P, 1 a Orestes
Painter G A, 120 a Summitville
Painter S P, 160 a "
Payne M, 57 a "
Pepper G P, 20 a "
Perdue G W, 120 a "
Plow J M, 25 a "
Potts J M, 143 a "
Price J E, 40 a "
Price Sarah, 40 a "
Price W & C, 4 a "
Prigg M, 74 a "
Pulley W & M, 140 a "
Ratliff J M, 79 a "
Rilfe W H, 40 a "
Roberts H H, 50 a Fairmount
Robertson B H, 3 a Summitville
Robertson G H, 75 a "
Rosaboom W, 103 a "
Rothell L, 1 a "
Robb M & G, 1 a "
Runyan H J, 20 a Anderson
Stanley E E, 40 a "
Sapp L A, 1 a Summitville

George B. Epperson, Paints, Oils, Varnishes and Painters' Supplies.
30 E. 9th St., - - ANDERSON, IND.

Schultz M M,158 a Summitville Trice I M, 26 a Summitville
Searle E P, 3 a " Tucker J A, 32 a Anderson
Sloan J W, 40 a Anderson Vaness J, 123 a Summitville
Sluder A, 20 a Fairmount Vinson B, 75 a "
Smith B & wife, 40 a Union Co Vinson Elijah, 60 a Rigdon
Smith J W, 160 a Summitville Vinson E, 1 a Summitville
Smith S, 160 a " Vinson F, 50 a "
Spencer R, 80 a " Vinson G M, 120 a "
Stanley A, 158 a " Vinson M J, 61 a Muncie
Stanley H, 2 a " Vinson J, 120 a "
Stanley O C, 100 a " Wall S, 80 a Summitville
Stokes Selby 1 a " Waltz I, 1 a "
Sweber E, 1 a " Warner W, 37 a "
Tappin Imit, 40 a " Webster D, 118 a "
Tappin Mary, 35 a " Webster G, 120 a "
Thawley J F, 11 a " Webster L, 26 a "
Thawley J, 20 a " Webster R W, 119 a "
Thomas L, 20 a Fairmount Webster R, 120 a "
Thomas M, 80 a Summitville Webster W, 120 a "
Thompson T, 76 a " Wehr S M, 39 a "
Thorn E M, 80 a " Whitney G, 90 a "
Thorn J, 8 a " Wilkins W, 41 a "
Thorn A, 39 a " Wilkins W, 95 a "
Thorn C M, 239 a " Williams A, 40 a "
Thornburg M, 320 a Cambridge Williams J, 20 a Alexandria
    City Williams J, 20 a "
Thurston G, 100 a Summitville Winn M E, 20 a Summitville
Thurston J F, 40 a " Witter F W, 60 a "
Thurston J & G, 80 a " Wood C S, 40 a "
Thurston J P, 160 a " Wood C, 40 a "
Thurston R, 40 a " Worth Peter, 4 a "
Tomlinson H, 99 a " Worth E, 55 a "
Trader O, 41 a Fairmount Zedaker C, 80 a Marion
Trader R, 160 a " Zedaker D, 30 a Summitville
Trice F, 27 a Summitville Zedaker D, 30 a "

PICTURE FRAMES of all sizes and prices at **Hugh Fisher's Novelty Works,**
198 and 200 N. Milton St.,   -   -   -   ANDERSON, IND.

www.ingramcontent.com/pod-product-compliance
Lightning Source LLC
Chambersburg PA
CBHW050844300426
44111CB00010B/1127